THE FRAUD

THE FRAUD

KEIR STARMER, MORGAN McSWEENEY, ND THE CRISIS OF BRITISH DEMOCRACY

PAUL HOLDEN

New York • London

Published by OR Books, New York and London

Visit our website at www.orbooks.com

All rights information: rights@orbooks.com

First printing 2025

The manufacturer's authorised representative in the EU for product safety is Authorised Rep Compliance Ltd, 71 Lower Baggot Street, Dublin D02 P593 Ireland (www.arccompliance.com)

Typeset by Lapiz Digital. Printed by BookMobile, USA, and CPI, UK.

paperback ISBN 978-1-68219-598-7• ebook ISBN 978-1-68219-599-4

For Zoe and Farah

CONTENTS

Cast of Characters and Notes may be consulted online at:
www.thefraud.info

PREFACE

On the evening of Thursday February 8, 2024, *The Guardian*'s political editor, Pippa Crerar, informed me by email that the paper was twenty-four hours away from publishing an article that I feared would significantly damage, if not destroy, my professional reputation. Crerar explained:

> We are planning on running a story on the *Guardian* site tomorrow, and in Saturday's paper, that the National Cyber Security Centre (NCSC) is investigating whether information obtained from an Electoral Commission hack may have been used to target the Labour Party. We understand the NCSC probe centres on a series of private legal emails between the political think tank Labour Together, which was previously run by Morgan McSweeney, and the Electoral Commission.

McSweeney is the chief of staff to UK Prime Minister Sir Keir Starmer and arguably the most powerful person in British politics. I have been investigating McSweeney and his secret, dodgy projects for the past three years, scrutinising how he used a seemingly anodyne think-tank called Labour Together to pull them off. This book is the result of that investigation.

'*The Guardian* understands that part of the NCSC's investigation is whether emails (subsequently leaked to you) came from that cyber hack', Crerar wrote.

I was given a deadline of less than fourteen hours to respond.

My first reaction was confusion. I had literally no idea what Crerar was talking about. I quickly Googled 'electoral commission hack' and discovered that the Commission had, indeed, been hacked in 2021, likely by a hostile foreign actor such as Russia or China. I wrote back to Crerar to make sure that this is what she was referring to. She confirmed that, yes, this was the hack she was talking about.

My second reaction was dismay. I feared that *The Guardian*'s huge global readership would soon believe that I was being seriously investigated for receiving documents from an illegal hack, likely by a hostile foreign country, targeting a Labour Party just about to sweep to power. While Crerar confirmed that *The Guardian* would not allege that I had *participated* in a hack, and would only say I was being investigated, I worried it would not take long for social media users and columnists to collapse this distinction and start wondering how and why I'd received hacks from a foreign power.

My third reaction was anger. I'd never even heard of this hack, let alone received materials from it. I was painfully aware of how *The Guardian*'s story would undermine my investigation into McSweeney and the Labour Party he effectively controlled, and how, more broadly, it would be immensely useful to some truly gnarly people: organised crime figures, money launderers, crooked politicians, and corrupt titans of industry. I also knew it would be politically damaging to good people in my country of birth, South Africa.

I've been investigating grand corruption and serious economic crime for fifteen years. My work has featured in newspapers and TV documentaries around the world and in multiple books. In fact, one of my investigations into how organised crime was moving billions via HSBC in Hong Kong and China had been featured in *The Guardian* itself only three years prior.[1] I didn't hesitate to tell Crerar this fact, also pointing out that I'd been the source of numerous stories in *The Guardian* where I hadn't been credited.

Some of my most important work has unfolded over the past six years. Starting in 2018, I've been investigating what has been called 'state capture' in South Africa, where I lived until my mid-twenties. For close to a decade, a family called the Guptas had worked with the government led by Jacob Zuma, South Africa's former president, to loot and pillage the state with the eager assistance of some of the world's biggest multinational companies. I worked with an incredible team of investigators, advocates, and auditors, using big data analysis and forensic techniques to unearth huge troves of evidence. We used that evidence to unravel the complex money laundering systems that had been used to hide the Guptas' loot.

I set out this evidence in a lengthy report that was underpinned by thousands of pages of raw financial data. I provided days of oral testimony under oath before a judicial commission of inquiry headed by South Africa's most senior judge, Raymond Zondo. Judge Zondo ultimately accepted my evidence and used it as the basis of a substantial part of his mammoth final reports.

Zondo's investigation, findings, and recommendations have had enormous legal and political consequences in South Africa and in many other countries, too. Most notably, his findings and my evidence have been fed into a stream of criminal and civil recovery cases. I have worked closely—and still work closely—with law enforcement and civil recovery agencies around the world to help build those cases. They have allowed the country to claw back close to a billion dollars in fines and seizures and have catalysed criminal proceedings in multiple jurisdictions. I am inexpressibly proud of this work, not least because the money that has been recovered can be used to build South Africa's sometimes infuriating and sometimes inspiring post-apartheid future.

I believed the Electoral Commission hack story would be a godsend to the network of criminal actors that had been the focus of my investigations. The pro-Zuma faction, still powerful in South Africa, would have loved to exploit these allegations to discredit me and my work, to undermine the efforts of Judge Zondo, and to attack the independence and credibility of the agencies now cleaning up a decade of corruption based on Zondo's findings.

I took two hours to collect my thoughts, contact my lawyer, and compose my reply. 'I want to make this very, very clear', I wrote to Crerar. 'If there is any hint in your reporting that I received material from the hack of the Electoral Commission referred to above, whether knowingly or unknowingly, I will immediately be bringing defamation proceedings against you and the Guardian. . . . The allegation that I have received information from a hack of the Electoral Commission is not only false, but I can positively prove it to be false'.

Crerar acknowledged my response but did not ask me how I could prove it to be false. 'I'll let you know what we do', she said. But she never did. Instead, I waited up anxiously overnight, checking *The Guardian* website to see if anything had appeared. Nothing. I wrote to Crerar the next day asking what was going to happen. She said that she would get back to me in a few days.

I never heard from her again.

And, of course, I have never heard from the NCSC—neither before nor since Crerar's email.

*

I have been investigating Morgan McSweeney and Labour Together for about three years. As a result, I now believe that I have enough evidence to plausibly argue that Morgan McSweeney may have purposefully broken the law when he failed to report hundreds of thousands of pounds to the Electoral Commission as required by statute between 2018 and 2020. McSweeney then used those undisclosed funds to propel Sir Keir Starmer to the leadership of the Labour Party, transforming both the party and British politics.

In investigating how McSweeney and his allies have transformed the Labour Party, I have come across evidence pointing to serious wrongdoing over an extended period, some of which I believe requires further investigation by regulatory agencies and law enforcement. Indeed, I have come to the opinion that the political project that delivered us a Starmer government has been a reckless and arguably lawless endeavour whose misconduct threatens the health of British democracy.

I came to these conclusions after I was given access to a substantial leak of documents from within the Labour Party. That story is a bit twisty, but don't worry—the documents were a legitimate public interest leak, and I hold them legally as a journalist. And while the size and richness of this leaked treasure trove is unusual, it is hardly an uncommon event for internal documents from the Labour Party to make their way into the hands of political reporters. That's a regular Tuesday.

In mid-2023 I took some of those documents to Gabriel Pogrund of *The Sunday Times*, which ran a story about the undeclared money on its front page in mid-November. It was a good story but ultimately did not pull the trigger quite as I'd hoped. The article concluded by citing me as the source of documents, noting that I was writing a book. On the day of the *Sunday Times* article, my publisher put up a short blurb that made it clear I was deep into an investigation of McSweeney and Labour Together.

At the same time, I started publishing a series of articles with the prominent US journalist Matt Taibbi. Not long before, he had been given access to the so-called 'Twitter Files' and had been writing disturbing stories about government overreach and censorship across the pond. I contacted Matt in 2023 when I realised his investigations were crossing over with mine. One of the organisations Matt came across in that work was the Center for Countering Digital Hate (CCDH), which had also attracted the angry attention of Twitter's new owner, Elon Musk. My investigations and subsequent articles with Matt revealed that CCDH, together with its dodgy sister project Stop Funding Fake News, had been incubated by Labour Together under McSweeney—and resourced by Labour Together at the time that it was failing to report donations as required by law.

This book irrefutably documents McSweeney's involvement in CCDH. That secret history now sits like a volatile piece of unexploded ordinance that could blow up the relationship between the current Donald Trump administration and Starmer's office.

In late December 2023, the Electoral Commission responded to a Freedom of Information request that I had submitted while working with Pogrund. The documents, which I describe in detail in Chapter One of this book, shed further light on Labour Together's breach of electoral law.

This time I took the story to *The Telegraph*, which had contacted me after the *Sunday Times* report with a view to taking it further. By late January 2024—just days before Crerar's email arrived in my inbox—*The Telegraph* had sent 'right of reply' notices to Labour Together and Morgan McSweeney ahead of its forthcoming article.

A few days after I had seemingly seen off the 'Electoral Commission hack' story, I reread Crerar's emails and noticed something I'd missed. There was no independent, self-initiated NCSC investigation into how I might have received hacked material. What had happened, Crerar told me, was that Labour Together had reported 'their concerns' to the NCSC. This means that Labour Together had raised 'concerns' about me to the British security services at about the same time that *The Telegraph* was asking questions about Labour Together's undisclosed money, based on the new evidence I'd provided.

Odd things had been happening ever since it was made public that I was investigating Labour Together and McSweeney. Two days prior to the Crerar email, I was contacted by a young man who claimed to be a journalist from the progressive news and investigative website *openDemocracy*. He was lying. But I trusted him because he had got in touch via a family connection that would be difficult if not impossible to discover through open records. I still wonder how he made that connection, and whether it was based on the sort of human intelligence gathered by private investigators.

The imposter asked me about my investigations into McSweeney, Labour Together, and the Labour Party. I gave him an overview but without a huge amount of detail. He then started asking pointed questions about Anonyvoter. As I discuss later, Anonyvoter was the internal Labour Party voting system that at least two MPs believed was being abused to stitch up their selections.

At this point my alarm bells started ringing and I ended the call. Something didn't feel right about the conversation. When *openDemocracy* confirmed that the young man had nothing to do with them, I contacted my lawyer. On his advice, I reported the call to the police as a case of fraud. I still have no idea who this person really was and how I had come onto their radar. I also have no evidence that Labour Together had anything to do with it, and a well-placed source indicated that it was highly unlikely that they would. But it was mighty strange.

A few months later, I was contacted by an old friend, a formidable researcher with a stellar investigative record. She had been looking into how reputation management agencies based in the UK (and the private intelligence firms they subcontracted) were used by rich clients and multinationals to manage problematic allegations—as well as the whistleblowers and journalists that made them.

'Your name came up', she said. 'One of these firms is looking at you'.

I still didn't quite believe it. I thought that perhaps my name had come up because of my close working relationship with my long-time friend and colleague, Andrew Feinstein, who has upset more arms dealers around the world than is strictly healthy. No. My friend was adamant: '*You* are the focus of the investigation. They call you a "significant person of interest". They have been looking into you and your family and your colleagues. They've been writing reports about you'.

'Since when?' I asked, my heart racing.

'November 2023', my colleague confirmed—the same month that *The Sunday Times* had cited me as a source of documents for its exposé of Labour Together's unlawful failure to disclose donations.

'Who was the client?' I asked.

'Labour Together', came the reply.

'Is there anyone from Labour Together on any of the emails?' I asked.

'Some young guy called Josh Simons'.

Simons was appointed a director of Labour Together in late 2022. He became the organisation's public face as the 'provisional wing' of Starmer's incoming government in late 2023 and the first half of 2024. In 2024, Simons was parachuted into a safe seat during the general election. He now sits as the MP for Makerfield, in which role he has appeared on the popular online politics channel *PoliticsJOE* lamenting how politicians have lost the trust of the public.[2]

Corroborating evidence soon emerged. Reports I saw confirmed that the investigation into me was launched after the *Sunday Times'* Labour Together exposé that cited me as a source. The firm used a mixture of human intelligence and expensive data scraping tools to find out where I lived and with whom, and who I associated with professionally. They had to use such approaches to find this stuff out about my private life because I have for many years purposefully kept a low profile, including foreswearing social media. I have done this because information about my private life had previously been used by bad actors I investigated in South Africa to target me for harassment.

The investigations paid for by Labour Together lingered on my colleague, Andrew Feinstein. They sought to discover who funded the small anti-corruption organisation that we use to investigate and expose the sort of criminals and kleptocrats who loot states and destroy democracies. The funding I received from the Open Society Foundation to undertake my work on South African state capture was noted as a point of potential 'leverage'. Colleagues and fellow journalists who worked at my shared office space in London or who served on our small board also came under scrutiny; some of them were subjected to deep dives into their family histories stretching back decades. Minor infractions of presumed political etiquette were then woven into a caricature alleging political malevolence or improper bias on the part of myself and my associates.

To widespread mirth in my office, I was told that the 'investigation' had eventually alighted on the allegation that—wait for it—Andrew and I were connected to Russian state actors via South African intelligence structures. This came as a huge surprise to Andrew and I: our previous investigations into Russian oligarchs had left us facing years of legal and extra-legal threats while Russian president Vladimir Putin was famously allied with the former South African president Jacob Zuma—the guy Andrew and I have been trying to get prosecuted for over a decade. Indeed, if Zuma's long pending and infuriatingly delayed corruption case ever takes place, Andrew is slated to appear as the first witness for the prosecution.

While I have not seen everything written by the company that Labour Together hired, none of the materials I *had* seen from the investigation claimed that my evidence was wrong, or that my information was incorrect, or that my leaked documents were inauthentic. Instead, they primarily indicated a burning desire to understand where I was getting my information from—and what else I might have.

As the following pages show, Labour Together had good reason to worry. I invite every citizen concerned with the fairness of British democracy to read on as I reveal the sordid inner workings of the Starmer machine, discover the serious wrongdoing I unearthed, and then join me in an effort to hold the culprits and their enablers to account.

Paul Holden
London
June 2025

INTRODUCTION

In early April 2020 Sir Keir Starmer was elected leader of the Labour Party, following a campaign that amounted to 'the biggest political con' in recent political history.[1] This fraudulent victory plunged British democracy into a crisis from which it has yet to escape.

For four months between January and April 2020, Starmer presented himself as an inheritor and guardian of the socialist Corbynite tradition that preceded him, as well as a conciliator determined to end the factionalism that had riven the party. He did so to win the votes of a Labour membership that leaned left on policy and yearned for an end to electorally ruinous fighting between the party's internal factions.

Starmer posed as a fervent eco-socialist who promised to 'make the positive case for immigration', vowed to shun *The Sun* during his leadership campaign, and decried the 'trickle-down' economics of Tory neoliberalism. He said Labour's left-wing 2017 general election manifesto was his 'foundational document' and pledged live on television to nationalise rail, mail, water, and energy. He signed up to pledges brought by LGBTQ+ Labour to recognise trans men as men and trans women as women and to implement gender self-identification (self-ID). He promised to abolish the undemocratic House of Lords. He warmly referred to Labour's outgoing leader—the socialist anti-war campaigner Jeremy Corbyn MP—as a friend. And he undertook to protect and extend democracy by allowing local branches to select their parliamentary candidates rather than imposing these from above.

Progressive, internationalist, democratic, green, socialist—this was the basis upon which Starmer became leader of the Labour Party, the springboard for his subsequent election as Britain's prime minister.

In the July 2024 general election, Starmer would lead his party to a 'loveless landslide', winning 411 out of 650 seats on a vote share of just 33.7 percent and on the lowest voter turnout (as a proportion of the total adult population) since the introduction of universal suffrage.[2] Starmer's 2024 platform was a neat, mirrored inversion of his 2020 offer.

'Starmer 2024' opened his general election campaign by writing tough on immigration in the reactionary tabloid he had once snubbed, *The Sun*, which then endorsed his campaign. Climate change barely featured in Labour's anaemic election manifesto as the party committed relatively little funding to the issue. The same manifesto used the word 'inequality' just once, even as reducing inequality had been the central theme of the 2017 manifesto Starmer previously endorsed as 'foundational'. The party now rejected gender self-ID while party officials started arguing that single-sex spaces should exclude trans women. Nationalisation of energy, mail, and water was rejected outright. Increased state spending to end the two-child benefit cap or ameliorate fourteen years of economic austerity were ruled out for the foreseeable future in the name of fiscal discipline. Any long-term ambitions to remove the cap—which is the primary driver of child poverty in the UK—were made contingent on economic growth. Indeed, rather than increase the majority's living standards by redistributing wealth, Starmer's vision for improving people's lives rested almost entirely on the prospect that revived economic growth would lift all boats. This presumed that economic growth would pick up—to say the least, a risky gamble—and effectively rehashed the 'trickle-down' Tory economics he previously argued had been disproven.

By this point, Corbyn, who Starmer once proclaimed his friend, had been turfed out of the party and forced to run as an independent, while left-wing candidates had been systematically excluded as potential MPs. Many of the MPs that were newly admitted to parliament in the 2024 election had been hand-picked by a Labour leadership cabal that refused local party members a vote. The candidates were simply parachuted into safe seats in a mockery of democratic process and in direct contradiction of Starmer's leadership campaign pledge to end this practice.

In the half-decade between his election as Labour leader in 2020 and as Britain's prime minister in 2024, Starmer and his advisors asserted an iron grip over the party. This authoritarian reconstruction is what enabled Starmer's leadership to campaign on a right-wing electoral platform in 2024. Many of the candidates manoeuvred into safe Labour seats during that election had participated in Labour's undemocratic transformation.

Labour under Corbyn had grown to more than half a million members, becoming Western Europe's largest political party. Starmer's ferocious attack on party democracy and uninspiring programme threw this historic expansion into reverse: his leadership oversaw the exodus of over two hundred thousand paid-up members, which continued even after Starmer's 2024 general election victory. By mid-2025, the membership had declined so precipitously that the new general secretary introduced measures to limit who would be shown the party's membership numbers.

Starmer's enforcers began by targeting the party's left flank but soon extended their censorious attention to the emollient 'soft left', as even minor deviations from the will of the controlling faction became intolerable. During the Corbyn years, Labour had played host to vibrant, fierce, and sometimes bitter political debates that generated acrimony but also ideas and ingenuity. In sharp but dismal contrast, as the political project around Starmer moved Labour policy ever rightward, the party became ever more hostile to internal dissent.

Importantly, the party's remaking under Starmer led to a striking drop in support from ethnic minorities, traditionally a key component of Labour's electoral coalition.

Starmer's leadership justified its assertion of internal control as an attempt to reduce the prevalence of anti-Jewish prejudice within the party—a claim that will be scrutinised in this book. Yet many observers concluded that the party was simultaneously engaging in or overlooking other forms of bigotry; that it was operating a 'hierarchy of racism' in which anti-Muslim and anti-Black discrimination were relegated to the bottom rung.

As the Starmer project repelled paying members and alienated minority communities, the flipside was Labour's renewed openness to lobbyists and big business. After all, *someone* has to pay the bills. From 2022 onward, lobbying firms assiduously hired party insiders with the aim of influencing Labour policy—and with the hope that doors would open once a Labour government was elected. This was accompanied by an influx of monetary donations as well as gifts from a super-rich donor class and other private interests. Starmer personally accepted tens of thousands of pounds in luxury holidays, clothing, and other freebies in the years following the Covid pandemic. All of this raises serious questions about how, and for whose benefit, Labour policy is now made.

In short, there is compelling evidence that the political project which propelled Keir Starmer to first party and then national leadership was authoritarian, deceptive, and open to corporate capture, and that it lacked a principled approach to the struggle against racism. As this book shows, the Starmer project has also repeatedly skirted the edges of the law.

This is the machine that now runs the UK.

*

This book tells the story of two overlapping projects. The first ran from approximately July 2017 through to April 2020. I call this the 'Labour Together Project', after the organisation through which it was largely carried out.

The political operators who made up the Labour Together Project used it to wage a contemporaneously undisclosed fightback against Corbynism. They then worked to get Starmer elected as leader of the Labour Party so as to gain control over it. This operation was driven primarily by a man named Morgan McSweeney and by Steve Reed, a Labour MP. They worked peripatetically alongside a group of anti-Corbyn MPs who now exercise huge influence within the party and therefore the government. They include Chancellor of the Exchequer Rachel Reeves, Health Secretary Wes Streeting, and the Lord High Chancellor Shabana Mahmood. Another key player was Imran Ahmed, a former Labour Party spin-doctor who would play a central role in covert projects deployed to discredit the Corbynite left.

It is worth noting at the outset that certain members of Labour Together appear not to have been aware of everything the organisation was doing behind the scenes. Those seemingly left in the dark include some of the group's founders, such as Jon Cruddas MP and Jonathan Rutherford, a Labour advisor aligned with the party's communalist 'Blue Labour' tendency. Labour Together's avowed mission was uncontroversial: to promote party unity and the need to reconnect with Labour's working-class base. For McSweeney and his associates, these commitments were used as cover for a far more ideologically divisive and factionally aggressive agenda. But the likes of Cruddas appear to have been authentically committed to the group's formal objectives.

When this book speaks of the 'Labour Together Project', therefore, this does not refer to Labour Together in corporate terms or to every Labour Together director and employee. Instead, it more precisely designates a group *within* Labour Together that appears to have used the organisation as a vehicle for its own ends. This project was helmed by McSweeney and Reed, with ample support provided by Ahmed. How much other figures—even the organisation's largest funders, Martin Taylor and Sir Trevor Chinn—were aware of is unknown.

From April 2020, the book turns to an investigation of what I call the 'Starmer Project'. I do so because this tight political network selected Starmer as its frontman, installed him as leader of the Labour Party, and then guided him to his current role as prime minister of the country. Even as Starmer became the face of this project, he was not its driver or even its most important member. As this books shows, the main motive forces behind the Starmer Project were McSweeney, his allies and associates in the party bureaucracy, a handful of trusted MPs, and McSweeney's financial backers.

The election in 2015 of a left-wing leader supported by an energised popular movement terrified not just the Labour right but also the full breadth of Britain's political and media class. The Starmer Project's top priority was to ensure nothing like the Corbyn experiment could ever happen again. To this end, the project has radically reshaped the Labour Party at every level, primarily to neutralise oppositional forces and disempower party members. One small, right-wing element of the Labour coalition effectively captured the whole party. This process freed the Starmer leadership to move Labour to the right on nearly every policy issue; to embrace big business; and to vigorously defend the UK's dominant national security paradigm, including support for Israel's destruction of the Gaza Strip.

I start the clock on the Starmer Project at the date of Starmer's election as leader of the Labour Party in April 2020 primarily for narrative ease, and because once McSweeney and his allies took over the party bureaucracy, Labour Together was no longer needed as McSweeney's primary political vehicle. But to be clear, the Starmer Project is coloured by the Labour Together Project that preceded it, while Labour Together still exercises influence within and through it. Indeed, the projects are linked by strong continuities in their political methodology and personnel.

After a period of relative quiet between mid-2020 and early 2023, Labour Together subsequently became an increasingly active participant in the Starmer Project. In April 2023, Labour Together relaunched as a de facto 'adjunct of the Leader's

Office', as Jon Cruddas described it to me, acting in practice as a defender of the Starmer leadership, a gatekeeper on party policy, and an incubator of politically aligned MPs and researchers. All this was enabled by a handful of wealthy donors who bankrolled the Labour Together operation. In 2024, Labour Together bragged of its role as 'Keir Starmer's provisional wing'.[3] Key players in Labour Together, or figures whose political careers were incubated by the organisation, were rewarded with safe seats in the 2024 election. They included Josh Simons, who was hired to lead the organisation on its relaunch in 2023 and who was parachuted into a safe seat in the first weeks of the 2024 election campaign. It was Simons, recall, who was on the correspondence with the reputation management firm that Labour Together hired to investigate my colleagues and I. Labour Together would donate resources valued at an astonishing £1.5 million between January 2024 and July 2024 to the party, including funding dozens of new and incoming MPs. This may seem like pocket-change to American readers, but in the UK, where political spending is much more constrained, it was an enormous sum.

*

This book tells the story of the Labour Together and Starmer projects in seven parts.

It begins by exposing Labour Together's failure to report hundreds of thousands of pounds in donations to the Electoral Commission between mid-2017 and late 2020, in violation of electoral law. This failure to report donations meant that the public was unaware of Labour Together's funding and where it came from, even as Labour Together was incubating Starmer's future leadership bid. I present evidence that has led me to believe that it is possible that Morgan McSweeney chose to not report donations—that is, to cause Labour Together to fall foul of its legal requirement to report donations.

I then show how the Labour Together Project publicly presented itself as a force for party unity and cross-factional reconciliation even as, behind the scenes, it aggressively targeted the Corbyn leadership in pursuit of its own ambition to control the party. Some of this manoeuvring involved working with anti-Corbyn figures whose positions in the party were threatened by the surge of new members. These were people who had joined in support of Corbyn's anti-war, redistributive platform and who then sought to select Labour candidates more to their liking. Labour Together's machinations against the Corbyn leadership arguably damaged the party's electoral prospects.

Perhaps the Labour Together Project's most consequential intervention was to insert itself into the high-profile Labour Party 'antisemitism crisis' that embroiled the Corbyn leadership from 2018. Further investigation is needed to establish the full extent of the project's involvement in what became a protracted national controversy, but there is now little doubt that its role was profound, wide-ranging, and at times despicable. This involvement was also entirely covert and at least partly funded with the money McSweeney was failing to properly declare to the Electoral Commission.

What is known for certain is that the Labour Together Project worked closely with national media to place arguably alarmist stories that painted the Corbyn project as irredeemably tainted with antisemitism. With the passage of time, many of these stories have not withstood scrutiny. There are also indications, not yet fully fleshed out, that the project helped 'engineer'[4] the Equality and Human Rights Commission (EHRC)'s investigation into antisemitism in the Labour Party. The resulting report, published October 2020, served as a critical pretext and justification for McSweeney and his allies to reshape the party in their image.

Still more significantly, Labour Together figures oversaw the creation of what may be called an 'astroturf campaign' called Stop Funding Fake News (SFFN). Astroturfing is where an entity or group claims to be made up of grassroots activists when, in fact, the organisation is created or run by people from undisclosed corporate or political backgrounds.

SFFN intervened in the Labour 'antisemitism crisis' yet insisted that its 'activists' remain anonymous. As a result, the public was unaware that key elements of the controversy were being driven by the Labour Together Project—a factional grouping that had plausible ulterior motives for discrediting the Corbyn leadership, whose not-so-grassroots membership included the current chief of staff to the prime minister, a former Labour Party spin-doctor, and a sitting MP: about as far away from being grassroots activists as one can imagine. The SFFN campaign set out to destroy the burgeoning left-wing media ecosystem that had buoyed Corbynism and which the Labour Together Project identified as a primary obstacle to its mission of permanently destroying the Labour left. The campaign bragged that it had 'eviscerate[d]' the economic viability of *The Canary*, an independently regulated left-wing media outlet, by pressuring advertisers to abandon the platform. The news site was forced to change its entire fundraising model, while many of its diverse roster of journalists and editors were let go.

SFFN displayed a chilling disdain for small and alternative media, as well as a propensity to undermine rigorous alternative or non-mainstream journalists who reported critically—but largely accurately—on the right-wing Labour Party faction that Labour Together's McSweeney and Reed were guiding back toward control of the party.

SFFN also intervened in the 2019 European parliamentary elections, when it attempted to convince people not to vote for right-wing candidates associated with the Brexit Party and Nigel Farage. I have little time for the politics espoused by Farage and his associates. But whichever party one supports, it is hugely problematic that an astroturf project like SFFN—resourced in part by Labour Together's unlawfully undisclosed donations—attempted to influence the outcome of an election in this underhanded way.

The book's second part tells the story of Starmer's April 2020 election as leader of the Labour Party. As a candidate,

Starmer committed to policies that made him almost indistinguishable from Rebecca Long-Bailey, his left-wing opponent and the presumptive Corbynite heir. The Labour Together Project played a critical role in executing this campaign. Notably, Morgan McSweeney served as company secretary of Labour Together and as Starmer's leadership campaign chief between January and April 2020. This means that, during the very period he was directing Starmer's campaign, McSweeney was simultaneously breaking electoral law by failing to properly report donations being made to Labour Together.

We then look behind the misleading performance to examine the 'real Keir Starmer'. Even at this early stage, Starmer's political and professional record should have rung alarm bells for the party's left wing as well as the broader membership. So how did his progressive posturing fool them? One plausible reason is that, in this critical period, SFFN intensified its astroturf campaign to discredit independent media outlets that urged their Labour readerships to back Long-Bailey over Starmer. This campaign was linked to the very man, McSweeney, who had helped set up SFFN and who was personally directing Starmer's election bid. These materially relevant affiliations went entirely undisclosed.

The book's third part turns to the Starmer Project. In Starmer's first eight months as Labour leader, McSweeney and his allies gained influence over Labour's bureaucracy and helped banish left-leaning ideas as well as people from the party. This factional purge culminated in the suspension of Corbyn himself as a Labour MP. The book describes how the party exploited a slapdash investigation into antisemitism in the Labour Party by Britain's statutory equalities regulator—the EHRC—as leverage to demoralise and exclude left-wing members, some of them Jewish. We now know that McSweeney had a direct role in 'engineer[ing]' the EHRC investigation during his time at Labour Together.[5]

I also explore the Starmer Project's response to the 'Leaked Report', a document prepared by officials in Corbyn's leadership team that was leaked in April 2020. The Leaked Report alleged serious wrongdoing by anti-Corbyn bureaucrats who had run Labour's headquarters between 2015 and 2018. The report threatened the Labour Together and Starmer projects, not least because it seriously disrupted a narrative on the 'antisemitism crisis' that the Labour Together Project had played a significant and undisclosed role in fomenting. Some of the bureaucrats fingered in the Leaked Report had also worked closely with both McSweeney and Imran Ahmed. The result, I argue, was that the party sought to manage the fallout from the Leaked Report in ways that protected the Starmer Project's factional allies while putting the report's authors—who had uncovered serious and material wrongdoing—through expensive and ultimately fruitless legal proceedings.

As a result of adopting this approach, the party has never seriously investigated the so-called 'Ergon House scheme' revealed by the Leaked Report, or earlier plans in a similar vein. The Ergon House scheme involved right-wing bureaucrats hostile to Corbyn's leadership secretly diverting party funds to their factional allies during the 2017 general election. The effect was to deprive the formal campaign of funds it wanted to use to target marginal seats. This might have materially impacted the outcome of the election and the number of seats the Labour Party eventually won.

Previously unseen documents show how truly explosive this covert plot was and continues to be. I raise serious concerns about how the scheme may have involved violations of electoral law, and highlight how Unite the Union—one of the largest donors to the campaign—raised material concerns about potential criminal wrongdoing up to and including fraud (although I do not presume to pass judgment on Unite's claim). The party has *never* meaningfully addressed these grave concerns as—more than five years after the scheme was revealed—it has still failed to conduct a serious, independent audit. Documents revealed for the first time in this book show that the scheme (and its predecessors) appeared to articulate a plan to benefit people who have become some of the country's most senior political figures. They include the likes of Shabana Mahmood, Rachel Reeves, and Yvette Cooper—all appointed cabinet ministers in the 2024 Starmer government—as well as Prime Minister Starmer himself. The party's failure to meaningfully investigate prima facie evidence of serious misconduct must raise questions about the Starmer Project's commitment to good governance, democratic integrity, and the rule of law.

The party also did not properly investigate the extent of the apparent racism, sexism, and other misconduct that was revealed in the Leaked Report. I draw on new documents to expose additional problematic conduct by individuals who now occupy senior positions in the British government, beyond what the Leaked Report already disclosed. This includes a chat log involving Paul Ovenden, a party official who after the 2024 election was appointed as the special advisor to Prime Minister Starmer and director of strategy at Number 10. Ovenden's chat log shows him joking with another Labour staffer about an incident in which party employees imagined performing sex acts on Diane Abbott, the country's first Black woman MP.

The book moves forward, in its fourth part, to the Starmer leadership's growing assertion of control up to the end of 2021. I investigate three case studies that shed light on the Starmer Project's approach to party management: the deselection of Anna Rothery as a mayoral candidate for Liverpool, the handling of hacked material from *Inside Croydon* (a dogged local media outlet), and the decision to shut down two Constituency Labour Parties (CLPs) in East London based on a dodgy secret dossier.

I scrutinise these episodes for two reasons. First, they illustrate what the Starmer Project's victory meant for the Labour Party: the installation of an authoritarian regime that excluded alternate voices by means that skirted the edge of the law and in ways that raise legitimate concerns about the party's commitment to combating racism and Islamophobia. Second, they are a useful corrective to mainstream commentators who breezily assert that Starmer 'changed the party', but who rarely acknowledge the political, democratic, and ultimately human cost of this 'change'. The Starmer Project did not oversee some bloodless, bureaucratic rationalisation; it waged a ruthless assault on basic principles of fairness and perhaps even legality that racked and wrecked real people's lives.

In the book's fifth part, I examine the Starmer Project's first big crisis and then consolidation. In 2021, the project nearly failed under the weight of Starmer's unpopularity as Labour barely held on to the constituency of Batley and Spen in a close-run by-election. This victory was achieved in part because *The Guardian* did not publish a damaging story until after the election was over.

Having weathered that storm, the Starmer Project redoubled its efforts to entrench the right's factional control within the party. The Starmer leadership engaged in bureaucratic machinations to rewrite Labour's rule book at the annual conference in September 2021. The revisions drastically circumscribed internal party democracy so as to ensure that the membership would not be able to use their democratic vote to choose a left-wing candidate like Corbyn again.

The book's sixth part spans the period from early 2022 until the July 2024 general election. Its subject is the Starmer Project unleashed. The Tories' electoral collapse under the ill-fated premiership of Liz Truss, together with the expulsion and exodus of Labour's own left wing, enabled the Starmer Project to more aggressively assert itself on policy and other matters. Labour accordingly adopted a platform that emulated the authoritarian Tory right on issues such as welfare, crime, and immigration; eschewed taxes on the wealthy or meaningful redistribution; and envisaged a drastic reduction in funds allocated to the fight against climate change. These positions became the basis of the Labour Party's 2024 election manifesto. As Labour lurched right on policy, the Starmer Project simultaneously embraced corporate lobbying, glad-handing, and freebies.

I conclude Part Six with Labour's response to Hamas' appalling attack on Israel on October 7, 2023, and Israel's devastating retaliation, which the International Court of Justice (ICJ) considered to have plausibly breached the Genocide Convention. Under Starmer's leadership the party defended Israel's criminal destruction of Gaza, despite overwhelming evidence that Israeli forces were targeting civilians and civilian infrastructure and notwithstanding a torrent of brazenly genocidal rhetoric from the most senior Israeli officials on down. To acquiesce in or enable so grave a breach of international law was bad enough. But Starmer also flouted British parliamentary convention to water down a Gaza ceasefire initiative in February 2024. This marked the first time that the Starmer Project's undemocratic and opportunistic political mode—previously confined to purging internal party dissent—was applied to the country at large. This response to Gaza exacerbated the unravelling of Labour's traditional electoral coalition, the consequences of which played out dramatically during the 2024 general election.

In the seventh and final part, I dissect Labour's 2024 general election campaign and then examine the Starmer government's first hundred days in power. I reveal how the leadership parachuted factionally aligned candidates into safe Labour seats while undemocratically deselecting left-wing and ethnic minority candidates. So blatantly and thoroughly did the Starmer Project rig the selection process that Michael Crick—a veteran political correspondent and self-identified Blairite—branded the campaign 'one of the most disgraceful episodes in modern Labour Party history'.[6]

After the election, Starmer partisans exulted in their massive parliamentary majority. But sober analysis reveals the election to be an expression of Britain's profound democratic crisis, manifested in historically low turnout and pervasive voter apathy. This deep disconnect was exacerbated by the country's first-past-the-post electoral system, which returned Labour seats in gross disproportion to the party's actual vote share.

Finally, the book turns to the Starmer Project's conduct in government. By the end of a tumultuous first hundred days, popular support for Starmer and the Labour Party had cratered while, within the government, Morgan McSweeney had ascended to a position of unparalleled influence. Part of the explanation for this collapse in support lies in the government's decision to introduce austerity-like conditions by cutting the Winter Fuel Allowance at the same time as the leadership was embroiled in a freebie scandal centred on Starmer's predilection for luxury gifts.

But I argue that the primary driver of public disillusion and disgust with the Starmer Project was the fact that Starmer and the Labour Party had made promises during the election campaign to win public support which they then rapidly and unashamedly betrayed. This fuelled a widespread sense that the party had offered the country a false bill of sale in pursuit of power—just as Starmer had done in 2020 to win over Labour Party members with a left-wing pitch he would instantly abandon upon victory. When Starmer and McSweeney used this methodology to win in 2020 they eventually provoked the exodus of nearly half the party's membership, which revolted at the cynicism and dishonesty of Starmer's path to power. When Starmer and McSweeney deployed the same stratagem against the whole country in 2024, they powerfully undermined the standing of the Labour Party among British citizens at large, many of whom now wonder whether voting makes any difference—or whether their vote is best given to the wrecking ball of Reform.

I conclude by reflecting on what the success of the Labour Together and Starmer projects means for the UK's economic, political, and social future. There is much to be concerned about.

*

This book is substantially based on leaked documentation from within the Labour Party, without which the twin Starmer and Labour Together projects would remain shrouded in mystery.

Such leaks, like all archives, are merely fragments of a larger whole. There is much more to be uncovered and understood—perhaps by regulatory authorities who might be minded to investigate what I consider to be the extensive wrongdoing outlined in this book.

The book is thoroughly referenced with nearly eight hundred footnotes. To avoid taxing the reader's arm strength as well as patience, I have decided to place this material online. The endnotes can be viewed on the website that supports this book: www.thefraud.info.

I have generally limited the endnotes to citations. A minority also include explanatory information, where I felt this was important but technical. This is particularly true in relation to the so-called Ergon House scheme as well as evidence that an earlier plan was already in place to allocate party funding during the 2017 general election along factional lines. I believe the Ergon House scheme is one of the most alarming cases exposed in this book. There is an urgent need for it to be properly investigated, which the Labour Party has so far failed to do. I encourage interested readers to consult the detailed endnotes that evidence this section via the website.

This will be the first time that many readers, especially those outside the UK, encounter an assortment of political actors who have previously been known only within Labour Party circles. Such readers may find a 'Cast of Characters' on the book's website: www.thefraud.info.

At the time of writing, there are four existing books that have substantively examined the political history of Keir Starmer and his rise to power: Oliver Eagleton's *The Starmer Project*, Tom Baldwin's Starmer biography, Anushka Asthana's post-election *Taken as Red*, and the substantial *Get In* by Gabriel Pogrund and Patrick Maguire. Each of these works is commendable in its own way and puts considerable evidence into the public domain. I draw on each of them to some extent.

As will become clear to the reader, I approach the same historical period from a different perspective, not least because

I draw on a unique set of primary materials unavailable to other writers. With the exception of Eagleton, I often disagree with the analysis or framing of the preceding writers and, sometimes, with their factual presentations too. It would however be tedious to construct my book as an ongoing back-and-forth, and so I have endeavoured to keep direct comment on their findings to a minimum.

PART ONE

THE POISONED TREE

CHAPTER 1

THE RISE OF LABOUR TOGETHER

Labour fought the December 2019 general election with a base split by Brexit and a party divided against itself. It went down to a heavy defeat. After Jeremy Corbyn resigned the helm, Keir Starmer wasted no time in putting his own name forward for the role of new party leader. Starmer's leadership campaign was a slick affair, launched and defined by a well-produced video that touted his leftist credentials and values. One campaign insider described how, from the outset, it was streets ahead of any contenders in terms of messaging, organisation, infrastructure, and funding.

Starmer could launch his candidacy so quickly thanks to years of preparation largely outside the public eye. This work was done by a political project operating through an organisation called Labour Together. The project had likely started preparing for a leadership contest before Starmer was even aware of its existence. Labour Together provided access to funders. It would also supply Starmer's key officials including his Svengali, Morgan McSweeney, and many of his future shadow cabinet and cabinet ministers.

Starmer's left-wing Labour leadership pitch was based on polling undertaken by McSweeney and Labour Together throughout 2019. This equipped Starmer's campaign with an in-depth understanding of party members' views. Indeed, as

Times reporters Gabriel Pogrund and Patrick Maguire have written, Starmer effectively 'subcontracted' his leadership campaign to Labour Together.[1]

McSweeney, a Labour Together director both before and during Starmer's leadership bid, was the head of Starmer's leadership campaign. He was later appointed Starmer's chief of staff in the Leader of the Opposition's Office (commonly referred to as LOTO). After Starmer formed a government in July 2024, McSweeney became arguably the most powerful unelected official in the UK as Starmer's chief of staff in Number 10. Before his stint at Labour Together, McSweeney had worked with David Evans, who was appointed general secretary of the Labour Party less than two months after Starmer's election as party leader.

From its formation in 2015, Labour Together had presented itself as a unifying body that sought to heal Labour's internal divisions. It even claimed, in February 2020, that it had no horse in the Labour leadership race. Between 2016 and 2018, its website claimed that Labour Together sought to 'provide a space for members and representatives across the party to discuss and debate the future of the Labour Party'. It also promised that 'our aim is to be broadly inclusive, and to involve people right across the movement. Jeremy Corbyn has rightly challenged the Labour Party to re-think the way it does politics'.[2] This complimentary nod to Corbyn was striking in light of what Labour Together now acknowledges it was actually doing behind the scenes.

In 2023, Labour Together would tell a very different story. On the social media platform Twitter (since rebranded as X), it claimed that a 'brave band' of eight MPs had '[b]uilt' Labour Together in 2017 in order to make Labour 'electable again'.[3] These MPs provided the spine of Starmer's shadow cabinet, and then his cabinet: Rachel Reeves (now chancellor), Steve Reed (secretary of state for environment, food, and rural affairs), Shabana Mahmood (lord chancellor and secretary of state for justice), Wes Streeting (secretary of state for health and social care), Bridget Phillipson (secretary of state for education), Lisa Nandy (secretary of state for culture, media, and sport), and Jim McMahon (minister of state in the department for levelling up, housing, and communities). Only Jon Cruddas, the eighth MP, has not subsequently served in Starmer's shadow cabinet or government.

Labour Together's retrospective claim to have been established in 2017 was curious on at least two counts. First, as discussed above, the group in fact formed in 2015. Second, it would have been most odd to found an organisation to make Labour 'electable again' in 2017—the year that Labour achieved the party's highest vote share in any election since the Blair heyday of 2001.

It *was* in 2017, however, that Labour Together became the vehicle through which McSweeney would run a 'secret' campaign to 'seize' the Labour Party back from its ascendant left wing.[4] One of Labour Together's central figures, the MP for Streatham and Croydon North Steve Reed, later bragged that '[i]n 2017 Labour Together developed a strategy for defeating the Hard Left and reconnecting Labour with the voters it had abandoned. In 2020, it played a key role in Keir Starmer's leadership campaign, and Keir has since transformed our party'.[5]

The Starmer Project is thus, in every sense that matters, a product and continuation of the Labour Together Project that preceded, guided, and enabled it.

As a result, the Starmer Project is both illuminated and condemned by Labour Together's history of financial murkiness, undisclosed influence campaigns, and attacks on citizen media, as well as its role in inflaming Labour's manipulated 'antisemitism crisis'. Starmer's leadership of the Labour Party—and the government he went on to form—is the fruit of Labour Together's poisoned tree.

LABOUR TOGETHER

Labour Together was formed in the shadow of Jeremy Corbyn. Its corporate precursor, Common Good Labour, was registered with Companies House on June 9, 2015, only six days after

Corbyn announced his intention to run for the party leadership. Its sole director was John Clarke, who would later turn up as a director of Blue Labour.[6] Blue Labour advocated a mixture of redistributive economic policy and social conservatism.

Party emails show that many of the people who would go on to form Common Good Labour (later Labour Together) had collaborated closely for years beforehand. They included Jonathan Rutherford, Jon Cruddas, Steve Reed, and Morgan McSweeney, the last drafted into discussions about localism and local government because of his role in the Local Government Association (LGA). In late 2014 and prior to Labour's embarrassing electoral defeat in 2015, this group engaged in constant correspondence about creating a project to centre Labour strategy based on a 'values model'.

The same emails reveal that the key movers behind the creation of Common Good Labour were Sir Trevor Chinn and Jon Cruddas. Cruddas, an MP well-liked across the party's factions, was also broadly sympathetic to the Blue Labour tendency. One email from early July 2015 shows that Chinn had initially wanted the Blairite MP Chuka Umunna to head the organisation. Umunna was at one point the leading light of sweet-talking Labour centrists and considered potential leadership material, before he immolated his political career by abandoning Labour for the ill-fated breakaway party Change UK in 2019. Umunna rejected the overture and Steve Reed or Tristram Hunt (the idiosyncratic MP for Stoke Central between 2010 and 2017) were mooted instead; Reed would become a director a few months later. Reed, who would serve on Corbyn's front bench as shadow minister under various portfolios between September 2015 and April 2020, would emerge as one of the key figures alongside McSweeney in the Labour Together Project, and in its undisclosed schemes that, amongst other things, stoked Labour's 'antisemitism crisis'.

Chinn, who would become a major donor to both Labour Together and Keir Starmer, is a wealthy entrepreneur with a long history of funding figures on the Labour right. Chinn made donations to Tony Blair (while MP), Ruth Smeeth, Tom Watson, Rachel Reeves, Ian Austin, and Wes Streeting—all of whom would express hostility to the leadership of Jeremy Corbyn. He has long been associated with Labour Friends of Israel and has an extended history of involvement in pro-Israel causes. For twenty years between 1973 and 1993 he chaired the Joint Israel Appeal (now United Jewish Appeal), which raised funds for cultural and educational endeavours in Israel.

In June 2016, a year after Common Good Labour was formed, Chinn was re-elected the vice chair of the Jewish Leadership Council (JLC), which engages in advocacy for Israel (among other things).[7] As of November 2023, Chinn was a member of the executive committee of the Britain Israel Communication and Research Centre (BICOM), a pro-Israel lobby group.[8] BICOM's sister project, We Believe in Israel, was run by Luke Akehurst prior to Akehurst's election to parliament in 2024. Akehurst is the Labour right's most effective campaigner and a dedicated warrior against the left. The JLC was fiercely critical of Corbyn when he was leader of the Labour Party.

In November 2024, Chinn was awarded the Israeli Presidential Medal of Honour. The award recognises individuals 'who have made an extraordinary contribution to the State of Israel or to humanity through their talents, their service, or in any other way'.[9] The award was the gift of President Isaac Herzog, who, in January 2024, had been cited by the International Court of Justice as making statements that plausibly violated the Genocide Convention. Herzog rejected the ICJ's judgment as a 'blood libel' that had 'twisted' his words.[10] By the time Chinn was awarded the medal, Israel's plausibly genocidal assault on Gaza had killed at least 43,000 Palestinians, including more than 13,000 children and 7,200 women.

Labour Together's first foray into public life made little impact. Cruddas announced in *The Observer* in October 2015 that Labour Together aimed to 'bring together all sections of our party to discuss and debate the future of our party'.[11] He promised that Labour Together would 'learn the lessons of defeat so that we can win again' and acknowledged that Corbyn had 'rightly challenged the party to rethink the way it does politics'. Cruddas confirmed that his colleagues in Labour Together included Steve Reed, Lisa Nandy, and Baroness Judith Blake.

Emails show that Corbyn's team in LOTO was concerned about Labour Together but was mollified when Nandy explained that the group was not 'anti-Jeremy'. Perhaps this was true at the time; McSweeney had not yet joined Labour Together or united forces with Reed. Nevertheless, the assurance that Labour Together was not 'anti-Jeremy' stands out in retrospect as a moment of poignant historical irony.

In March 2016, John Clarke, the original sole director of Labour Together, resigned. He was replaced by Chinn, Reed, Nandy, and Cruddas. They remained directors of Labour Together until a clear-out and reshape of the organisation in 2023.

The October 2015 launch was so forgettable that Labour Together felt comfortable unveiling itself a second time. That re-launch was announced in *The Guardian* in May 2016 with quotes from Lisa Nandy.[12] *The Guardian*'s coverage made no mention that Labour Together had already debuted the previous year. The new launch was boosted by articles from Jon Cruddas and Sharon Taylor.[13] Taylor was head of Stevenage Borough Council and deputy leader of the LGA Labour Group—then led by Morgan McSweeney. Nandy, Reed, and Taylor were described as Labour Together's vice chairs. Another supporter was Nick Forbes, the Labour leader of Newcastle City Council between 2011 and 2022—a matter of relevance later in our story.

Labour Together's second outing made almost as little public impact as its first. The group hosted a function at Labour's annual conference in September 2016 and established a £40,000 fund for projects advancing localism. It also co-hosted a one-day conference in November 2016 with the Fabian Society. Speakers included Nandy, Reeves, Taylor, and Tom Kibasi, the last of whom was a director of the Institute for Public Policy Research, a left-leaning think-tank and charity. Kibasi would go on to play a key part in linking Starmer's leadership campaign to the Labour left—a role for which he would later express his remorse.

And then: silence. Labour Together effectively disappeared from public view. Although it claims to have done extensive work behind the scenes in setting up meetings and campaign groups, whatever happened unfolded outside the public eye. Neither of the organisation's Facebook or Twitter accounts posted between November 3, 2016—the day of the conference—and February 17, 2019.

MCSWEENEY TAKES CONTROL

The 2017 general election was a shot across the bow for the Labour right. Shattering expectations, Corbyn's party won thirty seats more than in 2015 and, for only the third time since 1974, achieved 40 percent of the national vote. Within the Labour Party, the 2017 election left the Corbynite faction at its most powerful since Corbyn had been elected leader in 2015, while the right-wing faction that McSweeney represented was at its nadir.

The 2017 election result was the backdrop to a radical transformation of Labour Together. According to Anushka Asthana, ITV's deputy political editor whose 2024 book *Taken As Red* traced Starmer's rise to power, McSweeney took up employment at Labour Together the very day after the 2017 general election results came in.[14] What is certain is that the following month, on July 10, McSweeney was appointed Labour Together's company secretary, leaving the LGA.

According to Labour Together legend, 2017 was the year its eight 'brave' MPs formed the organisation to lead Labour back to electability through 'secret planning'.[15] As the above account shows, this is not true. Labour Together was created in 2015 out of a very different impulse—to hold the party together as the right wing revolted against a Corbyn leadership. During Labour Together's first years, the Labour Party's right wing had gone into overdrive to undo Corbyn's election, feeding endless attack lines to the media and using the pretext of the UK's vote to exit the European Union in 2016 to launch the so-called 'chicken coup'—a leadership challenge to Corbyn that was roundly defeated by a Labour membership that rallied behind its embattled leader.

But as with most legends, there is fact amidst the fancy: The organisation did fundamentally change character in 2017. It was then that McSweeney came on board and started working to undermine the Labour left.

I interviewed Cruddas for this book in 2023. His disappointment at the direction Labour had taken at the hands of Starmer and McSweeney was palpable. Cruddas' long-time friend, Neal Lawson, had been suspended from the party on contentious charges (his story is discussed in more detail later). Lawson hailed from Labour's so-called 'soft left'. Cruddas was highly critical of the authoritarian style that Labour had adopted under Starmer's leadership.

During the interview, I presented Cruddas with quotes from Labour Together figures retrospectively claiming credit for 'defeating the Hard Left' and playing a 'key role' in Starmer's leadership campaign. Cruddas seemed genuinely flummoxed. He speculated that this was a rewriting of history to cast Labour Together as more central to Starmer's leadership than it really was and thereby cement the group's influence in government.

I then asked Cruddas whether he had ever heard of an entity called the Center for Countering Digital Hate. CCDH, as shown in considerable detail later, was created by the Labour Together Project without any public disclosure. CCDH played an arguably ugly and certainly undisclosed role in the Labour Party 'antisemitism crisis' that would engulf the party under Corbyn's leadership. Cruddas, again, looked flummoxed. He had never heard of it, or of the people that Labour Together worked with to create CCDH.

'What, do you think Morgan and others were creating secret campaigns or projects or something?' he asked, seemingly betraying his own ignorance of the projects that McSweeney and Reed, via Labour Together, had launched and run for years.

The extent of Cruddas' ignorance appears to have been matched by Jonathan Rutherford, a veteran Labour figure who was invited to various Labour Together meetings and get-aways. In November 2023, *The Sunday Times* ran a front-page story about Labour Together, based in part on documents I gave to the paper. The story looked at the way Labour Together had transformed politics 'under the cover of darkness and in breach of the law', a reference to Labour Together's unlawful failure to declare its donations—discussed below.[16]

The article prompted a bemused response from Rutherford, who appears to have been involved in Labour Together's more respectable early endeavours. Rutherford wrote an article in the *New Statesman* denying that there was anything secret or nefarious about the group.[17] By then, a brief blurb for this book had been published, and, on the basis of a scant three-hundred-word summary, Rutherford declared that it leaned toward the 'conspiratorial'.[18] Rutherford then went into colourful detail about all the wonderful things Labour Together did behind the scenes to unite the party, like organising rural retreats for MPs and hosting them for private dinners à la Winston Churchill's The Other Club. Rutherford insisted Labour Together had 'developed bridge-building for a common-good politics'. It all sounded positively bucolic—and a world away from the disturbing projects that McSweeney and Reed actually launched via Labour Together, such as CCDH.

Assuming that Rutherford, like Cruddas, was speaking in good faith (and there is no reason to believe otherwise), both suffer from striking gaps in knowledge about what Labour Together was being used for in the period between 2017 and 2020—and precisely what sort of character they were dealing with in Morgan McSweeney.

To be fair to both Rutherford and Cruddas, they were not the only people who the Labour Together Project would lull or misdirect with soothing pieties about unity. In April 2019, McSweeney arranged a meeting with Jeremy Corbyn; Cruddas also attended. By then, McSweeney was already intervening covertly in the party's 'antisemitism crisis' that was undermining Corbyn's public reputation. McSweeney used the meeting to assure Corbyn that Labour Together was a project of 'renewal', not rivalry—even as McSweeney was actively plotting to destroy Corbyn and his politics, which McSweeney 'despised'.[19]

THE REAL McSWEENEY

Multiple insiders have described McSweeney as charming, polite, and serious, and there is no doubt he was exceptionally skilled at convincing the very people whose politics he was actually conspiring against that he was a reasonable man who had their best interests at heart.

One of these people was Gráinne Maguire, an Irish comedian and political commentator. In 2018, Maguire co-hosted a podcast series, *Changing Politics,* which put out twenty episodes before being shuttered in December 2018. Maguire confirmed to me that the podcast was largely McSweeney's brainchild and was generously funded by Labour Together, which paid for her time. Maguire said that McSweeney also played a central role in scripting the content of different episode segments. Labour Together's role in funding the podcast, and McSweeney's role in writing it, were not publicly known at the time, making the podcast one of a number of undisclosed projects McSweeney had a hand in directing after joining Labour Together.

Maguire had voted twice for Corbyn as Labour leader and openly identified with the party's left. By the time I caught up with her in 2024, Maguire had been so put off by Labour's direction under the Starmer Project that she voted Green in the July general election. Like many, she was upset by the party's approach to Gaza and trans rights, and by its decision to retain the two-child benefit cap (discussed in more detail later).

Maguire was clearly taken with McSweeney, their shared Irishness underpinning an instant rapport. 'He seemed like such a pure boy', she recalled, 'with his little bright cheeks'. After a long time in the party, Maguire had become finely attuned to 'Progress types', a reference to the Blairite group that was implacably opposed to Corbynism. She detected no hint that McSweeney was aligned with this faction or that he 'despised' Corbyn and Corbynism. In fact, she found him 'so fantastic, so intelligent, so articulate'. She recalls thinking that 'if only somebody like Morgan was running the country', everything would be alright. Little did she know that, even as McSweeney was penning scripts about trans rights and other right-on causes, he was simultaneously incubating plans to drive her worldview out of the party for good.

McSweeney joined Labour in the mid-1990s as a receptionist and then a member of the party's media operations. During the 2001 election he was given the task of feeding data into Peter Mandelson's famed *Excalibur* computer that stored information to be used by the party's rebuttal unit. But according to a *New Statesman* profile by Rachel Wearmouth, McSweeney's first real dive into Labour politics came when he worked alongside Steve Reed, then leader of Lambeth council. Under Reed, McSweeney 'led a revolt against the far-left factions for which the authority had become notorious'.[20]

Following a period in Dagenham—where retrospective hagiography has him single-handedly routing the far-right British National Party (BNP)[21]—McSweeney ran Liz Kendall's disastrous 2015 campaign for Labour Party leader. Kendall ran as a Blairite and received just 4.5 percent of the votes against Corbyn's landslide. McSweeney then returned to the LGA, where he would stay until leaving to join Labour Together in 2017. Kendall's career would undergo a renaissance after McSweeney had guided Starmer to victory.

For an organisation supposedly committed to internal harmony through cross-party unity, McSweeney was plainly an odd choice. Nick Forbes, who had been one of Labour Together's first public supporters, explained in 2021 that McSweeney 'doesn't have room for compromise with the hard left. He thinks that they need to be eradicated from the party because they are so dangerous'.[22] That doesn't sound very harmonious. McSweeney is a long-time protégé of Peter Mandelson, the architect of New Labour who, in February 2017, publicly bragged that he was 'working every day' to bring down Corbyn's elected leadership.[23] That doesn't sound very unifying. Mandelson has been quoted saying of McSweeney: 'I don't know who and how and when he was invented, but whoever it was . . . they will find their place in heaven'.

Asthana puts it bluntly: McSweeney and his close ally Reed 'despised' Corbyn and the 'hard-left' politics he represented.[24] Pogrund and Maguire similarly relate that, for McSweeney, 'Corbyn's politics were not just wrong. They were evil'.[25] A man of such uncompromising views plainly could have no interest in bringing the party's factions together.

Indeed, almost as soon as McSweeney became the company secretary of Labour Together and its employee, he set his sights on destroying Corbyn and the popular movement he had inspired. These plans were laid out in a SWOT (Strengths, Weaknesses, Opportunities, Threats) analysis authored by McSweeney that set out the lay of the land for the Labour Together Project in the post-2017-general-election environment. McSweeney distributed the analysis to Labour Together insiders at a meeting in Steve Reed's office on June 20, 2017—less than two weeks after the Labour Party had achieved its best national vote share since 2001. The document argued that Labour Together had to undertake a project of 'renewal' to remake the Labour Party as representative of the working class and remove it from Corbynite hands. McSweeney would use that same word, 'renewal', in his fabled meeting with Corbyn two years later, but this document shows what he really meant by the word—the permanent defeat of Corbyn and his politics, even as Corbynism had nearly doubled the party's membership and substantially increased its share of the popular vote.

The document noted that Corbyn was unassailable as party leader in the wake of the impressive 2017 election result, which had secured the left's ascendancy throughout the party. McSweeney would experience the bitter reality of the left's growing influence in Streatham, the constituency of Chuka Umunna, where McSweeney was a right-wing fixture in the CLP. At this local level, McSweeney worked closely with Matt Pound, who in turn was close to Luke Akehurst. Pound was the 'national organiser' for Labour First from January 2017 to January 2020.[26] Whereas Labour Together under McSweeney engaged in covert efforts to sabotage the Corbyn leadership, Labour First was base camp for the Labour right's overt fightback. Pound would subsequently join the Labour bureaucracy under Starmer; McSweeney, Pound, and Akehurst would all play important roles in the selection of Labour's parliamentary candidates for the July 2024 general election, a process which (as noted) was heavily criticised for excluding left-wing candidates on controversial grounds.

Streatham's CLP was the site of fierce factional confrontation following a surge of left-wing members who joined (or began to participate) after Corbyn's election. The contest came to a head in February 2019, when the CLP voted by the slimmest margin to adopt an all-member-meeting model that was seen as a way of short-circuiting the right's grip on the CLP. The fight played out on the pages of *LabourList*, the party's de facto in-house journal, with Pound making an impassioned plea for all constituencies to reject the model.[27] One left-winger active in the community recalls that, until that point, McSweeney had cut a modest figure, with Pound considered more personally combative. But when the Labour right lost the vote in Streatham, McSweeney was seen losing his temper for the first time: he shouted 'blue murder' about the voting process, according to one person who attended on the night.

Just under three weeks after the left had won its desired changes to the structure of the CLP, Umunna would leave the

Labour Party to join the short-lived breakaway party Change UK. The CLP's ascendant left would select the left-wing Bell Ribeiro-Addy to replace him as their local MP candidate. Ribeiro-Addy would be elected to parliament in December 2019 and join the Socialist Campaign Group of MPs.

Back in Reed's office, McSweeney explained that the Labour Together Project had two missions: First, it had to prepare for when Corbyn eventually stepped down, identifying and developing a candidate who could swoop in to take Corbyn's place. This role would eventually be played by Keir Starmer. While there was no need to immediately pick Corbyn's successor, McSweeney explained that Labour Together would have to transform itself into a vehicle for a leadership bid at the appropriate time. If they succeeded, the rewards would be immense: with a new hand-picked leader in place, the Labour Together Project could capture the party for the right—and, per the testimonies quoted above, 'eradicate' those 'evil' left-wing tendencies that McSweeney 'despised'.

Second, Labour Together had to 'ensure' that Corbyn 'lost badly', according to Maguire and Pogrund.[28] Only Corbyn's resounding defeat in a general election would remove him from the scene and trigger a new leadership contest. There is no doubt that the Labour Together Project viewed electoral success for the Labour Party under Corbyn as anathema. McSweeney's SWOT analysis listed 'a Labour government' in the category of 'threats'. As Asthana notes, this made 'explicit that [McSweeney's] concern was not whether Corbyn could win, but that if he were to become Prime Minister it would prevent the renewal they were focused on'.[29] McSweeney and his allies would burn down the party to inherit the ashes.

Indeed, Labour Together was bent on engineering this 'renewal' even though it meant giving the Tories another five years to oversee widening inequality and biting austerity as they drove through a hard Brexit. It is one of the striking ironies of the Labour Together Project that it would select Starmer to replace Corbyn in part because it could trade on his popular image as the party's 'Mr. Remainer'—even as the Labour Together Project had worked for years to ensure that the party 'lost badly' to a Tory government that promised to deliver Brexit on the most uncompromising terms.

McSweeney was clear in his briefing that the conspiracy to destroy Corbynism would have to be conducted in utmost secrecy. Indeed, McSweeney's SWOT analysis identified the discovery of the true work of the Labour Together Project as one of the greatest threats it faced. But Labour Together couldn't disappear altogether. Instead, the project set out to mislead all but a small coterie of insiders about what it was really doing. It would do so by curating its public image as a well-meaning, cross-factional think-tank convening convivial dialogues to help the party navigate and transcend its factional divides. McSweeney dubbed this protective manoeuvre 'Operation Red Shield'.[30]

From the outset, then, the Labour Together Project acted with premeditated misdirection and deceit.

In years of investigating McSweeney and Labour Together, I've only ever found one clip of McSweeney talking to camera: a recording of his introductory remarks to a small gathering hosted by Labour Together on July 15, 2019. It is chilling to re-watch the presentation knowing, as we now do, what McSweeney was up to behind closed doors.

McSweeney stands in a natty suit in front of a big-screen TV broadcasting the subject of the event: 'How can we build a 21st Century Labour Party?' He is positioned behind three speakers spanning the breadth of political opinion in the party: Nathan Yeowell, director of the Blairite think-tank Progress, is ironically seated on McSweeney's left. To McSweeney's right is Laura Parker, a former Corbyn aide and director of the left-wing campaign group Momentum, which had been established following Corbyn's shock leadership victory in 2015. Sandwiched between them is Neal Lawson, the director of Compass. Compass is devoted to the Sisyphean task of getting progressive left-wing and liberal forces to work together.

As will be seen later, both Parker and Lawson would eventually fall foul of the political project being incubated by McSweeney, having being lured into giving it their tacit and sometimes explicit support. Both came to denounce the authoritarian and factional project that McSweeney would incubate. Both were played like a fiddle.

To be fair, McSweeney was utterly convincing. 'The Labour Party has always been a party that has brought traditions together: our Labour unionist tradition, our radical socialist tradition, our reforming and social democrat tradition', McSweeney told the meeting in his soft Irish lilt:

> But too often and for too long these traditions are in a state of angry estrangement. Too often [and] for too long the focus has been on our differences, and that can come at a cost. The party is divided, and unity requires reconciliation. The best place to start this journey is by revisiting our founding principles. Labour was built on the principle of justice. We stand for decency in how we treat one another, and fairness in how we share out the advantages and burdens in society. The moral heart of justice is equality: each person is of equal worth. We must embed into our systems and actions this principle that all members are equal . . .
>
> Sometimes some people seem to make it their mission to try and kill off the traditions that are not theirs. But you can't do that, because these traditions are always with us. They're like our souls. When those three souls stand together is when our party comes to life.

By this time, McSweeney's secret plot to 'kill off' the party's Corbynite 'soul' was well-advanced. But to put it into action, McSweeney needed cash.

McSweeney's work with Labour Together, so important for Starmer's rise, was made possible by hundreds of thousands of pounds in donations. The public was totally unaware of this because McSweeney failed to report these donations as required by law. Serious questions need to be asked about whether McSweeney may have failed to report the donations on purpose—in my opinion, there is evidence that strongly suggests that possibility.

The Electoral Commission is a statutory body that regulates elections in the UK. It is of fundamental importance to UK democracy as it provides vital information about who funds politicians, parties, and related organisations like think-tanks. Its remit includes regulating and monitoring political donations. Individuals and organisations that fall under the ambit of the Commission are supposed to report any donation made or received over £7,500. Details of the donation are made public via the Electoral Commission's register, which is searchable. It is not difficult to report donations or search the Commission's public register.

One consequence of McSweeney's failure to report donations as required by law was that the donations were not contemporaneously published. This meant the public had no way of knowing that Labour Together was receiving hundreds of thousands of pounds, or who it was receiving the money from. This will have helped the organisation to fly under the radar as it pursued its 'secret planning' and 'strateg[ising]' to defeat the 'Hard Left'. If the donations had been made public, questions would certainly have been asked about why Labour Together, with its limited public presence, was receiving such huge pots of cash, and what it was doing with it.

Prior to McSweeney's arrival Labour Together was modestly funded. Between October 2015 and June 2017 it received £121,000 in donations, all from Martin Taylor. Taylor, a hedge fund manager with interests in private healthcare, would become a major funder of Starmer's Labour Party. Taylor's financial records reveal an affinity with anti-Corbyn causes, including a £180,000 donation to an outfit called Labour Tomorrow that was reportedly being used to 'fund campaigners against Jeremy Corbyn' during the 2016 Labour leadership contest.[31] Taylor's 2015 and 2016 donations to Labour Together were properly reported.

After the 2017 general election, which suggested that Corbynism could be electorally viable, Taylor and Chinn poured resources into Labour Together. Between June 2017 and September 2020, Labour Together received £862,492 in cash and non-cash donations. Taylor donated £585,992 in cash and non-cash donations; Chinn donated £175,500 in cash. The vast bulk of these donations—£849,429—was made between June 21, 2017, and March 18, 2020: two weeks before the vote in which Starmer was elected as Labour Party leader.

This date range is revealing. It spans the time between Labour's unexpectedly good showing at the June 2017 general election, the devastating results of the 2019 general election, and Starmer's Spring 2020 Labour leadership campaign. It thus covered the exact period when McSweeney secretly worked first to undermine Corbyn and then to secure the Starmer succession.

Additional, smaller donations to Labour Together were made by Baron Clive Hollick (£10,000), a co-founder of the Institute for Public Policy Research; Simon Tuttle (£10,000), a private equity executive and director of the anti-racism campaign group Hope Not Hate;[32] Baron Paul Myners (£25,000), a 'City grandee' and former Labour minister under Gordon Brown;[33] Richard Greer (£10,000), reported to be an investment banker; and Sean Wadsworth (£10,000), the founder of the Nigel Frank recruitment company and a donor to Owen Smith's leadership campaign.[34] Smith had unsuccessfully challenged Corbyn for the leadership in 2016 in the so-called 'chicken coup', after revolting MPs triggered a contest.

Labour Together failed at the time to report fully £739,429 of the cash and non-cash donations it received between June 2017 and September 2020 to the Electoral Commission, as required by law. Of this amount, £143,992 consisted of three non-cash donations made by Taylor. The remainder (£595,000) were cash donations made by Chinn, Taylor, Myners, Tuttle, Greer, and Wadsworth. Electoral law requires that all donations must be reported within thirty days of receipt. There is no evidence that the donors were aware their gifts were not being properly reported.

In September 2021 the Electoral Commission fined Labour Together £14,250 for these failures, after Labour Together's new company secretary (who replaced McSweeney) reported the matter to the Commission. The fine was levied following an investigation by the Commission. The implication of this finding is profound: the Commission found that Labour Together had incontrovertibly broken the law. That is now beyond dispute. What remains to be settled, I believe, is why.

Labour Together has claimed that it was all a big mistake—that it broke electoral law for two years by accident. Hannah O'Rourke, a long-time employee of Labour Together and company secretary at the time of the self-report, told the media following the outcome of the Commission's investigation that the failure to report had been 'entirely unintentional' and an 'administrative oversight'. She further claimed that Labour Together had contacted the Electoral Commission 'as soon as we became aware of the error'.[35]

Documents show that this was also the story that Labour Together told the Electoral Commission directly. Labour Together explained to the Commission that, 'put simply, a number of donations should have been reported but were not: it appears, as a result of human error and administrative oversight'. It further explained that 'enquiries have been made with those involved at the material time and frankly it was assumed that donations were being properly reported'. Most importantly, correspondence reiterated that 'there was absolutely no intention to make a false declaration, nor to fail to report'.

The Electoral Commission has refused to disclose the full basis on which it reached its decision to levy only a very modest fine on Labour Together, or any details of the investigation it conducted. It has refused at least three Freedom of Information (FOI) requests for copies of its investigative report. It has claimed—wrongly, in this author's view—that disclosure of its investigative report in this instance would dissuade others from self-reporting wrongdoing.[36] The Commission has maintained this position despite publishing detailed investigative reports on other matters, like its investigation into Momentum in 2019 and Vote Leave/BeLeave/Veterans for Britain/Darren Grimes in 2018.[37]

However, having looked at the documents from the Labour Party, the more limited number of documents released to me by the Electoral Commission based on FOI requests, and new details about what the Labour Together Project was doing behind the scenes, I don't find Labour Together's version convincing. Or, more precisely, it is my opinion that the totality of evidence about the Labour Together Project, not least its capacity and appetite for misdirection and subterfuge, when read alongside the FOI requests and Labour Party files, could just as plausibly give rise to the suspicion that McSweeney's failure to report donations was intentional.

We turn to the FOI disclosures first. In late December 2023, the Commission finally released documents to me showing that it had explicitly told McSweeney that Labour Together needed to report its donations.

The FOI disclosures included records of a call between McSweeney and an unidentified person at the Commission dated November 14, 2017. The call was logged in the Commission's contact system and appears to have been initiated by McSweeney. At the time of the call, Labour Together had received three donations that it had yet to report, including one donation of £10,000 from Chinn and two donations totalling £38,000 from Taylor. McSweeney had by this time already set in motion his secret plan to destroy Corbynism.

Under the heading 'detail', the call log records that 'Labour Together have not been reporting donations to us, Mr McSweeney was under the impression that Labour Together did not have to report because they do not campaign. However, Labour Together is a registered MA [members association] on our system. Mr McSweeney says that they are not a members association and this is where the confusion started'. The unidentified Commission advisor told McSweeney 'to report the donations to us with a cover letter saying why they had not been reported sooner and said that if the details in the system were wrong, we can review it'.

A members association is an 'organisation that is not a political party, but is wholly, or mainly, made up of members of a political party', the Commission would later tell McSweeney. Members associations are required by law to report to the Electoral Commission donations they make and receive above £7,500.[38]

McSweeney's claim that Labour Together 'did not campaign' is striking. By the time of this call in November 2017, McSweeney had already told Labour Together insiders that it should prepare to incubate a future leadership bid once its undisclosed political projects had contributed to the defeat of Corbynism.

McSweeney's plan also involved fostering an ecosystem of influencers and publications to rival pro-Corbyn alternative media in order to achieve his political aims. Indeed, McSweeney would literally script a podcast called *Changing Politics*! Furthermore, this podcast engaged directly in political campaigning, without any public acknowledgment that it was funded by Labour Together and part-written by McSweeney. 'So excited for @changingpolipod', Hannah O'Rourke, an employee of Labour Together, tweeted one day before the first episode was released in late June 2018. '[It is] the first all female presented [*sic*] political podcast that connects politics to actually campaigning', she enthused.

The first episode of the podcast focused on Seni's Law: a laudable piece of legislation to improve the treatment of people with mental health issues. Seni's Law was submitted as a Private Members' Bill by none other than Steve Reed, McSweeney's long-time ally and collaborator on the Labour Together Project, as well as the shadow minister for civil society. Reed was given five minutes of the tight thirty-minute runtime of the first episode to sell the bill. The episode closed with a call for members of the public to contact their MPs to push for them to attend the next reading of Reed's bill the following week and vote it through the Commons.

The podcast's Twitter feed also extolled Seni's Law and prominently featured Steve Reed. 'Steve's the MP for Croydon North who is pushing Seni's Law through Parliament', the *Changing Politics* Twitter account explained, sharing Reed's own endorsement for the show. 'Follow him for updates'. The podcast's Facebook account was also used to set up a Facebook group called 'Changing Politics Campaign for Seni's Law'. In February 2019, the podcast's Twitter account shared a video produced by Labour Together that extolled the historic virtues of the Labour Party.

This was an extraordinary situation, regardless of the virtue of Seni's Law. Just over seven months after McSweeney had told the Electoral Commission that Labour Together 'did not campaign', the organisation was using its undeclared donations to pay for and launch a podcast, scripted in part by McSweeney himself, that was explicitly 'campaign[ing]' for a bill introduced and backed by Steve Reed, a shadow cabinet minister and McSweeney's fellow Labour Together director—all without any public disclosure of these connections.

On December 6, 2017, an unidentified Commission staffer wrote to McSweeney. They informed him that Labour Together was correctly registered as a members association and that Labour Together was therefore required to continue to declare donations. 'As the Board of Labour Together is made up of Labour

Party members, it is considered to be a Members Association', the Electoral Commission confirmed. The response went into considerable detail about what donations members associations were supposed to report and provided guidance on what forms to fill in and where to download them. It reminded McSweeney that donations had to be made within thirty days of receipt.

Further correspondence in February 2018 shows McSweeney engaging with an Electoral Commission official about how to report donations; the Commission pointed out that he had filled in a form incorrectly when reporting a single donation.

This correspondence has potentially serious legal consequences. When the Electoral Commission began its investigation into Labour Together in 2020, Labour Together was asked to provide the Commission with any and all information relevant to the matter. Party emails show that McSweeney receive the correspondence in which this request was made clear. They also show that McSweeney was being consulted about Labour Together's response to the Electoral Commission in February 2021, as the Electoral Commission investigation was ongoing, even though he had already stepped down from Labour Together as a director. McSweeney was pencilled in to meet Labour Together's lawyers to discuss the issue the following month, apparently ahead of sending a response to queries raised by the Electoral Commission.

Emails show that McSweeney was told that it was possible that the Electoral Commission had failed, during its investigation, to identify the existence of his call to the Commission in November 2017. If it is true that the Commission was unaware of the call, it is something the Commission is going to have to work extremely hard to explain and justify.

Email correspondence shows that the idea was floated with McSweeney that no mention should be made of his call to the Commission. Emails also show that Labour Together's initial correspondence with the Commission made no mention of McSweeney's call, or the clear and explicit directions that the Commission gave to McSweeney of the need to report donations and how to do so.[39] Email correspondence also shows that McSweeney was sent copies of the Electoral Commission's correspondence with Labour Together up until March 2021, as well as Labour Together's response to the Commission, quoted above, all of which neglected to mention McSweeney's call and asserted that the failure to report was due to an 'administrative oversight'.

One important caveat: the available documentation concerning how the Commission and Labour Together addressed this issue does not go beyond March 2021. It is possible that Labour Together decided, at some later point, to acknowledge McSweeney's call. The Commission has failed to answer whether this is so—all the more reason why it is so imperative that the Commission release the investigative report it drafted in preparation for levying its fine.

On the available evidence, there is an urgent need to establish precisely what Labour Together told the Commission.

More alarmingly still, there is evidence that, in my opinion, raises serious questions as to whether McSweeney may have deliberately chosen not to report donations to the Electoral Commission:

First, we have the correspondence between the Electoral Commission and McSweeney. This indisputably establishes that McSweeney had put it to the Commission that Labour Together did not have to report donations as it did 'not campaign' and that the Commission repeatedly informed McSweeney that Labour Together was indeed required to report donations, and how to do so.

Second, as noted above, *The Sunday Times* reported in November 2023 on McSweeney and his failure to report donations.[40] The article was prompted by my decision to give certain documents to *Times* reporter Gabriel Pogrund. The paper spoke to a well-placed MP who had attended a Labour Together meeting in parliament in 2019. This source claimed that the issue of reporting donations was raised in that meeting, and that McSweeney was directly asked in front of the assembled MPs whether Labour Together was properly reporting its donations to the Electoral Commission. McSweeney, according to the source, affirmed that Labour Together was reporting its donations properly. In reality, Labour Together failed to report even a single donation as required by law throughout the entirety of 2019.

As McSweeney was reportedly misinforming MPs, Labour Together was simultaneously misinforming the public. From at least April 2019, Labour Together's website claimed that 'we are funded by donations small and large from activists, trade unions and members who recognise our network needs to exist'.[41] It then directed readers to the Electoral Commission's donation register, providing a hyperlink to the Electoral Commission's searchable database with the phrase 'Labour Together' pre-filled in. Of course, anybody clicking that link in April 2019 would not have seen the majority of the donations Labour Together had received in 2018 and 2019, because McSweeney had not reported them. Labour Together would repeat this claim, and again direct people to the Electoral Commission's register, in an article published by *LabourList* in February 2020,[42] when McSweeney was still neglecting to report donations while acting as the campaign chief for Starmer's Labour leadership bid.

The February 2020 article, written on behalf of Labour Together and incorrectly telling the public that Labour Together was reporting its donations, was penned by Shabana Mahmood, who would later be appointed the lord high chancellor and secretary of state for justice. As discussed later, this was not the only inaccurate or incomplete claim Mahmood made in that article, which, taken together, must raise questions about her suitability for her current role as the safekeeper of the UK's legal system.

The FOI documents, the MP's testimony, and the Labour Together website all indicate that the organisation in general and McSweeney himself were repeatedly informed of the legal requirement to report donations and were simultaneously testifying that this was taking place—*when it was not*. Is it really credible that, in light of these repeated reminders and public statements, Labour Together just absent-mindedly forgot to disclose more than *half a million pounds* in politically sensitive donations?

A third relevant piece of evidence is what we now know about what McSweeney was actually doing. As the following chapters will show, while Labour Together was failing to report donations it also helped set up an astroturf campaign that fuelled the Labour 'antisemitism crisis'. It did so without any public disclosure—and, it appears, without informing Jon Cruddas MP, its own erstwhile director. It also worked to place damaging stories in the media about the same issue—again, without any public disclosure. At the same time, McSweeney was purposefully misleading all but a small group of insiders about what Labour Together was really doing, curating a façade of cross-factional bonhomie that would deflect close or critical scrutiny.

We also now know that McSweeney was upfront about the biggest threat to his secret projects: discovery. As noted above, his 2017 SWOT analysis had warned that, if anybody found out what he and his allies were really doing, the initiative would fall apart. In my opinion, the SWOT analysis provides compelling evidence of motive: a need to avoid scrutiny and fly under the radar, so as to free the Labour Together Project's hands to pursue its secret mission to destroy the Corbyn movement.

The Labour Together Project under McSweeney's direction was arguably defined by this propensity to misdirect, obscure, plot in secret, and—as in the case of its February 2020 *LabourList* article—mislead the public about its work and activities. As we've seen, Labour Together now brags about having strategised to destroy Corbynism whereas, at the time, it had adopted a public posture of studied neutrality and pretended to seek unity. Similarly, it now celebrates its part in Keir Starmer's election as party leader, a role it explicitly denied playing at the time. Indeed, its secret projects, as McSweeney set out in the SWOT analysis, were *entirely contingent* on misleading people.

In these circumstances, would it be so surprising that Morgan McSweeney, who was incubating secret campaigns and misdirecting the public about his objectives, would take the exact same approach to his funding?

There is another crucial aspect to this: when the Electoral Commission conducted its investigation into Labour Together in 2020 and 2021, there was no hint that Labour Together was anything other than the anodyne, well-meaning think-tank it was claiming to be in public. The true nature of McSweeney's projects being run via Labour Together have only very recently come to light. This constitutes substantive new evidence that altogether recasts Labour Together's failure to report donations; evidence indicating that McSweeney and his allies were comfortable with using deception to achieve their political objectives. This is one reason why I believe the Electoral Commission must not only release its investigative reports but also reopen its probe. The integrity of British democracy and the rule of law require it.

STARMER'S LEADERSHIP BID

One way that Labour Together helped Starmer's Labour leadership campaign was with access to polling.[43] By the time McSweeney hooked up with Starmer in mid-2019 to incubate his candidacy, Labour Together had spent hundreds of thousands of pounds on intensively polling the party membership. Polling was a declarable benefit under parliamentary reporting rules at the time. Starmer, if he did receive this sort of benefit above a certain value, would have been required to report it in his parliamentary spending declarations.

As of the end of 2023, not a single donation or benefit-in-kind flowing between Starmer and Labour Together appeared on the Electoral Commission's donation register or in Starmer's parliamentary declaration of interests.

Perhaps this is true. Perhaps Labour Together's support was merely of the moral, or financially negligible, variety. Perhaps it was spending its undeclared pot of funding on matters wholly unrelated to the very campaign that McSweeney was running while simultaneously sitting on the board of Labour Together, and even as Labour Together was helping Starmer win the leadership election—per its own subsequent online boasting.

Regardless, questions must arise about how McSweeney has been able to retain his roles in the Labour Party and as chief of staff to the prime minister. It is now incontrovertible that McSweeney caused Labour Together to break electoral law by failing to report donations over a long period of time.

Then there is the matter of Labour Together breaking the law by failing to report donations valued at £147,500 during the period of Starmer's Labour leadership campaign—while the organisation was secretly backing Starmer's campaign (as it subsequently admitted) and while McSweeney still figured as its company secretary.

Three donations were made to Labour Together in January 2020, while a fourth was made in February (see Table 1). Labour Together failed to report the donations within the mandated thirty-day period, and still had not reported them by the time McSweeney resigned as Labour Together's company secretary on April 4, 2020. In fact, Labour Together only reported these four donations in December 2020. Between January and April 2020, McSweeney served as the campaign chief for Starmer's Labour leadership bid.

To reiterate: McSweeney was the company secretary of Labour Together while he was running Starmer's Labour leadership campaign. During this period, Labour Together was breaking the law during by failing to report donations; it was also secretly backing Starmer's campaign while telling the public it was not supporting any particular candidate. During this period, Steve Reed and Lisa Nandy were also serving as directors of Labour Together; both were later appointed shadow ministers and then cabinet ministers under Starmer's leadership. This means that two of Starmer's future cabinet appointments, as well as his future chief of staff, served as the directors of a company that was breaking electoral law while secretly backing his Labour leadership campaign.

What a mess.

TABLE 1. Undisclosed Donations to Labour Together During Starmer's Labour Leadership Campaign

Donor	Amount	Date Made and Accepted	Legal Reporting Date	Date Actually Reported	Days Late
Trevor Chinn	£12,500	17/01/2020	16/02/2020	10/12/2020	298
Martin Taylor	£70,000	20/01/2020	19/02/2020	10/12/2020	295
Trevor Chinn	£15,000	23/01/2020	22/02/2020	10/12/2020	292
Martin Taylor	£50,000	28/02/2020	29/03/2020	10/12/2020	256

ORIGINAL SIN

McSweeney's failure to report donations as required by law was the original sin of the Labour Together Project. Everything the project did between mid-2017 and at least April 2020 must be understood as having been done with a pot of money that Labour Together was failing to report to the authorities and the public in violation of the law—with compelling (albeit not conclusive) evidence suggesting that he might plausibly have done this on purpose.

In order to grasp precisely what the Labour Together Project was up to, and how problematic its interventions were, one has to understand, at least in broad outline, the nature and content of the Labour 'antisemitism crisis' that raged for years under Corbyn's party leadership. That controversy contributed to Labour's 2019 electoral drubbing and, arguably, haunted and constrained how Starmer's party navigated the 'plausible' genocide Israel went on to inflict in Gaza.

CHAPTER 2

THE CRISIS

In April 2023, Labour Together came clean about its long involvement in the fight against Corbynism. 'In 2017, Labour Together developed a strategy for defeating the Hard Left', as Steve Reed MP matter-of-factly explained.[1]

Much remains unknown about what this factional 'strategy' concretely entailed. What is clear is that, behind closed doors and away from public knowledge, the Labour Together Project inserted itself directly into a national media furore centred on allegations of antisemitism in the Labour Party. The project's interventions inflamed this controversy, which dogged Corbyn's leadership and was later cited by the Starmer regime to justify suppressing the party's left flank.

THE CRISIS: AN OVERVIEW

Labour's 'antisemitism crisis' comprised many strands. Fierce condemnation of Israel from many on the left of the party was undoubtedly painful for those Jewish members who had profound emotional ties to that country. Sometimes, albeit much less often than alleged, left-wing criticism of Israel took antisemitic forms. Sometimes it lacked sensitivity to the intergenerational trauma many Jews carry. Sometimes it raged with the fury of the oppressed. Sometimes the truth hurts.

Broadly, the 'antisemitism crisis' wove a series of discrete allegations of anti-Jewish rhetoric or discrimination, levelled against individual Labour members as well as the party's leadership and institutional practices, into a comprehensive indictment: that Corbyn's Labour Party was deeply antisemitic, and that this antisemitism flowed from the left-wing ideology Corbyn espoused.

In the main, and with a forewarning that this is a brutally reductive summary, the 'antisemitism crisis' was composed of four related allegations:

- That Labour's elected leader Jeremy Corbyn MP was personally antisemitic, as illustrated by statements he made and the company he kept;[2]
- That the Labour Party had become infested and overrun with antisemites since Corbyn's election as party leader in September 2015, inferentially because Corbyn's politics were antisemitic and because his leadership tolerated antisemitism;[3]
- That the Labour Party had received a huge volume of complaints alleging antisemitic conduct by members, which the party was either failing to properly process[4] or in which Corbyn's office was unduly interfering,[5] inferentially either to support allies accused of antisemitism or because Corbyn and his leadership team were insufficiently concerned about antisemitism;
- That any person or organisation questioning the substantial truth of any of the above allegations, or suggesting that any of them were driven by antipathy to left-wing politics or Palestine solidarity, was engaged in 'denialism', which was its own form of antisemitism.

As the 'crisis' unfolded over the years, emphasis was placed on different aspects, and certain allegations flitted into and out of relevance or were redefined, sharpened, and sometimes even totally inverted depending on how particular stories developed. This dynamic process ensured that the 'crisis' retained political momentum and salience across the full span of Corbyn's leadership.

In 2016, for instance, commentators primarily focused on the claim that Corbyn's associates were antisemitic, based largely on contemporary reporting. This was the year when, for example, Ken Livingstone made remarks defending a Labour MP, Naz Shah, for having once shared a controversial cartoon about Israel. The image had previously been posted online by Norman Finkelstein, a leading scholar of the Israel-Palestine conflict and well-known American Jewish critic of Israel. Livingstone's comments led to feverish media coverage demanding his expulsion—and then further media coverage demanding answers as to why this had not already happened. Livingstone was the former mayor of London and, at the time of his comments, a member of the party's highest organ of elected governance, the National Executive Committee (NEC). He was also a prominent supporter of Corbyn.

The media hubbub quietened in 2017 but reignited the following year, just as the Labour Together Project turned its attention to the issue. This revival of the controversy was predicated on the unearthing of historical examples of alleged wrongdoing through a process of digital archaeology. Stories began circulating that accused Corbyn personally of antisemitism based on old social media posts or comments he had made at events years prior. Meanwhile, online campaign groups such as Labour Against Antisemitism (LAAS) began scouring the social media records of actual or presumed Labour Party members so that they could submit formal complaints to the Labour Party. When the party failed to process such complaints to the groups' satisfaction, case details were leaked to the media, driving lurid coverage about obscure councillors sharing dodgy 'Rothschild' memes and the narrative that Corbyn's administration was letting antisemites off the hook.

We now know that McSweeney and Labour Together Project insiders were also engaged in this online trawling. Unlike LAAS, they did so behind the scenes, anonymously placing stories in the media rather than publicising them directly.

By about late 2018, and certainly from mid-2019, the primary alleged sin of the 'antisemitism crisis' was one of 'denialism', which could, at times, give the whole controversy a Kafkaesque air. The coverage from 2016 through early 2019 had, it was implied, established an impossible-to-deny bedrock of evidence supporting the three primary allegations so conclusively that they could not be denied, rejected or contextualised in good faith. It followed that anyone who tried to do so was indifferent to Jewish well-being, blinded by factional devotion to Corbynism, or—and this was the most common inference—either tolerant of antisemitism or antisemitic themselves. Furthermore, anyone who defended someone else accused of antisemitic denialism found themselves charged with the same offence. This discursive structure ensured that the allegation of antisemitism spread with the speed, ferocity, and relentlessness of a contagion.

This chronology is important for appreciating the role of the Labour Together Project. As shown in more detail below, the project went to work in 2018 and early 2019 placing media stories about alleged antisemitism in the Labour Party, creating that bedrock of 'facts' which all decent people thenceforth simply had to accept. In March 2019, the Labour Together Project initiated a campaign to 'completely eviscerate the economic base'[6] of alternative media outlets that investigated or reported on aspects of the 'antisemitism crisis' in ways that did not chime with or directly undermined the mainstream narrative. This campaign stigmatised such reporting as antisemitic denialism.

Importantly, the Labour Together Project's interventions recast 'denialism' as being not just antisemitic but also a form of misinformation. Questioning aspects of the 'antisemitism crisis' could then be construed as part of a broader threat to the fabric of Western democracy—akin to, say, claims that the 2020

American presidential election was fraudulent. The chutzpah of this campaign was impressive: even as it was busy plotting to destroy Corbynism, using money it was unlawfully failing to declare to the Electoral Commission, the Labour Together Project secretly fuelled a moral panic about antisemitism in Corbyn's Labour Party, then set up a seemingly unconnected entity that delegitimised any questioning of this moral panic as antisemitic. All in the name of fighting 'misinformation'!

Indeed, when independent reporters or commentators speculated or reported on a hidden hand or ulterior agenda driving the 'antisemitism crisis' narrative, the astroturf entity covertly associated with the Labour Together Project would brand them antisemitic conspiracists—even as the Labour Together Project was *itself* a hidden hand! A still crueller irony was that the thought-crime of 'denialism' would become a web that ensnared large numbers of left-wing *Jews* who questioned aspects of the 'antisemitism crisis', or who worried that the prevalence of antisemitism in the Labour Party was being exaggerated in order to undermine socialism as well as pro-Palestinian activism.

The 'antisemitism crisis' also became a proxy battle in a long-running conflict between establishment Jewish community organisations, on the one hand, and non-conformist as well as non-Zionist Jews on the other. Resolving the 'antisemitism crisis' on terms acceptable to the Jewish communal establishment required the performative and ugly exclusion of Jewish people from the Labour Party on the basis that their dissenting opinions amounted to denialist antisemitism.

A MORAL PANIC

The problem with the charge of 'denialism' is that it stigmatised scepticism toward media narratives on antisemitism, even where there was evidence that these narratives rested on claims that were sometimes untrue, incomplete or patently absurd.

To be sure, there was and is antisemitism in the Labour Party, while there are particular forms of antisemitism that appear disproportionately in left-wing circles. Indeed, the Corbyn leadership repeatedly acknowledged that social media trawling by various groups had unearthed clear-cut cases of antisemitic speech, such as Holocaust denial or conspiracies about sinister Jewish involvement in a New World Order. A 2022 Al Jazeera documentary, *The Crisis*, also unearthed evidence that some party members had engaged in clearly antisemitic exchanges. It would therefore be untrue to dismiss all claims of antisemitism in the Labour Party as politically motivated smears.

But it was another thing entirely to allege that these examples of antisemitism defined Corbynism, that it was pervasive throughout the party, or that it was a logical outcome of left-wing progressivism—all claims made repeatedly by the likes of the Jewish Leadership Council and the Board of Deputies of British Jews, two leading Jewish community organisations that also engage in pro-Israel advocacy.[7] The Al Jazeera documentary referred to above also discovered that substantial numbers of party members were accused of antisemitism merely for having engaged in legitimate criticism of Israel, while multiple studies found that anti-Jewish prejudice is lower among Labour supporters than among supporters of other political parties.[8]

What's more, many of the high-profile concrete stories making up the 'antisemitism crisis' were questionable, involving double standards or inaccurate reporting. This helped generate unwarranted hysteria and grievously hurt those left-wing Jews who found themselves pasted across tabloids as defenders of antisemitism, or even as antisemites themselves.

Even in cases where the reporting may have been largely accurate, some stories were just plain dumb. Take the example of 'Jew process'.

In March 2019, a Jewish Labour Party councillor named Jo Bird was suspended and then swiftly readmitted after *The Jewish Chronicle* had whipped up a froth. . . about a pun.[9] The

Chronicle, which was stridently critical of Corbyn's leadership, reported on a 'shocking recording' of a meeting of Jewish Voice for Labour (JVL) at which Bird was said to have made a number of 'shocking comments'.[10]

JVL was founded in 2017 as a pro-Corbyn counterweight to the Jewish Labour Movement (JLM), a formal affiliate of the Labour Party that had been critical of Corbyn. We now know that JLM figures worked closely with Morgan McSweeney from at least 2019 onward. JVL's leadership team was entirely Jewish and the group counted well-known Jewish anti-Zionist activists among its ranks. JVL contested aspects of the mainstream narrative around the 'antisemitism crisis' and for this reason became the target of ferocious condemnation from the pro-Israel and anti-Corbyn Jewish establishment.

What so 'shocked' *The Jewish Chronicle* were remarks by Jo Bird in defence of Marc Wadsworth, a Black member of the Labour Party who Bird and others believed had been unfairly accused of antisemitism. Bird said that JVL was 'calling for disciplinary hearings to be paused until a due process has been established based on principles of natural justice. What I call Jew process'.[11]

The pun was not only a little bit funny but also implied a positive comment on Jewish identity. Bird was saying that JVL wanted an unfair process to be reformed so that it upheld what Bird considered to be a positive Jewish trait, namely a respect for natural justice. For this innocuous bit of wordplay, Bird—a Jewish woman—was subjected to multiple days of damning media coverage and suspended from the Labour Party.

But things would become even more absurd. In May 2020, the newly minted shadow minister and Labour Together Project alum Steve Reed submitted dossiers on ten individuals to the head of Labour's Governance and Legal Unit (GLU), which handled membership complaints. Reed demanded that all face immediate suspension and investigation for engaging in allegedly antisemitic conduct. Four of the people on Reed's list were Jewish. One of them was Jonathan Rosenhead, an esteemed emeritus professor at the London School of Economics, who had a long history in anti-racist activism, including in the anti-apartheid movement. Reed is not Jewish.

Reed's complaint then prompted Labour Party bureaucrats to dredge up every complaint ever submitted against Rosenhead and subject him to an investigation on suspicion of antisemitism. One of the charges that Rosenhead was forced to answer—to prove that he, a Jewish professor with a lifelong history of anti-racist activism,[12] was not antisemitic—was that he had repeated Jo Bird's pun. In fact, Rosenhead, during a party meeting, had simply retold the story of what had happened to Bird.

The party would eventually find that he had no case to answer on this charge. But in the febrile crucible of the 'antisemitism crisis', the party found itself interrogating an elderly Jewish professor on charges of antisemitism because he had recounted how another Jewish member had been suspended, because she had made a pun that cast Jewish identity in a positive light.

Rosenhead's written response to the party is one of the most authentically moving pieces of writing about Jewish identity one is likely to encounter. Rosenhead detailed his family's history of antisemitic persecution, including how one branch of his father's family had been entirely wiped out in the Holocaust. 'The awareness of the provisionality of tolerance has a taproot stretching back centuries', Rosenhead wrote in response to the party's investigation:

> That is why all my parent's friends were Jewish; and why all *their* friends were Jewish . . . I am telling you all this to give you a take on how outrageous it feels, in effect, to be accused of antisemitism. Outrageous. It actually gives me the sense that whoever drafted this Notice [of Investigation] has quite simply failed to grasp the enormity of antisemitism as a concept or practice.

Sadly, this sort of deeply silly and cruel stuff was a routine feature of the 'antisemitism crisis'. It is no mystery why many observers would see such absurdities and conclude that the alleged 'antisemitism crisis' was not nearly so clear-cut as some claimed, that not every allegation of antisemitism was true or even reasonable, and that the people making those allegations should not be taken seriously or should have their motives examined.

To recap: it is wrong to say that there was no antisemitism in the Labour Party. But it is also wrong to say that every allegation of antisemitism in the Labour Party was true. Questions about the prevalence of antisemitism in the party remain a difficult, but important and necessary, subject for rational debate. The charge of 'denialism' killed this nuance. It demanded that anyone exercising scepticism be ejected from the political and moral community as anti-Jewish bigots—even when the sceptics in question were themselves Jewish.

The crusade against 'denialism' also upped the stakes. It became nearly impossible for well-meaning people to sift through the welter of claims about antisemitism and to have a reasoned discussion about what conduct was truly antisemitic. It chilled into frosty silence precisely the discussions that needed to be had. It created a sense of panic and fostered a political environment in which the safe option for many people was to tactically concede that, for example, robust criticism of Israel was antisemitic, or to cede the ground on that issue and not engage at all. It also incentivised party officials to err on the side of unfairly sanctioning members because it was more politically expedient to deliver 'results' than it was to properly examine the cases against them.

It is perhaps for this last reason that Corbyn's faction would eventually over-compensate for earlier procedural failings, rushing to discipline members even where the evidence against them was scanty—or where accused individuals merely had the temerity to question a flawed narrative, some of which was being written, behind a veil of anonymity, by a Labour Together Project that 'despised' Corbynism itself.

LABOUR AGAINST ANTISEMITISM AND THE ZIONIST FRINGE

One more feature of the 'antisemitism crisis' needs to be understood before moving on to the nuts and bolts of Labour Together's interventions in this arena: the role played by the online group Labour Against Antisemitism. The astroturf project that the Labour Together Project created would succeed with the support of LAAS activists and supporters. Its most prominent cheerleader was the British television celebrity Rachel Riley, who was also close to LAAS activists.

LAAS formed around late 2016 or early 2017 as a loose network of affiliated activists. An open letter of LAAS members, signed in March 2018, suggested it had at least fifty-five members at the time.[13]

The primary (but not exclusive) focus of LAAS' work was to engage in deep digs into the social media histories of real or apparent Labour Party members to discover alleged evidence of antisemitism. This evidence would be compiled into dossiers that were sent into the Labour Party demanding the expulsion of alleged antisemites.

An audit of complaints files for Al Jazeera's 2022 documentary, *The Crisis*, found that approximately 12 percent of all antisemitism-related complaints submitted to the party during Corbyn's leadership had come from LAAS-affiliated actors.

When the party failed to expel and suspend LAAS' targets, LAAS would inform the media that it had made thousands of complaints that had been ignored.[14] This, in turn, would drive the key narratives that the party was both overwhelmed with antisemites and that it was failing to meaningfully deal with complaints. Party files, discussed below, suggest that far more critical scrutiny should have been applied to LAAS' allegations.

LAAS was controversial for two reasons. The first was that the organisation and its members had a history of attacking the conduct of left-wing and non-Zionist Jews and accusing Jewish figures of antisemitism.[15] Many of these allegations were made by non-Jews.

In 2022, Al Jazeera reported on documents leaked from the Labour Party which showed that LAAS' spokesperson and one of its most well-known activists, Euan Philipps, had created a fake persona called 'David Gordstein', which many readers would take to be a Jewish name. Philipps is not Jewish. Philipps admitted to Al Jazeera that he was David Gordstein but insisted that 'he never claimed to be Jewish when doing so'.[16] 'David Gordstein', as shown below, would play a material role in the success of the astroturf campaign that was incubated by the Labour Together Project. Philipps remained a prominent member and spokesperson of LAAS even after his Gordstein persona was exposed.

Previously unseen documents from the Labour Party show that the Gordstein persona was used to make hundreds of complaints of antisemitism to the Labour Party between 2017 and 2021. The reports are detailed, but perhaps the most important feature was the number of times the persona was used to accuse left-wing Jews of antisemitism. The outrageous story of Gordstein's complaint about the elderly Jewish party member Riva Joffe, which led to the party investigating her on her death bed, is dealt with in Part Three below.

One of the more absurd Gordstein complaints was directed against Miriam Margolyes, the idiosyncratic national treasure and garlanded Jewish actress who played Professor Pomona Sprout in two of the film adaptations of *Harry Potter*.

One of Margolyes' allegedly antisemitic acts, according to 'Gordstein', was to use her Facebook profile to share an impassioned article written in 2019 by the highly regarded Jewish social anthropologist and London School of Economics professor David Graeber. Graeber challenged aspects of the mainstream narrative alleging a 'crisis' of antisemitism in the Labour Party.[17] He argued that the way the Labour Party 'antisemitism crisis' had been covered was itself antisemitic, because it generated unjustified 'rancour, panic and resentment' that 'creates terror in the Jewish community'. Ironically, Graeber had written in despair about how many of the 'protagonists' of the antisemitism crisis 'were not Jewish'.

So, to recap: an invented Jewish-sounding persona (Gordstein), created by a non-Jew, charged a Jewish actress with antisemitism, because she had shared an article by a left-wing Jewish academic, which argued that non-Jews telling scare stories about antisemitism was itself a form of antisemitism. This same non-Jewish activist would play a key role in amplifying the astroturf Stop Funding Fake News campaign, also led by non-Jews, that would implicitly accuse media outlets of being antisemitic for interviewing and recording the views of Jewish people who questioned aspects of the 'antisemitism crisis'. That astroturf campaign was run by an organisation established by the Labour Together Project.

I contacted Margolyes for this book to get her response to the Gordstein complaint. In an entertaining potty-mouthed tour of world politics, Margolyes bemoaned the conflation of anti-Zionism and antisemitism. On Gordstein she was amusingly frank: 'I'm an old cunt and I know what's what, and if he thinks I'm an antisemite he is speaking out of his bottom'.

Another, previously unseen document indicates that contempt for left-wing Jews emanated not merely from this or that LAAS figure but was one of the group's core commitments. It is one page of a longer text, prepared with a LAAS logo, which appears to be a training document or a preparation of press lines. The document endorses the use of the phrase 'as a Jew'. This is a derogatory play on how (often progressive or non-Zionist) Jews might open their critique of Israel, or some other related matter, with the qualifying clause: 'As a Jew . . . '. Some Jews find the phrase hurtful, even offensive, as they feel it can imply an accusation that they only recognise or inhabit their Jewish identity when it is politically convenient to do so.

LAAS was apparently very comfortable with deploying the as-a-Jew epithet to mock Jewish people guilty, in their view, of either engaging in or defending antisemitism. Thus, under the heading 'As-a-Jew antisemitism', the LAAS document alleges that 'racist Jews tend to underline their identity as a defence and to separate themselves from non-Jewish antisemites'. An illustrative example tells the reader that 'Jackomi and her friends commonly say they are talking "as a Jew"—as if that gives them more authority to make antisemitic statements'. This is quite something from an organisation whose most prominent spokespeople and many of whose most active members were not Jewish.

In May 2023, *Novara Media* broke the story of how Julie Cattell, a LAAS member, had been selected by the Labour Party as a councillor candidate in Brighton and Hove to contest the 2023 elections—despite a history of using the phrase 'As a Jew' on Twitter. In one 2019 exchange, Cattell was asked why a range of Jewish public figures—such as Noam Chomsky, John Bercow, and Miriam Margolyes—questioned aspects of the mainstream narrative of the antisemitism crisis. 'I asked for proof. Not a list of AsAJews', she responded.[18] Cattell is not Jewish.

The second controversial aspect of LAAS was that it was connected to a group of fringe pro-Israel activists who had historical links to the far right. One of those activists was a man called Jonathan Hoffman, who was an early advisor to LAAS.[19] The same 2022 Al Jazeera documentary that exposed David Gordstein[20] also established Hoffman's links to figures on the far right. It included footage of Hoffman and a fellow member of this fringe network called Damon Lenszner hectoring a Palestinian woman in 2018, for which they were both convicted of 'aggressive, bullying behaviour' in a North London court the following year.[21] Hoffman was connected to a broader group of equally fringe pro-Israel activists who harboured what some might call *robust* opinions about Muslims.

To give a flavour of Hoffman's milieu: in 2010, he was pictured protesting alongside a woman named Roberta Moore. Moore was one of the founders of the far-right English Defence League (EDL). She parted ways with the EDL in controversial circumstances in 2011, the year after she was pictured with

Hoffman. Moore would claim that she quit the EDL because of 'Nazi elements' within it.[22] But this had come after the EDL's leadership rebuked her for developing a working relationship with the far-right American Jewish Task Force, whose leader had been imprisoned for terrorism offences.[23]

When the photo of Hoffman and Moore was published, Hoffman attempted to claim in his *Jewish Chronicle* blog that the photo was a photoshopped fake, but embarrassingly he was forced to retract the claim.[24] Moore would subsequently write articles trying to contextualise the murderous attacks by Anders Breivik, the terrorist who killed dozens of children and teenagers on the Norwegian island of Utoya, which she described with near-comic understatement as 'regrettable'. 'I hold the same amount of sympathy for those on Utoya as I would if somebody committed this act on a Hitler Youth camp in the 1940s', she would write.[25]

Moore was an assiduous contributor to the comment section of a blog run by a man called Richard Millett, who worked closely alongside Hoffman for years. Moore posted repeated rants using Islamophobic slurs on Millett's blog. She also referred to liberal or anti-Zionist Jews as 'kapos', a reference to Jews who collaborated with the Nazis.

Together, Hoffman and Millett formed a double team: Hoffman would disrupt pro-Palestinian meetings, provoking confrontations that Millett would record. Millett would then post the recordings on his blog. During the 'antisemitism crisis', Hoffman and Millett's videos and stories were the source of a number of scandalised articles targeting the Labour Party and Corbyn. Indeed, Hoffman and Millett were at the centre of one of the defining scandals of the 'antisemitism crisis': the unearthing of a video (albeit not sourced from Millett or Hoffman) that showed Corbyn telling an obscure meeting in 2013 that certain 'Zionists in attendance' at a previous meeting did not understand 'English irony'. Corbyn was referring to four individual 'Zionists', two of whom were Hoffman and Millett. Much media coverage was canny in cutting up Corbyn's comments to make it seem as if he was casting aspersions against *all* Zionists, rather than four specific people, at least two of whom (Hoffman and Millett) had a history of disruptive behaviour at pro-Palestine events.

Another key advisor to LAAS was the libel lawyer Mark Lewis, who was also a director of UK Lawyers for Israel (UKLFI) between 2014 and 2017.[26] Mark Lewis' role in advising LAAS was not well known until 2023, when a video of LAAS activists speaking on a platform in 2020 was discovered.[27] A LAAS spokesperson confirmed during the event that 'we could not have functioned without him'. After the video was discovered by journalists in 2023, it was quickly set to private on YouTube. Richard Millett was appointed the operations manager of UK Lawyers for Israel (UKLFI) in February 2020.[28]

Lewis also represented, amongst others, Rachel Riley, who would play an important role in amplifying the work of Stop Funding Fake News—something she agreed to do after meeting directly with McSweeney and his closest collaborator, Imran Ahmed, in February 2019.

CHAPTER 3

THE SECRET PROJECTS

What was the Labour Together Project *doing* with Labour Together's huge pot of unlawfully undisclosed donations? Thanks to previously unseen Labour Party documents and more recent contemporary disclosures, we now know at least part of the answer: the project was fanning and fuelling the Labour 'antisemitism crisis' that would besmirch Corbynism's reputation and enable the Starmer Project to impose an iron grip on the party.

How did the Labour Together Project intervene in the 'antisemitism crisis'? First, McSweeney and his allies, including Imran Ahmed, seeded and placed a raft of media stories alleging that the Labour Party under Corbyn had a serious antisemitism problem that a Corbyn-aligned bureaucracy was failing to properly address. Details of the Labour Together Project's role in fuelling the controversy were only revealed in 2025—a shocking lack of disclosure about a crisis that helped transform British politics.

Second, internal party documents and recent revelations confirm that Labour Together was directly involved in creating an organisation called the Center for Countering Digital Hate and its deeply problematic astroturf campaign, Stop Funding Fake News. SFFN played a frankly unforgivable role in inflaming the Labour 'antisemitism crisis' well beyond what the evidence warranted. SFFN also evinced a disturbing hostility to free speech and democratic media as it set out to destroy the livelihoods of hard-working journalists on the basis of claims that were at best contentious.

Third, even while SFFN was destroying the careers of journalists at left-wing news outlets with largely unfounded allegations of misinformation, McSweeney worked 'secretly' with the Jewish Labour Movement to 'engineer' the Equality and Human Rights Commission investigation into the Labour Party over allegations of antisemitism.[1] I deal with this aspect of the Labour Together Project's involvement in the 'antisemitism crisis' in Chapter Eight.

For many of the people who have been caught up in the antisemitism controversy, or witnessed how it disoriented and demoralised Labour's briefly ascendant left wing, there was always a lingering sense that there was some hidden hand guiding and stoking a moral panic that raged for years in the media—much of it powered by claims that were misleading and, at times, absurd.

The truth is more complicated. There was no single organising force, no one smoke-filled room in which all conspirators met to plot their next move. Like most things in politics, the antisemitism controversy was propelled by diverse impulses and actors. Some of the furore was genuine and organic, as many people were authentically hurt and alarmed by evidence of undeniable antisemitism that was uncovered. Some of it, though, was disingenuous, as antisemitism claims were opportunistically exploited by people who treated a profoundly important issue as a cudgel to beat a political movement they opposed for other reasons and which they could not best through democratic means.

But we also now know, many years later, that there was at least *one* hidden hand orchestrating the 'antisemitism crisis': the Labour Together Project. And there was also at least *one* room in which plotting took place: Room 216 at the China Works hot-desking offices in South London, where McSweeney and his closest allies covertly inflamed the 'antisemitism crisis' and undermined the elected Corbyn leadership so that they might one day rule over the ashes of the party they had set alight.

And when the Starmer Project took up the baton as the Labour Together Project's next act, it would cynically use the 'antisemitism crisis'—a controversy that the Labour Together Project had itself exacerbated—as a pretext to marginalise the Labour left while disempowering the party's membership at large.

FACTIONAL BEDFELLOWS

McSweeney's plot to undermine Corbynism and incubate its replacement was carried out in utmost secrecy. Only a handful of insiders were ever allowed access to the inner sanctum where McSweeney's schemes unfolded. Indeed, the need for secrecy was so overwhelming that only a tightly controlled selection of people ever visited Labour Together's office, the aforementioned Room 216. Only three people, besides McSweeney, were allegedly allowed to work from there. Two were junior staffers: Hannah O'Rourke and Will Prescott. The third was McSweeney's contemporary and a man who shared his visceral antipathy to Corbynism: Imran Ahmed.

McSweeney, Ahmed, and Steve Reed MP would together establish CCDH and SFFN, both of which would declare war on what they dubbed online 'misinformation'. Ahmed, now based in the US, is the current CEO of CCDH, in which capacity he rails against alleged misinformation in *The New York Times* and on CNN while endorsing censorship legislation that many human rights groups consider a draconian threat to democracy. Since 2020, CCDH has grown into one of the most influential groups tackling 'misinformation' on both sides of the Atlantic, supported by millions in donations (the sources of which CCDH often does not identify).

As I have extensively detailed elsewhere,[2] Ahmed had a long history in the Labour Party—and a long history of butting heads with the Corbyn movement. After an initial stint with Andy

Slaughter MP he went to work for Hillary Benn, another MP and son of the famous Labour left-winger Tony Benn. Hillary Benn had been drafted into Corbyn's first shadow cabinet. When he defied Corbyn's position by delivering an impassioned speech arguing for British bombing raids in Syria, in December 2015, he was reading words allegedly written by Ahmed. Corbyn eventually sacked Benn in July 2016 after it emerged that he had been encouraging ministers to resign if Corbyn refused to accede to a motion of no confidence. By then, Ahmed's name was already the subject of dark whispers in Corbyn's office. One LOTO insider described Ahmed to me, with admittedly knowing hyperbole, as 'an absolute agent of horror'. Ahmed was widely suspected (albeit with no hard proof) of being the source of a raft of damaging leaks about the Corbyn project.

Ahmed's career would appear to make him an unlikely choice for organisations claiming to fight misinformation. For example, while working for Hillary Benn MP, Ahmed collaborated with a *Guardian* journalist on a story that would run during the 2015 general election about Grant Shapps. Shapps was a prominent minister in the Tory-Lib Dem coalition government and co-chairman of the Conservative Party. The article alleged that Shapps had created a fake Wikipedia profile (called Contribsx) to edit his own Wikipedia page. In an internal party email Ahmed claimed that the piece was based on a joint investigation by himself and *The Guardian*. Alas, the story fell apart in spectacular style a few months later after an investigation by Wikipedia's arcane audit committees comprehensively repudiated the claims.

Ahmed then moved to work with Angela Eagle MP, who would soon challenge Corbyn for leadership of the Labour Party. During this period, Ahmed amplified an allegation that angry Corbynites had smashed Eagle's window with a brick after she announced her leadership challenge. This incident had been dubbed 'Brickgate' in the media. In the midst of the resulting furore, Ahmed released a press statement on behalf of Eagle's office that included numerous questionable claims for which he was later chastised by independent media. Ahmed's statement, for example, alleged that a planned event at a Luton hotel where Eagle was slated to appear had been cancelled because the venue received threats. Alas, the hotel quickly pooh-poohed the story. 'Brickgate', an entirely ludicrous affair, would nevertheless bolster the media narrative that left-wing members of the Labour Party who supported Corbyn were intolerant reprobates. It was a narrative that Ahmed and McSweeney would continue to foster, covertly, when they started working together in 2018.

Dogged investigations by independent bloggers and media outlets revealed that Eagle's office window had *not* been smashed (it was instead a window on the ground floor in a shared office stairwell); the police had *no* evidence this incident was linked to Eagle; and there was *no* evidence the window had been broken by a brick. It eventually emerged that there wasn't even a brick on the scene—just a stray piece of masonry on the road, which may or may not have played a role in the damage. Nobody knew, in fact, what had broken the window, or who had done it, or why—yet the incident still somehow retains its force as a shorthand for the alleged thuggishness of Corbynism.

Brickgate was part of a broader attempt to defend Eagle's position against the real prospect that her mostly left-wing constituency would organise and vote to deselect her. It coincided with an allegation made by Eagle's supporters, and then by Eagle herself, that, at a critical meeting where left-wingers won control of the local Constituency Labour Party (CLP), members had engaged in rampant homophobia, including limping their wrists at a young gay man. The claim was never properly substantiated. It was also fiercely disputed by people who, unlike Eagle, were physically present at the meeting.

Emma Runswick, the self-identified 'queer' daughter of the CLP meeting's chair Kathy Runswick, wrote in the *New Statesman* of how unimaginable it would be that her loving, accepting mother would ever tolerate such gross and blatant homophobia. In fact, the day after the meeting at which Kathy was said to have allowed homophobia to run amok (and at which she was elected chair of the CLP), she attended her daughter's wedding—to another woman.[3] Unsurprisingly, despite years of investigations and alarmist reporting, not a single individual was ever sanctioned or found guilty of homophobia in this case.

Nevertheless, Eagle's supporters flooded the bureaucracy with complaints alleging that homophobia at the meeting, alongside a generalised air of left-wing menace, meant it was no longer safe or appropriate for the CLP to convene meetings. Of course, if the party agreed, the newly elected left-wing leadership of the CLP would be unable to move motions that could censure Eagle—or seek to replace her as an MP. Emails show that at this time, Labour Party bureaucrats opposed to the Corbyn leadership were working with Eagle to ensure her CLP remained suspended in order to prevent her deselection. The same emails show that Ahmed was frequently corresponding with Labour Party bureaucrats—including the now-infamous Sam Matthews, an official in the party's internal disciplinary unit, whose activities are discussed in more detail later. Documents show that Matthews was frequently at the coalface of a bureaucratic fightback against the Corbynite left. In one email, Matthews acknowledged speaking to Ahmed and described how Ahmed was involved in desperately trying to manage processes in Eagle's CLP to protect her position from the presumed wishes of local party members.

Even as he was working with Eagle and anti-Corbyn bureaucrats to undermine party democracy, Ahmed was also using his connections to try and convince the Labour Party to expel journalists who happened to be party members. By this point, Eagle's office was framing expressions contesting the claims of homophobia as a form of—you guessed it—homophobic denialism.

Ahmed left Eagle's office in late 2017 or early 2018. From there he went to work with Morgan McSweeney.

Ahmed's history in the party is important for three reasons: First, it showed that Ahmed was a factional, anti-Corbyn spin-doctor. He was responsible for seeding and amplifying contentious stories in the media that damaged the left by depicting it as a hotbed of hate, bullying, and abuse. Second, it revealed Ahmed's intolerance of alternative media outlets that constrained the ability of the Labour right to foster political narratives unhindered. Third, it illustrated Ahmed's uncanny ability to recode the legitimate contestation of controversial controversial claims as 'bullying' and 'libelous' conduct spread via '"conspiracy theory" channels'.

Ahmed would bring all of these qualities to the table when he joined McSweeney in Room 216.

CONSTRUCTING THE NARRATIVE

McSweeney and Ahmed got to work. Starting in either January or February 2018, Ahmed and McSweeney joined a raft of Corbyn-supporting Facebook groups, many of which had tens of thousands of members. McSweeney used Labour Together's money to commission YouGov to poll two of the largest groups, in order to develop a picture of members' demographics and beliefs. At the same time, McSweeney and Ahmed trawled the Facebook groups and recorded every post they could find that they deemed to constitute 'hate' of one kind or another: racism, misogyny, violent language, or—most consequentially—antisemitism.

'McSweeney ensured the most disturbing examples found their way to the *Sunday Times*', Pogrund and Maguire write in their 2025 book recounting Starmer's rise to power.[4] How McSweeney achieved this is not clarified. But unstated in their book is that the *Sunday Times* reporting that resulted from McSweeney's efforts was written up by Pogrund himself, who was one of four journalists credited on the stories.

'Exposed: Jeremy Corbyn's Hate Factory', the *Sunday Times* front-page headline screamed on April 1, 2018.[5] A second article on the inside pages, headlined 'Vitriol and Threats of Violence: The Ugly Face of Jeremy Corbyn's Cabal',[6] fleshed out the story. Presented in an air of breathless scandal, both stories were examples of the arguably alarmist reporting on the 'antisemitism crisis' that would make it such an ungainly muddle and fuel much left-wing scepticism of how the media addressed this complex topic. As such, they merit a detailed deconstruction.

At the heart of the stories was a 'dossier' comprising two thousand incidents of 'hate', which had been identified by *Sunday Times* journalists working alongside unidentified 'whistleblowers' for two months—McSweeney and Ahmed. These had been found by combing through twenty Corbyn-supporting Facebook groups, which had a combined membership of four hundred thousand people. Many of these groups were 'open', meaning that anyone in the world could post to them. The 'incidents' largely consisted of comments posted by Facebook users in the groups. The article quoted a professor dubbing these groups 'online hate factories': the implication being that the groups, which were also said to be central to Corbynism's on-the-ground political operations, were pumping out filth on an industrialised scale. The article hinted that the rhetoric in such groups could eventually give rise to political violence.

A very different picture was painted by Wendy Patterson in a rebuttal published by *openDemocracy* four days later but universally ignored in the mainstream press.[7] Patterson was an administrator of a Facebook group that fell within the scope of the Labour Together Project's investigation. She estimated that there were approximately four million user posts across the twenty Facebook groups identified in the investigation. While the existence of two thousand 'hate' posts was of course to be regretted, they constituted a miniscule fraction of the groups' total activity. Far from being 'online hate factories' churning out antisemitic bile, the scale of hateful content was so small, she believed, that it was virtually 'impossible to find on the groups unless you conduct a 2 month investigation specifically searching for antisemitism'.

Patterson was also troubled by the implication that administrators of the Facebook groups were either supportive of 'hate' posts or else delinquent in their duties as moderators. She described her extensive efforts alongside other administrators to develop codes of good practice for her group—what they referred to internally as the 'Corbyn standards' of 'zero tolerance for racism, antisemitism, sexism, homophobia, all discriminatory language or personal abuse'. She explained how there was a meta-group where administrators from multiple Corbyn-supporting groups met to exchange insights and guidance on best practice, and how administrators repeatedly encouraged ordinary users to report every breach they came across so they could refer them to Facebook. Considering the scale of activity on the groups, she argued, there was always the chance that problematic posts could fall through the cracks—but it was not for want of trying.

The *Sunday Times* articles, like much mainstream media reporting of the 'antisemitism crisis', would mix together real and serious incidents with others that were less-than-convincing. In the former camp, one user was identified as posting that Hitler 'should have finished the job' while another claimed the Holocaust was a 'big lie'. Ian Love, a Momentum organiser, was rightly excoriated for posting that Tony Blair was 'Jewish to the core' and for telling *The Sunday Times* that the 'Rothschilds control all the money in the world'.

But then the article lingered on the fact that Corbyn staffers were members of the group, including Laura Murray (then a stakeholder manager in Corbyn's office) and James Meadway, a staffer in Shadow Chancellor John McDonnell's office and now a respected left-wing economics commentator. The article noted that Murray had 'seen' a post by another user that dismissed claims of antisemitism in the Labour Party as a 'Blairite to far-right' conspiracy designed to damage the party. The article disclosed that the offending material had been posted by Naomi

Wimborne-Idrissi, but failed to mention that Wimborne-Idrissi was herself Jewish and a prominent voice in pro-Palestinian activism. Murray told the paper that she had no recollection of ever seeing Wimborne-Idrissi's post.

Readers were thus invited to be scandalised by the claim that a junior official in Corbyn's office had seen, but neither endorsed nor interacted with, a solitary post made by a Jewish Labour Party member that expressed scepticism about how claims of antisemitism were being used to undermine Corbynism. And how outrageous were Wimborne-Idrissi's comments, really, considering that we now know her posts were identified and reported as part of a project led by an associate and protégé of Peter Mandelson using undeclared donor funds and premeditated misdirection to destroy Corbynism?

A COLLABORATIVE AFFAIR: LABOUR TOGETHER, PRO-ISRAEL GROUPS, AND THE CREATION OF CCDH

While McSweeney and Ahmed were secretly feeding alarmist stories to journalists to build the narrative that Corbyn's Labour was awash in antisemitism, they were simultaneously establishing what I believe to be the Labour Together Project's most problematic known initiative: the Center for Countering Digital Hate and its sister campaign Stop Funding Fake News.

I first exposed Labour Together's undisclosed role in creating CCDH and SFFN in articles published by Matt Taibbi's *Racket News* in 2023 and 2024. These were based on three sets of documents discovered in Labour Party files.

The first set of documents was drafted by Owain Mumford, a parliamentary assistant to Labour Together's Steve Reed MP. Mumford wrote two briefing documents that were intended to be given to *Jewish Chronicle* journalist Lee Harpin, seemingly in preparation for an interview or profile of Reed. The profile and interview did not materialise. The documents extolled Reed's role in tackling antisemitism in the Labour Party.

One of the briefing documents was titled 'Steve's Record on Fighting Anti-Semitism'. It said that Reed had 'created Labour Together to bring together people across the Labour Party to combat the threat of extremist politics and antisemitism'. This was an odd claim given that, for the first four years of its existence, Labour Together barely mentioned antisemitism in public at all.

According to Mumford's briefing, Labour Together's role in fighting 'antisemitism' focused on the creation of CCDH. 'Labour Together set up the Campaign for Countering Digital Hate [*sic*] by raising start-up funds and providing office space', the briefing explained. At the time, remember, Labour Together was not declaring its donations, in violation of the law. The briefing further noted that CCDH

> started life with a campaign to stop corporates from paying for advertising space on anti-Semitic websites and political blogs. These sites deploy a form of micro-advertising farmed out by marketing firms who pay per websites or click. CCDH would take a screenshot of a corporate's advertising on a page alongside anti-Semitic propaganda and would then bombard the image at the corporate's social media channels, using celebrity endorsers to call on them to stop funding hate.

This description is important because it actually describes the work of SFFN and not CCDH, as shown below. On this version, at least, it would appear that CCDH emerged out of SFFN. This was striking both in describing the questionable roots of CCDH and because, for the first year of SFFN's existence, the campaign did not publicly acknowledge any connection to CCDH.

The founding of CCDH was a collaborative affair. Mumford's briefing claimed that 'Steve Reed MP engaged directly with the Community Security Trust (CST) and the Jewish Leadership Council for consultation and advice on setting it up'. This involvement of the CST and the JLC has never been publicly disclosed. At the time, Trevor Chinn—a Labour Together director and the group's second largest donor—was vice president of the JLC. Neither the CST nor the JLC replied substantively when *Racket News* approached them with the allegation.

The CST is a charity that 'protects British Jews from antisemitism', according to its website. This includes monitoring antisemitic incidents and providing, or overseeing the provision of, physical protection for Jewish schools and other Jewish cultural meeting points. The CST relies heavily on funding from the UK government. Serious questions must be asked about whether it was appropriate for the CST, as a charity with significant ties to the government, to be advising a party political faction behind closed doors on such a divisive (and as we will see, disreputable) project.

The second set of documents was also drafted by Mumford and comprised his minutes of a meeting convened on December 2, 2020, between Reed—then shadow communities secretary—and several Jewish community organisations. Attendees included Amanda Bowman, vice president of the Board of Deputies in charge of the organisation's Defence and Group Relations division; Daniel Sugarman, also of the Board of Deputies; Trevor Chinn, appearing along with two colleagues on behalf of the JLC; and Dave Rich, head of policy at the CST.

'Dave Rich remarked that the CST saw first-hand the importance of Labour Together's work tackling Anti-Semitism [*sic*] in left-wing spaces', the minutes recorded. It is not known what 'work' this referred to. Rich refused to be interviewed for this book, claiming that I had already made up my mind about the issue of antisemitism in the Labour Party.

In 2016, Rich published a book called *The Left's Jewish Problem: Jeremy Corbyn and Antisemitism*. Rich was a strident critic of Corbyn. His book argues that left-wing critiques of

Israel can amount to coded expressions of antisemitism, and that Corbyn's Labour was allowing this distinct form of antisemitism to flourish. In 2019, Rich made the same point in a bombshell BBC *Panorama* documentary entitled 'Is Labour Anti-Semitic?':

> if you look back at the antisemitism that existed in the 1930s—Jews using their money, Jews controlling governments. Instead you see the same ideas being directed . . . toward Israel. These kinds of ideas are much more acceptable on the left and in pro-Palestinian campaigning circles because they talk about Israel, they don't talk about Jews—but actually, underneath the surface, it's the same thing.

Less than six months prior to the minuted meeting, Reed had caused a mini-scandal when he tweeted that Richard Desmond—a British Jewish businessman—was 'puppet master to the Tories'. This comment had been condemned as an antisemitic trope and Reed apologised profusely the following day. In a gesture of striking magnanimity, Amanda Bowman kicked off the Board of Deputies' contribution to the meeting by reassuring that she was 'confident that Steve was unaware he [i.e., Desmond] was Jewish and of the context of his remark'.

Bowman's remarkably lenient attitude towards an offence that would have terminated the careers of lesser—or leftier—Labour figures teed-up Reed to present his record of fighting antisemitism. Reed referenced the work of Labour Together, assuring the assembled parties that 'he was active in the fight internally against anti-Semitism through Labour Together' while he served on Corbyn's shadow front bench. Chinn burnished Reed's reputation by affirming that 'Steve for many years had been a very good friend to the Jewish community' and noted that Labour Together had 'played a significant role' in getting Starmer elected as Labour leader.

The third set of documents comprises emails shared in 2021 between Reed, Mumford, and Ellie Robinson, the latter serving as deputy political director in Starmer's office. The context of the email exchange was that Reed had been selected to address parliament for Holocaust Memorial Day. Reed drafted a speech and distributed it for feedback.

Reed's original draft was striking in its self-regard:

> I could not bear the thought that over 100 years of my party's story could end in a cesspit of racism. So I chose to find my own way to resist . . . I helped establish the Centre [*sic*] for Combatting [*sic*—actually 'Countering'] Digital Hate, which ran a hugely effective operation to identify, expose and disable online antisemitism . . . This project tackled anti-Semitic extremism on the left and right, but where it identified anti-Semites who were Labour members I reported them immediately for expulsion.

Reed's draft, and the speech he finally delivered, failed to mention Labour Together's central role in creating the organisation, as reported by Mumford.[8]

Reed's involvement in CCDH is both instructive and disturbing; indeed, he is one of the more chilling figures encountered in researching this book. Two things are worth noting here, both of which are set out in more detail later.

First, party files show that Reed had a history of accusing people of antisemitism on the basis of arguably tendentious evidence; as noted above, this included submitting complaints dossiers to the party that demanded the immediate suspension of four left-wing, anti-Zionist Jews. Party files also show that Reed submitted complaints about left-wing members of his local constituency, accusing them of antisemitism for, amongst other things, sharing factually accurate news stories. In one case, Reed accused a party member of antisemitism for having shared a well-researched article about how Labour MP Margaret Hodge's family company had run a profitable South African subsidiary during the era of apartheid. The company had helped to market South African steel to Chile, then under the fist of the brutal dictator Augusto Pinochet. (Hodge happens to be Jewish, but this is not mentioned in or relevant to the article.)

Second, Reed took what I consider a disturbing approach to alternative and citizen media. As is shown in much more detail below, Reed tried to get the editor of local outfit *Inside Croydon* suspended or expelled from the Labour Party. Reed claimed that reports alleging gross dysfunction in Croydon's local government—reports I consider accurate and well evidenced—amounted to a campaign of 'hostility, distortion and abuse' designed to 'misrepresent facts' and thereby 'undermine public confidence and support in the Labour Party': fake news, in other words. At one point, Reed submitted to party officials a complaints dossier that cited, as an example of the editor's alleged 'harassment', *Inside Croydon*'s use of a satirical photo that Reed took exception to—because it photoshopped a Tory party rosette onto a smiling picture of him.

Party files show that Reed would later be copied into exchanges in which emails hacked from *Inside Croydon* were shared. Those hacked emails were being used to identify and punish the news website's confidential sources. Importantly, these sources were helping *Inside Croydon* reveal how Croydon's local government had become so dysfunctional under the leadership of Reed's political allies that it required a £120 million bailout to remain afloat after declaring bankruptcy in 2020.

Party files thus paint a worrying picture of Reed: of a man who reframed investigative journalism sounding the alarm over serious governance failures in Croydon as harassment and misinformation, and who showed a penchant for trying to get left-wingers in his constituency booted from the party for antisemitism on highly contestable grounds.

McSweeney, Reed, and Ahmed—these were the political operatives who came together to create CCDH and SFFN with the purported aim of tackling misinformation and hate. It is hard to imagine three people less suited to the task.

McSweeney, at that very moment, was breaking the law by failing to report hundreds of thousands of pounds in donations, and using premeditated misdirection (in fact: disinformation) to mislead people about the nature of Labour Together and his secret mission to defeat Corbynism. Ahmed was a factional spin-doctor with a long history of making contentious claims of bullying against left-wingers and railing against independent media outlets that challenged his versions of events. Finally there was Reed, who was not only collaborating in McSweeney's conspiracy of deception, but who had himself attempted to get a bona fide journalist expelled from the Labour Party for the temerity of trying to hold Reed's local political allies to account.

CREATING CCDH

There is some confusion as to when CCDH was established. Imran Ahmed claims on his LinkedIn that he became a director of the organisation in December 2017.[9] At the time, however, there was no corporate entity called CCDH. Across multiple interviews, Ahmed has given slightly different versions of when the idea for CCDH first came to him, or when he started putting the plan into action. His most recent story is that the idea for CCDH was seeded in 2016 when he was working with Angela Eagle. On this version, the impetus for establishing CCDH was the death of Jo Cox, the Labour MP who was killed in June 2016 by an adherent of the far right. If true, this would mean that Ahmed was considering the need for the organisation just as his work levelling unsubstantiated allegations of abuse and discrimination against the political opponents of Angela Eagle was being challenged by independent media asking difficult questions.

The corporate entity that would eventually become CCDH was originally called Brixton Endeavours.[10] Brixton Endeavours was set up in October 2018 and shared its address with Labour Together. Morgan McSweeney was its sole director. This is also the date that McSweeney has provided on his LinkedIn for when he became a director of CCDH.[11]

McSweeney ran this LinkedIn account for years, listing his role in CCDH. But in November 2024, as this book was being finalised and just after Donald Trump swept to victory in the US presidential election, McSweeney's LinkedIn profile suddenly went dark. This happened two weeks after a story broke in the US media about how CCDH had targeted Elon Musk's Twitter, based on leaks from within the social media company. That exposé was written by the American journalists Paul Thacker and Matt Taibbi, with whom I'd been working for about year on CCDH. It quoted extensively from my work on CCDH's prehistory and highlighted McSweeney's role in creating CCDH.[12] The story caught the attention of Elon Musk who announced that he was declaring 'war' on the organisation.[13] Trump campaign insiders told Taibbi and Thacker that CCDH would be 'investigated from all angles' if Trump was elected.[14]

Was it a coincidence that McSweeney's longstanding LinkedIn profile disappeared just as Trump was entering the White House and critical attention began to be trained on CCDH? Certainly, Thacker and Taibbi's article had set the cat among the pigeons and there were hurried attempts to distance Labour Together and McSweeney from CCDH. On October 24, two days after their story came out, Taibbi appeared on the *Times* podcast to talk about the history of CCDH. He was told that Labour Together claimed they had 'nothing to do' with CCDH. 'What can we say in response to that?' Taibbi texted me. I sent him a raft of screenshots, company reports, and extracts from the documents we had already published. Amongst them were screenshots of McSweeney's LinkedIn page, which I had fortuitously saved after Taibbi reached out to me. Soon thereafter, McSweeney's LinkedIn profile disappeared. About a year later, McSweeney's LinkedIn was reactivated, with subtle but interesting changes to how he described his overlapping occupational arrangements at Labour Together and CCDH, and as Starmer's campaign director (see Figure A).

FIGURE A. The Two Versions of Morgan McSweeney's LinkedIn

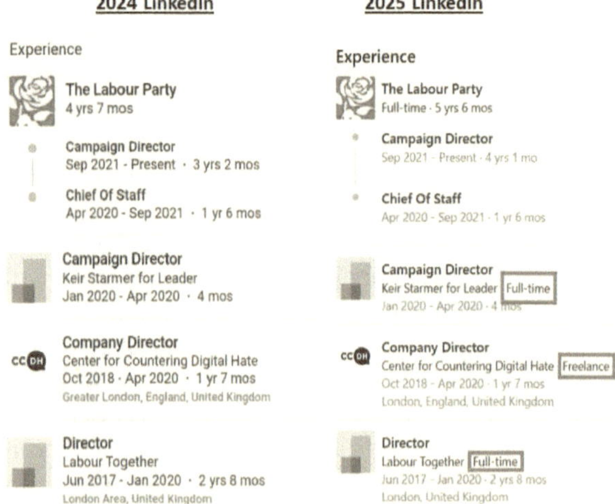

The day after Taibbi appeared on the *Times* podcast, *The Guardian* ran a lengthy story about how Ahmed and CCDH were determined to continue their work despite Musk's threats. *The Guardian* explained that McSweeney had simply helped Ahmed out by 'providing a shell company to house the organisation' and that McSweeney 'had no operational role at CCDH'.[15] Then why had McSweeney listed his directorship in CCDH for years on his LinkedIn? It was hard to credit.

As noted, CCDH started life as Brixton Endeavours; it shared an address with Labour Together and listed McSweeney as its sole director. This enterprise would eventually be renamed CCDH in September 2019, coinciding with the outfit's public launch via the publication of a thin pamphlet entitled 'Don't Feed the Trolls'. McSweeney would remain a listed director of CCDH until April 2020, giving up the role only after Starmer won the Labour leadership election.

Another company that shared its address with Labour Together and Brixton Endeavours/CCDH was Labour Campaigns.[16] Labour Campaigns' sole director was none other than Imran Ahmed. He changed the registered address of Labour Campaigns in January 2019 to that of CCDH and Labour Together. This was the same month that some unknown person or entity registered the web domain of Ahmed's first public foray into the world of disinformation: Stop Funding Fake News.

There is, however, a striking lack of detail known about how CCDH has been funded. When the organisation first launched in late 2019, its website said it received funding from five philanthropic foundations: the Joseph Rowntree Charitable Trust, the Pears Foundation, the Laura Kinsella Foundation, Barrow Cadbury Trust, and Unbound Philanthropy.[17] In June 2020, CCDH changed its website so that individual funders were no longer listed; it now simply stated that CCDH 'is a non-governmental organisation (NGO) that is funded by philanthropic trusts and members of the public'.[18] The current incarnation of CCDH's website, launched after the creation of a US affiliate company registered in Washington, does not identify any funders.[19]

CCDH has never publicly acknowledged that it was created by Labour Together, or that it received resources from the think-tank while being set up (including 'office space' and 'help' with raising start-up funds)—or that Labour Together was failing to report its donations as required by law at the time.

In March 2019, five months after the formation of Brixton Endeavours, Stop Funding Fake News was born. As noted above, Mumford's briefing suggested that CCDH had emerged out of SFFN's work. But in 2020, Ahmed would give a talk to a US State Department conference on antisemitism opened by such storied fighters for civil liberty and moderation as Mike Pompeo, Michael Gove, and Israeli prime minister Benjamin Netanyahu. Pompeo served as the director of the CIA and then secretary of state under Trump. His contributions to global free speech included plotting with CIA officials to abduct and assassinate *WikiLeaks* publisher Julian Assange. Gove, a long-time Tory MP and cabinet minister, has been robustly criticised for his views on Muslims. One of his critics is the Tory grandee Lady Warsi, who was genuinely 'fearful of the idea of Michael Gove becoming prime minister' because of 'his views on British Muslims'.[20] Ahmed suggested in his speech that SFFN had emerged out of research work done by CCDH—not the other way around.[21]

In reality, there seems to have been little distinction between these entities behind the scenes. In 2021, for example, Ahmed noted on Twitter that he was the 'founder/CEO' of both CCDH and SFFN.[22] Historical website registration data for the now-defunct SFFN website shows that it was previously registered as belonging to Imran Ahmed and under his personal email address. In fact, in light of what we now know about McSweeney and Ahmed's long-term collaboration, there does not appear to be any real distinction between SFFN, CCDH, and the Labour Together Project itself.

The purview of SFFN extended beyond alleged antisemitism. SFFN also tackled what it called 'fake news'. In a Twitter thread from April 2019, SFFN explained that 'fake news . . . means lies & deliberate misleading, particularly when designed to fuel hate'. This definition is important, because it meant that SFFN, in effect, defined fake news as *dis*information rather than *mis*information. Disinformation refers to the creation and spread of false information with the intention to deceive; misinformation refers to false information spread without such intention.

The irony was that SFFN, run by a man who had made his career as a factional spin-doctor, could itself be regarded as a prime example of fake news. SFFN did not disclose the actors behind its creation and operation; it was only in May 2020 that SFFN declared any relationship with CCDH. For the first year of its public existence, SFFN explained to readers of its website that 'we would like to be open about our identities, but doing so could put our activists at risk'.[23] SFFN was thus presented as a group of anonymous 'activists' inspired by a US campaign called Sleeping Giants, which had targeted the right-wing *Breitbart News* in the US. But the contrast between the two initiatives is stark: Sleeping Giants was initiated and run by grassroots campaigners, while SFFN was resourced from undeclared funding provided by millionaires to Labour Together, which itself featured three Labour MPs on its board alongside Morgan McSweeney—who subsequently became perhaps the most powerful non-elected official in the country.

SFFN was assiduous in cultivating this grassroots image in profiles of its work. In April 2019, the *Jewish News* described SFFN as a 'small group of friends' and 'activists'. Explaining why they had remained anonymous, these plucky underdogs said they 'didn't want the levels of hate that far braver people than ourselves have been subjected to'. They then neatly deflected attention away from their anonymity by explaining that 'the campaign isn't about us' but relied on ordinary people taking a 'stand for truth and tolerance'.[24]

SFFN's failure to disclose its true origin, funding, and political leanings makes it a textbook example of what is known as *astroturfing*. As an academic article from 2019 explains, political astroturfing involves 'a centrally coordinated disinformation campaign in which participants pretend to be ordinary citizens acting independently'. The article warned that such campaigns can 'influence electoral outcomes and other forms of political behaviour'.[25] As this definition indicates, astroturfing is not just considered ethically dubious but is a form of disinformation. SFFN was thus an astroturf disinformation campaign purporting to target disinformation.

SFFN's astroturfing had a profound impact on how it was received. The group's work would surely not have resonated as widely as it did if audiences had known the group was founded by Labour Party insiders who despised Corbyn's leadership and run by a man with a long history of battles against the independent media outlets he was now trying to demonetise. Its studied secrecy allowed SFFN to pass as non-partisan, a false impression that would have rendered its activities more credible.

Anonymity also made SFFN and its controlling minds unaccountable to public scrutiny and, most importantly, the law. Because no-one knew who was behind SFFN, it would have been difficult to bring claims of libel against it. To do so would have required getting Twitter or SFFN's website registrars to disclose confidential information, which may have ultimately needed court applications. There is a good case to be made that SFFN may have defamed media outlets, their editors, and journalists when it accused them of making up 'lies' and being 'deliberate[ly] misleading', especially when such allegations were directed against outlets like *The Canary* that were independently regulated and whose survival depended on public trust. Yet these targets were, on account of SFFN's anonymity, effectively denied their legal right to defend their reputation at the time.

SFFN launched its online campaign on March 5, 2019, with a series of Twitter posts directed at advertisers. SFFN targeted four sites from what it presented as 'both sides' of the political spectrum: *Evolve Politics* and *The Canary* on the left, *Westmonster* and *Politicalite* on the right. Its methodology was strikingly similar to that employed by the likes of LAAS. SFFN compiled virtual 'dossiers' against their targets based on deep dives into social media posts. The dossiers were then posted in long Twitter threads as evidence of fake news and antisemitism.

For a budding new campaign of disconnected grassroots activists with no obvious political connections, SFFN was able to secure some remarkably quick endorsements from niche Labour Party figures. 'Fantastic new campaign to persuade advertisers to stop funding fake news sites that spread hatred, bigotry, and warp our politics towards extremism stopfundingfakenews.com',[26] Steve Reed tweeted out on the evening of March 6. The following day, Hannah O'Rourke, the long-time Labour Together staffer, posted her own endorsement.[27]

By far the most consequential endorsement came from Rachel Riley. 'Just had a look at your website @SFFakeNews and actually burst into tears seeing where all the hate I get daily is coming from. With you in any way I can be, you have my full support', Riley posted at 6:18 p.m. on March 6, 2019, ending her post with a link to the SFFN website.[28]

Riley had agreed to front the SFFN campaign a month earlier. She had been taken to meet McSweeney and Ahmed at Labour Together's offices in February 2019, brought there by Adam Langleben. Langleben was a prominent member of the Jewish Labour Movement, a Labour Party affiliate that was sharply critical of Corbyn and his supporters. As discussed later, Langleben would work closely with McSweeney to 'engineer' the JLM's submissions to the EHRC, whose slapdash findings would prove devastating to the long-term reputation of Corbynism. 'McSweeney and Ahmed made a modest proposal. Might Riley be the face of a campaign to defund *The Canary*? She agreed with alacrity', Pogrund and Maguire write.[29]

Both *Evolve Politics* and *The Canary* had emerged in reaction to what was perceived as a media environment hostile to left-wing ideas and, specifically, the Corbyn leadership. *The Canary*, formed in 2015 by Kerry-Anne Mendoza and her wife Nancy Mendoza at a cost of £500, grew spectacularly in its first year. By July 2016, it was listed as the seventy-ninth-most-viewed UK Media Publishers website, attracting over 7.5 million views a month.[30] Both outlets grew their reach and impact in the crucible of the 2017 election, where their pro-left and generally pro-Corbyn stance garnered significant social media support. *The Canary*'s revenue allowed it to employ twenty-five editorial staff.[31] Numerous studies have argued that *The Canary*, in particular, played a significant role in Labour's better-than-expected showing at the 2017 general election. Two weeks after SFFN launched its campaign, *The Canary* celebrated publishing its ten-thousandth article.[32]

The two other sites targeted by SFFN were *Westmonster* and *Politicalite*. Both were right-wing and accused by SFFN of posting Islamophobic material. *Westmonster* was funded by Arron Banks, the controversial Brexit backer.

But SFFN's 'both sides' approach, and its explicit decision to target these four websites first, was a striking act of unfair conflation. *Westmonster* and *Politicalite* had never agreed to be regulated and both received mixed reviews from services that monitor media bias and trustworthiness.

By comparison, both *Evolve Politics* and *The Canary* had been regulated by the independent regulator Impress since 2017. Impress was the first regulatory body approved by the Independent Press Review Board, itself created by Royal Charter to implement the recommendations of the Leveson Inquiry. The combustible first phase of the Leveson Inquiry had looked into historic cases of media abuses, including phone hacking. It made recommendations about setting up robust systems for press regulation that were properly independent of media proprietors. Impress was thus the first media regulator that actually met the stringent tests and guidelines suggested by Leveson. Its regulation arguably represents the gold standard of press accountability in Britain.

In April 2019, not long after SFFN launched its campaign against *The Canary*, the independent and often-cited Media Bias/Fact Check service described the site's reporting as manifesting a liberal 'bias' but gave its factual content a 'high' rating for accuracy. In the same month, *The Canary* was one of the first media websites in the UK to be awarded a green trust mark for credibility by Newsguard.[33] And while *Evolve Politics* has not been reviewed by either service, it was considered sufficiently credible that, in 2018, it was given a press pass for 'the lobby': the political reporting centre of Westminster.

But it was *The Canary* that was the real target of SFFN's early operations. Indeed, as Anushka Asthana tells it, *The Canary* was one of McSweeney's 'obsessions'. It had featured prominently in McSweeney's 2017 SWOT analysis, which had decried the power of independent media outlets in buttressing Corbynism. With no little hint of irony, one of the biggest threats that McSweeney identified in the same analysis was that *The Canary* might discover what the Labour Together Project was really up to. Or, seen another way, one of the biggest threats to his project was that *The Canary*'s dogged investigative journalists might discover the truth and report it accurately. As Asthana tells it, McSweeney's warning to Labour Together insiders was stark: 'Destroy *The Canary*, or *The Canary* destroys us'.

This background must, of course, raise questions about whether SFFN was established out of an authentic impulse to challenge disinformation and hate—or whether it was created to neutralise an obstacle to the success of the Labour Together Project, cynically deploying anonymity and widespread concern about disinformation as its weapons of choice.

SFFN's focus on *The Canary* is clear in retrospect: between its first post and the 2019 general election, SFFN posted no fewer than 176 tweets about *The Canary*,[34] which it branded a 'Fake News website'.[35] In its first anti-*Canary* broadside, it highlighted stories published by the website that questioned aspects of the alleged Labour 'antisemitism crisis', as well as a story about the poisoning of former Russian intelligence agent Sergei Skripal.

When *The Canary* rejected the allegations that it purveyed fake news, SFFN responded by listing a number of articles with which it took issue. The number of pieces that SFFN highlighted amounted to a tiny fraction of the site's output. But in an approach that characterised much reporting of the 'antisemitism crisis' more broadly, this unrepresentative sample was used to justify a sweeping delegitimisation.

The paucity of SFFN's claims against *The Canary* was revealed when SFFN cited an Impress adjudication as evidence against *The Canary*. What this judgment actually showed was that *The Canary* had voluntarily submitted to rigorous regulation and assiduously corrected errors in its reporting.[36]

To summarise a somewhat complex case:[37] The headline of a *Canary* article claimed that Laura Kuenssberg, the political editor of BBC News, was speaking at a Tory party conference. *The Canary* asked the BBC for comment but the BBC did not provide one by the noon deadline, when *The Canary* hit publish. The BBC then responded in the late afternoon, noting that Kuenssberg was not a speaker but merely an invitee. *The Canary* fixed the article and put out a correction on social media.

Impress investigated *The Canary* after a complaint from the public. The regulator found that *The Canary* should have done more to put questions to the BBC prior to publishing. It also commented that *The Canary*'s note of correction should have appeared at the top and not the bottom of its amended article. Impress directed *The Canary* to apologise and publish Impress' decision, which it duly did.

This was a strange form of 'fake news', indeed: not only had *The Canary* contemporaneously corrected an error in its reporting, but it also then voluntarily submitted to an independent investigation and swiftly carried out the remedial measures required. This was best practice, not fake news.

SFFN followed up its screenshots of the Kuenssberg article by quoting a *New Statesman* headline that accused *The Canary* of running a 'misogynistic' campaign against Kuenssberg. This was a remarkable accusation to level at the only independent media outlet in the country edited by a lesbian woman of colour. Later, in May 2019, SFFN would share a link to a *Press Gazette* story reporting that among outlets regulated by Impress, *The Canary* had received the most complaints—again effectively attacking *The Canary* for having submitted to robust oversight.[38] SFFN failed to note that of the eighty complaints received, only *two* were upheld by the regulator—including the Kuenssberg case.

SFFN also accused *The Canary* of antisemitism based on social media comments made by *Canary* journalists in their personal capacity as well as a handful of *Canary* articles. By way of illustration, SFFN was scandalised by a social media post from *Canary* journalist Emily Apple. 'Israel is a cunt', she had written in 2010, a full nine years before SFFN's campaign (they really scraped the barrel). This comment accompanied a link to a protest march against Israel's killing of nine activists involved in the Free Gaza Flotilla.[39] In SFFN's fevered imagination, this off-colour epithet directed against a state that had just killed unarmed civilians was not only antisemitic but sufficiently egregious to warrant the closure of an entire independent media website that the writer would contribute to nearly a decade later. In another four-part exposé, SFFN criticised an article written by Apple that had the temerity to criticise Britain's chief rabbi for contentious comments he had made about Jeremy Corbyn.

It should be noted that Emily Apple was raised in a Jewish family (her father is Jewish) and has written movingly about how her Jewish upbringing forms a central part of her identity.[40]

Elsewhere, SFFN pointed to multiple *Canary* headlines that supposedly demonstrated the publication's antisemitic tendency. One of these purportedly incriminating headlines read: 'Jewish Voters Are Done with the Bogus Antisemitism Smears Against Jeremy Corbyn'.[41] The accompanying article was based almost entirely on comments by left-wing Jews that contested media allegations about the Labour 'antisemitism crisis'. The Labour Together Project's secret astroturf campaign was effectively amplifying claims that left-wing Jews were antisemitic, such that giving space to their perspectives constituted a form of antisemitic denialism.

In 2021, Impress launched an investigation into *The Canary* alongside *Skwawkbox*, another independent, pro-Corbyn political website. Impress acted pursuant to a report published by Lord Mann, a vehement Corbyn critic and former Labour MP who was promoted to the House of Lords by the Tories. Mann's report had accused both online publications of antisemitism. The accusation was based, in part, on the research of Daniel Allington, an academic based at King's College London. Allington was also 'Head of Online Monitoring' for the Campaign Against Antisemitism (CAA) between June 2016 and September 2018.[42] The CAA had been a fervent critic of Corbyn and had submitted the founding complaint that led to the EHRC investigation into the Labour Party, which is dealt with in more detail later. Allington was thanked in CCDH's first publication, the aforementioned 'Don't Feed the Trolls'.[43]

Impress approached Allington and asked for the entirety of his evidence implicating both sites. This was, in effect, the case for the prosecution against *The Canary*.

The accusations were reviewed by Impress' Regulatory Committee whose conclusions were confirmed by the Board. Both bodies were staffed by some of the most well-respected figures in journalism and law, such as Board chairperson Richard Ayre. Ayre was the former deputy chief executive of BBC News and later the chair of the BBC Trust's editorial standards committee.

On reviewing the material, Impress noted that the majority of Allington's chosen articles centred on the 'defence of Jeremy Corbyn or Corbynism (and in some cases criticism of Israel), criticism of the British Board of Deputies, and hypocrisy surrounding the reporting of the antisemitism crisis'. After considering all of this material, Impress found that it 'did not amount to discrimination against Jewish people'. It felt moved to add that those who 'disagree with the Publisher's views on subjects such as Zionism may find these views offensive, adversarial or provocative but this in itself does not rise to the level of threat to, or targeting of, persons or groups on the basis of their protected characteristics'.[44]

SFFN, RACHEL RILEY, AND LAAS

SFFN's campaign was tendentious, untransparent, censorious—and startlingly successful. In August 2019, *The Canary* announced that, partly as a result of SFFN's hostile campaign, it had been forced to downsize its workforce and move to an entirely new funding model.[45] SFFN celebrated the coming unemployment of a number of young journalists. The following year, in his address to the State Department conference opened by Netanyahu, Imran Ahmed boasted of how SFFN's methodology could 'completely eviscerate the economic base of a website'. Ahmed cited *The Canary* as a case study of success, gloating that the website 'went down from twenty-two staff to one member of staff within a few months of us targeting it'.[46] In December 2019, SFFN posted an update to a (largely unsuccessful) crowdfunding campaign in which it took credit for massively reducing the impact of *The Canary* and *Evolve Politics* during that year's general election. 'In 2017 the Fake News site *The Canary* received 6m views a month—in this general election it was cut to 1.4m', SSFN trumpeted. 'In 2017, the Fake News site *Evolve Politics* received 2m views a month—it is now 170,000'.[47] In a further call for funding, SSFN argued that it was now time to 'finish the job'. While changes to Facebook's algorithm also had an impact on the reach of *The Canary* and *Evolve Politics*, it seems likely that both sites did not wield the same influence in 2019 as they had in the 2017 general election, and that SFFN played a significant role in this diminution.

This may be obvious, but it is important to emphasise that both *The Canary* and *Evolve Politics* were pro-Labour Party websites when the party was led by Jeremy Corbyn. They both wrote favourably about the Labour Party and published information as well as arguments that would persuade voters to back Corbyn's Labour over the Tories. Within Britain's media ecosystem, which overall skewed heavily to the right, *The Canary* and *Evolve Politics* were isolated bastions of pro-Corbyn progressivism. Amidst a non-stop barrage of absurd and unproven media allegations against the Labour Party, these websites functioned as fact-checkers. SFFN's campaign was thus attacking a key source of support for the Labour Party. Indeed, it can be compellingly argued that the Labour Together Project's offspring, SFFN, was effectively dedicated to undermining Labour's own prospects during the 2019 general election. This would be unsurprising, considering that McSweeney's own SWOT analysis had identified the election of a Labour government under Corbyn as an obstacle to achieving Labour Together's so-called 'renewal'.

One reason SFFN succeeded was that it harnessed the power of celebrity, as public figures with outsized platforms ensured that SFFN messages reverberated across social media. Rachel Riley was SFFN's biggest asset. She maintains a strong relationship with Ahmed and CCDH. Shortly after CCDH was publicly launched in September 2019, Riley was appointed its sole 'patron'. At the time of writing, Riley still describes herself on X (formerly Twitter) as 'CCDH Ambassador'.[48]

Working with Riley, SFFN and CCDH found themselves at the coalface of the Labour 'antisemitism crisis'. By the time Riley began amplifying SFFN content, she had become close to LAAS, with whose members she repeatedly conversed on social media and which she endorsed on Twitter (alongside other contentious accounts such as the anonymous and pugnacious @gnasherjew).[49]

Riley's interactions with LAAS were not limited to social media. In late November 2019, only weeks before the general election, Riley caused outrage amongst some when she wore a shirt that featured an edited photograph of Jeremy Corbyn. The picture showed Corbyn being led away from an anti-apartheid protest by police in the mid-1980s wearing a large placard around his neck. In the original photograph, Corbyn's placard read: 'DEFEND THE RIGHT TO DEMONSTRATE AGAINST APARTHEID JOIN THIS PICKET'. This text was deleted on Riley's shirt and replaced with the phrase: 'JEREMY CORBYN IS A RACIST ENDEAVOUR'.

Facebook posts reveal that the shirt was designed and printed by a LAAS member, Zoe Kemp, who had given it to Riley in February 2019. Kemp shared a photo of Riley wearing the shirt in Riley's kitchen, holding her Ragdoll cat. Kemp bragged to her Facebook friends, 'I had dinner at hers last night. We are both anti racist activists too, so we do politics'. Like many LAAS activists, though unlike Riley, Kemp is not Jewish.

Kemp, incidentally, had been stridently criticised in a 2016 *Canary* article after Kemp and a *Guardian* columnist, Nicholas Lezard, had joked on Facebook about an assassination plot against Corbyn. In the same exchange, Kemp also dismissed the UK's first Black woman MP, Diane Abbott, as Corbyn's 'ex-shag'.[50] This was just one example of *The Canary*'s critical reporting on the activities and political histories of people connected to LAAS, such as Hoffman and Kemp.[51] Indeed, the site was one of the only outlets in the country to subject LAAS to journalistic scrutiny. *The Canary* had also run comments directly and explicitly critical of LAAS.[52] This meant that when LAAS activists amplified SFFN's attacks on *The Canary*, they were targeting a news outlet that had reported critically on their own organisation.

The extent of LAAS' connection to Riley was further revealed during a libel case brought by Riley against the Labour Party staffer Laura Murray, who had previously been highlighted in the *Sunday Times*' 'hate factory' article that had been covertly seeded by McSweeney and Ahmed. As noted previously, Murray was the stakeholder manager in Corbyn's office. Shortly afterward, she moved to the Labour Party's Governance and Legal Unit to help process antisemitism complaints.

The libel case had its origin on March 3, 2019, when Corbyn visited the Finsbury Park Mosque, which had recently been the site of a terrorist attack by a far-right figure. Corbyn was attacked and punched in the head by a man holding an egg. Later that day, Riley tweeted out a screenshot of an old tweet by left-wing commentator Owen Jones. In that tweet, Jones had discussed the egging of Nick Griffin, former leader of the BNP. Jones had commented, 'If you don't want to be egged, don't be a Nazi'. Riley retweeted Jones' post, commenting 'Good advice' alongside a picture of a rose—the symbol of the Labour Party—and an egg. Murray responded later that day. 'Today Jeremy Corbyn went to his local mosque for Visit My Mosque day and was attacked by a Brexiteer', Murray tweeted. 'Rachel Riley tweets that Corbyn deserves to be violently attacked. She is as dangerous as she is stupid. Nobody should engage with her. Ever'. Riley sued Murray claiming that this libellously misrepresented the content of her tweet.

Court records show that Riley's legal team relied heavily on the evidence of a LAAS activist and spokesperson, Emma Feltham (alias Emma Picken), to prove that Murray's tweet had spread widely. Feltham provided screenshots for use by Riley's legal team. Feltham/Picken explained that she was a member of LAAS and had been 'very concerned about the rise of antisemitism in the Labour Party and chose to take an active role in monitoring what was happening in that respect'. The evidentiary basis of Riley's trial thus rested heavily on the work of Feltham/Picken, a spokesperson for LAAS.

Riley posted her 'Good advice' tweet only two days before SFFN launched its public campaign, and three days before she began amplifying their work. The judge found in Riley's favour, stating that Murray had failed to capture that there were two 'obvious' meanings that could be inferred from Riley's tweet. In one meaning, Riley could be seen to be criticising Owen Jones, effectively claiming that it was hypocritical of him to cheer on the egging of Griffin but deplore the egging of Corbyn. Nobody deserved to be egged, according to this version, and to celebrate one and criticise another amounted to hypocrisy.

The second 'obvious' meaning was that Corbyn 'deserved to be egged for his political views'.

But the court found that Riley's tweet '. . . falls to be characterised as provocative, even mischievous. It was calculated to provoke a reaction and it did'.[53] The court further found that Riley 'was quite aware that [her tweet] was capable of being read in both senses', even if she intended only to convey the 'hypocrisy' meaning. And she could 'not complain' that her tweet provoked a furious reaction after many people interpreted it to mean that she believed Corbyn deserved to be egged.

'DAVE GORDSTEIN' AND THE ENGINE OF HATE

In late March 2019, SFFN scored its first major success when the Macmillan Cancer charity responded to its campaign against *The Canary*. Macmillan was alerted to the fact that one of its appeals for donations appeared at the bottom of an article in which *The Canary* criticised the former Labour MP Joan Ryan. Ryan had left the Labour Party to join The Independent Group, the breakaway splinter that became Change UK. Prior to this defection, Ryan had been the chair of the pro-Israel lobby group Labour Friends of Israel. She had previously received donations from Labour Together's Trevor Chinn. She is not Jewish.

The *Canary* article in question recounted how Ryan had travelled to the US to address a meeting of the American Israel Public Affairs Committees (AIPAC), a leading pro-Israel advocacy group. *The Canary* reported that Ryan's presentation before AIPAC had 'smeared' Corbyn with claims of antisemitism, including the allegation that he was 'friends' with Hamas and Hezbollah.[54]

Whether or not one agrees with *The Canary*'s argument, it is an extraordinary stretch to suggest that it was an exercise in fake news. The article was sourced and its factual basis was true. To be sure, *The Canary*'s interpretation of those facts was up for debate, but such is the nature of all political media. Nevertheless, Macmillan was urged to 'please stop funding fake news' in a tweet that copied *The Canary* headline and included a picture of Macmillan's ad. The tweet tagged SFFN's Twitter account and included the hashtag #sffnews. It was sent by an account with the username @ed_derwent on March 25.

The appeal was amplified by Rachel Riley the following day. Within hours, Macmillan announced that 'we are taking action to remove this placement whilst we review the platforms used for our online ads'. SFFN would tweet out their fulsome thanks for 'Dave'. But who was Dave? Dave was none other than David Gordstein: the Twitter account, @ed_derwent, which only had a handful of followers, used the descriptor name 'Dave Gordstein', the strikingly Jewish-sounding pseudonym of LAAS' non-Jewish Euan Philips.

To recap: *The Canary*, arguably the most widely read alternative media outlet that supported Corbynism, was being demonetised at the behest of a fake Jewish-sounding Twitter profile run by a non-Jewish man, as part of a broader SFFN astroturf campaign that hid its connections to CCDH, Labour Together, Imran Ahmed, and sitting MPs. This, at least in part, was what the Labour Together Project was presumably doing with Labour Together's undisclosed pot of funding: celebrating the 'David Gordsteins' of the world as they destroyed the careers and livelihoods of young journalists, some of whom had written proudly of their Jewish cultural roots—all in the name of fighting antisemitism.

Macmillan's decision infuriated many left-wing Twitter followers. Within hours, Twitter users reacted with their own campaign organised around the hashtag #BoycottRachelRiley, which began trending on Twitter. The hashtag was treated as antisemitic by, amongst others, the Board of Deputies of British Jews. The hashtag 'tells you just about everything you need to know about these people', the Board was quoted as having said in *The Jewish Chronicle*. 'Racists and racism-apologists, attacking a Jewish woman for speaking out against antisemitism'.[55]

Dave Rich of the CST commented that '#BoycottRachelRiley is what happens when you speak out about antisemitism. It's a double-punch: first the antisemitism, then the bullying to shut you up'.[56]

Rich's response presaged an astonishing report published by the CST in August 2019 called *Engine of Hate: The Online Networks Behind the Labour Party Antisemitism Crisis*.[57] The report purported to track a web of 'antisemitic' networks backing the Labour Party under Corbyn and charged that articles published by the likes of *The Canary* had fuelled this bigotry. The report traced accounts using hashtags implicated in the party's antisemitism controversy. One of those hashtags was #BoycottRachelRiley. CST claimed that the hashtag was developed and used to 'promote the online bullying of a public personality who had repeatedly spoken out against antisemitism'.[58]

This was chilling. #BoycottRachelRiley was, after all, a defensive response to a campaign launched by SFFN and housed inside or alongside CCDH—a campaign the CST itself has discreetly advised. This campaign was based on the smear that a popular, left-wing, and independently regulated media website was nothing more than a 'fake news' factory 'deliberately' making up 'lies' to spread 'hate', including antisemitism.

When CST published *Engine of Hate*, garnering fulsome coverage in *The Guardian* and *Jewish Chronicle*, it had the effect of linking numerous people to allegations that seriously tainted their reputations. Some of these people were Jewish—like Heather Mendick, who woke up one morning to lurid coverage of how she, a Jewish Labour Party member, was part of an antisemitic 'engine room'.[59]

Seen in this context, what the CST report represented was the hostile surveillance of left-wing social media users, many Jewish, who had been provoked by an inflammatory astroturf campaign in which the CST had played its own undisclosed role. More importantly, the SFFN's dishonest and anti-pluralist campaign had been incubated by the same team that would deliver Keir Starmer to the leadership of the Labour Party, and, upon Starmer's 2024 election victory, be elevated to the highest levels of state power.

ELECTORAL INTERFERENCE

As well as demonetising Labour-supporting websites, SFFN also staged a problematic intervention in the European parliamentary elections of May 2019.

On May 23, SFFN posted a lengthy thread about participants in the election.[60] 'We're not party-political', SFFN absurdly promised, 'but we do campaign against fake news . . . Here are the fake news merchants involved in today's #EUelections2019'.

SFFN's thread targeted two right-wing figures, Tommy Robinson and Michael Heever. Heever, a journalist, was also the Brexit Party candidate for the East of England and co-founder of SFFN's target *Westmonster*. He would be elected to the European Parliament in the 2019 campaign alongside the Brexit Party chairperson, Richard Tice. Tice subsequently formed and ran the Reform Party with former UK Independence Party (UKIP) leader Nigel Farage. SFFN complained that Heever was the editor of the 'fake news website' *Westmonster*, also pointing out that he had previously worked as Farage's press officer. SFFN's 'evidence' threads against *Westmonster*, posted when SFFN was launched and thereafter, included numerous allusive photographs of Farage and Donald Trump, amid complaints that 'fake news website Westmonster, co-founded by Arron Banks, is now effectively a propaganda channel for Nigel Farage's #Brexit Party'.

'Please don't vote for those who spread lies, bigotry or hate', the May 23 thread implored. 'And make sure you vote today!'

I do not support the politics and opinions of the likes of Farage and Heever. But this is beside the point. SFFN's Twitter thread was a direct and material intervention in a UK election, which sought to convince people who they should and should not vote for. It is manifestly problematic for an astroturf campaign funded with resources not declared to the Electoral Commission in violation of electoral law, and secretly created by an organisation that counted multiple sitting Labour Party MPs among its directors, to attempt to influence electoral outcomes.

What a fillip to Farage, Tice, and Reform, who can now legitimately claim that the current chief of staff to the prime minister was responsible for creating a secret astroturf campaign that tried to 'cancel' a news website sympathetic to their views, and which used its censorious mode to try and influence the outcome of a major national election to the detriment of the Brexit Party—all in the name of fighting 'misinformation'. But for those concerned about the rise of Reform and the health of British democracy, and those who fear that SFFN's history could be turned to Reform's advantage, the real question is: How could McSweeney and Ahmed have been so irresponsible?

STARMER'S PEOPLE AND THE IMPLICATIONS OF LABOUR TOGETHER

The story of the Labour Together Project, CCDH, and SFFN is important for a host of reasons:

First, there is little doubt that the Labour Together Project drove major stories in the Labour 'antisemitism crisis', without public knowledge of their involvement and based on a melange of serious and sensationalised claims. It did so both by working directly with the media and indirectly by launching the SFFN campaign, which itself fuelled media coverage conveying that there was a serious problem with antisemitism on the Corbyn-supporting left. As discussed later, the Labour Together Project also helped the Jewish Labour Movement to 'engineer' the EHRC investigation into Corbyn's Labour Party. The Labour Together Project was thus a major hidden hand driving a crisis that would have devastating consequences for not just the British left but also the very fabric of British democracy and those people in Britain who *needed* a redistributive, democratising government to help them get by. In addition, as I show later, the 'antisemitism crisis' would also frame and haunt the Labour Party's response to Israel's destruction of Gaza.

Put otherwise, there were indeed powerful and hidden actors driving the 'antisemitism crisis'. Those actors were simultaneously engaged in a premeditated, politically motivated campaign to destroy Corbynism and then recapture the Labour Party for the right. This campaign—including those elements intended to foment the 'antisemitism crisis'—unfolded under the cover of purposeful misdirection and was funded by illegally undeclared donations. While all this played out, those same actors were working secretly with other important players in the 'antisemitism crisis' like the Jewish Labour Movement and the Jewish Leadership Council, on whose board one of Labour Together's key funders sat. It would be obtuse not to acknowledge that the 'antisemitism crisis' narrative has to be problematised and understood in this light.

At the very least, promiscuous allegations of antisemitic 'denialism' have to be rethought. It was never persuasive to reflexively stigmatise as antisemitic any speculation about ulterior political agendas driving the 'antisemitism crisis'. Such an attitude is now wholly unpersuasive because this is just what the Labour Together Project was doing. When left-wingers railed against 'fifth columnists', 'Trojan horses' or 'wreckers' when confronted by allegations of pervasive antisemitism in the party, perhaps they weren't engaging in Jew-hate but instead divining a truth that had been deliberately obscured and which has taken years to emerge. Or, maybe they were engaging in Jew-hate. Who knows? The water has been so muddied by the Labour Together Project that it may forever be impossible to tell.

Second, SFFN's covert machinations showed how unethical the Labour Together Project's modus operandi was. SFFN targeted factional opponents while presenting itself as non-partisan; smeared independent, fact-based journalism as 'fake news'; and implicitly pilloried left-wing Jews in the name of fighting antisemitism. It will be forever to the Labour Together Project's discredit that it helped to create such a shameful operation. It says much about Starmer's leadership of the Labour Party that his candidacy emerged from, and was embedded in, a project that could conceive of and execute a campaign as appalling as SFFN.

Third, SFFN proved a brutally effective method of policing so-called 'denialism'. By demonetising *The Canary*, SFFN sent a powerful message that anyone who questioned the dominant narrative about Labour's 'antisemitism crisis' would be destroyed—a narrative being manufactured, at least in part, by McSweeney and Ahmed themselves. Meanwhile, the lack of publicly available information about who was running SFFN precluded effective rebuttal.

Establishing 'denialism' as a thought-crime would have profound implications. As the rest of this book shows, countless Labour Party figures, including many left-wing Jews, would be accused of antisemitism for alleging that the 'antisemitism crisis' was at least partially driven by a political impetus to destroy Corbynism; or, alternatively, that reporting on the alleged crisis tended to overstate the prevalence and severity of the problem. Corbyn himself would eventually be turfed out of the Parliamentary Labour Party for making this precise claim in October 2020—a decision in which Morgan McSweeney would play a key role. But our knowledge of the Labour Together Project now confirms that these claims were credible, and, indeed, that McSweeney must have known them to be so.

Finally, the murky history of SFFN and CCDH could come back to bite Starmer, now sitting as prime minister. Ahmed and the CCDH would migrate to the US after the spectre of Corbynism had been vanquished. From this new perch, they began targeting populist politicians, including Robert F. Kennedy Jr. Their influential advocacy for censoring social media sites provoked X's owner Elon Musk into a 'war' against the organisation and attracted the ire of the incoming Trump administration, which promised that CCDH would move to the 'top of the list' of investigative targets upon election.[61] If and when the notoriously vindictive Trump administration, in which Musk and Robert F. Kennedy Jr. have played a key role, realises that one of its 'top' investigative targets was created by the man who is now chief of staff to the UK prime minister, who knows what might happen.

PART TWO

THE LONG CON

CHAPTER 4

THE CAMPAIGN

Keir Starmer launched his campaign for leader of the Labour Party on January 4, 2020. Four months later, as British citizens were isolated in Covid lockdown, he was announced as the winner of a three-way run-off between himself, Lisa Nandy, and the left's preferred candidate Rebecca Long-Bailey. In the final poll of Labour Party members, Starmer took nearly 60 percent of the vote: an impressive achievement secured by one of the most mendacious political campaigns in modern political history.

COMING CLEAN

Starmer's leadership campaign was incubated and run by the Labour Together Project and financed by its donors. This reality was obscured from the public during the campaign itself and for a number of years thereafter.

At the time, Labour Together was adamant that it had no stake in the leadership contest. This was explicitly relayed to members by Shabana Mahmood in February 2020 in an article published by *LabourList*. 'Labour Together is not supporting any particular leadership campaign',[1] she said.

Labour Together was still broadcasting its public image as a kumbaya circle promoting collaboration, listening, and party unity. Between 2020 and 2022, the Labour Together website carried an anodyne 'About Us' section that described a 'network of committed Labour Party members, supporters and politicians' and listed Labour Party MPs who 'are helping to coordinate our projects'. The website recommended that political challenges be resolved through 'conversations face-to-face, in living rooms and around kitchen tables' and by creating a 'space' in the Labour movement 'for us all to step forward, to be heard and to listen'.[2] The website made no mention of Labour Together's funders, its history, or the candidate it had secretly backed.

In April 2023, Labour Together broke cover, updating its website to coincide with the launch of *Red Shift*—the group's first substantial research publication since 2020. The new organisational biography now boasted about elements of Labour Together's pre-2020 history and claimed credit for Starmer's leadership win.

'Labour Together was built by a group of MPs—Shabana Mahmood, Steve Reed, Bridget Phillipson, Wes Streeting, Lucy Powell, Rachel Reeves, Jim McMahon, Jon Cruddas and Lisa Nandy—who wanted to see Labour back in power', the site now read. In a nod to the group's historical roots, the site recalled that 'Labour Together fought to make the party electable again' during 'Labour's wilderness years' under Corbyn. Those years in the 'wilderness' were ending because Labour Together had put a winner in the leader's office:

> In 2020, with Morgan McSweeney as Director, it united the party behind Keir Starmer's leadership campaign. In the years since, Keir Starmer has reformed the party, placed the country's best interests at heart, and put Labour on the path to power.[3]

The Labour Together website thus confirmed that McSweeney 'united the party behind Keir Starmer's leadership campaign' as a 'Director'—that is, as director of Labour Together, not as Starmer's campaign chief, as he also was.

If there was any ambiguity about what Labour Together meant by crowing that it had 'united' the party behind Starmer, this was dispelled by Steve Reed MP, in a quote also featured prominently on the group's website:

> In 2017, Labour Together developed a strategy for defeating the Hard Left and reconnecting Labour with voters it had abandoned. In 2020, it played a key role in Keir Starmer's leadership campaign, and Keir has since transformed our party.[4]

And on Twitter, Labour Together would brag that 'we backed @Keir_Starmer & helped him win the leadership'.[5]

In November 2023, *The Sunday Times* ran an article probing Labour Together's failure to report donations and the role of Labour Together in running Starmer's campaign, based in part on documents I provided and which had been discovered as part of research for this book. Not long after, Labour Together deleted Reed's quote from its website and replaced it with a new one. Reed 2.0 made no reference to Starmer.[6] All mention of McSweeney was also scrubbed from the website, although Labour Together neglected to take down or edit the PDF of its 2023 report *Red Shift*, which had featured the same organisational hagiography that emphasised McSweeney's role.[7]

Back in 2020, this information about Labour Together's support for Starmer would have been useful for Labour Party members contemplating who to elect as their next leader. Streeting and Reeves were known for their open hostility to Corbyn and Corbynism, and widely seen as part of a Blair-adjacent right wing. Reeves, in particular, had long set out her right-wing ideological stall. During the Cameron-Osborne austerity years, she promised that the Labour Party would cut public spending faster than the Tories.[8] In 2015 she infamously told a *Guardian* interviewer that Labour 'are not the party of benefits . . . We don't want to be seen [as], and we're not, the party to represent people out of work'.[9]

As we will see below, Starmer pitched himself to the party's left-leaning membership with a policy platform that differed little from that of his closest rival, the left-wing standard bearer Rebecca Long-Bailey, as he promised not to 'oversteer' away from Corbynism.[10] Starmer's pitch would have appeared much less credible had Labour members known that he was anointed by a collection of MPs who had been at the forefront of undermining the Corbyn project. Of course, had Labour members known what McSweeney had been up to behind the scenes to ensure that Corbyn's Labour lost as badly as possible to a Tory Party that most members held in utter contempt, Starmer's progressive posturing would have been laughed out of the room.

INCUBATION

By late 2018, there was a growing sense that Corbynism was on borrowed time. The opinion poll leads of late 2017 had given way to a see-sawing balance in which first Labour and then the Tories took the advantage. For those who had access to substantive constituency-based polling, it was clear that the decisive moment came during the party's annual conference in September 2018.

In a 2016 referendum, the British public had narrowly voted for 'Brexit'—to leave the European Union. The implications of this vote still dominated British politics two years later. The Corbyn leadership's line at the time was to rule out a second Brexit referendum that included 'Remain' as an option. On the eve of Labour's 2018 conference, shadow chancellor John McDonnell MP was dispatched to explain the leadership's position. He clarified that, if there was going to be another referendum, it would not offer the choice of 'Remain'—this having already been rejected by the referendum in 2016—but would instead focus on the terms of whatever Brexit deal had been negotiated with Brussels.[11] Simply: the Labour Party would pull the country out of the EU, honouring the 2016 result, even if the final terms were up for debate and would be settled by a confirmatory referendum.

This policy dismayed pro-Remain campaigners. These had the support of most Labour Party members but also prominently included the likes of the People's Vote Campaign, which was populated by former Labour politicians and staffers who had a long history of attacking the Corbyn movement. This tension is important for understanding the political events that unfolded: whereas the push for a second Brexit referendum was led by figures hostile to Corbynism, its core demand was supported by a majority of Labour's pro-Corbyn membership.

Two days after McDonnell's intervention, Starmer—Labour's shadow Brexit secretary—unveiled a very different programme. Starmer's office had prepared and confirmed a carefully calibrated speech that had been vetted by Corbyn's leadership office. It stuck faithfully to LOTO's political line as expressed by McDonnell. But in his appearance at Labour's annual conference, Starmer decided to deviate from his approved speech, and instead put forward his own Brexit policy: 'Conference, it is right that parliament has the first say, but if we need to break the impasse, our options must include campaigning for a public vote, *and nobody is ruling out Remain as an option*'.[12] Starmer received a standing ovation on the conference floor and was heralded in the press. Martin Kettle wrote in *The Guardian* that Starmer's maverick intervention was a 'Brexit zinger' that 'hit the spot'.[13]

Starmer's intervention helped to burnish his own reputation as the Remainers' great hope and grew his public profile immensely. Within the Labour Party, and in the Remain press, he instantly became the sober saviour who would fight for the civility and decency that many Remainers associated with the EU. But Starmer's speech also guaranteed that Labour's fragile and regionally heterogeneous voting coalition would fall apart as so-called 'Red Wall' seats—traditional Labour-voting constituencies in the north that had voted Leave in 2016—baulked at this fresh insult to their democratic decision. Of the sixty seats

Labour went on to lose in the 2019 general election, fully fifty-two had voted Leave.[14] Of the other eight constituencies, all of which voted Remain, six were in Scotland, lost in part due to the consolidation of the Scottish National Party (SNP) bloc following Labour's Scotland wipeout in 2015.

It was in this context that Labour Together began to publicly re-surface. In February 2019, the group hosted a 'cross-factional take over'[15] of the *LabourList* website. It published articles from fifty contributors, including MPs from across the party's political spectrum. The organisation's Facebook and Twitter pages, so long dormant, sprang back to life.

In May 2019, British voters used the European parliamentary elections to express distaste with both major parties for their failure to negotiate some form of Brexit. The Tories came in fifth, their support eviscerated by Farage's Brexit Party, which won over 30 percent of the vote. It seems few voters were persuaded by pleas from Stop Funding Fake News to shun Farage. Labour limped in third with 13.6 percent of the vote, well behind the Liberal Democrats (19.6 percent) and just barely ahead of the Greens (11.8 percent).

According to Labour insiders, these results panicked Corbyn and led him to soften on a second referendum platform. The Tories also took fright, removing Theresa May as prime minister and eventually electing Boris Johnson as party leader. Boris' appointment as prime minister, and his relentlessly repeated promise to 'get Brexit done', saw the Tories' poll ratings soar. Labour failed to keep up.

This was the background to the announcement of Labour Together as a parliamentary force. In the aftermath of the European elections, Labour Together declared it had set up a parallel policymaking group of MPs. The news was delivered as an exclusive in *The Independent* and cast as a 'fresh challenge' to Corbyn.[16] The MPs released a statement arguing that 'populism divides our country' and that 'shouting through megaphones and setting up single issue protest parties' would not heal these divides. Despite these backhanded criticisms, the MPs were nevertheless still careful to paint themselves as non-factional. The group was 'committed to working with members who support the current leadership and those who do not', the statement professed. 'No one has a monopoly on wisdom or morality'.[17]

At around the same time, and unbeknownst to the public, the Labour Together Project also began secretly preparing for a future tilt at the Labour leadership.

According to Starmer's sympathetic biographer, Tom Baldwin, Starmer's leadership ambitions were incubated by a loose network called the 'Arlington Group'. The name referred to the road in Camden that was home to Jenny Chapman MP, who would help Starmer's leadership bid and become a fixture in Starmer's office after his election. Chapman was elevated to the House of Lords in March 2021 at Starmer's nomination, after losing her parliamentary seat in the 2019 election (partly as a result of the Brexit policy Starmer championed).

The group met weekly on Monday mornings. Chapman's husband, Nick Smith MP, was one frequent attendee. Another was Tom Kibasi, founder of the left-leaning Institute for Public Policy Research, although it is not quite clear when he joined. As noted, he would eventually express remorse for his role in getting Starmer elected as party leader. Labour Together's Steve Reed joined in at some point, although it's not clear exactly when; Baldwin claims that he was part of the group from the beginning whereas Pogrund and Maguire suggest that he was only invited from mid-2019.

Baldwin's account is vague on dates, but he claims the Arlington Group convened after Chapman had been disgusted by Corbyn's response to the poisoning of Sergei Skripal in March 2018. Skripal, a former Russian military officer and double agent for British intelligence services, barely survived a poison-based assassination attempt in Salisbury. In the immediate aftermath, Corbyn urged caution before rushing to blame Russia without investigation. Chapman told Baldwin that many like her were at the end of their tether and that they needed some 'light at the end of the tunnel'. She placed a call to Starmer and asked if he had ever considered standing for leadership. He affirmed that it was something he might be minded to do.

If this timeline is accurate, the Arlington Group was set up to discuss matters related to an eventual leadership bid in early 2018.

It appears there was a step change in the Arlington Group's discussions in June 2019, when McSweeney was invited to a meeting. Reed made the connection. McSweeney presented a slide deck based on extensive polling by an unidentified polling firm. Labour Together had commissioned the polling at the same time as it was failing to report donations to the Electoral Commission. The polling amounted to an 'MRI' of the party membership, Baldwin notes.

The essence of the analysis was that the Labour Party's membership was not 'composed of the ideological Corbynites of popular imagination'.[18] Roughly one quarter of the membership was ideologically committed (20 percent on the left, 5 percent on the right), another quarter would support whoever they believed would win a general election, some 10 percent were 'identitarians' concerned with diversity, and the remaining 40 percent were idealistic types for whom 'politics was an expressive, emotional and values-led exercise: on Brexit but also austerity'. If Starmer could win that 40 percent, he would win the leadership election, just as Corbyn had before him.

McSweeney impressed all attendees. He was rapidly drafted into the Arlington Group and put in charge of matters related to the party membership.[19] From the outset, then, Starmer's leadership bid was crafted with the direct support of Labour Together.

Baldwin's revelations are noteworthy for two reasons. First, they show that, at an early stage, Labour Together's unlawfully undeclared funds were presumably being put to uses that would benefit Starmer, as he was being given access to polling data from Labour Together. (There was nothing wrong with Starmer using this data, of course, on the assumption he didn't know that Labour Together had funded its collection and analysis improperly. Questions might, however, be raised about whether Starmer should have reported the polling as a benefit-in-kind to parliament.)

Secondly, they suggest that McSweeney was getting on board with Starmer only three to four months after the Labour Together Project had helped launch SFFN's anti-Corbyn astro-turf campaign. Starmer's leadership campaign and McSweeney's secret project to destroy Corbynism were tightly linked.

As an aside: it is perhaps uncouth to criticise a fellow chronicler, but Baldwin's light-touch treatment of Labour Together's massive pot of undisclosed funding does his book a disservice. Baldwin addresses this serious matter in a single paragraph, noting that Labour Together figures had excused their failure to disclose as an administrative error. Baldwin comments that the story 'went virtually unnoticed at the time but made front-page news in the build-up to the 2024 election, when McSweeney's political opponents realised he had been running the organisation for much of that time'.[20] This dismissively implied that an originally inconsequential story was opportunistically disinterred for political reasons. Baldwin's account does not mention the discovery of new documents or revelations from closely placed sources as a reason for the belated investigative interest. He also does not consider what it meant for democracy if Starmer's campaign had benefitted from an organisation that was breaking electoral law.

Anushka Asthana also underplays the issue, which her book disposes of in a single paragraph that breezily concludes: 'mistakes were made'. Asthana devotes more words to describing what songs Reed and McSweeney belted out at karaoke than to discussing Labour Together's unlawfully undeclared donations. Does the integrity of British democracy mean so little?

But it is Pogrund and Maguire whose treatment of this scandal most disappoints. They, too, expend a single, lone paragraph of their nearly five-hundred-page tome to McSweeney's failure to report Labour Together's funding. 'The oversight ultimately served its strategic interest. It kept the secret', they write. But

> it was also informed by a desire to protect Trevor Chinn, Labour Together's greatest benefactor and a lightning rod for antisemitism. The explanation they eventually offered in public had the advantage of ringing true to anyone who had worked with McSweeney: that he was simply too disorganised to have known what to declare and when.[21]

This paragraph is full of holes, and it is disappointing that Pogrund and Maguire do not point them out. First, Chinn was not Labour Together's only, or even largest, donor during this period. That was Martin Taylor, who is not Jewish. Second, one of the only donations that McSweeney properly reported in 2018 was a £50,000 donation *from Chinn*—the man who supposedly needed protecting from 'antisemitism'. Third, Chinn would tell *The Telegraph* in 2024 that he had no idea his donations had not been reported—the implication being that he made them in the expectation they would be reported, a prospect that apparently did not trouble him.[22] Fourth, if Labour Together was trying to protect Chinn, this means that it was, in fact, *purposefully* deciding not to report donations. That is straightforwardly illegal. This excuse reads like just another example of concern over antisemitism being instrumentalised to defend the indefensible.

The notion that McSweeney was just too disorganised to comply with the law is also hard to credit. McSweeney was plenty organised enough to call the Electoral Commission back in November 2017 to make the argument that Labour Together shouldn't have to report donations. He was also organised enough to run a multi-year campaign of political sabotage and subterfuge, before guiding the Labour Party to electoral victory, and then, if commentators are to be credited, effectively running the country as Starmer's chief of staff. It is hard to believe that such a seasoned and reputedly effective operator was bamboozled by basic administration and online forms, despite having them patiently explained to him by helpful Electoral Commission staff.

Returning to the matter at hand: the last action of parliament before its recess on October 29, 2019, was to approve the calling of a general election that December. Polling predicted a solid Tory victory, thanks in no small part to the Labour Party's confusing offer on Brexit. Labour Together's support for Starmer was by then sufficiently developed that it began hosting planning sessions, the earliest of which took place in late October or early November 2019, according to well-placed sources.

Labour Together also hosted a lavish dinner in a West London hotel around the same time, attended by a smattering of journalists from papers and magazines on the centre-left of the political spectrum. Other attendees included Starmer and the Labour Together MPs (excluding Reeves) as well as Morgan McSweeney and Labour Together staffer Hannah O'Rourke. Participants were clear that Starmer was their choice in a future leadership contest, and discussions centred on his prospective platform.

One attendee recalled that each MP present gave their elevator pitch for how to win over the membership. However, it seems likely that the dinner's real function was to introduce key journalists to the 'real' Labour leadership campaign, sending them a coded reassurance that—whatever radicalism Starmer might signal to the membership—his candidacy was rooted in the kind of politics that offers presentations from the likes of Reed and Wes Streeting over lavish three-course meals.

The scale and intensity of these preparatory meetings reportedly increased as soon as the general election campaign began in earnest. According to Pogrund and Maguire, Tom Kibasi started hosting discussions in his kitchen attended by Starmer and McSweeney. The sessions undertook scenario planning for a potential leadership bid and organised seven distinct groups tasked with identifying supportive MPs and fundraising routes. Further sessions were held at St Barnabas House, a private members' club in Soho.

As early as mid-November, and while he was being briefed by McSweeney, Starmer began putting out feelers with Labour colleagues. One left-winger recalled being approached by Starmer to go for a coffee. Starmer approached the meeting as if he was seeking an opinion and advice, but in retrospect it read as both an attempt to suss out a left-wing reaction to his candidacy and as a means of seeding the idea. 'We want Labour to win, of course we do', Starmer told his interlocutor. 'But, if it doesn't, some suggest I might run for leader. What do you think?' The answer was non-committal.

By the time the final results confirmed Labour's collapse to just 202 seats on December 12, Starmer's campaign was almost ready to go, supported by Labour Together. A *Daily Mail* article on December 14 confirmed that Starmer, who had not yet announced his candidacy, was the favourite. 'It is understood he has donors and a campaign team ready', the paper reported.[23]

On December 20, 2019, Movement for Another Future Limited was formed. The company would act as Starmer's campaign vehicle, employing campaign staff and holding data. The sole director of the company was Alex Barros-Curtis. Barros-Curtis acted as the Starmer campaign's legal and financial compliance chief, as he had previously done for anti-Corbyn challenger Owen Smith. He would go on to play a key role in the Starmer Project. In the 2024 general election, Barros-Curtis was selected into a safe Labour seat in Wales and now sits as an MP.

Keir Starmer's personal website, keirstarmer.com, was discreetly updated around December 21, 2019, according to captures from online archiving tool The Wayback Machine. The formerly humdrum constituency page was replaced with a striking image of Starmer in profile addressing a crowd. Accompanying text—bold white on a black background—announced: 'Keir Starmer. Another future is possible'.[24] The pieces were in position and the stage was set—but for what?

Starmer's 2020 Labour leadership bid has been called the 'most dishonest campaign for the leadership of a major political party in British political history',[25] and it is not hard to see why. In retrospect, the campaign appears to have been an efficiently executed plan to invent a 'green-socialist' persona that not only diverged from Starmer's real project but was the virtual antithesis of it. Once Starmer had extracted the votes he needed from Labour Party members, he jettisoned the platform they voted for almost immediately. Indeed, the unifying and radical environmentalist version of Starmer that was curated in early 2020 would bear almost zero resemblance to the right-wing and hyper-factional Starmer who would run the Labour Party shortly thereafter.

Starmer launched his candidacy on January 4, 2020, with a slickly produced social media video, followed the next day by an article published under his name in the *Sunday Mirror*. Together, these announcements set the tone—the mood music, as one Starmer campaign insider described it—for Starmer's invented identity and position.

Starmer's *Mirror* piece confirmed that he endorsed and supported the tenets of leftist Corbynite policy, as well as the 'radicalism' of his predecessor:

> We must not lose sight of our values, or retreat from the radicalism of the past few years . . . We must push for a Green New Deal to tackle the climate crisis, demand dignity at the heart of our social security system and make the case for a radically transformed economy that empowers trade unions and communities that have been left behind. And we should lead the fight for peace and justice around the world with a human rights approach to foreign policy and international relations.[26]

The video, meanwhile, set out to establish Starmer's supposedly progressive legal background. Across a nearly pitch-perfect four minutes, viewers were told of Starmer's assorted good deeds, from representing the McLibel defendants to standing up for unions and defending environmental campaigners. A lengthy endorsement from Doreen Lawrence—the mother of Stephen Lawrence, who was murdered in a racist attack in 1993—set up Starmer to deliver direct to camera a humble and sober address on the need to unite the party.

These voiceovers were complemented by evocative images, all designed to imply Starmer's support for, and location within, progressive social movements. They included shots of Stop the War's march against the 2003 Iraq War; grainy footage of historical trade union confrontations with the police; and, most notably, shots of Starmer standing with Diane Abbott or being embraced by Corbyn. The video thus eerily foreshadowed the social movements and individuals that Starmer's Labour would soon betray: Abbott and Corbyn would both be refused the Labour whip, for example, while Starmer would prohibit MPs from standing on union pickets and threaten them with losing the whip if they signed a Stop the War statement on Ukraine.

But in the period between January and April 2020, these betrayals were still over the horizon. Powered by nearly £700,000 in donations—mostly undeclared, unlike those of his competitors—Starmer was able to punctuate his campaign with launches at the Roundhouse and an astonishing direct mail campaign that saw his poster sent to *every* Labour Party member; a 'mailshot' that commentators estimate must have cost hundreds of thousands of pounds. Starmer kept up his progressive patter with strict message discipline throughout the campaign.

MOOD MUSIC

Starmer's campaign confected a left-wing ambience by regularly emphasising five key themes.

First, it referred positively to radicalism and, in particular, to the radicalism Starmer claimed had been introduced by Corbyn. 'We should treat the 2017 manifesto as our foundational document, the radicalism and the hope that inspired across the country was real',[27] Starmer said in mid-January. Starmer's 'Labour Even MORE Radical?' the *Daily Express* asked in wild-eyed response.[28] 'I'm very concerned that we retain the radicalism of the last four years. I don't want to throw the baby away with the bathwater', Starmer told the *Manchester Evening News* a few days later.[29] To the BBC, Starmer explained:

> What I've said is, we don't trash past Labour governments. All Labour governments made very important changes to the lives of millions of people. But nor do we trash the last five years . . . Jeremy Corbyn made the Labour Party a clearly anti-austerity party, a party that stood up against cuts to public services. And I think that was important.[30]

Starmer's rhetorical support for Corbyn was consistent and powerful. In a barnstorming segment during the first hustings event in Liverpool, Starmer lustily criticised the mainstream media and its attacks on Corbyn:

> They vilified him, and they knew what they were doing, and they know why they were doing it. We just lost the election, and it's going to happen again, and we need to cut through that. This city has been wounded by the media . . . and I certainly won't be giving any interviews to *The Sun* during the course of this campaign.[31]

The speech earned Starmer the biggest round of applause of the whole event. Starmer would write for *The Sun* on multiple occasions after being elected leader and would eventually be endorsed by the paper in the 2024 general election because 'Sir Keir has distanced himself from crazy Marxist Corbynista policies and MPs'.[32]

The campaign also hammered home Starmer's commitment to socialist environmentalism, with a particular focus on the climate crisis. Starmer repeatedly claimed that a Green New Deal should be at 'the heart' of any government programme and deployed a line that was striking in its bald radicalism: 'If it's bad for the environment, it's bad for the economy'.[33]

This fearless eco-socialism was accompanied by a forthright critique of neoliberal economics, its third theme. 'We have to be bold enough to say the free-market model doesn't produce, doesn't work', Starmer told an audience in Manchester. 'The trickle-down effect didn't happen. We have to rebuild an economic model that reduces inequality and protects working people'.[34] A few days later, Starmer wrote a lengthy article in *The Guardian* that pitched his vision of a 'moral socialism':

> There are two parts to being Labour. First, enabling everyone to get a decent education, the best job they can, better standards of living and a fulfilling life. The free market has failed in this endeavour. We have to fight to put wealth, power and opportunity in the hands of all.[35]

The campaign's fourth theme was a powerful defence of immigration, which was tied to Starmer's post-Brexit support for continued freedom of movement. 'We need to make the wider case on immigration', Starmer argued in late January 2020:

> We welcome migrants, we don't scapegoat them. Low wages, poor housing, poor public services, are not the fault of people who come here: they're [a] political failure. So we have to make the case for the benefits of migration; for the benefits of free movement.[36]

In late February 2020, Starmer criticised the Tories for introducing a points-based system for immigration that included a minimum-salary threshold. 'They are equating the worth of an individual coming to this country by how much money they earn', Starmer charged. 'I think that's profoundly the wrong approach'.[37]

The final theme was Labour Party unity. 'The whole of the party wants to be united', Starmer told the first hustings audience in Liverpool. 'We have to end factionalism. Stop asking the question "which bit of the party are you from?" and start asking, "what are you saying?" . . . We are unstoppable when we are united'.

Starmer's unity pitch was anchored in a promise to reform how Labour's internal democracy functioned. In early February, Starmer published an eight-point plan to 'reform and unite our party'.[38] His leadership would oversee the recruitment of 'a truly representative set of candidates for future elections', ending top-down 'imposition of candidates' by the National Executive Committee on the understanding that 'local party members should select their candidates for every election'. It would also scrap the National Constitutional Committee (a body that sat above the NEC and was the final stop in complaints hearings), encourage 'more party members to become active in their trade unions', and launch a 'transparency revolution' so that 'any member can see what decision is made, where and by whom'.[39]

Starmer couched his case for party unity in terms (*reconciliation, respect*) calculated to resonate with Labour's membership:

> Our party is divided, and unity requires reconciliation. The best place to start this journey is by revisiting our founding principles. Labour was built on the principle of justice. We stand for decency in how we treat one another and fairness in how we share out the advantages and burdens in society. The moral heart of justice is equality: each person is of equal worth. We must embed into our systems and actions this principle that all members are equal.

If these stirring words sound familiar, you're not hallucinating. They repeat almost verbatim the presentation by McSweeney to the July 2019 meeting of Labour Together insiders that I described earlier. In that meeting, recall, McSweeney had earnestly beseeched his Labour-supporting audience to embrace unity and reconciliation at the very same time as he was executing his secret plan to marginalise and erase those Labour factions he abhorred. In fact, as Table 2 documents, the preamble to Starmer's 'reform and unite' platform was liberally lifted from two sources: McSweeney's July 2019 speech and text that had appeared on Labour Together's website since April 2019.

TABLE 2. Starmer's Borrowed Unity Pitch

Starmer's 'Reform and Unite Platform'[40] (Matching text *italicised* or underlined)	**McSweeney's Speech and the Labour Together Website**[41] (Speech in *italics*, website underlined)
The Labour Party has always been a place where different ways of thinking come together. Our trade unionist, reformist social democrat and radical socialist traditions are still at the heart of our movement, and over the decades Labour has also become a home for feminists, environmentalists, internationalists, LGBT+ movements and more. *But too often we find ourselves focusing on our differences rather than the values and principles that brought us together, and that comes at a cost. Our party is divided, and unity requires reconciliation. The best place to start this journey is by revisiting our founding principles. Labour was built on the principle of justice. We stand for decency in how we treat one another and fairness in how we share out the advantages and burdens in society. The moral heart of justice is equality: each person is of equal worth.*	*The Labour Party has always been a party that has brought traditions together: our Labour unionist tradition, our radical socialist tradition, our reforming and social democrat tradition. But too often and for too long these traditions are in a state of angry estrangement. Too often [and] for too long the focus has been on our differences and that can come at a cost. The Party's divided and unity requires reconciliation. The best place to start this journey is by revisiting our founding principles. Labour was built on the principle of justice. We stand for decency in how we treat one another and fairness in how we share out the advantages and burdens in society. The moral heart of justice is equality: each person is of equal worth. We must embed into our systems and actions this principle that all members are equal . . . Sometimes some people seem to make it their mission to try and kill*

(continued)

Starmer's 'Reform and Unite Platform'[40] (Matching text *italicised* or underlined)	**McSweeney's Speech and the Labour Together Website**[41] (Speech in *italics*, website underlined)
We must embed into our systems and actions this principle that all members are equal. I am clear: reconciliation does not mean shying away from the real political differences that exist. Reconciliation is not submission to the strongest or loudest, nor is it compelling others to conform to an ideological norm. Unity cannot be forced and is entered into willingly, with open hearts and minds. Working together does not mean surrendering our own personal views about how our values are put into practice; that debate and those differences are what keeps us alive and relevant. We need our party to function like friends round a table, where each of us can be confident that our ideas are valued while we work together to find a way forward. Unity can only be achieved through respect for others and the recognition that no individual, group or faction has all the answers. *Labour's traditions will always be with us, they are a part of us.* The future of our party must be built on a new, more inclusive, more democratic culture of dignity and respect.	*off the traditions that are not theirs. But you can't do that, because these traditions are always with us. They're like our souls. When those three souls stand together is when our party comes to life.* Now more than ever Labour must create a democratic politics that can build a broad national coalition. It must be based on a reconciliation of our differences. Reconciliation does not mean avoiding the real political conflicts that exist. Unity cannot be forced. Labour needs to create at all levels of its organisation, the kind of political leadership that can build bridges, respect difference and reconcile opposing interests. Working together does not mean surrendering our own values. Consensus has to be worked for. Labour must be the space where we can create relationships in which we each know our difference and we each recognise the difference in the other. We have our own identities but we also share a common bond. Our party needs to function like a table where each can keep their own identities while working together to find common ground and work out how we can belong.

Starmer was literally reading from McSweeney's dishonest script. Is it any surprise, then, that these passionately delivered promises were among the first to be broken once Starmer took over the party?

Starmer's campaign cemented his position as the unity candidate with a canny hiring policy that hinted at a rapprochement with Corbynites. The press was quickly informed that the campaign had hired Simon Fletcher, who directed Corbyn's leadership bids in 2015 and 2016. Starmer's campaign also cultivated left-wing figures like Laura Parker, who was invited to join an informal group to provide feedback on the campaign via WhatsApp. Parker had been Corbyn's private secretary in LOTO between May 2016 and November 2017, before becoming the national coordinator for the pro-Corbyn campaign group Momentum. She would later endorse Starmer[42] and, not long after, express remorse for having believed him.[43]

These choices were counterpointed by the hiring of much more aggressively right-wing campaigners. Among them was Matt Pound, a close ally of Luke Akehurst. As noted previously, Akehurst is one of the most effective organisers on the party's right, who often takes delight in aggravating left-wingers. Pound was also one of Labour First's earliest employees, dedicated to fighting an anti-Corbyn ground war in the latter years of the Corbyn movement. Another appointee was Ben Nunn, a previous Starmer advisor and former lobbyist for private healthcare. Nunn's appointment drew pointed questions from left-wing members, to which Starmer responded with a righteous refusal to pass comment on his staff.

The emptiness of Starmer's unity platform would be illustrated by the divergent career trajectories of these early appointments. By the end of 2021, every noted left-winger who had joined Starmer's campaign had either resigned as party employees (Fletcher and Bond) or denounced Starmer's betrayal (Kibasi and Parker). But Starmer's right-wing appointees flourished. Pound wound up working closely with McSweeney and Akehurst to oversee the selection of MP candidates, in a process that has been widely criticised for its alleged factionalism.

SHADOWING AND THE TEN PLEDGES

For all its importance, the Labour leadership contest was a quiet affair. Polls put Starmer in the lead from the off and he never looked likely to lose it.[44] All candidates agreed to conduct themselves in the spirit of comradeship in an attempt to prevent factionalism and model unity from the top. The result was that, across multiple hustings, candidates rarely attempted to knock out their competitors. Any attack on Starmer, no matter how gentle, invited condemnation for breaching the peace.

But even as the candidates kept their powder dry, Starmer's approach did reveal something important about his modus operandi. His campaign—'subcontracted' to Labour Together, as Pogrund and Maguire put it—adopted a strategy of 'shadowing'. This involved consistently moving to the left on policy whenever Long-Bailey threatened to differentiate herself from Starmer on brass-tack deliverables. The purpose was not to necessarily deliver on these promises but rather to preclude any public debate over them that threatened to lose Starmer support before the vote.

Starmer would later adopt the same strategy in his general election contest with the Tories (and especially Rishi Sunak)—either agreeing with, or doubling-down on, whatever right-wing policy, decision or talking point they wheeled out. It says much about the cynicism of the Starmer and Labour Together projects that Starmer would present as virtually indistinguishable on policy from Corbyn's 'woke' socialist heir Long-Bailey *and* from the sharply right-leaning and culture-war-baiting leadership of Sunak, all within the space of three years.

For Long-Bailey's campaign team, Starmer's shadowing was both blatant and exasperating. Matt Zarb-Cousin, the former Corbyn speechwriter who led Long-Bailey's communications team, described how Starmer's policy evolved during the leadership campaign. 'It was just impossible to draw any space between us and him. He would box us out on any policy differences, follow us along, and agree with everything we suggested'.

The result was that Starmer's policy platform, unlike his rhetorical 'mood music', changed during the campaign, becoming more left-wing and radical in response to moves made by Long-Bailey. This was especially obvious in relation to nationalisation and constitutional reform.

At Starmer's campaign event in Manchester on January 12, he endorsed the renationalisation of rail but 'refused to commit to taking energy, water and postal services back under state control'.[45] At the end of January, Long-Bailey laid down the gauntlet on the issue during a speech in Leeds. 'Other candidates say they agree with the transformative programme, but now I'm calling for specific, concrete commitments you can trust', she said. 'Public ownership of key utilities is the foundation for a more fair and equal society, and any candidate for Labour leader should endorse them without hesitation'.[46]

Similarly, in mid-January, Long-Bailey announced her plans to scrap the House of Lords, which she wanted to replace with an elected senate based in the North. Starmer's response was initially cautious, promising a vague 'constitutional convention' that would explore devolving power and introducing federalism.[47] There was no mention of abolishing the House of Lords—for another two weeks.

On February 11, Starmer unveiled his now-infamous 'ten pledges' designed to put meat on the bones of his supposed radicalism. The pledges were considerably more progressive and concrete than what Starmer had previously committed to. Under the theme of 'radical devolution of power, wealth and opportunity', Starmer now promised a devolved 'federal system' and to 'abolish the House of Lords', which would be replaced with 'an elected chamber of regions and nations'.

By the end of February, Starmer was promoting his opposition to the House of Lords especially hard. In an interview for the left-wing Scottish website *Red Robin* (now defunct), Starmer recommitted to an elected senate and appended an attention-grabbing promise: 'All new Labour appointees to the Lords in the interim will sign a declaration committing themselves to vote for the abolition of the Lords and we will enshrine this in party policy', he announced.[48]

It proved to be just another pledge that was dumped after Starmer's election as party leader and then directly contradicted by his decisions as prime minister: whereas candidate Starmer said he would abolish the House of Lords because it was undemocratic, Prime Minister Starmer would end up elevating Angela Smith and Poppy Gustaffson to the Lords to enable them to become (unelected) ministers.

On nationalisation, too, Starmer radicalised his rhetoric over the course of his leadership campaign. Starmer's fifth pledge, under the theme of 'Common ownership', stated that 'public services should be in public hands, not making profits for shareholders' and called for 'common ownership of rail, mail, energy and water'.[49] These commitments would be jettisoned nearly as soon as Starmer was elected party leader, and entirely erased from the platform on which Starmer was eventually elected prime minister in 2024.

TURNCOAT

Starmer, in short, is a turncoat.

For four months, he donned the mantle of socialism to win the leadership, drawing on its language, policies, and symbols. After winning the election, that coat was swiftly discarded and a new one tailored. This new garb was cut to fit a man who would mimic the language and policies of a Tory party drifting ever closer to the far right.

There is a danger that, with the passage of time, the profundity of Starmer's about-turn might be forgotten, trivialised or reduced to the begrudging gripe of a disgruntled left. This would be a catastrophic mistake. To guard against this, a full table setting out every pledge, promise, and principle that Starmer backed in the leadership campaign and subsequently dumped is available on the website that accompanies this book: www.thefraud.info.

There are at least *twenty* instances during the leadership campaign where Starmer made a direct and material policy commitment, or gave a firm opinion about a policy position, that was subsequently abandoned. These were hard commitments to specific policy outcomes (abolishing tuition fees, for example), or expressions of opinion on concrete policy issues (for instance, that the UK should pursue a customs union with the EU following Brexit), or promises to reform the Labour Party itself in a specified way (such as ending the NEC's top-down imposition of parliamentary candidates on local CLPs).

In the years after his election as Labour Party leader, Starmer was often criticised for having ditched his campaign promises. Starmer and his outriders developed two main defences against this charge. Both are worth examining.

The first response was to argue that 'changing circumstances' tied Starmer's hands in ways he could not have predicted during the campaign. In particular, the economic downturn following the disastrous seven-week premiership of Liz Truss in 2022 supposedly meant there was no longer enough money to deliver on his promises. It was on this basis that Starmer would dump his leadership pledges to scrap university tuition fees[50] and to nationalise mail, water, and energy.[51] Perhaps most disgracefully, this was also the excuse offered for why Starmer jettisoned his commitment to 'build a new social-security system, which supports families by scrapping the two-child limit'.[52]

The two-child benefit cap was introduced to widespread dismay from anti-poverty campaigners by the Tory government in 2017. The cap prevents families from claiming benefits for third and subsequent children and is widely understood to be a key driver of childhood poverty. Starmer's government retained the cap and even went so far as to remove the whip from seven left-wing MPs who voted against this decision.

The chaos of the Truss period was also cited to explain why the party needed to reassure the rich and big business, leading Starmer to drop his leadership pledge 'to increase income tax for the top 5% of earners' and 'reverse the Tories' cuts in corporation tax'.[53]

This defensive rationale was wholly unconvincing:

First, Starmer and his defenders were unable to explain why the party's response to economic hardship was to adopt more conservative economic policies—the sort of policies that had led to these economic hardships in the first place. There was no attempt to explain why, for example, the party felt that a cost-of-living crisis driven by energy price increases did not make the argument for nationalising energy stronger rather than weaker.

Second, this approach addressed specific policy pledges but failed to acknowledge that Starmer's pitch was a combination of both policy and principle. This was important because Starmer's positioning on certain issues after his election was *incommensurate* with the principles he had espoused during his bid for the leadership.

Take, for example, the topic of licenses issued by the Tory government for offshore oil and gas developments in the Rosebank oilfield under the North Sea. It is estimated that the carbon dioxide emissions generated by Rosebank are equivalent to the annual output of the world's twenty-eight lowest-income countries.[54] Starmer, confronted with the Tory plan to grant these licences in 2023, argued that it would be inappropriate for the Labour Party to commit to reversing them as it would be bad for the economy to make things unstable for business. Put in simpler terms, it would be bad for the economy if the Labour Party stopped something that was bad for the environment.

This, of course, was quite literally the opposite of one of Starmer's most oft-repeated leadership campaign principles: 'if it's bad for the environment, it's bad for the economy'.[55]

Third, economic imperatives cannot explain why Starmer abandoned pledges on matters that had no bearing on the economy. It could not, for example, explain why Starmer promised to abolish the House of Lords in 2020 but then said in 2023 that he would not be able to do so during his first five years in government,[56] or why he elevated unelected politicians to the House of Lords after his election as prime minister so that he could appoint them as cabinet ministers. This rationale also failed to explain why Starmer told the country in January 2020 that Scotland would be justified in having another independence referendum if the Scottish National Party won the Holyrood elections the following year,[57] but then said in December 2020 that, in fact, 'no responsible first minister should contemplate [an independence referendum]—and no responsible prime minister would grant it'.[58]

It is also worth examining Starmer's reversal on trans issues. In February 2020, he signed on to ten pledges put forward by the Labour Party LGBT+ network. One of these was to

> campaign to reform the Gender Recognition Act to introduce a self-declaration process and for the introduction of legal recognition for non-binary gender identities. I believe that trans women are women, that trans men are men, and that non-binary gender identities are valid and should be respected.[59]

In December 2023, however, Starmer would tell BBC Radio Five that 'a woman is an adult female, so let's clear that up', and that 'we don't think that self-identification is the way forward'.[60] The party would formally abandon self-ID in its 2024 general election manifesto.

Then there is the fact that Starmer dropped, abandoned or failed to deliver on promises to reform the Labour Party itself. He had, for example, committed to ending 'the NEC's imposition of candidates' on local parties, a promise that was flagrantly breached in 2024 when Starmer used the NEC to block Jeremy Corbyn from standing as a parliamentary candidate, contrary to the wishes of Corbyn's local party. Indeed, as will be seen in the last chapter of this book, this promise was systematically broken when the NEC appointed a whole raft of MP candidates during the 2024 general election—including a number of sitting NEC members.

SMALL-PRINT POLITICS

The second defence offered by Starmer was perhaps even more discreditable: to deny that he had made pledges and commitments that everyone had heard him make, or to protest that people should have read the small print.

Consider Starmer's decision to drop his campaign pledges to nationalise rail, mail, water, and energy. When confronted by the journalist Andrew Marr in September 2021 on his decision to drop the pledge, Starmer argued that he had never committed to nationalisation per se. Marr presented him with the text of his leadership pledge: 'Public services should be in public hands, not making profits for shareholders. Support common ownership of rail, mail, energy and water'. Starmer gestured with a dramatic flourish toward the TV on which the pledge was shown: 'I don't see nationalisation there'.[61] When asked what he meant by 'common ownership' if not nationalisation, Starmer did not explain but deflected with a non-sequitur about pragmatism versus ideological purity.

In fact, Starmer had explicitly backed nationalisation twice during the leadership race. In a televised leadership debate on

Newsnight on February 13, 2020, candidates were requested to raise their hands if they intended to include a given policy in the 'next manifesto'. 'Renationalising water and electricity?' the host asked. Starmer, along with every other participant, raised his hand.[62]

Then, during an interview in March 2020, Andrew Neil asked Starmer, 'Can you guarantee that under your leadership the 2019 Labour commitments to nationalise water, energy, rail, the Royal Mail—they'll all be in Labour's next election manifesto?' 'I've made that commitment', Starmer affirmed. When Starmer attempted to hedge by arguing he could only write a 2024 manifesto closer to the time, Neil made sure: 'those four industries [water, energy, rail, and mail] will be in the Labour manifesto for nationalisation come 2024?' 'They will', Starmer again confirmed. Directly thereafter, Starmer was asked, 'Will you remain committed to scrapping university tuition fees, will you remain committed to scrapping them?' 'They are pledges, Andrew, so the answer to these questions is yes'.[63]

The second example of Starmer's dishonest small-print politics related to his campaign pledge to introduce a 'Prevention of Military Intervention Act'. He had explained in an interview with Andrew Marr in February 2020 that, as prime minister, he would 'pass legislation that said that military action could [only] be taken if first a lawful case for it was made, secondly there was a viable objective, and thirdly you got consent of the Commons'.[64]

In 2023, as the crisis in Gaza escalated and Yemeni forces began blocking Israeli shipping lanes, Britain's Conservative government joined the US in bombing Yemen. Starmer supported the bombing, even though Prime Minister Sunak had neither sought nor received the consent of parliament.

Starmer explained that there was no contradiction between his commitment to pass legislation requiring 'consent of the Commons' for any military action and his support for a military action that MPs had not voted on. Starmer's reasoning was that the strikes in Yemen did not involve a 'sustained campaign' or 'troops on the ground' and thus could not be considered 'military action'.[65] Acting directly contrary to his campaign promises, Starmer did not forthrightly acknowledge and try to explain the contradiction but sought refuge in lawyerly tricks as he baldly claimed that scrambling jet fighters and drones to bomb another country didn't constitute 'military action'.

CHAPTER 5

THE REAL KEIR STARMER

Starmer's victory in the Labour leadership campaign was predicated in large part on ignorance. Most Labour voters were unaware of Starmer's professional and political history, the latter arguably deeply inflected with right-wing factionalism. Indeed, the real Starmer was a very different beast from the progressive persona deployed during his campaign, as shown by his record as director of public prosecutions (DPP) at the Crown Prosecution Service (CPS) as well as his association with the hyper-factionalism that paralysed the Labour Party during the Corbyn years.

DIRECTOR OF POLICE PROTECTION

Starmer's time as DPP (2008–13) revealed a disturbing tendency to enable the worst aspects of Britain's security state, including by protecting police as well as security forces from accountability, as comprehensively detailed by Oliver Eagleton in his book *The Starmer Project*. Starmer's fealty to the state apparatus was particularly noticeable after the election of the Tory-Lib Dem coalition government in 2010, with which Starmer developed a friendly working relationship. 'The consensus among Conservative ministers was that Starmer had their interests at heart', Eagleton reports.[1]

Many of Starmer's decisions as DPP would have likely discomforted the Labour Party's left-leaning membership, had it only known about them. Consider, for example, Starmer's roles in the persecution of *WikiLeaks* founder Julian Assange, the Gary McKinnon extradition case, and the establishment of 'night courts' after the 2011 London riots.

—Night Courts

In August 2011, Mark Duggan was killed by police forces deployed as part of Operation Trident, which targeted gun crime in Black communities. His killing ignited days of angry protests and riots throughout London.

Prime Minister David Cameron's framing of the riots as 'criminality, pure and simple' set the tone for the government's response. This relied on harsh treatment of offenders as a deterrent to further unrest. Even as the riots had been triggered by a police shooting, the possibility that authentic political and social grievances had played a role in the upheaval was dismissed.

Starmer's intervention was two-fold: First, he argued that lengthy sentences for offenders caught in the riots were not an effective deterrent; what mattered was prosecuting people *quickly*, in part so as to rapidly take offenders off the streets.[2] Starmer backed the introduction of night courts, where cases were heard around the clock; one *Guardian* article described Starmer's 'morale-boosting visit' to the Highbury Magistrates Court at 4:00 a.m.[3] Many commentators considered the courts a disaster, because they created an environment that encouraged harsh and arguably disproportionate sentences.

This draconian response was also driven, in part, by Starmer's second intervention: to issue new guidance to CPS prosecutors on August 15, 2011, four days after the last embers from the riots had cooled. The guidance was patently aimed at providing a framework for how the CPS would deal with participants in the riots. The new guidance advised prosecutors to charge people engaged in looting with burglary rather than theft, when the offence was committed in the context of public disorder. Burglary, considered a more serious crime, carried a longer prison sentence. The result was that offenders caught up in the riots sometimes received sentences four times longer than was usual for similar offences.

The majority of those facing the full might of the courts—'the shock and awe of the law', as one senior prosecutor called it at the time—were young people. A retrospective review found that 27 percent of those prosecuted in relation to the riots were aged between eleven and seventeen and another 26 percent were aged eighteen to twenty. Among those prosecuted was an eleven-year-old who was convicted of burglary for stealing a cap.[4]

The Guardian, in conjunction with the London School of Economics (LSE), ran an extensive research programme called 'Reading the Riots'. Numerous *Guardian* articles raised serious concerns about how the night courts had been run and about the sentences they had imposed on juveniles. 'Many defence lawyers were shocked watching children who had never been in trouble before being sentenced to custody, something that normally happens only if they had been convicted of a serious crime', one article reported.[5] One solicitor told the story of a vulnerable eighteen-year-old sent to a Young Offender Institution for stealing electrical items from outside a shop. He was sentenced to custody despite being in remission from cancer and after attempting suicide while on remand.[6] He was bullied extensively while serving his term. Another article, by an LSE professor, questioned whether the night courts had led to abuses of due process.[7]

Starmer's August 2011 guidelines had serious knock-on effects when it came to other forms of protest. In addition to pushing for burglary instead of theft, the guidance advised CPS prosecutors to consider, in relation to suspects involved in public disorder, whether 'there is evidence that a person had equipped themselves with clothes or masks to prevent identification, items that could be considered body protection, or an item that can be used as a weapon'. The reasoning was that 'such evidence may indicate the person anticipated disorder or there was an element of planning'.[8]

This was hugely problematic. As Nadine El-Nany noted in *The Guardian*, given previous police violence against anti-austerity protesters, taking pre-emptive defensive measures might reflect prudent planning rather than violent intent.[9] (El-Nany is a Reader in Law at Birkbeck University and co-director of the Centre for Research on Race and Law.) Similarly, given that police routinely conducted surveillance on protestors while allegations of police spying were rife, it was arguably a sensible precaution to preserve one's anonymity when protesting, irrespective of any intention to breach the law. The failure of Starmer's guidelines to specify what constituted a 'weapon' was also notable; anything, if used offensively, can be a weapon, as the same *Guardian* piece noted. Indeed, the CPS under Starmer did successfully convict one nineteen-year-old protestor for throwing two placard sticks at police during a protest, even though the sticks did not hit anyone.[10]

—Gary McKinnon

Oliver Eagleton has described how DPP Starmer developed a close working relationship with Barack Obama's attorney general, Eric Holder. Holder was responsible for, among other things, developing legal opinions that greenlit the US programme of drone strikes that killed civilians during the 'war on terror'. Starmer frequently went to bat for the US when it pursued questionable extradition requests.

One of the more egregious cases involving Starmer was that of Gary McKinnon, an autistic IT expert. In 2001, McKinnon had hacked into US military databases looking for information about UFOs. The US responded with an indictment that would have led to a seventy-year sentence, and then sought McKinnon's extradition. Starmer reportedly made a personal pledge to Holder that he would make it happen. McKinnon's extradition was widely opposed for fear that McKinnon would not survive prison in the US.

McKinnon's case wended its way through the courts for years. Starmer was unmoved by public opposition to the extradition, even when it was expressed by McKinnon's mother. She recalled her astonishment at Starmer's cold response to her heartfelt pleas when she was able to confront him person. Starmer rebuffed her approach, stating that he was 'uncomfortable' with the discussion. 'Did he have any idea how that sounded to me, when he was supporting the extradition of my son to some foreign hellhole?' she asked.[11]

In 2009, amid judicial reviews about the decision to extradite, McKinnon's lawyers wrote to Starmer.[12] They submitted a request for McKinnon to be tried in the UK—a reasonable ask, considering that the offence was committed there.[13] A UK trial would have immediately halted the extradition proceedings.[14] To bolster the application, McKinnon submitted a plea of guilt under the Computer Misuse Act. This meant that if Starmer agreed to the application, the CPS could rest easy knowing that a conviction was assured.[15]

But in February 2009, despite admitting that McKinnon could have been charged in the UK for nine violations of the Computer Misuse Act, Starmer and the CPS ruled that prosecuting him for the offence in the UK would not 'come near to reflecting the criminality that is alleged by American authorities'.[16] McKinnon's mother decried a decision that would facilitate his extradition 'to a high-security prison knowing he won't survive'.[17] Starmer had the chance to save McKinnon and chose not to, even though McKinnon's conviction in the UK would have been guaranteed.

McKinnon was ultimately rescued by an unexpected saviour: Theresa May. She used her authority as Conservative home secretary to block the extradition, explaining that it 'would give rise to such a high risk of him ending his life that a decision to extradite would be incompatible with Mr. McKinnon's human rights'.[18] Starmer, reportedly furious, flew to the US to meet with Holder's deputies, according to sources quoted by Eagleton, where he sought to emphasise that the decision had nothing to do with the CPS.

If this story had been told during the leadership election, it is hard to see how Labour Party members would not have been perturbed by the fact that Theresa May—architect of the harsh, anti-immigrant 'hostile environment'—evinced more basic human compassion than Starmer. A still less flattering comparison could have been made with Boris Johnson, Starmer's prospective opponent across the dispatch box. Even Johnson, while serving as London mayor, had called on the US to drop the case, branding the extradition demands 'brutal, mad and wrong'.[19]

—WikiLeaks

But the case that would have truly rung alarm bells for many Labour Party idealists was that of Julian Assange, the founder of *WikiLeaks*. In 2010, Holder approved a raft of charges under the Espionage Act flowing from Assange's revelations of US war crimes in Afghanistan and Iraq. Simultaneously, authorities in Sweden pursued an investigation into Assange related to sexual assault allegations against him. Assange stated that he was happy to answer questions about the Swedish charges but did not want to travel to Sweden for fear that the Swedes would render him to the US. Assange's lawyers requested that he be interviewed in London, which the Swedes were amenable to. Yet this eminently reasonable request was blocked by Starmer's CPS, which then lobbied to ensure that the Swedes did not close their investigation despite the misgivings of Sweden's most senior prosecutor. One CPS lawyer infamously excoriated the Swedes in private, imploring, 'Don't you dare get cold feet!!!!'[20]

Extensive destruction or withholding of documents by the CPS[21] has hampered subsequent attempts to identify the extent to which the CPS colluded with the Obama administration to ensure that Assange remained trapped in the Ecuadorian embassy, where he had fled in panic. A United Nations rapporteur would later determine that Assange's treatment amounted to torture.[22] CPS obstruction has also protected Starmer from a full accounting for his role in the Assange affair. But it would be truly remarkable if Starmer had not been directly involved in it, given his direct and personal interest in matters pursued by Holder and given that he had directed CPS staff to regularly brief him on high-profile cases.

FACTIONAL FIGHTER

Starmer's pitch for party unity and an end to internecine factional warfare was attractive for a Labour Party membership exhausted by years of internal battles. Yet here, too, Starmer's promises would have rung false had members been aware of Starmer's own deeply factional record.

Starmer's factionalism was no secret in his own constituency of Holborn and St Pancras. Local members described how the CLP had descended into ugly internecine conflict after Corbyn's election as party leader in 2015. Whereas the party had previously struggled to muster enough delegates to attend the local General Council meetings, AGM elections now became hotly contested on factional lines. Slates were introduced—on both left and right—for the first time, excluding many veteran campaigners from positions they had held for decades alongside fellow party members, now turned factional enemies.

Such factionalism extended to Starmer's home branch of Kentish Town, where slate politics came to dominate proceedings. Left-wing organising ahead of a key meeting in 2019 raised the prospect that branch leaders—many of whom were personally close to Starmer—would be removed from their positions. On the night of voting, Starmer and his wife reportedly participated in order to vote for Gill Black—Starmer's election agent—who was standing against the left-wing Labour staffer Laura Murray for the role of branch secretary. This was highly unusual, even more so given the timing: Starmer, then Labour's shadow Brexit secretary, took time out of his schedule to attend this local vote for a junior position in the midst of a crisis in Brexit negotiations.

In January 2020, the progressive news site *Novara Media* interviewed Sienna Rodgers, the erstwhile editor of *LabourList*. In an unexpectedly candid interview, Rodgers told *Novara*'s Michael Walker that whereas Starmer himself was apolitical and lacked strong ideological convictions, his factional alignment at the local level was clear. 'I find it genuinely unbelievable and a huge failure of the "Labour left" that people are actually swallowing this narrative of, "he really wants to be more left-wing secretly but he's being held back as he builds this broad coalition". I think that's absolutely laughable', she commented. 'You only need to look at what he's like in his own Constituency Labour Party to know that he is on the right of the party. He keeps out of a lot of fights but the right know in that CLP, when they vote, they will rely on Keir and his wife to come and vote for them'.[23]

Local left-wingers in the CLP were desperate to inform their fellow party members of Starmer's true allegiances. In mid-January 2020, a few days before Rodgers' interview, all fifty attendees at a Camden Momentum meeting agreed to release a public statement. Noting that Starmer had launched his campaign with a 'tilt to the left', it warned fellow Labour members that 'we do not trust him to follow through on these gestures and warm words . . . He has not sought to engage with, encourage or welcome the left at a local level. In Holborn and St Pancras, he has built a team around him that has worked tirelessly to marginalise the left in the CLP, yet he now calls for an end to "factionalism"'.[24] The statement concluded with a stark plea:

> If you are a member or supporter of the Labour Party who has been inspired or enthused by Jeremy Corbyn's leadership; if you want our movement to continue travelling in the direction of socialism, internationalism and solidarity: we urge you not to vote for Keir Starmer.[25]

Camden Momentum's statement was carried in full in the *Islington Tribune* and summarised in the *Camden New Journal*.

One lone article described it briefly in *The Telegraph*. And that was it. One can only imagine the extensive coverage that would have ensued if Rebecca Long-Bailey had been disparaged in such strong terms by activists from her constituency.

Local party members had also developed an unease about Starmer's character: he was prone to telling stories that many found hard to believe, especially in the context of a potential confrontation. One example that many left-wingers still discuss related to Starmer's decision in 2016 to join the so-called 'chicken coup' by Labour MPs against the Corbyn leadership. The leadership challenge had been triggered by a vote of no confidence in Corbyn following the EU referendum result. Most of Corbyn's shadow cabinet members resigned to support the no-confidence motion. They synchronised their resignations to take place one every hour, evidently with the intent of driving constant coverage in the media. Starmer joined the resignations.

Some left-wing members in Starmer's constituency were upset by his decision and questioned Starmer about it during a meeting of the CLP. Starmer's response has become something of a local legend. Explaining that he felt morally obliged to resign when Corbyn had whipped the party to trigger Article 50 (and thus the beginning of the Brexit process), Starmer claimed that when the mass resignations unfolded, he had been in the countryside camping with his son and had had limited access to the internet. The intended implications of this were not entirely clear, but one member believed it was an attempt by Starmer to disavow the accusation that he had discussed or coordinated his resignation with fellow quitters.

Left-wing attendees of this meeting were incredulous at the idea that Starmer had not discussed resigning with his shadow cabinet colleagues, not least because a resignation plot had been trailed in the media weeks previously. A number of attendees at the event also recalled that Starmer looked genuinely afraid and anxious, which they found odd because the questioning was not inquisitorial and the left-wing was far from locally dominant.

An equally surreal story is relayed in Lord Ashcroft's otherwise confused Starmer biography, *Red Knight*. A lawyer, Jon Holbrook, explained to Ashcroft that he had booked Starmer to a 'Battle of Ideas' law debate in October 2014, when Starmer was just throwing his hat into the ring to become the Holborn and St Pancras MP. A few weeks prior to the meeting, Starmer wrote to Holbrook to withdraw from the event. Starmer explained that he had taken on a client and that the only time he could consult with this client was during the period of the debate. Holbrook was perturbed because he believed that Starmer had not told him the 'real reason' for not attending. On the day of the event, Starmer's Twitter account posted about how great it had been to meet the mayor of London Sadiq Khan at a rally of the Trades Union Congress (TUC).

Holbrook's response was typical of many who had encountered Starmer's apparent aversion to conflict: 'it always struck me as the actions of a weak man. If he had simply said to us, as organisers, "I'm sorry, I now realise that, particularly as an aspiring Labour MP, I need to attend the TUC march and rally", I would have entirely understood'.[26]

'NOT A TRUE BELIEVER'

Local leftists were not the only people who realised where Starmer's true loyalties lay. This was also abundantly clear to the right-wing bureaucracy that had run the Labour Party from its headquarters (HQ) in Southside under General Secretary Iain McNicol between 2015 and 2018.

In April 2020, only days after Starmer was elected leader, unidentified individuals leaked a report that had been drafted for submission to the Equality and Human Rights Commission. It was a response to the EHRC's investigation into antisemitism in the Labour Party. The document became known, creatively, as the Leaked Report.

The EHRC's investigation required the Labour Party to dig deep into its servers to reconstruct how antisemitism complaints had been handled from 2016 onward. Searches revealed hitherto unseen emails, chats on the party's internal messaging system, and transcripts from two WhatsApp groups, one of which had only six participants: the most powerful members of the party bureaucracy, including General Secretary McNicol.

The Leaked Report and its revelations are dealt with in more detail later. Suffice it to note here that the document presented compelling evidence that the Labour Party bureaucracy under McNicol's watch had been zealously hostile to Corbyn's leadership and to the surge of new members Corbyn had attracted. This included evidence of what became known as the Ergon House scheme, in which party funds were allocated to right-wing allies of the bureaucracy, without the knowledge of the elected party leadership, during the 2017 general election campaign.

What has not previously been revealed is that the Ergon House scheme had a lengthy and important pre-history, the details of which are presented later. Party documents show that almost as soon as the election was called, the most senior anti-Corbyn Labour bureaucrats distributed spreadsheets showing that a pot of discretionary funding was being allocated to certain seats, *most of which were not under electoral threat*. Party insiders linked to Corbyn's LOTO have confirmed that they were not given contemporaneous sight of these spreadsheets at the time that they were being shared internally by McNicol-era bureaucrats.

The spreadsheets list seventeen MPs as having been allocated discretionary funds. These included a raft of right-wingers linked to party headquarters, such as Jonathan Ashworth, the husband of senior party bureaucrat Emilie Oldknow; and Tom Watson, who had been a node of resistance against Corbyn since 2015. When Ashworth eventually lost his seat, in a shock 2024 general election upset, he was subsequently appointed to lead Labour Together.

Keir Starmer was also slated to benefit as, according to the spreadsheets, his constituency was allocated £13,000. Crucially, there was no evidence that Starmer's seat was under any sort of electoral threat, notwithstanding the party's poor early polling. In fact, Starmer's seat was classified as 'D5', or 'defensive 5', which put it in the category of *least*-threatened seats. According to the spreadsheets, other, more imperilled seats were not allocated the discretionary funding.

There is no evidence to show that Starmer or his campaign team were aware that they had been allocated funding in this way, or that they were aware they had received more than their other parliamentary colleagues; it is equally true that this has never been properly investigated and should be. But what these allocations showed was that the Labour Party's factional bureaucracy had decided that Starmer was worthy of support. The most natural inference is that Starmer was viewed by the right-wing bureaucracy as an ally, or, at the very least, as the sort of candidate who could be relied upon to push through a right-wing factional agenda.

Importantly, the WhatsApp chats confirm that the bureaucracy was aware that Starmer, despite his position in Corbyn's shadow cabinet, was not of the left. In December 2016, the chat discussed an interview by an unnamed person who, from the context, was clearly viewed as a Corbynite. This Corbynite had complimented Starmer and suggested that he could pose a threat to Theresa May. Tracey Allen, the head of General Secretary McNicol's office, commented: 'Irony that she is citing Keir as "brilliant" and a threat to the PM, when he's not a true believer'.

In January 2020, Lord Iain McNicol (he was knighted after he stopped serving as general secretary in 2018) wrote a column lambasting Corbynism in the *Financial Times*.[27] With enviable brass neck, McNicol claimed that the 2017 general election campaign had returned a good vote for Corbyn only because the party bureaucracy, which McNicol had led, had delivered a 'professionally-run [*sic*] campaign with strategic goals'. In 2019, by contrast, the Corbynite bureaucracy had failed because, 'with many long-serving and experienced members of staff no longer employed at the party's headquarters, targeting of resources was not based on strategy but on a fanciful belief that Labour was going to win a majority'. It was only three and a half months later that headquarters' 'targeting of resources' in the service of a hyper-factional 'strategy' under McNicol's own watch was revealed.

McNicol insisted that 'Corbynism must end with Corbyn' and urged Labour members to rebuff Rebecca Long-Bailey. In passing, he agreed that Lisa Nandy and Jess Phillips were 'capable of driving the transition Labour needs'. But his most enthusiastic endorsement was reserved for Starmer:

> Keir Starmer is already attracting the bulk of support from MPs, has the backing of Unison, the largest trade union, and has appointed a campaign team drawn from both left and right of the party, bringing together Morgan McSweeney and Simon Fletcher, key figures from the Liz Kendall and Jeremy Corbyn leadership campaigns respectively.

The endorsement contained a strange and revealing slip: McNicol claimed that all traces of Corbynism had to end but then cited the appointment of Simon Fletcher in approving tones. McNicol must have sensed—or indeed known, based on his long-term admiration of Morgan McSweeney (discussed later)—the reality of Starmer's pitch. Because given McNicol's visceral hostility to the Labour left, as revealed by the Leaked Report and the WhatsApp groups from which it quoted, one thing is certain: there is no way that McNicol would have backed Starmer if there had been even the slightest prospect that any aspect of Corbynism would survive on Starmer's watch.

LESS HONEST THAN TONY BLAIR

The idea that Starmer would recant on his pledges and pivot to Labour's right wing after becoming party leader was apparently promoted by Starmer's own backers behind the scenes, according to a number of insiders.

Margaret Hodge MP is one of the Labour Party's most right-wing, unreconstructed Blairites, and accordingly one of the fiercest critics of Jeremy Corbyn. She was interviewed about Starmer by the *Financial Times* during the leadership election. 'He's triangulating like mad', she said. 'Somebody said to me, I don't mind what he does as long as he wins, he beats Rebecca Long-Bailey. And I thought, you know, Tony [Blair] never did that. Tony was completely straight, completely honest'. Being considered less forthright than Tony Blair is quite some achievement, and there was a germ of truth to Hodge's claim: whatever Blair eventually became, and whatever horrors he unleashed abroad, he came to power proudly extolling the pro-market ideology he went on to implement.

'So is Keir lying to get the job? And will he then change?' Hodge asked. 'That's what this person was saying to me as a way of promoting Keir'.[28]

Sebastian Payne of the *Financial Times* told much the same story in an interview on LBC radio in 2022. When a listener questioned Starmer's trustworthiness given that he had betrayed his leadership pledges, Payne responded:

> I remember speaking to somebody who was involved in Keir Starmer's campaign, and you will remember he did Ten Pledges, which pretty much echoed what was in Labour's 2019 manifesto. I recall this person saying to me, 'look at those ten pledges, there's not a single one of those that will tie our hands when we've won this leadership'. And that has proven to be exactly the case, and I think, the fact is, I think Keir Starmer was probably misleading when he ran that leadership [campaign].[29]

Payne and Hodge were hardly unique in having been shown behind the curtain of the project to install Starmer on a phoney prospectus. As discussed above, we know now that many journalists were invited to meet, dine, and drink with Labour Together's assorted right-wing MPs behind the scenes as Starmer prepared his tilt at the leadership.

The question is: Why did none of those journalists think to tell the public?

CHAPTER 6

DEMOCRACY DIES IN DARKNESS

Starmer's leadership campaign was marked by a striking lack of transparency, most notably about his funders. This secrecy was exacerbated by a media environment that failed to meaningfully engage with Starmer's mixed history as director of public prosecutions—an environment in which one of the only progressive, anti-Starmer media outlets in the country was being aggressively targeted by Stop Funding Fake News, the Labour Together Project's astroturf campaign.

A HIATUS ON SCRUTINY

In early January 2020, Stephen Bush, editor of the *New Statesman*, wrote about Starmer's campaign launch and its packaging. Bush noted that 'Facebook and the *Guardian*'s website are, along with the BBC, the main outlets where the Labour leadership race will be fought and won'.[1] It is striking that during the leadership campaign, neither the BBC nor *The Guardian* reported on the controversial decisions made by Starmer in his previous role as DPP. This was despite the fact that, having entered politics only recently, Starmer's legal career culminating in his role as DPP was the obvious place to look for insight into his convictions and character.

Matt Zarb-Cousin, head of communications for Rebecca Long-Bailey's leadership campaign, found the media uninterested in reporting on Starmer's history. Zarb-Cousin said that he had tried repeatedly to place stories about Starmer's past in an attempt to alert party members to the reality of his politics. No outlet would touch them. 'It was an effective hiatus on scrutiny', Zarb-Cousin recalled:

> In a normal climate, you would expect the media to interrogate somebody like Starmer in the moment. It was like living in a country without a free press. We just didn't expect such a total lack of scrutiny. And for anyone who would have spent some time lifting the lid, there was a goldmine of stories.

Nowhere was this clearer than at *The Guardian*, a primary source of news for Labour Party members. A review of *The Guardian* archives reveals extensive contemporaneous comment about cases like Gary McKinnon, including damning quotes about Starmer's conduct. *The Guardian* had, as noted above, also run a substantive research programme with the LSE about the 2011 London riots, which had produced multiple articles criticising Starmer's endorsement of night courts.

But even as *Guardian* reporters had this extensive institutional archive on hand, the paper made barely any reference to Starmer's record as DPP during his leadership campaign. Throughout the entire Labour leadership contest, from January to April 2020, only two *Guardian* articles even acknowledged one of Starmer's controversial cases: the killing of Ian Tomlinson, who died of a heart attack after being struck by a police officer in 2009 during protests against the G20 summit.[2] The killing caused an outcry, but Starmer initially refused to bring charges, only changing his mind after a series of bruising inquests into Tomlinson's death.

The only article that dwelt on this episode in any depth—a profile by the barrister David Renton—commented that there were some decisions Starmer had made as head of the CPS that 'had been criticised' but that 'it is difficult to say whether the criticisms were justified'.[3] Criticism of Starmer was deferred on the basis that it was impossible to know what advice Starmer had been given, effectively fobbing off bad decisions onto his juniors. Reviewing Starmer's career, Renton's primary criticism was that Starmer had sometimes briefed the press using right-wing talking points.

Strikingly, despite the McKinnon case being of national import and receiving considerable contemporaneous coverage in *The Guardian* and elsewhere, *The Guardian* did not mention the case once during the Labour leadership election. It also neglected to mention Starmer's role in the treatment of Julian Assange and establishment of night courts, or the role that Starmer's guidance had played in encouraging the prosecution of an eleven-year-old for stealing a cap.

The same omertà marked the BBC's coverage. A search through the BBC News website finds not a single mention of Starmer in relation to McKinnon, Assange, or even the London riots in the entire period between January and April 2020.

The only profile of Starmer that appraised his CPS career in any depth was a March 2020 long-read by Patrick Maguire in the *New Statesman*. Maguire's piece was commendable for mentioning Starmer's decisions not to prosecute in two notable cases (Jean Charles de Menezes, a Brazilian man killed by Metropolitan Police officers in 2005; and the above-mentioned Ian Tomlinson) as well as the CPS' decision to charge anti-austerity protestors. But even in this lone, lengthy piece, Starmer's career as DPP was dispatched in a few paragraphs, which contained no mention of the London riots, McKinnon or Assange. Assange was a particularly notable omission considering that his case, alongside that of the notorious sex offender Jimmy Savile, was the most high-profile to be handled by the CPS while Starmer was in charge.

The result was that it was only in late 2020, and thanks to the left-wing writer Oliver Eagleton, that the concerning aspects of Starmer's time at the CPS were thoroughly set out. Eagleton's book was the first time many had encountered these stories.

The Guardian would persist in its myopia. In late 2023, the paper published details of a brand-new 'investigation' into Starmer's time as DPP. This was framed as a deep dive into Starmer's professional history, conducted in light of 'Conservative officials . . . poring over Starmer's record as a human rights lawyer and DPP for material to use against Labour in the general election'.[4] The author was perhaps unaware that some readers might infer from this context that *The Guardian* was acting like Starmer's unofficial rebuttal unit, rather than an independent newspaper. The so-called 'investigation' primarily comprised some light chuntering about difficult decisions, buttressed with respectful quotes from former colleagues. It did not mention Assange, McKinnon or the London riots and night courts.

PSY OPS AND SPY COPS

Whereas most media outlets, and especially *The Guardian*, did not interrogate Starmer's background, or else covered stories with a pro-Starmer slant, *The Canary* took the opposite approach. Indeed, during the period between January and April 2020, *The Canary* was the only media outlet in the country to interrogate Starmer's professional history from a critical perspective and use this to contextualise his leadership pitch.

At the same time, SFFN relaunched its campaign against *The Canary* to deprive it of advertising income and, perhaps even more importantly, create the impression that it was a fringe outpost of cranks and nutjobs.

McSweeney was company secretary of Labour Together and a director of CCDH when SFFN relaunched its campaign against *The Canary*. He only resigned these positions in April 2020. This means that for the full duration of the Labour leadership contest, Starmer's campaign director was also leading a company linked to an astroturf campaign that targeted the only media outlet attempting to subject Starmer to critical scrutiny.

As set out above, there was no way that Labour members could know the links between the Labour Together Project, CCDH, and SFFN, because these relationships had not been disclosed at the time. It was only in mid-2020 that SFFN would update its website to explain that, '[f]rom May 4, 2020, SFFN has been a project of CCDH'.[5] The date chosen in this disclosure was both specific and revealing. While company filings indicate that McSweeney had resigned from CCDH on April 6, 2020, his resignation form was only submitted electronically to Companies House on May 4, 2020.[6] So, from literally the first possible day when McSweeney's involvement in CCDH could be said to have ended, SFFN and CCDH publicly acknowledged their relationship. Those inclined to cynicism might wonder whether this reflected how problematic it might have proved if McSweeney had been linked in the public mind to an astroturf campaign that was undermining media outlets critical of the man whose leadership campaign he was running.

SFFN sprang back into life on January 8, 2020, following a period of relative quiet. McSweeney was officially announced as Starmer's campaign chief on the same day. SFFN launched a fresh salvo against *The Canary*, replacing and updating the original thread of 'evidence' it had compiled in March 2019. On the afternoon of the eighth, SFFN posted a seven-tweet thread attacking an article run by *The Canary* in May 2017.

The SFFN critique was unconvincing. *The Canary*'s article dealt with the murder of the Democratic Party staffer Seth Rich in the US, and speculation about how it had come about.[7] *The Canary* did not endorse the speculation or indicate that the claims made were factually accurate; the essence of the article was to summarise ongoing reporting in the US on the matter and then examine the political consequences of these claims *if* any of them turned out to be accurate.

SFFN's aghast coverage implied that *The Canary*'s repetition of claims it did not endorse amounted to promoting an 'alt-right conspiracy theory'. SFFN presented evidence debunking these claims but failed to mention that such evidence had only emerged after *The Canary* had run its article. SFFN also failed to acknowledge that *The Canary* had subsequently published articles explaining how the speculative claims had been debunked.[8]

SFFN argued that, once the speculative claims were disproven, *The Canary* should have gone back and deleted the offending article. One wonders whether SFFN wanted *The New York Times* to do the same with articles quoting sources that attested to Saddam Hussein's weapons of mass destruction.

On the same day that SFFN launched its new attack on *The Canary*, the latter published an article by a veteran campaigner and reporter, Emily Apple. Apple, who is of Jewish heritage and has written about the importance of Jewishness to her identity, had been accused by SFFN in 2019 of having published antisemitic social media posts nearly a decade prior (discussed above). Apple was also a victim of undercover police spying due to her history of activism against the global arms trade. In 2018, the UK government confirmed that two activists who had been good friends of hers were undercover police officers.[9]

Apple's January 2020 article was titled, 'A Message to Anyone Thinking of Voting for Keir Starmer in the Labour Leadership Race'.[10] It set out, in stinging terms, Starmer's role in the undercover policing scandal, claiming that as DPP he had not done enough to uncover the truth. Apple was clear that Starmer's role in the whole 'Spy Cops' affair made him an unsuitable candidate for Labour leader:

> We don't know exactly what Starmer knew. But he was DPP. Even if he didn't know all the details, he was one of the few people in the country who had the power to find out and with the power to deliver justice ... He didn't. And this lack of integrity means I could never vote for him as Labour leader.

Apple's article also noted that Starmer had worked with Nick Paul, the national coordinator for 'domestic extremism' at the CPS, who had designated a range of protestors and activists as 'domestic extremists'. For Apple, this made Starmer's campaign references to his former progressive lawyering cynical and misleading: 'As someone with a domestic extremist file going back to the time Starmer was DPP, Starmer's radical history tour is grossly offensive and disingenuous'. After noting Starmer's role in the Jean Charles de Menezes and Ian Tomlinson cases, Apple concluded that 'supporting Starmer would be a betrayal':

> If you're voting in the Labour Party leadership election, please listen to how victims of police spying feel. Not just out of solidarity—but because of what our experiences, and how Starmer is using his radical past, tell us about his honesty and integrity.

Apple's article was notable not only for its passionate argument, based on deep personal knowledge, but also because, as noted, virtually no attention was being paid during the leadership campaign to Starmer's record as DPP. Apple's article was *literally* the only time during the leadership contest that Starmer's CPS career was subjected to a thoroughgoing analysis from a critical perspective.

The Canary ran multiple articles criticising Starmer on a range of issues throughout the election campaign, and urged support for his erstwhile challenger, Rebecca Long-Bailey.[11] All the while, *The Canary* was under attack by SFFN—the astroturf offshoot of the very same Labour Together Project that was guiding Starmer to party leadership.

TRANSPARENCY FAILURES

Between early September 2019 (around the time Starmer's leadership ambitions were being discussed in meetings) and March 2020, Labour Together received £235,000 in donations:

£170,000 from Martin Taylor and £65,000 from Trevor Chinn. These donations were only reported to the Electoral Commission in December 2020;[12] as we have seen, there is compelling evi-dence that this unlawful non-disclosure by McSweeney may have been intentional (although there is no evidence that Taylor and Chinn were aware of the failure to report).

In total, Keir Starmer took £683,435.43 in donations between January and April 2020; a further £24,500 was donated in March and April but only formally accepted by Starmer after the leadership results had been announced.[13] Rebecca Long-Bailey, his left-wing competitor, received £438,978.36. Long-Bailey's donations were made either by sympathetic unions (Unite, the Communications Workers Union, and the Fire Brigades Union) or by Momentum.

Both Long-Bailey and Lisa Nandy, who from late February joined Starmer in what had become a three-horse race for the leadership, declared their funding and donations contempo-raneously. Long-Bailey published the figures on her website. Starmer refused to follow suit.

Jon Trickett, a member of the Socialist Campaign Group of MPs, pointed out that Starmer's failure to publish donations contemporaneously was 'anti-democratic' because 'voters deserve to know what lies behind the candidates they are being asked to vote for, before they cast their vote, not afterwards'.[14] In an uncomfortable interview that same month, Starmer was pushed on his failure to report by the broadcaster Andrew Neil. Starmer explained that he was abiding by parliamentary report-ing requirements, as if that ended the matter. He refused to be drawn on issues of transparency and accountability.[15]

According to Starmer's parliamentary filings, he started taking donations toward his leadership campaign on December 30, 2019. The final donation he received was dated April 6, 2020.[16] From January to April 2020, Starmer was forced to report to parliament on four occasions: February 10, March 2, March 16, and April 14. Starmer's campaign processed the majority of his donations such that they were only made public on April 14, 2020, twelve days *after* the deadline for the submission of ballots and ten days after he was declared the winner of the contest.

The result was that, by the time Labour Party members were due to submit their ballots for an April 2, 2020, deadline, only a third of Starmer's donations had been publicly disclosed: just over £223,000 in total. Of this amount, £150,000 came from three large donors: £100,000 from Robert Latham, a barrister at Starmer's chambers, and £25,000 each from Martin Clarke and Clive Hollick.[17]

The donation from Latham did not challenge Starmer's narrative as a unifying centrist and would not have alarmed Labour Party members. The same was not necessarily true of Clarke and Hollick. Clarke, a former executive at the roadside recovery firm AA, had long criticised Corbyn and had openly supported the anti-Corbyn breakaway party Change UK in 2019. Hollick was a long-time donor to right-wing Labour causes and had funded Labour Together (although nobody could have known the latter at the time, as it had not been declared). As the former owner of the *Daily Express*, Hollick and his ties to Tony Blair were widely known.

For left-wing Labour Party members, and perhaps also for the 'idealists' targeted by Starmer's strategy, these donations might have been cause for concern, or at the very least for discussion. But they flew under the radar, hardly reported on at all. The only notable mention of Hollick's donation, and Hollick's political background, came in a Twitter post by *Evolve Politics* on March 30, 2020—mere days before the polls closed.[18] Like *The Canary*, the *Evolve Politics* news site had been relentlessly targeted by SFFN.

A further £509,479.80 in donations to Starmer were only declared on April 14. Nearly half of this amount came from three donors: Baron Waheed Ali (£100,000), Martin Taylor (£95,000), and Trevor Chinn (£50,000).

Ali, a wealthy media entrepreneur who had co-created the *Survivor* television series, was sufficiently close to Blair to be dubbed one of 'Tony's cronies'.[19] He was made a Labour life peer in 1998, becoming the youngest peer in the House of Lords. He had funded Liz Kendall and Andy Burnham in the 2015 Labour leadership contest and donated £3,000 to Angela Eagle when she emerged as a contender following the anti-Corbyn 'chicken coup' in 2016. When Eagle fell away, Ali donated to Owen Smith. In 2022, Starmer appointed Ali to lead the party's fundraising efforts with sights on a general election.[20] Ali would figure centrally in the explosion of coverage about Starmer's predilection for freebies following the 2024 election after it was reported that he had given Starmer expensive clothing and accessories.

Taylor and Chinn's donations to the Starmer campaign supplemented the sums they had already contributed to Labour Together. This amounted to £235,000 between September 2019 and March 2020, of which £160,000 was donated during the leadership contest itself. Chinn and Taylor thus contributed a total of £305,000 during the leadership campaign period to both Starmer and Labour Together, the latter of which now claims to have been central to Starmer's election campaign. The combination of Labour Together's unlawful failure to declare donations until December 2020 and Starmer's belated declarations meant that the Labour Party membership voted for Starmer in total ignorance of the fact that, if Labour Together donations are considered alongside Starmer's, Chinn and Taylor were the largest funders of Starmer's leadership bid.

Incidentally, Starmer received a further £25,000 from Hollick and £15,000 from Paul Myners, both of which were declared on April 14 and thus after the election had concluded. Both donors had previously funded Labour Together.

The donations made to Starmer by Chinn, Taylor, and Baron Ali were all made long before they were eventually declared. Taylor's donation was made on February 11 but only 'accepted' by the campaign on March 9; Ali's donation was made on February 24 but only 'accepted' by the campaign on March 23; and Chinn's donation was made on February 26 but only 'accepted' on March 23—the same date as Ali. It was these gaps between the making and the formal acceptance of donations that allowed the Starmer campaign to delay their disclosure until after the vote.

The timing of Ali's donation was particularly important in light of Starmer's interview with Andrew Neil, which took place in early March. During that interview, Starmer was adamant that the £100,000 he had taken from Robert Latham was the biggest donation he had received.[21] But this was not entirely accurate. It was, in fact, the *joint* largest donation he had received, as he had already been given £100,000 from Ali on February 24, about which he said nothing to Neil.

Starmer's camp may claim that the gap between the donation being made and 'accepted' was due to the campaign's rigorous compliance regime (as Starmer had tried to hint in his interview with Neil). But it seems surprising that it would take over a month for them to conduct due diligence on extremely well-known public individuals who had a history of donating to Labour Party causes. Taylor's donation, moreover, was 'accepted' on March 9, which was seven days *prior* to the March 16 reporting date. Starmer's team only registered that payment with parliament on March 31, a full twenty-two days after it had been 'accepted'. Considering that the donation had passed compliance checks and had already been accepted, questions deserve to be asked as to why Starmer's team would take so long to inform parliament and thus the public.

Was there a fear that Starmer's unity pitch would have fallen apart if it had emerged that almost half of his funding came from Ali, Chinn, Taylor, and Hollick, all of whom vehemently opposed Corbyn and the politics he represented?

LABOUR TOGETHER GATHERS DATA

On November 11, 2019,[22] McSweeney was appointed director of the website *LabourList*. Within days, the formal general election campaigning period would begin. McSweeney was appointed alongside Sienna Rodgers, also a director. Rodgers had been the editor of *LabourList* since February 2018. Both McSweeney and Rodgers were reported to have 'significant control' over LabourList Ltd. McSweeney held the position of director until April 4, 2020, the day that Starmer was announced as leader of the Labour Party.[23]

McSweeney's appointment as director of *LabourList* went without contemporary mention in the media, even though it might have been considered strange that a man with zero media experience had been elevated to this senior position. It wasn't even mentioned in *LabourList* itself. Most importantly, McSweeney's directorship was not once mentioned during the Labour leadership election, even though McSweeney was directing Starmer's leadership campaign. Nobody, in public at least, seems to have thought it appropriate to question whether there might have been a conflict of interest for McSweeney to direct a media organisation targeted at Labour Party members while simultaneously leading Starmer's campaign.

On December 23, 2019, in the wake of the general election and three days after the formation of Starmer's campaign vehicle, an article in *LabourList* announced the launch of a Labour Together commission to review the party's election defeat. The review had been '[j]ointly commissioned' by *LabourList* itself, in order to 'learn the lessons of our seismic election defeat'.[24] The commission would gather evidence from the Labour Party grassroots to find out what went wrong and how to fix it.

The commission was pitched as a non-factional project. 'Labour Together says that the commission will be independent, and is made up of people who believe that Labour will only be successful if it moves past factionalism', the article clarified.[25] The commissioners would be drawn from all wings of the party, and the exercise would 'involve' everyone from Momentum on the left to Progress on the right. The non-factional character of the commission and of Labour Together was underlined in a piece published on December 27 by Hannah

O'Rourke, Labour Together's long-time staffer,[26] and again in a February 18, 2020, update that decried 'the factional rancour that hobbled the party in recent years' and declared: 'The Labour Together review is by and for the whole labour movement', to help us 'move forward together'.[27] The author of that last article, Daniel Jackson, was a director of The Campaign Company, a polling and consultancy firm for which McSweeney had previously worked and which had been founded by Labour's future general secretary, David Evans.

At its heart, the Labour Together election review was a massive data gathering exercise. In addition to soliciting written feedback from losing election candidates, the commission would conduct 'a wide-ranging survey of Labour members and activists, with the help of *LabourList*'.[28] *LabourList* and Labour Together repeatedly circulated a link to an online survey in which 'Labour members and supporters' were 'encouraged to take part'.[29] The uptake was remarkable: by early February 2020, over ten thousand people, most of them party members, had taken the survey.[30] When Labour Together published its final report on the election in mid-2020, it confirmed that it had received over eleven thousand survey responses from 638 out of 650 constituencies across the country.[31]

The survey questions asked respondents to discuss their feelings about the effectiveness of Labour's campaign. It asked how effective the 2019 manifesto was, which policies did or did not resonate with the general public, and what Labour's most effective messages were and weren't. In a section called 'the future', the survey asked what the Labour Party needed to do to be effective in parliament, and 'what one change' Labour needed to make 'to win the next election'.[32]

Labour Together seemingly felt compelled to address concerns about whether this invaluable survey data would be shared with any of the campaigns and thus tilt the Labour leadership contest. On February 12, 2020—shortly after Starmer had published his Ten Pledges—Shabana Mahmood wrote for *LabourList* on behalf of Labour Together, to address 'frequently asked questions' about the review 'so that we can assuage any concerns people may have, and encourage all members to take part in how we move forward'.[33] Mahmood's answers, supposedly delivered as part of an article clearing the air, conveyed three key pieces of misleading information.

The first two misrepresentations related to Labour Together's funding and corporate structure. Mahmood explained that 'Labour Together is not a membership body or faction, so we are funded by donations small and large from activists, trade unions and members'. In fact, Labour Together *is* a membership body, registered against Companies House code 94990: 'Activities of other membership organisations not elsewhere classified'. Labour Together was also, as discussed above, registered as a members association for the purposes of electoral law.

Mahmood went on to assert that '[o]ur funding is registered on the Electoral Commission's website'. The Labour Together website, from which much of the copy of Mahmood's article was taken, carried the same text, and even linked to the Electoral Commission's site. Any interested reader who clicked on this link would thus have done so on the understanding that the Electoral Commission page displayed the full details of Labour Together's funders.

But this was not the case. As I have set out, Labour Together had failed to declare the vast majority of its donations since mid-2018, including sizeable donations from Chinn and Taylor made during the Labour leadership contest. When Labour Together published the results of its commission in 2020, Chinn and Taylor were the first two people they thanked in the report's acknowledgments. Party members who engaged with the survey did so in ignorance of these important facts—a grave failure of transparency.

Third, and perhaps most importantly, in a section about the use of data from the survey, Mahmood assured that 'Labour Together is not supporting any particular leadership campaign, and the data from our survey is not and will not be shared with any campaign'. Indeed, Labour Together's commitment to neutrality was so profound that it was 'not planning to launch our final report until after the leadership ballot has closed because we don't want our findings to influence the result in any way'.[34]

But this was patently untrue, according to Labour Together's own subsequent admission: 'We backed @Keir_Starmer & helped him win the leadership',[35] they bragged as part of an eleven-tweet thread on April 2, 2023. 'In 2020, [Labour Together] played a key role in Keir Starmer's leadership campaign', Labour Together noted, quoting Steve Reed.[36]

Mahmood's article also sought to calm fears that data gathered by the commission would be used for anything but its intended purpose, pre-empting concerns that the results could be fed into leadership campaigns. 'The survey data is being held by a separate organisation who are administering the survey for us, and is not accessible to anyone other than the commissioners', she wrote.[37] But Mahmood's article failed to mention that she herself was a commissioner (to be fair, other *LabourList* articles did mention this). Labour Together's website confirmed that Lucy Powell was also both a commissioner and part of the Labour Together group. Labour Together did not identify which 'separate organisation' was administering the survey. But as we will see, it did subsequently disclose that the survey data had been analysed for Labour Together by The Campaign Company, whose founder and director was a close political ally of both McSweeney and Reed.

This is serious stuff. The collection, retention, and processing of data in the UK are governed by data protection laws. Two key parts of this legislation are important here. First, the laws (and published guidance) make it clear that political information—on political views and affiliations, for instance—is considered 'special category' data that must be processed with extra care. Second, the laws emphasise the need for full disclosure and transparency. Organisations are forbidden from gathering data on false pretences. Questions need to be asked about whether Labour Together fell afoul of these provisions when it failed to inform survey respondents of both its sources of funding and its involvement in Starmer's leadership campaign. And questions will also have to be asked about whether Mahmood's conduct in this episode was befitting of a current secretary of state for justice.

There is circumstantial evidence that the survey data was being gathered with the leadership election in view. On February 18, five days after Mahmood's article appeared, *LabourList* reported that Labour Together had extended the deadline for people to submit responses. The survey would now conclude on February 23. *LabourList* explained this extension as a response to 'news uncovered by *LabourList* that ballots in Labour's leadership contests have been delayed by the party, and will now not be sent out until February 24th—leaving a gap of ten days between the close of nominations and the start of voting'.[38]

But if Labour Together did not intend to report the survey results until after the leadership election was over, what did the timing of the leadership election matter? Surely, if the commission wanted to gather as much useful data as possible, Labour Together could have run the survey for any length of time it wanted. The odd linking of the leadership election and Labour Together survey timelines would make more sense if the organisation was primarily interested in getting hold of data it could use for the last part of the leadership election.

Slightly more information about who got to handle the survey data was provided when Labour Together finally published its election review in mid-2020. In the report's acknowledgments, Labour Together credited The Campaign Company as having conducted the 'brilliant analysis of our member's survey'. The data had been shared with the review commissioners, who included two Labour Together MPs. It would have been an act of remarkable restraint for these players not to share the insights they had gathered with the Starmer campaign. And, of course, it was impossible for these players to simply delete this knowledge from their brains if they had had any discussions about the campaign and its progress, even if they did not mobilise it directly.

Interestingly, the survey data was being processed as the responses were being received. On February 18, for example, Daniel Jackson's article in *LabourList* encouraged people to participate in the Labour Together survey. Jackson noted that thousands of responses had been received and that 'our team is busy reading each of these responses, to provide an honest, accurate analysis of how Labour Party members feel and their ideas of their future'.[39] He did not make clear what he meant by 'our team'. (His author bio presented him as both 'director of The Campaign Company' and 'a Labour Together review commissioner', so it was unclear from this article in which capacity he was reviewing the data.) Jackson gave a broad overview of the responses received up to that point and themes that had been identified in them.

It was, in fact, The Campaign Company, which Jackson directed, that evaluated the survey responses and provided a report to the Labour Together commission. That report was eventually published in June 2020 as an appendix to Labour Together's *2019 Election Review*. But the report itself was dated March 2020—when the Labour leadership election was still ongoing. Previously unseen emails, described here for the first time, show that The Campaign Company report was received by Labour Together in March: the report was emailed to review commissioners in the second week of March by Labour Together's Hannah O'Rourke. Commissioners were also provided with a spreadsheet presenting hundreds of (anonymised) notable quotes extracted from survey responses, helpfully organised by theme. Finally, commissioners were provided with an eight-thousand-word report drafted by The Campaign Company based on in-depth interviews with twenty-three candidates who had either lost, or failed to win, their seats during the 2019 general election. It was a rich trove of information. The emails confirm that these materials from The Campaign

Company were received in the second week of March by Shabana Mahmood and Lucy Powell—two of Labour Together's eight 'brave' MPs said to have rescued the party from Corbyn and delivered Starmer in his place.

To recap: Morgan McSweeney served as the chief of Keir Starmer's leadership campaign, during which time he also acted as a director of both *LabourList* and Labour Together. At the same time, Labour Together and *LabourList* launched an election review, a central part of which involved convincing over eleven thousand Labour Party members and supporters to provide detailed insights into their views about the Labour Party, which they were providing as the Labour leadership contest was unfolding. These members were asked to share this data on the basis of insufficient information about Labour Together's funding and its political alignment, which disguised the fact that Labour Together 'backed' Starmer and 'helped him win', as it later admitted. Labour Together was then given access to the results of this massive data gathering exercise while the leadership challenge was ongoing.

FOR THE 5 PERCENT, NOT THE MANY

When McSweeney presented Starmer with his slides describing the composition of the party, he identified 5 percent of the membership as unreconstructed Blairites: the types to defend the Iraq War and the legacy of Blairite neoliberalism. This was, most likely, the same rough 4.5 percent who had voted for arch-Blairite Liz Kendall in the 2015 leadership campaign that McSweeney had directed.

What many failed to realise at the time was that the Labour Together Project, and the Starmer Project that would succeed it, represented just this marginal 5 percent of the party. If the Labour Together Project operated in secret and crafted a misleading leadership pitch that was unceremoniously dumped upon victory, this modus operandi arguably reflected a clear-eyed understanding that this faction's beliefs, ideologies, and political language were deeply unpopular with the Labour members it needed to win over. Implementing this deceptive strategy required a candidate like Starmer: a man who felt no compunction about posturing as a radical during the campaign and then dropping the act once in power.

PART THREE

KILLING CORBYNISM

CHAPTER 7

NO REST FOR THE WICKED

On April 3, 2020, *The Guardian* reported that Keir Starmer would be announced as Labour leader the following day.[1] For followers of the Starmer campaign and many of the Labour members who had voted for his unity ticket, the article would have come as a shock.

The article did little to extol Starmer's virtues. Instead, it focused primarily on how a Starmer leadership would expunge all that came before. 'Allies' of Starmer were said to be closely watching the scale of his impending victory, which would determine how 'quickly he can remake the party in his own image, with a clear-out of those responsible for the damaging 2019 election defeat'. MPs said to support Starmer also hoped that a 'resounding victory' would put pressure on Corbyn's bureaucratic chiefs—Karie Murphy (who ran LOTO, the leader's office) and Jennie Formby (the general secretary)—to step down without delay. The article also noted that a Starmer victory would allow him to remove three Corbyn-era appointees to the party's ruling National Executive Committee: Rebecca Long-Bailey, Jon Trickett, and Diane Abbott.

Starmer's victory was not pitched as a moment of rapprochement but, instead, as the beginning of the left's disembowelling.

The anonymous sources quoted in the article practically vibrated with vitriol. The urge to punish, humiliate, and traduce the bogeymen of the Corbyn era was almost physically tangible. For them, the prospect of putting the likes of Corbyn advisor Seumas Milne back in their box was so delicious that they could not even wait to brief the press until Starmer had taken over the party. No more would these leftist upstarts be calling the shots. The 'grown-ups' were back in charge.

Or, more accurately, the Starmer Project—and the man who pulled its strings, Morgan McSweeney.

TAKING CONTROL

The *Guardian* preview was unerringly accurate. McSweeney, the head of Starmer's leadership campaign, was quickly appointed chief of staff in Starmer's LOTO. McSweeney formally resigned his role as a director of Labour Together. Labour Together had still not declared the funding it had started receiving in 2018 from the likes of Martin Taylor and Trevor Chinn, both of whom had also funded Starmer's leadership bid directly. McSweeney also resigned his directorships in *LabourList* and the Center for Countering Digital Hate.

On April 4, 2020, in the middle of the UK's first Covid lockdown and the same day that he was officially appointed leader of the Labour Party, Starmer placed a call to Jennie Formby, a Corbyn ally who was still the party's general secretary. The Labour Party general secretary heads up the bureaucracy and wields significant power over internal governance, including managing (and sometimes massaging) internal party contests.

After some rudimentary pleasantries, Starmer told Formby that he did not want to work with her and that he wanted a new general secretary to herald a new era. Technically, the leader has no power to remove the general secretary; they are appointed by and report to the party's NEC. Starmer's behaviour was thus technically outside of protocol and arguably aggressive. Formby, who had recently recovered from breast cancer, agreed to step down.

Although Formby formally stood down in early May, in practice, general secretary functions passed to LOTO almost immediately after Starmer's call. In the period before a new general secretary took over, Morgan McSweeney shared the duties (if not the formal position) of acting general secretary with Simon Mills, the party's executive director of finance. Mills, as set out in considerably more detail below, was also the executive director of finance during the Corbyn period, in which role he had participated in the so-called Ergon House scheme, as well as its predecessor. Thus, in April and May 2020, the party was helmed by two men who had controlled controversial and concealed pots of funding from which Starmer might have benefitted. As discussed below, McSweeney and Mills were replaced as general secretary by David Evans, whose polling firm, The Campaign Company, had participated in Labour Together projects at the same time as Labour Together was unlawfully failing to report donations to the Electoral Commission.

The party also appointed Alex Barros-Curtis as its acting executive legal director in early May 2020, following a stint by him in LOTO. Barros-Curtis was understood by a number of party employees to be a McSweeney hire. He was also the sole director of the company—Movement for Another Future Limited—set up to manage Starmer's leadership bid and control its data, a position he retained after his appointment by the party.

Movement for Another Future Limited, at the time of writing, was still registered as a live company, of which Barros-Curtis remained the sole director. Its persistence beyond the 2020 Labour leadership campaign is likely because it has acted as a useful repository for the data gathered via Starmer's website, which could be used in a future leadership contest. This means that between May 2020 and the July 2024 general election, the head of the party's internal legal functions—which includes overseeing the handling of disciplinary complaints—was at all times the sole director of a company set up to benefit Starmer.

Arguably, Barros-Curtis' dual role in the party and as the sole director of Starmer's campaign vehicle meant that there was effectively no meaningful distance or separation between Starmer's office (headed in the first year by McSweeney) and the party's legal and governance bureaucracy—a fact of particular significance, as shown in more detail below, with regards to how the party handled disciplinary complaints and the vexed issue of alleged 'political interference' in that process. At the very least, questions have to be asked about whether Barros-Curtis' dual role might constitute a material conflict of interest.

On May 26, 2020, it was announced that the NEC had appointed David Evans as general secretary upon recommendation from Starmer. Starmer and the NEC did not have the power to unilaterally appoint the general secretary; technically, the general secretary's appointment had to be endorsed by party conference, which did not convene until September 2021. Evans thus technically filled the role of general secretary without ratification for over a year.

Evans was a political ally of McSweeney, and it is more than likely that McSweeney was crucial to his appointment. Evans was steeped in Croydon politics. He had been a Labour councillor in Croydon in the late 1980s. After serving as the party's assistant secretary general between 1999 and 2001, he stepped down to form his strategic advice firm, The Campaign Company, based in Croydon. This firm processed the member survey data that had been solicited by Labour Together through its post-2019 election review. McSweeney had himself been employed by The Campaign Company as its 'director of communities' between October 2007 and November 2009, following a stint as the head of the leader's office in Lambeth when Steve Reed was leading the borough. Reed had become the MP for Croydon North in a 2012 by-election.

Emails show that McSweeney and Reed were working closely with Evans' Campaign Company as late as April 2017, only a few months prior to McSweeney becoming a director of Labour Together. In April 2017, the Labour Party was asked to deliver training and briefing sessions to representatives of South Africa's ruling party, the African National Congress. This appears to have been facilitated by The Campaign Company. Minutes from the meeting show that the first session was opened by David Evans, who was followed by McSweeney and then Reed.

But the best evidence that Evans was a McSweeney appointee was that he was *not* Starmer's choice for general secretary. Starmer's choice was Anneliese Midgley. Midgley had a long union background and was Unite's political director at the time of Starmer's election. Under the leadership of Len McCluskey, Unite had been a key institutional supporter of the Corbyn project. In his own recounting, McCluskey notes that he was in frequent personal contact with Starmer after the latter took office. Midgley's transition from Unite to the party was approved by McCluskey and plans were put in place for Midgley to take on the role. Midgley formally resigned from Unite in anticipation of taking up the position, giving up a stable senior role at the union. McCluskey recalled in his memoirs: 'I agreed to release her but then, just like that, Keir changed his mind'.[2]

What had happened behind the scenes to end Midgley's appointment was instructive. As news filtered through that Midgley was likely to take up the position, objections were raised by a well-known and well-connected member of the party's right wing. Starmer swiftly backtracked. Midgley, who had been left in the lurch after quitting Unite, was offered the position of deputy general secretary by way of compensation. One insider, however, recalls that McSweeney was given responsibility for making this happen. 'He just sort of didn't do anything', the insider recalled. As a result, Midgley drifted in limbo until her appointment as an advisor was announced only a week before Evans took up his role.

The Midgley incident is curious. Considering the hyper-factionalism that unfolded under Starmer's leadership, it is surprising that he would have opted for Midgley, a Unite stalwart (albeit with collegial relationships across the party's factions), to take on the general secretary role. Certainly, it is hard to imagine that Midgley would have hounded the party's left with as much vigour as what in fact unfolded, or that she had any backing from such factional warriors as McSweeney. One plausible inference to draw is that in his first few weeks as party leader, Starmer attempted to operate with a degree of independence from McSweeney, and that perhaps his immediate instinct was to appoint a more emollient, balanced figure to steer the party through a transitional period.

If this is true, the spiking of Midgley's appointment would have been a bruising lesson for Starmer and an early indication of just how powerful the alumni of the Labour Together Project, now running his office, would be. It would have also been a telling illustration of how easy Starmer was to push around, and how this spinelessness could be exploited by the Labour Together Project to place its key allies into positions of influence.

The party membership was thus saddled with Evans, who would turn out to be just as factional as the rest of the Starmer Project. 'The left suspected Evans of being a factional warrior', McCluskey notes. 'They were right'.[3]

If there was any doubt that Labour Together's alumni and allies were in control of the party machinery, this was dispelled by a party staffer who worked close to Evans' office. They recalled that, after Evans was appointed as general secretary, he held weekly meetings with McSweeney and Reed. Reed held a shadow cabinet position as the shadow communities secretary. It was hardly the sort of role that would ordinarily require weekly planning sessions with the two most senior Labour bureaucrats. But as a director of Labour Together and a participant in its secret projects, his attendance makes considerably more sense.

Over the next six months, the Starmer Project was forced to deal with a bursting in tray of pressing issues and inheritances from the Corbyn era. Three knotty matters loomed largest in terms of Labour's factional wars: the libel case brought by the BBC *Panorama* antisemitism 'whistleblowers' and journalist John Ware, the so-called Leaked Report, and the Equality and Human Rights Commission investigation into the party's handling of antisemitism complaints.

These issues were a litmus test of how factional Starmer's regime intended to be. That they ended with Corbyn losing the party whip, a purge of prominent left-wing members, and mass resignation in the grassroots proved that Starmer's unity pitch had been decisively dumped.

In order to understand just how factional and problematic Labour's response to these matters was, some background is required.

CHAPTER 8

INHERITANCE

Starmer inherited from the Corbyn era an ongoing investigation into the Labour Party's handling of antisemitism complaints by the Equality and Human Rights Commission.

The EHRC was established under Tony Blair's premiership and given statutory responsibility to monitor and enforce anti-discrimination laws. The EHRC's Labour investigation had been triggered by complaints submitted to it by the Campaign Against Antisemitism in September 2017, March 2018, and July 2018. The CAA was invited to make detailed legal submissions to the EHRC in August 2018, and it filed these in November. As noted previously, the CAA's Daniel Allington had been linked to the Center for Countering Digital Hate and played a prominent role in levelling charges of antisemitism against *The Canary*—a target of McSweeney's Stop Funding Fake News astroturf campaign.

The CAA's complaints were supported by additional submissions from the Jewish Labour Movement and Labour Against Antisemitism. LAAS, of course, had played a key role in amplifying the SFFN campaign to 'eviscerate' the economic viability of *The Canary*, while McSweeney is reported to have assisted the JLM with the preparation of their own EHRC submission (discussed below).

In March 2019, the EHRC announced that it was opening a preliminary investigation into the Labour Party pursuant to claims of antisemitism. By the end of May 2019, this was elevated into a full statutory inquiry. The EHRC published a note that gave its investigation a broad scope but did not make any specific allegation. It was clear, though, that the investigation would centre on the party's handling of antisemitism-related disciplinary complaints: the very types of complaints that had been submitted in bulk by the likes of LAAS and Euan 'David Gordstein' Philipps, SFFN's boosters.

McSweeney's fingerprints were all over the EHRC investigation, too, as revealed for the first time in Pogrund and Maguire's 2025 book *Get In*. They report that McSweeney worked extensively with Adam Langleben of the Jewish Labour Movement after the EHRC announced the statutory inquiry. In meetings held in the offices of Labour Together, McSweeney helped Langleben identify Labour councillors and other insiders who might have been willing to provide testimony about their experiences of antisemitism in the party. McSweeney could draw on his prior experience as a member of the Local Government Association for this task.[1] These testimonies were collated and formed a substantial part of an omnibus submission that the JLM made to the EHRC in late 2019, which argued that the Labour Party was institutionally antisemitic.

According to Pogrund and Maguire, Imran Ahmed also stepped up his briefing operation on the issue of antisemitism at around this time. 'Armed with 10,000 leaked emails supplied by Corbyn-sceptic staff, Ahmed disseminated some of their most shocking content to political journalists'.[2] By May 2019, the Labour Together Project, it seems, had become a major node driving and shaping the Labour 'antisemitism crisis'. Put otherwise, the 'antisemitism crisis' was being fanned at least in part by a body that had its own factional interests at stake. The public was unable to factor this potential ulterior agenda into consideration when evaluating the antisemitism allegations because the project's involvement was kept secret. It would be fascinating to discover what media stories Ahmed's work led to and the extent to which they can withstand scrutiny.

On December 5, 2019, only a week before voters went to the polls, JLM's summary submission to the EHRC was leaked to the press. This drove a damaging news cycle that foregrounded the claim that Corbyn had allowed his party to become institutionally antisemitic. It is still not known who leaked the document, in which the names of certain individuals accused of antisemitism—more than one of them Jewish—were left unredacted.

The EHRC's investigation would eventually home in on the allegation that Jeremy Corbyn's Labour leadership office had interfered in the handling of antisemitism complaints. Importantly, such 'interference' had not originally been viewed as a bad thing by Corbyn's critics and by Jewish communal organisations. In February 2019, for example, Tom Watson MP revealed that he had submitted a dossier of complaints to the party and publicly called on Corbyn to 'take a personal lead in reviewing those cases, and recommending to the National Executive Committee what needs to be done'.[3]

It was only in March 2019 that a new narrative of improper political involvement in complaints handling began to be constructed. This novel charge originated primarily as a 'gotcha'. In response to Watson's call for Corbyn's personal involvement, the party briefed that it would be inappropriate for the leader to be involved, claiming further that Corbyn's office had not been involved in complaints handling.

But this wasn't entirely true because, for a period of two months between February and April 2018, as Jennie Formby was settling in as general secretary after taking over from Iain McNicol, the leader's office had provided input on some complaints of antisemitism. Importantly, and as the Forde Inquiry would later find, LOTO's involvement mostly took place because anti-Corbyn staff in the party's Governance and Legal Unit had repeatedly forwarded cases to LOTO to ask for its input and guidance.

Suddenly, it became politically opportune to criticise Corbyn's office for intervening in complaints rather than for having failed to do so. The new attack line was based, in large part, on email leaks to *The Times*, *The Sunday Times*, and *The Observer*, which showed LOTO providing input on a handful of cases in 2018. According to Pogrund and Maguire (the former of whom had worked on *The Sunday Times* article that now cast LOTO's involvement in complaints as a problem), the emails were leaked by a member of the Labour Party bureaucracy named Sam Matthews. As noted previously, Matthews had worked with Imran Ahmed to shut down Wallasey CLP and rescue Angela Eagle MP from the threat of local democracy. Matthews had worked in the GLU, the unit in Labour Party headquarters that handles complaints and other disciplinary matters. The leak was coordinated by Tom Watson's office. The 'political interference' narrative, which would ultimately prove one of the most potent tools for discrediting Corbynism by association with antisemitism, was thus being written through leaks provided by the Labour Together Project's long-time bureaucratic and factional allies.

After years in which Corbyn was told to 'get a grip' on antisemitism complaints and intervene personally to expedite their resolution, any involvement by LOTO in the handling of complaints was now itself construed as evidence of the party's antisemitism. This narrative was most powerfully expressed in *Panorama*'s 2019 documentary, 'Is Labour Anti-Semitic?' The legal fallout from this programme was another unresolved legacy of the Corbyn era that fell to Starmer to resolve.

JOHN WARE AND THE 'WHISTLEBLOWERS'

The new Starmer leadership faced the problem of two libel suits threatened by BBC *Panorama* journalist John Ware, along with a host of former Labour Party employees and officials who featured as 'whistleblowers' in Ware's *Panorama* documentary.

Ware's film 'Is Labour Anti-Semitic?' aired on July 10, 2019, about six weeks after the EHRC announced its inquiry.[4] The former party officials it featured included Matthews, Kat

Buckingham, Michael (Mike) Creighton, Dan Hogan, Louise Withers Green, Benjamin (Ben) Westerman, and Martha Robinson. As noted above, Matthews had been the source of the spate of articles early in March 2019 that attacked LOTO interference in complaints; Withers Green had joined Matthews in at least one background meeting with the journalists who would break the stories. Former general secretary Iain McNicol, who also appeared in the programme, did not join the libel claim.

The *Panorama* programme was the culmination and distillation of the new 'Labour antisemitism' attack line that had been developed leading up to the EHRC's announcement of its investigation. As discussed, this narrative alleged that Corbyn's leadership team had problematically intervened in antisemitism-related complaints. In the media, it was treated as the hard evidence needed to effectively condemn Corbynism as an antisemitic endeavour.

This argument got a receptive hearing at the EHRC. Indeed, it is arguable that the *Panorama* programme framed the nature and direction of the EHRC's investigation and eventual findings, by further reinforcing the 'political interference' narrative promulgated through previous leaks orchestrated by Tom Watson's office and supplied by the Labour Together Project's long-time bureaucratic and factional allies. Emails show that, two days after the documentary aired, the EHRC wrote to Gordon Nardell, the party's executive director of legal affairs. The EHRC explained that it had

> noted the allegations and information featured on the BBC *Panorama* programme '*Is Labour Antisemitic?*' aired on July 10, and ensuing media coverage. The programme raised very serious issues about the approach taken to antisemitism complaints in the party. We will consider this evidence, and the party's response to it, insofar as it relates to the Terms of Reference.

Nardell responded with alarm that the EHRC had taken this approach. He pointed out that the party had already complained to the BBC that the documentary had breached its editorial guidelines. 'The programme cannot properly be regarded as "evidence" for the purpose of a statutory investigation', Nardell implored. The EHRC was having none of it. They argued that it was 'surprising' that the party was arguing this point. And while the EHRC would decide what weight to place on the film, the Commission would 'reject entirely the suggestion that we should disregard it as "evidence" entirely'.

THE LIBEL CASES

John Ware took umbrage at a statement put out by the party when *Panorama*'s film was broadcast. 'The Panorama programme was not a fair or balanced investigation', the statement read. 'It was a seriously inaccurate, politically one-sided polemic, which breached basic journalistic standards, invented quotes and edited emails to change their meaning. It was an overtly biased intervention by the BBC in party political controversy'.[5]

The Labour 'whistleblowers' were aggrieved by a statement provided by the party to the BBC for use in the documentary. In response to the allegation that LOTO staff had improperly interfered in antisemitism complaints, the party asserted that '[t]hese former disaffected employees sought the view of staff in the Leader's Office, which was complied with in good faith. These disaffected former officials include those who have always opposed Jeremy Corbyn's leadership, worked to actively undermine it, and have both personal and political axes to grind'.[6]

Ware and the Labour 'whistleblowers' sued the party for libel.

The Labour Party's primary concern with the *Panorama* programme then became how to deal with these libel claims.

Many on the Labour right had argued that the cases should be settled immediately, even treating this as a litmus test of how seriously the party leadership took the issue of antisemitism.[7]

The case for libel on the part of some of the 'whistleblowers' (Sam Matthew and Mike Creighton in particular) was far from slam-dunk. The first claim—that LOTO had answered queries raised by GLU staff—appears well-evidenced. When he reviewed the documentary record, the respected barrister Martin Forde KC concluded that LOTO had, for the most part, responded to requests for input on complaints 'reasonably and in good faith'.[8]

The second claim—that some of the 'whistleblowers' were factionally hostile to Corbynism—would be buttressed by considerable evidence presented in the Leaked Report, set out below. This evidence was particularly compelling in respect of Matthews and Creighton, as a trove of emails and messages reproduced in the Leaked Report evinced their disdain for Corbyn and his team. Matthews, in particular, was central to the Ergon House scheme, mentioned above and discussed in detail below.

Of course, it is possible that if the cases had been brought to trial, the whistleblowers might have succeeded—libel law is complicated terrain and there is no way of knowing how a judge would construe both the meaning of the Labour Party's statement and whether it was fair. The central point, however, is that within the Labour ecosystem, Starmer's position on the libel case was seen as a test of his approach to party factionalism. The right argued for the immediate payment of damages to the 'whistleblowers' whose testimony had damned Corbynism, while the left baulked at the idea of paying off 'whistleblowers' whose credibility had been challenged by the Leaked Report.

Ware's libel claim was a more vexed subject and this book does not presume to judge whether Labour's allegations of bias or flawed journalism were true. The party had sought legal advice by the time that Starmer took over the leadership. This legal advice, written in strikingly robust terms, argued that the party had a good chance of defending itself: 'In my opinion, the party is likely to successfully defend these claims. The defamatory meaning identified by the claimants can be shown to be fundamentally flawed'.[9] But as the saying goes, 'two lawyers, three opinions'.

Again, it is beyond the scope of this book—or the competence of its author—to comment on the strength of Ware's case from a strictly legal point of view; it is not provable or really even important whether Ware's journalistic approach was biased and flawed, which he has denied. What is clear is that, as time has gone on, evidence has emerged that calls into question certain facts and claims put forward by *Panorama*. This is not to suggest that Ware's approach necessarily led to these errors, but rather that the errors must raise questions about the factual accuracy and cogency of the piece.

Consider the case of Izzy Lenga.

One of *Panorama*'s key threads was that many Jewish party members had experienced antisemitism in party spaces. This was substantiated by a series of unidentified talking heads who testified about their personal experiences. It subsequently emerged that many were members or officers of the Jewish Labour Movement, which was hostile to Corbyn. Amongst the unidentified talking heads was Adam Langleben, whose testimony featured prominently at the outset of the episode. At the time, Langleben had been working with McSweeney to develop JLM's evidentiary submissions to the EHRC in 'secret', having also previously introduced Rachel Riley to McSweeney and Imran Ahmed. Ahmed then asked Riley to front the SFFN campaign against *The Canary*. Another of *Panorama*'s unidentified talking heads was Philip Rosenberg. Rosenberg was director of public affairs for the Board of Deputies of British Jews in addition to being a former Labour councillor. The Board is a communal representative body that takes a strongly pro-Israel line. It had been extremely critical of Corbyn personally and Corbynism in general.

In 2022, Al Jazeera broadcast a documentary on the Labour 'antisemitism crisis' that criticised Ware's film and raised questions about the cogency of certain aspects of it. This led the BBC to issue a clarification about the testimony of one of *Panorama*'s talking heads, Izzy Lenga. She appeared in Ware's documentary with a damning account of her experiences after she had joined the Labour Party in 2015: 'The antisemitic abuse I received was what I was subjected to every day . . . Telling me Hitler was right, telling me Hitler did not go far enough . . . In Labour Party meetings . . . We've seen people engage in Holocaust denial . . . and that's terrifying for Jewish members'. The natural inference was that the antisemitic abuse Lenga had suffered was logically related to her joining the party in 2015.

The BBC acknowledged that Lenga's testimony had been edited and that 'if the programme were re-broadcast, we would include some additional comments from Ms. Lenga's interview to give further context around her experiences'. The BBC reproduced the unedited text of Lenga's interview, which made it clear that her 'Hitler-was-right' experiences happened while she was a student, were unrelated to the Labour Party, and had nothing to do with Corbyn, who was not even party leader when Lenga was a student. The full, unexpurgated quote, with the parts excluded by *Panorama* highlighted in bold, ran as follows:

> I'm Izzy Lenga, I joined the Labour Party in 2015 . . . **When I was a student . . . being quite a high-profile Jewish woman student, I was subjected to quite a lot of, like, nasty vitriol and abuse** . . . The antisemitic abuse I received . . . was what I was subjected to every single day . . . **Predictably, a lot of it came from the far right . . . neo-Nazi abuse** . . . telling me Hitler was right, telling me Hitler did not go far enough **and even more** . . . **What absolutely baffled me, was at the same time, I was receiving . . . very similar and almost often the exact same tropes and anti-Semitic abuse . . . from the far left.**[10]

Another questionable segment concerned an email sent by Corbyn's director of strategy and communications, Seumas Milne, to GLU staff. Ware cited this email to prove that the leader's office had interfered in complaints. *Panorama* reproduced a copy of the email, most of which was blurred out. Two fragments were left in focus: 'we need to review' and 'muddling up political disputes with racism'. Ware's voiceover explained that 'an email from Mr Corbyn's director of communications asked for a review of disciplinary processes into antisemitic complaints. There was a risk, he said, of muddling up political disputes with racism'. Ware asked Sam Matthews how he interpreted this email; Matthews claimed that it amounted to a de facto 'instruction' that LOTO 'be involved directly in the disciplinary process'.

The full text of the email told an arguably different story. The email showed that Milne was referencing a specific case in which a *Jewish* member of the Labour Party had been accused of antisemitism, about which he made a seemingly reasonable point:

> This member is a Jewish activist, the son of a Holocaust survivor. If we're more than very occasionally using disciplinary action against Jewish members for anti-Semitism, something's going wrong, and we're muddling up political disputes with racism. Quite apart from this specific case, I think going forward we need to review where and how we're drawing the line if we're going to have clear and defensible processes.[11]

In 2023, Martin Forde KC gave his assessment of the *Panorama* documentary to Al Jazeera, all of which is discussed in much more detail below. Forde considered that Ware had 'filleted' Milne's email such that 'the context was lost and a more sinister interpretation could be placed upon that email than was ever intended'.[12]

THE LEAKED REPORT

The Starmer Project's third holdover from the Labour 'antisemitism crisis' was the Leaked Report—full title: *The Work of the Labour Party's Governance and Legal Unit in Relation to Antisemitism, 2014–2019*. As noted in the previous chapter, this report was written by Labour Party staff to answer questions posed by the EHRC, using software that could search the entire Labour Party server. The report presented evidence that raised serious questions about the credibility of some of the Labour Party 'whistleblowers' that featured prominently in Ware's *Panorama* documentary, in particular Sam Matthews, Mike Creighton, and Iain McNicol.

The Leaked Report was primarily written by the young GLU staffer Harry Hayball, with input from Laura Murray (the head of the party's complaints unit) and Georgie Robertson (responsible for media management). They were overseen by more senior officials including Karie Murphy, Seamus Milne, and General Secretary Jennie Formby, although Formby's involvement was limited by her ongoing treatment for cancer. The report appears to have been completed in early March 2020, with the expectation that it would be submitted to the EHRC. Later that month, however, the party decided not to submit the report. This decision may have reflected legal concerns as the Leaked Report found that complaints had indeed been mishandled by party officials during the McNicol era. It was duly shelved.

On April 12, 2020, Sky News reported details of the document, which had been leaked by unknown individuals. Murray, Hayball, Robertson, Milne, and Murphy—dubbed the 'Carter Ruck Five', after the law firm that has since represented them—have all denied leaking the document. Multiple investigations have been unable to establish the identity of the leakers. A copy of the report was placed online at roughly the same time as the Sky News report and widely shared on social media. Starmer had only been elected as Labour leader eight days previously, taking up the position just weeks after the first Covid lockdown was announced.

The Leaked Report was a bombshell that challenged the media narrative around the handling of antisemitism complaints in the party, which had previously reflected accounts and leaks by the likes of Sam Matthews and other GLU staff. As such, the report also served to undermine a narrative around the 'antisemitism crisis' that had been secretly promoted by Morgan McSweeney and Imran Ahmed. Across more than eight hundred pages, the Leaked Report produced astonishing evidence of what it called the 'hyper-factionalism' of party staff who worked under General Secretary Iain McNicol and who fiercely opposed Corbyn's leadership. Now-infamous WhatsApp chat records as well as previously unseen emails painted a picture of Labour Party staffers dead set on undermining Corbyn—not only because they thought he would lead Labour to electoral defeat, but also because they, like McSweeney, feared he might win.

In one example documented in the report, a Labour Party official responded to Labour's better-than-expected 2017 election result by writing that the result was 'the opposite of what I had been working towards for the last couple of years'. The official described themselves as 'ashen and grey-faced' and in need of counselling.

Another infamous example of factionalism was the way in which GLU staffers had, at various points, tried to prevent left-wing members being accepted into the party, in anticipation of future leadership elections in which Corbyn would stand. The officials would trawl social media records for reasons to exclude new members, a process they variously dubbed 'trot hunting', 'trot busting' or 'bashing trots'. 'Trot', a reference to the Russian revolutionary Leon Trotsky, was the Labour right's epithet of choice for perceived left-wingers in the party.

The Leaked Report made two core arguments. The first was that the Labour Party had become 'host to a small number of members holding views which were unarguably hostile to Jewish people and in some cases frankly neo-Nazi in their nature'.[13] The sad reality was that as the party had exploded in size to nearly 550,000 members—reaching 1 percent of the country's adult population—the instances of antisemitism within its structures had correspondingly increased. The party 'became more broadly reflective of the problems and prejudices of British society at large'.[14] The Leaked Report also identified a broader lack of understanding as to how anti-Jewish bigotry can 'be expressed on the left of politics, as well as the right'.[15]

The report's second core argument was that 'hyper-factionalism' under General Secretary McNicol had made the party's bureaucracy profoundly dysfunctional. In particular, the report argued that GLU staffers under McNicol had failed to properly investigate antisemitism complaints in the period between 2016 and April 2018. These officials included the Labour Party 'whistleblowers' upon whom Ware had relied: Mike Creighton, Sam Matthews, Ben Westerman, Kat Buckingham, and Louise Withers Green.

A retrospective review in the Leaked Report discovered that at least three hundred complaints of antisemitism had been submitted between November 2016 and February 2018, around half of which were 'actionable'. Yet the GLU under McNicol had initiated just thirty-four investigations. The review also found that there was no system for handling or logging complaints; at one stage, it said, an inbox receiving complaints went entirely unmonitored for months at a time. 'For the failures of this period, the party must apologise most profusely to Jewish members and the Jewish community', the report conceded.[16]

The report revealed that the rate of new investigations into antisemitism complaints increased substantially when Corbyn's ally, Jennie Formby, became general secretary in 2018. Formby oversaw the introduction of a more rigorous and effective process for handling complaints. Between 2016 and 2017, the party expelled one person for antisemitism; this increased to ten in 2018 and forty-five in 2019. The party also achieved a twenty-five-fold increase in the number of investigation notices issued between 2017 and 2019.[17]

The Leaked Report also revealed what it argued were disturbing levels of racism in the McNicol bureaucracy. It detailed how party staff had expressed disdain for Diane Abbott, Britain's first Black woman MP. One official had written that Abbott 'literally makes me sick'. When Abbott appeared on an episode of BBC *Question Time*, another staffer commented that 'Abbott is a very angry woman'. The Leaked Report commented that this was arguably engaging in a classic racist trope. 'Abbott is truly repulsive', another official responded. An inquiry chaired by Martin Forde KC would later find that party staffers' comments about Abbott were expressions of racism.

The report also presented exchanges that it characterised as sexist. In one exchange, three female staffers complained that young female colleagues had 'stopped wearing bras' and that there were 'nipples out' at a meeting. One young woman was attacked for wearing a 'flesh coloured, skin tight top and no bra. No wonder [MP John] Trickett speaks so highly of her'.[18]

ERGON HOUSE

As noted above, the Leaked Report identified another startling piece of 'hyper-factionalism' in Labour headquarters: evidence that, during the 2017 general election, senior party officials had rerouted party money to secretly fund right-wing MPs outside the knowledge or permission of LOTO. Under Labour Party rules, LOTO had authority over campaigning strategy, which was executed via a body called the National Campaign Committee that answered to LOTO. Party files now permit a much fuller reconstruction of what happened in the so-called Ergon House scheme, including striking details of its prehistory that implicate Keir Starmer's own constituency.

The secret funding scheme emerged out of a sense of panic in Labour headquarters after Prime Minister Theresa May had called a snap general election in 2017. Three factors appeared to drive this panic. The first was polling, which predicted a devastating wipeout for Labour. Internal polling data distributed by the party's targeting teams in early April 2017 predicted that the Tories would win 45 percent of the vote share (412 seats), while Labour would win just 26 percent (141 seats).

'We're in meltdown . . . 25 points down and they've not started on us', Heneghan commented in a WhatsApp group chat called 'SMT' on April 22, 2017, suggesting that staff believed this polling was understating the problem. 'SMT' stood for 'Senior Management Team'. The chat was restricted to six of the most senior party bureaucrats: Heneghan, McNicol, Emilie Oldknow (executive director of governance and membership services), Simon Mills (in charge of party accounting), Tracey Allen (McNicol's assistant), and Julie Lawrence (a director in McNicol's office).

The second factor was funding. In the lead-up to the general election, many of the large donors the party had previously relied on had abandoned it. Labour ultimately raised a huge election fund based on a deluge of small donations from ordinary members and generous donations from Unite. But at the outset of the election campaign, this seemed an uncertain prospect.

The third factor was a generalised antipathy toward Corbyn's team and a belief that the Corbyn project was unprofessional and unreliable. This found expression in the hatred shown by officials in party headquarters toward Steve Howell, who had been appointed by LOTO in February 2017 to oversee communications and who would be put in charge of Labour Party messaging and strategy during the election campaign. Howell had long run a successful messaging and strategy company. WhatsApp messages on the SMT group show senior party officials like Heneghan and Oldknow branding him a 'twat', 'ridiculous', 'appalling', and 'absolutely shit'.[19]

In April 2017, McNicol explained to staffers on the SMT group that the party was struggling to finance the campaign.

WhatsApp transcripts show that over the next five minutes, officials in party headquarters agreed to exploit their control of funding to 'protect' a key anti-Corbyn ally, Tom Watson MP:

> *22/04/2017, 22:43—Iain McNicol: We are now getting v tight on covering core ge [general election] costs. No union money in. Lets discuss monday but my gut is we cant afford it.*
>
> *22/04/2017, 22:43—Emilie Oldknow: Oh my god . . .*
>
> *22/04/2017, 22:43—Emilie Oldknow: Iain???*
>
> *22/04/2017, 22:43—Emilie Oldknow: Really . . .*
>
> *22/04/2017, 22:43—Patrick Heneghan: 500k digital in so far I'm told*
>
> *22/04/2017, 22:44—Patrick Heneghan: Ok. But we need to throw cash at Tom's seat*
>
> *22/04/2017, 22:44—Patrick Heneghan: Even if just 50k for that*
>
> *22/04/2017, 22:44—Emilie Oldknow: We should do this*
>
> *22/04/2017, 22:46—Patrick Heneghan: We can't let him lose for want of money*
>
> *22/04/2017, 22:46—Patrick Heneghan: We're in melt-down*
>
> *22/04/2017, 22:46—Patrick Heneghan: 25 points down and they've not started on us*
>
> *22/04/2017, 22:48—Iain McNicol: Lets talk monday. Am off to bed. But obviously protect toms seat.*

From its inception, this plan was based on secrecy. In this same conversation, McNicol told the SMT group that he was due to meet Len McCluskey in the coming days, partly to congratulate him on being re-elected as general secretary of Unite. Staffers pushed McNicol to ask McCluskey for money. Allen, in McNicol's office, added: 'Don't tell him any of it for Tom ha ha'. Watson, of course, was understood to be a fierce opponent of Corbyn, whom McCluskey had backed.

Four days later, a staff member sent a spreadsheet to Patrick Heneghan that set out allocations of party funding for the first phase of the election.[20] The spreadsheet would be regularly updated and circulated until May 4, the day after parliament was dissolved and the so-called 'short campaign' began. The spreadsheet was shared with McNicol, Oldknow, and Mills—the executive director of finance.

These spreadsheets show that the bureaucracy allocated Tom Watson more money than any other MP: £41,000 across three spending categories. This was almost double the next-biggest allocation. They also reveal that a select group of seventeen MPs were allocated extra funds for a 'mailer' (a pamphlet campaign) financed by party headquarters and for spending on Promote, the party's system for buying social media advertising.[21] The MPs whose constituencies were allocated these additional marketing funds included a raft of right-wingers, allies of the bureaucracy, and Corbyn-critics. Notable recipients included Jonathan Ashworth (then married to Oldknow, and the head of Labour Together between July 2024 and July 2025), Shabana Mahmood, Pat McFadden, Tom Watson, Yvette Cooper, Rachel Reeves (all currently senior ministers bar Watson)—and Sir Keir Starmer.[22]

Strikingly, none of the seventeen constituencies in receipt of this additional funding were in the category of seats considered to be most under threat according to the party's polling. In fact, Starmer would campaign for one of the party's safest seats, as would Mahmood and Cooper.[23]

There remain many unanswered questions about the allocation of funding to these seventeen MPs, largely because the matter has still not been properly investigated. It is still not known whether these allocated funds were actually spent or if the MPs designated as recipients were aware of this. What can be said with certainty is that Corbyn's LOTO and the National Campaign Committee were wholly unaware at the time that the allocations had been made.

For unknown reasons, a more sophisticated and detailed covert funding scheme was set up in early to mid-May, now widely referred to as the Ergon House scheme. This involved moving party staff into Ergon House, a Labour Party spillover office, and giving them the resources to run what amounted to a parallel election campaign. From this secret base, Sam Matthews, an ally of Imran Ahmed, led a team of junior staff in designing, printing, and sending off flyers as well as other campaign materials. The funds to pay for the scheme were transferred internally into a pre-existing budgetary instrument then being used for a hodgepodge of expenses: a 'spending code' labeled 'GEL001' or 'Generic Campaign Materials'.

In response to disciplinary charges brought against him (discussed later), Patrick Heneghan later claimed that the Ergon House scheme had been instituted after Karie Murphy, who ran Corbyn's office, had instructed Heneghan to cut funding for certain MPs and reallocate it to Corbyn allies during a meeting on May 19.[24] Murphy has denied that she issued these instructions.

Heneghan's public defence of the Ergon House scheme places significant weight on the May 19 meeting as the scheme's instigating event.[25] But Heneghan's account sits awkwardly with the available documents, which show that planning for the Ergon House scheme had actually commenced at least nine days earlier.

The first logistical emails setting up the Ergon House project were exchanged on May 10, after a passing reference to it had been made in the SMT WhatsApp group the day before.

They show Tom Geldard, the party's director of campaigns and communications, liaising with other senior staff, like Tammi Robson (the party's head of technology), to provide quotes for enhancing Ergon House facilities (Robson does not seem to have been aware of the Ergon House scheme, but was contacted for what would have seemed like routine logistical assistance).[26] An 'action plan' was drawn up shortly thereafter, with a logistics breakdown provided by Sam Matthews.

Discretion was the watchword. In one email between staffers, it was explained that 'this [is] to be kept relatively off the radar right now'. In another exchange between two staffers, dated May 10, one commented that 'there is a secret key seats team arriving in Ergon House permanently'. 'Key seats' is internal party jargon for constituencies being targeted for party campaigning. 'Lots of secret meetings going on here. I think it's all secret to LOTO', the same staffer commented. 'Brill. I endorse this plan. And will keep said plan v much to myself', the other staffer promised. The staffer who 'endorsed' the plan was Stephanie 'Steph' Driver, who would be appointed to LOTO as Starmer's communications director in March 2021 and then as director of communications in Number 10 from March 2025. I return to Driver's other problematic messages in the next chapter. LOTO staff in the Corbyn era would remain totally ignorant of the scheme until it was discovered in the Leaked Report investigation—an ignorance shared by members of the National Campaign Committee, which was literally running the party's election campaign.

By the end of May, Labour had begun to gain significantly in the polls. Seats that had seemed out of reach six weeks earlier were now entering into marginal territory. The party's last chance to send designs that could be printed and mailed out for a final 'Get Out the Vote' (GOTV) campaign was May 30.

Steve Howell was then overseeing a plan to print and deliver flyers as part of the formal campaign's GOTV drive. He wanted to target as many marginal seats as possible within the limits of what the party could afford. As far as Howell knew, he had just £50,000 at his disposal to fund the party's direct-mail GOTV campaign. The result was that only twelve of the marginal seats identified by Howell received the last set of GOTV flyers in the party's final week of campaigning.[27]

GOTV campaigns are rightly given serious weight by political parties. Studies show that they can significantly increase voter turnout, which can make the decisive difference between winning and losing marginal seats.[28]

At the very same time that Howell was operating on the assumption that only £50,000 was available to spend on the formal GOTV campaign, serious cash was secretly being assigned to the Ergon House scheme. Emails show that Matthews was given huge new allocations of funding on May 29, which took the budget for GEL001 from £75,000 to over £175,000.[29] Heneghan was copied into emails showing that the party's head of finance, Simon Mills, approved this allocation. A further increase was also approved on May 30; the amount is unknown.[30]

What *is* known is that, when the election was over, party bureaucrats prepared a spreadsheet that reviewed party spending over the election period. It showed that a whopping £225,852 had been allocated to the special budgetary code GEL001 during the life of the campaign. The Ergon House scheme would have received a very substantial portion of this.[31] From that budgetary allocation, only £135,014 had been spent, leaving an underspend of about £90,000. This bears repeating: unelected party bureaucrats secretly appropriated tens of thousands of pounds of donor money, diverted it from Labour's election campaign toward their own favoured candidates, and then left some £90,000 of it *just sitting there unspent*, even as the party's authorised campaign was scrabbling for funds. They did this during an election that would be marked by a preponderance of tightly marginal contests and in which LOTO's strategy would be vindicated by the party's remarkable election surge and better-than-expected results.

Here's the kicker: In the weeks following the general election, Matthews wrote to his fellow staff member and future GLU colleague Sophie Goodyear via the Labour Party chat facility. The chat logs show that Matthews intended to ask the party for a retrospective pay-out for all his work on the Ergon House scheme. Matthews was confident this could be afforded because 'I left £100k in that budget unspent'.

None of this, of course, was known to the official campaign team, including LOTO staff or Steve Howell. Howell is adamant that, had he only been aware that additional funds were available, he would have directed they be spent on targeting an additional thirty-five marginal seats—seats he could not target because he thought he had only £50,000 available. If just the underspend on GEL001 had been made available to Howell, it would have *tripled* Howell's budget from £50,000 to £140,000. If the entire GEL001 budget had been allocated to Howell's GOTV mailer campaign, in line with LOTO's electoral strategy, this would have increased his budget fourfold to £275,000.

This is huge. Howell calculated that it would have cost £135,000 to target the thirty-five additional marginal seats he believed he could not afford to target with a GOTV mailer: considerably less than had been allocated to the GEL001 budget code. Of those seats, fourteen were nevertheless won by the Labour Party. In a further seven seats, the party lost by an average of just *451 votes*.

If the money allocated on GEL001 had been given to Howell instead, could the party have been in a position to deny the Tories a majority and maybe even to negotiate a minority government?

I don't know the answer, and I suspect it could be endlessly debated. The more pertinent questions at this point are arguably these: Why was the Labour Party bureaucracy, including the general secretary and executive director of finance, concealing an expensive parallel election campaign from the National

Campaign Committee and LOTO? Did this violate the party's rule book? And did it break the law?'

My own firm opinion is that if the funds allocated to the Ergon House scheme in late May had instead been made available to the formal campaign, the party would have performed better than it did. This is because the funds would have been used to target marginal seats instead of either sitting there unspent or—as records show—being squandered by party bureaucrats on extremely safe seats.

The available documentation makes it somewhat difficult to reconstruct with certainty which MPs benefitted and by how much from the covert funding scheme, which had started by mid-May at the latest. What is known is that, on May 30, a key player in the Ergon House scheme, Tom Geldard, sent a list of priority seats to Sam Matthews.[32] This listed ten MPs selected to receive last-minute campaign materials via Ergon House, many of them hostile to Corbyn or close to the bureaucracy: Margaret Beckett, Yvette Cooper, Mary Creagh, Judith Cummins, Gloria De Piero, Caroline Flint, Emma Reynolds, Ruth Smeeth, and Angela Smith.[33]

Of the ten constituencies on this priority list, only one was eventually won by under a thousand votes (De Piero won her seat by a margin of 441). Every other seat on that priority list won by more than a thousand votes. This means they were much less marginal than the seven constituencies identified by Howell that the party ultimately lost by fewer than a thousand votes. In fact, the priority list included a range of seats that were comfortably safe: Reynolds would win by 4,587 votes, Flint by 5,169 votes, and Cummins by 6,700 votes. Some were *ultra*-safe. Yvette Cooper and Margaret Beckett, for example, would win by fully 14,499 and 11,248 votes respectively. Both won 60 percent of all the votes in their constituencies. These were hardly the sort of seats that needed scarce GOTV materials and were certainly nowhere near as deserving as those on Howell's target list.[34] By comparison, one of the seats Howell would have targeted if he'd had the money was Southampton Itchen, which the Tories held against Labour by just 31 votes.

To reiterate: Labour's campaign director was unable to send crucial election materials to marginal seats because the requisite funds had been secretly diverted by right-wing party staff, who wasted much of the money by leaving it unspent or by directing it to constituencies that were already safe.

Ongoing secrecy makes it difficult to determine with absolute certainty how much of the money allocated to Ergon House was actually spent.[35] In the absence of supporting invoices, some of which are not available, I would not want to hazard a guess. But what I have been able to confirm is that at least six constituencies *definitely* received money from Ergon House, and that this was used to buy flyers and printed materials for the general election campaign.[36] These beneficiaries were:

1. Mary Creagh (Wakefield)
2. Gloria De Piero (Ashfield)
3. Judith Cummins (Bradford South)
4. Margaret Beckett (Derby South)
5. Caroline Flint (Don Valley)
6. Angela Smith (Penistone)

It is possible that Ruth Smeeth's constituency also received funds from Ergon House, although the evidence is not conclusive.[37]

The spending on these constituencies raises another important (albeit technical) legal issue: the way this money was accounted for *may* possibly have broken electoral law. The Labour Party has refused to release the information that would allow this to be checked.

With apologies in advance for getting into the weeds—election spending in the UK is reported in two categories: 'national' and 'local'. Each category of spending is strictly controlled. During the 2017 general election, the amount that could be spent by each MP on 'local' spending was in the region of £12,000 to £16,000, depending on various factors.

How does one differentiate between the two categories, 'national' and 'local', in relation to the flyers and GOTV material that Ergon House was purchasing? Basically, spending on flyers counts as 'local' if it produces material in which an MP directly addresses constituents and appeals for their vote. If you live in the UK, you know the genre: a letter with your MP's face in the corner explaining that you should vote for them because they have lived in the area their whole life and run local charities and so on. 'National' spending, on the other hand, would fund a flyer from a political party that does not specifically mention any individual MP candidate but instead explains why the party as a whole deserves your vote.

My investigations confirmed that the constituencies listed above received money from Ergon House and that this was declared as 'national' spending by the Labour Party. The amounts spent on these constituencies were thus *not* declared against 'local' spending, with the result that they were not accounted for in the very tight local constituency spending limits.[38]

Why does this matter? Because the constituencies in question were being supplied with what the Labour Party bureaucracy called 'Individual Electors Letters'.[39] Party emails show that printing these 'Individual Electors Letters' was a key part of the GOTV campaign being undertaken by Sam Matthews. Contemporaneous emails and social media suggest that these 'Individual Electors Letters' may have been precisely the sort of thing that should have been declared as 'local'—but which the party instead declared as 'national'. Electoral law was thus *potentially* broken by both the Labour Party, which may have wrongly declared the spending as national spending, and by the MPs who received this benefit but did not declare it against their 'local' constituency spending limits.[40]

To establish this for certain, one would need to review the text of the flyers. To this end, I contacted Potts Print, the company that printed them. Their staff were extremely helpful. They confirmed that they still retained the original digital designs for the flyers, which they were happy to send to me. However, because the flyers were the intellectual property of the Labour Party, Potts could only release them to me if the party agreed. Potts staff repeatedly asked the Labour Party for this approval over the course of more than a month. Despite the party acknowledging the requests, the approvals were never granted. Simultaneously, a journalist I was working with wrote to the Labour Party's data protection team, requesting approval. They got no response.

If the flyers were indeed 'national' and not 'local', then the present situation is absurd: the party is refusing to authorise the release of text and designs that were previously printed in their thousands and distributed across the country, even as this release would remove rational suspicion that the party breached electoral law. On the other hand, if the flyers were in fact 'local', such that the covert schemes being run by Ergon House bureaucrats did violate electoral law, then the party's refusal to release them makes perfect—if sinister—sense. The party should release this material, and the entire Ergon House scheme should be investigated by the Electoral Commission.

CHAPTER 9

CONTAINMENT AND COVER-UPS

The Leaked Report had the potential to have a profound and lasting impact on the Labour Party and British politics. The details of the Ergon House scheme were explosive, while the Leaked Report provided detailed evidence that disrupted key elements of the 'antisemitism crisis' that had made national headlines for years. The report's reconstruction of Labour Party complaints data, for example, powerfully argued that it was the right-wing staff under McNicol—BBC *Panorama*'s vaunted 'whistleblowers'—who were at least partially responsible for the unsatisfactory handling of antisemitism complaints. The effect was to profoundly unsettle a narrative around Labour antisemitism that the Labour Together Project had secretly helped to construct.

The report also confirmed what many on the left had sensed but could not prove: that in the period from 2015 to 2019, the party's upper echelons had attacked, undermined, and potentially destroyed the Corbyn project from within. Indeed, the Leaked Report was revivifying for many on the left of the party, providing left-wingers with an evidence-based explanation for why Corbyn failed.

Yet the Leaked Report could have been an opportunity for an incoming Labour leadership. It identified a toxic culture of factionalism, bullying, sexism, and racism that undermined the party's effectiveness and which would be unacceptable in every other professional environment. In the right hands, the Leaked Report could have been a catalyst to lance this boil once and for all, providing the opportunity to clean up a dysfunctional bureaucracy. That opportunity wasn't taken. Instead, it was actively spurned.

Many of the staffers whose factional conduct was revealed in the Leaked Report would go on to have illustrious careers under Starmer in the party and then in Number 10—like Paul Ovenden, as discussed later, as well as Steph Driver. And when the party was presented with an independent report by Martin Forde KC in 2022, which confirmed the toxicity of party culture and provided a roadmap to fix it, the party instead sniffed at his findings and treated Forde in an appalling manner.

The reason why this opportunity was missed was not hard to understand: for the Starmer Project and the Labour Together Project that preceded it, the Leaked Report was a potentially mortal threat. It implicated a raft of actors in serious misconduct, many of whom were closely linked to the projects. It was also critical of many fomenters of the 'antisemitism crisis', such as LAAS, which had played a key role in amplifying the Labour Together Project's astroturf SFFN campaign.[1] And if the party started digging into how funds were allocated by the right-wing bureaucracy in 2017, it might have uncovered the spreadsheets showing that Starmer himself had been amongst those slated to benefit.

The bureaucrats exposed by the Leaked Report were also long-term allies of, and friends with, the likes of Morgan McSweeney and Imran Ahmed, the latter of whom had worked with Sam Matthews in Wallasey. When senior official Patrick Heneghan left the party in late 2017, he emailed himself a list of invitees to his leaving do. Among the hundred people he invited were Labour Together honchos like McSweeney, Steve Reed, and Rachel Reeves. In February 2019, McSweeney allegedly reached out directly to Heneghan, who was by then a leading figure in the People's Vote campaign for a second referendum on Brexit. McSweeney asked Heneghan to mobilise young Remainers to 'harangue' Corbyn as the Labour leader addressed students at the University of Warwick.[2]

Similarly, the WhatsApp chats reproduced in the Leaked Report showed that on two occasions in 2017 when vacancies arose in the party's bureaucracy, Labour's then-general secretary Iain McNicol both times identified McSweeney as a suitable candidate. McNicol had himself endorsed Starmer for leader of the Labour Party via an article in *LabourList*.

As will be discussed further below, after the Leaked Report was published, Heneghan became the only party official mentioned in it to be suspended from the party. It appears that Heneghan at least initially believed that McSweeney would have his back. In May 2021, Heneghan wrote an angry email to the Labour Party Disputes team, copying in General Secretary David Evans; Head of Legal Alex Barros-Curtis; NEC Chair Margaret Beckett; and NEC Complaints and Disputes Sub-Committee Chair Shabana Mahmood (the long-time Labour Together associate).

'Mr McSweeney told me on the phone the day the document [i.e., the Leaked Report] leaked that Labour knew the document was a stitch-up and that there would be no issues apart from a short statement from Mr. Starmer', Heneghan alleged.

While he griped that McSweeney then failed to call back, Heneghan was able to reach out to another key actor in the Labour Together Project to help his cause: Imran Ahmed. Heneghan had been charged under the party's social media policy in relation to the WhatsApp records exposed in the report. Heneghan claimed he had been in 'direct contact with' CCDH, whose CEO Ahmed confirmed that WhatsApp messages are 'not online abuse because it's not online. It's literally peer to peer data transfer'.

It is not known whether these calls actually took place. Heneghan, as we will see, is not the most reliable witness. But it would not have been a major leap for people like Heneghan to believe that McSweeney would have the back of bureaucrats who had worked so long with McSweeney's collaborator Ahmed to undermine the Corbyn project.

The Labour Party's response to the Leaked Report was to appoint an independent investigation into its contents as well as its unauthorised disclosure.

On April 23, 2020, the NEC selected Martin Forde KC to lead the investigation. Forde was a well-respected Black barrister, whose appointment was welcomed by many, including the Labour Party's BAME (Black, Asian, and Minority Ethnic) Staff Network. Forde featured in *The Lawyer*'s 'Hot 100' list of 2019, the year after he had been appointed an independent advisor to the Windrush Compensation Scheme.[3] Forde was to be supported by a panel comprising Lord Larry Whitty, Baroness Ruth Lister, and Baroness Debbie Wilcox.[4]

Forde's appointment took place in the small window between Starmer's victory and the establishment of control by the Starmer Project under McSweeney. This perhaps explains how Forde, who would go on to lead a credible investigation, made the cut. If a similar process had played out a year or two later, it is hard to imagine that such independence would have been tolerated.

Forde was given a wide remit. In addition to examining how the report was leaked, and looking into the party's culture, the Forde Inquiry was also asked to

> investigate and report on: The truth or otherwise of the main allegations in the Report (the Panel shall determine which are the most significant allegations but they shall include the extent of racist, sexist and other discriminatory culture within Labour Party workplaces, the attitudes and conduct of the senior staff of the Labour Party, and their relationships with the elected leadership of the Labour Party.[5]

Although no specific date was announced for when the inquiry would be published, it soon became clear that it would be substantially delayed. Ultimately, the Forde Report was only published in July 2022—more than two years later. Forde's findings are discussed in this book's penultimate section, as is the way in which the party alternately denigrated or ignored them and treated Forde in a generally appalling manner. Forde claimed, in his introduction to the eponymous report, that publication had been delayed because of ongoing investigations by the Information Commissioner's Office (ICO), which was also probing the leak.

With the Forde Inquiry's report kicked into the long grass, the party bureaucracy would use the opportunity to prejudge its findings and undermine its independence, taking a series of decisions designed to protect the right-wing McNicol-era party bureaucracy that had been exposed in the Leaked Report.

The real attitude of the party bureaucracy and LOTO to the Leaked Report was revealed in June 2020. On June 3, the academic Justin Schlosberg wrote to Simon Mills. Schlosberg intended to write an article about the Leaked Report, co-authored with Richard Sanders and Peter Oborne and appearing in *openDemocracy*. He sought Mills' reply. At the time, the full extent of Mills' involvement in the Ergon House scheme was not publicly known—this book reveals it for the first time—but he had been identified as a participant in the offensive WhatsApp groups, where he called Karie Murphy a 'fuckwit'. Schlosberg put this allegation to him, alongside another.

Mills immediately forwarded Schlosberg's query to Alex Barros-Curtis, Joseph Perry (Labour's head of human resources), and Cassie Mathers (Labour's data compliance officer). Mills requested advice on a response and whether it was possible to prevent publication of the WhatsApp messages. Mathers urged delaying a response and attached an important document: a letter that the Labour Party had sent on April 20, 2020, to media outlets including *The Guardian*, *The Times*, *The Telegraph*, the *Financial Times*, *The Canary*, *The Economist*, *Novara Media*, the *Evening Standard*, and *LabourList*.

The letter advised the media houses to consider whether they risked breaching the Data Protection Act by obtaining a copy of the Leaked Report. It also advised that 'insofar as you continue to publish/disseminate the Report and/or any Relevant Extracts, you will immediately be placing yourself at risk of legal action being taken against you by the party, as well as by the affected individuals and the Information Commissioner'. Of course, factionalism and bias could explain why the Leaked Report received limited coverage in the mainstream media, but the aggression behind the letter spoke to the party's determination to deter media coverage—even though it would later admit to the ICO that the contents of the Leaked Report were in the public interest.

The party ultimately decided against sending a legal response. Instead, an email was sent from the Labour Party Press Office account to Schlosberg, extracts of which were included in the article eventually published by *openDemocracy* at the end of June 2020. The party mounted a vigorous defence of Mills, noting that he had not taken any formal position as acting general secretary, but had merely helped out to assist the party in trying times. Taking its cue from inputs made by Perry, the response emphasised that 'Mr Mills does not exist in the public eye' and that it 'trusted' that any reporting 'will respect his non-political position within a political party and treat him like you would any private individual'.

Most importantly, the response also sought to defend the WhatsApp groups, even though the Forde investigation into them was still ongoing and despite their obnoxious content. Schlosberg had described some of the language used in the WhatsApp groups as 'infantile'; the party's response dismissed this characterisation as 'po-faced'. The party further defended the allegedly racist and sexist messages by claiming that they were 'exchanged between co-workers in the expectation that they remain private and confidential and the tone of the language reflects that'. The party thus appeared to be suggesting that it was no big deal for party employees to exchange allegedly sexist and racist messages about their colleagues so long as this was done in private.

Importantly, emails showed that, in preparing this line, the matter had been raised with Ben Nunn by Barros-Curtis; Nunn was then copied into further correspondence. Nunn was at that time an advisor in LOTO and particularly close to Starmer; he was not a part of the party bureaucracy. Nunn, as previously mentioned, was vigorously defended by Starmer when he was appointed to his leadership campaign having previously worked as a pharmaceutical industry lobbyist. Nunn was sent a copy of the party's response, confirming 'this is good for me'. The intense effort to protect Mills thus came not just from the party bureaucracy but also from Starmer's office itself, as did the defence of the WhatsApp messages. Considering the seriousness of the allegations in the Leaked Report, and the genuine distress and upset that many BAME members felt about the content of the WhatsApp messages (discussed later), it is extraordinary that Starmer's LOTO attempted to underplay their significance.

The episode provoked a furious response from Richard Simcox, a member of the Labour press team, who sent his complaints to Nunn and another member of LOTO, Paul Ovenden. Simcox argued that a query to Simon Mills should have been answered by Mills' own lawyer and that the party should have stuck to the usual line that it did not discuss staffing issues. Most importantly, Simcox was angry that the party's response 'goes significantly further than what Keir and Angela have said publicly' and that 'there is a serious risk of it being seen as an attempt by the party to influence or prejudice the [Forde] Inquiry—something Keir, Angela and the NEC have been clear we're not seeking to do'. Nunn defended the action but noted, with what would be an ironic foreshadowing of what would actually happen, that he had spoken to McSweeney and Barros-Curtis, who 'have given me the assurance that it does not prejudice any disciplinary process or inquiry in any way whatsoever'.

Simcox was not alone in his anger. Within a day of the *openDemocracy* article being published, thirteen members of the NEC sent a stinging letter to Starmer demanding a public apology and retraction of the statement. The NEC members argued that 'the Labour Party's statement was not only inexcusable in defending the racist, sexist and abusive comments in the WhatsApp groups, it also directly pre-judged the specific issues that Martin Forde's inquiry is considering'.

ERGON HOUSE AND THE WHATSAPP IMBROGLIO

The level of party protection afforded to Simon Mills vis-à-vis *openDemocracy* was striking, not least when compared to how relentlessly the party would hound the authors of the Leaked Report. Equally striking was the party's failure to properly investigate the Ergon House scheme, in which Mills was closely involved, despite exhortations to do so from Unite.

On April 22, 2020, Unite wrote to Starmer and Formby about the Ergon House scheme, which Unite identified as a matter of the 'utmost seriousness' that 'warrants particular attention'. Unite was the party's largest donor in the 2017 election and there were fears that Unite money had been diverted to Ergon House. It argued that, based on what had already been revealed by the Leaked Report, the Ergon House scheme 'represents at least a very serious breach of trust and democratic accountability, and at worst a prima facie case of fraud (by representation, failure to disclose information, and/or abuse of position) and false accounting'. Unite asked that the party investigate Ergon House by appointing a forensic auditor and that it report any financial irregularities discovered to law enforcement.

The party effectively replied that Unite did not need to worry because the matter would be thoroughly investigated by the Forde Inquiry. But this response was problematic for two reasons. First, the Forde Inquiry had been given a wide latitude to decide what to investigate—there was no guarantee it would consider Ergon House. Second, while Forde was a capable and competent barrister, he was not a forensic auditor. Nor were the other inquiry members.

Forde's report, published July 2022, did address the Ergon House scheme, and is to be commended for its serious-minded investigation into the welter of allegations appearing in the Leaked Report. But it was not based on a thorough inspection of the party's accounts. This is clear in the report's discussion of the budgets set aside for Ergon House, in which the inquiry admitted it was unable to establish what an amount of £45,000 had been spent on, while tracing the funds 'would require a forensic accounting exercise beyond the scope of this report'.[6] Forde's team had not felt able to conduct a forensic audit of the type requested by Unite. As the Forde Report acknowledged, this meant they were unable to establish whether Ergon House broke electoral law in relation to the 'national' vs 'local' spending issue identified in the last chapter.

The Forde Inquiry also did not mention the extended pre-history of the Ergon House scheme, which, as discussed above, involved senior members of the party bureaucracy allocating scarce party resources to a select group of MPs without the knowledge of the party leadership. I do not believe the Forde Inquiry would have avoided this topic if it had known about it. As a result, I have serious reservations about whether the Forde Inquiry was given access to all the documents that sat on the Labour Party server relevant to the Ergon House scheme or its predecessor.

To this day, the Ergon House scheme has never been investigated by a forensic auditor or accountant. The money has never been fully traced. The Labour Party was presented with serious and credible evidence pointing to potential irregularities and alleged fraud (as suggested by Unite's letter to the party) as well as potential violations of electoral law. Yet the party under Starmer's leadership has chosen not to properly investigate it. Labour neglected even to mount an internal investigation into Simon Mills, who retained until mid-2023 the same executive director of finance position he held while he was participating in the Ergon House scheme, and in which he had been copied into emails distributing spreadsheets showing that Starmer's constituency had been allocated substantial additional funds without the knowledge of LOTO. Serious questions must be asked about what this failure to properly investigate the Ergon House scheme says about the Starmer Project's commitment to good governance, democratic integrity, and respect for the law.

Mills was also at the centre of a mini-storm related to somewhat bizarre allegations (whose accuracy I could not verify) that WhatsApp group chats supplied to Forde had been edited.

As part of a longer chain of correspondence about certain aspects of evidence to be shared with Forde, Barros-Curtis informed the secretariat that the party had uploaded a copy of the infamous WhatsApp groups to the cloud for the secretariat to download in the first or second week of December 2020. Records show that the secretariat planned to review the WhatsApp messages and make summaries for the commissioners to read, and to make them available for witness interviews.

On December 18, Forde conducted a witness interview with Patrick Heneghan. That evening, a member of the Forde Inquiry secretariat wrote to Barros-Curtis to set an agenda for a discussion in the near future. Amongst the items for discussion was 'whether we [the inquiry] have access to the full set of WhatsApp messages. In interviewing, reference has been made to the fact that messages from a certain individual who was originally part of the WhatsApp group(s) seem not to have been included in the leak, but are nevertheless held by the party'. When Barros-Curtis asked for more details that would have allowed him to investigate further, the secretariat member wrote back explaining that 'the concern is the party may have (and supplied to a witness before the inquiry) a more complete set of messages [than] that which the panel has (including, for example, messages from Simon Mills)'.

The secretariat did not identify which individual they were referring to, but it is plausible that it was Heneghan. First, the email from the secretariat had been sent on the evening of the same day that Heneghan was interviewed, suggesting it was his interview that prompted the question. Second, the party's data protection officer, Cassie Mathers, had provided Heneghan with a full and unredacted copy of the WhatsApp group chats—an odd thing for a data protection officer to do.

Finally, Heneghan made the very same allegation. Heneghan wrote to the Labour Party in February 2021, after the BBC published a story in which it was claimed that Forde had not been given a copy of the WhatsApp chats. Heneghan explained that 'many of us have spoken to FORDE at length', that 'the inquiry did confirm' that 'they received what they were told was a full copy of our private whatsapp [*sic*] messages (unredacted)', and 'that the messages were edited by LPHQ [Labour Party headquarters] first—so for example the version you supplied him of the SMT group had all messages from Simon Mills removed—i.e. you edited the evidence before sending to him'.

A further email sent by Heneghan to the party in May 2021 was even more explicit. As part of a set of ten questions, he asked, 'did you edit/process my personal messages as the version of the SMT group you gave to Forde had been edited out to remove all messages from Simon Mills?'

The SMT group, recall, was the WhatsApp group that involved only the six most senior members of Labour's management team under McNicol, including Mills. The group texts could have been particularly important for any investigation into Ergon House—which Heneghan was most likely being interviewed about—because they showed Heneghan joking about the scheme in response to a conversation with Mills.

When Forde finally published his report, it included a seeming non sequitur that makes considerably more sense against this background. In a discussion about the WhatsApp groups, Forde confirmed that 'we are confident . . . that we received full copies of the WhatsApp messages referred to in the Leaked Report'.[7] No one had publicly suggested otherwise.

Emails show that considerable tension already plagued the relationship between the Forde Inquiry and the Labour Party bureaucracy by the time that the claim of doctored WhatsApp transcripts emerged. Members of the inquiry were frustrated by the length of time it took for them to receive documents and by the sometimes-obtuse answers to queries it had raised.

I have not been able to establish whether the WhatsApp logs provided by the party were truly altered. But the resolution that was reached was nonetheless striking: ultimately, the Forde Inquiry secured copies of the Whatsapp group from other sources and relied upon them instead of the version given to it by the Labour Party, in order to ensure the panel had access to an unexpurgated copy. What did that say about the levels of trust between the inquiry and the party machinery?

THE UNEXAMINED EVIDENCE AND THE CONDUCT OF STARMER LIEUTENANTS

In retrospect, the party's appointment of Forde primarily served as an excuse to carry on with business as usual—in ways that would undermine Forde's own inquiry. But it was also treated as an entirely sufficient response to the Leaked Report's revelations, obviating the need for the party to conduct its own inquiries, as seen in the party's response to Unite.

The result was that the party materially neglected to conduct its *own* internal investigations into whether other senior party staff had used the party's messaging system to exchange the sort of problematic messages that were identified in the Leaked Report. Indeed, it does not even seem to have reviewed the record of messages exchanged by people whose conduct had *already* been identified in the Leaked Report.

If the party had investigated, it would have uncovered additional evidence that Labour Party staff were sharing questionable and arguably unacceptable messages via the Party's internal messaging system—communications I reveal here for the first time.[8] Some of these messages were exchanged by people who would go on to serve in senior party roles under Starmer, despite having appeared in the Leaked Report. Some would also be appointed to senior positions in Number 10 after Starmer was elected as prime minister, while others would serve as elected Labour Party representatives. What does this say about the Starmer Project's concern with tackling the toxic culture identified by the Leaked Report and, later, Martin Forde KC's inquiry?

One of these individuals is Paul Ovenden. The Leaked Report claimed that Ovenden had exchanged messages that it alleged constituted evidence of factionalism. Ovenden worked as a press officer for the Labour Party between 2014 and September 2017. Following a stint for private PR and communications firms, he was rehired by the party in June 2020 to serve as its director of communications. That is, Ovenden was hired into a senior party position by the Starmer Project *after* he was mentioned in the Leaked Report. In July 2024, following the general election, Ovenden was appointed as a special advisor to the prime minister in Number 10. In January 2025, he was appointed as the director of strategy in Number 10, making him one of the most senior figures in Starmer's office.

One saved chat shows Ovenden referring to a left-winger as a 'trot'. In another, Ovenden joked about how, in August 2015, he had used access to the party's database to check whether his neighbour was a member. At the time, the party had seen a surge of new members on the back of Corbyn's insurgent campaign to become leader. 'I have a new neighbour. White with dreadlocks, smokes roll-ups. Just put my post code into memberscentre [the party's membership database]; she registered as a member yesterday. Ffs'.

But the most disturbing chat involved Ovenden talking to a young female staffer in May 2017 about Diane Abbott. Note that, in the copy of the chat below, I've anonymised some names in the interests of privacy and because what Ovenden relays about them could be considered hearsay. I have replaced them with letters instead.

The chat record reads:

> *Ovenden:*
> I've got something that will make you lol from last night. We were playing shag marry kill at PT. Honestly, I nearly wet myself from laughing.
>
> *Staffer:*
> What??? I love that game!
>
> *Ovenden:*
> X asking Y who would use the strap on out of her and Diane Abbott was the highlight/lowlight.
> and then X's physical demonstration of Y putting it on was amazing. 'what are you doing? It's so big it has shoulder staps'
>
> *Staffer:*
> Hahaha that's amazing!!! What was the answer? Some awful mental pics are assembling in my head.
>
> *Ovenden:*
> we spent a lot of time discussing Y going down on Diane. Honestly it was outrageous.
>
> *Staffer:*
> Oh my god.

'PT' in Ovenden's chat likely referred to 'Paedo Towers', the joking name that Ovenden and others gave to Dolphin Square, an apartment block in London. Media staff working for the Labour

Party during the 2017 election were put up at Dolphin Square in hired apartments.

Another is Stephanie 'Steph' Driver. She was cited in the Leaked Report on a number of occasions, usually in the footnotes. One internal party chat reproduced in the Leaked Report, noted above, involved her exchanging messages about how she 'endorse[d]' the 'brill' plan to install a secret 'key seats' team in Ergon House.

Driver, like Ovenden, had left the party in the Corbyn years, going into private practice in March 2019. In March 2021 she was hired back by the party (long after the Leaked Report was made public) to be appointed as Starmer's communications director in LOTO, holding the position until after the election in July 2024. Thereafter she was transitioned into Number 10, where she first served as the deputy director of communications and then as the director of communications from March 2025. Driver, like Ovenden, was thus one of the most senior members of Starmer's Number 10 team at the time of writing.

Party messaging records reveal a concerning conversation Driver had in May 2017 with another female staffer (incidentally the same staffer who shared the messages about Abbott with Ovenden). The chat focused on Georgie Robertson. Robertson was a key member of the late Corbyn-era press team. She was also one of the authors of the Leaked Report; the party would spend millions of pounds suing her based on the unproven accusation that she had leaked it.

The chat ran:

Staffer:
Who the flip is Georgie? Who are all these people?
Who's the old man?

Stephanie Driver:
God knows who the old man is
some hack from south wales but don't know what hes doing

> Georgie is the blonde girl who wears tiny skirts
> shes from momentum
> think she is one of Schneider's floozies
>
> *Staffer:*
> He's got a full on harem. They must have no sense of smell. I just hate them being here so much.

'Schneider' referred to James Schneider, who co-founded Momentum before moving into Corbyn's LOTO as a press advisor.

Then there is the case of Danny Adilypour. Adilypour was elected as a councillor in Lambeth in 2014 and is the deputy leader of Lambeth council at the time of writing. Adilypour was an advisor to Deputy Leader Tom Watson in the latter stages of the Corbyn years. He had played an important cameo in the Labour Party antisemitism crisis. When Sam Matthews chose to leak documents to *The Sunday Times* and *The Guardian* in March 2019, alleging LOTO interference in complaints, the leak was facilitated by Watson's office. Matthews delivered his documents into the hands of Adilypour.

Adilypour's name appeared an astonishing thirty-three times in the Leaked Report and its footnotes. Adilypour had referred to himself in one 2015 message as 'trot-smasher in chief' and, in a 2016 conversation about Momentum, told another party staffer that 'half our current membership have serious mental health problems, that's the frightening thing'.

But this was just the tip of the iceberg. In one previously unreleased chat, Adilypour laughed and joked while a white fellow staffer complained how working with BAME Labour (the official Labour group for Black, Asian, and minority ethnic members) had made this staffer 'racist':

> *Staffer:*
> Today is a depressing day! I hate BAME Labour, i swear I wasn't a racist before this job

Danny Adilypour:
Today has been a really depressing day
Haha I reckon there's always been a racist within you waiting to break out ☺

Staffer:
I used to be tolerant I swear
☺

Danny Adilypour:
I know what you mean, just had a member in the North West complaining about being asked to donate to the No campaign.

The chat continued the following day:

Danny Adilypour:
How are the BAME's behaving today?

Staffer:
Very naughty indeed

Danny Adilypour:
Haha

Staffer:
X [a male BAME staffer] is ignoring me because he hasn't sorted out the catering for next week

Danny Adilypour:
He's such a dick . . .

They returned to this rich conversational vein a few days later:

Danny Adilypour:
I've been dealing with crazy people all day again
It wastes so much time and energy.

Staffer:
Me too! It must be less than 48 hours till a BAME reception with this level of crazy . . .

Danny Adilypour:
It's gonna be a fun evening . . .

Staffer:
at least there is wine and paneer

Danny Adilypour:
We'll need lots of both

Is Danny Adilypour a suitable candidate to be a Labour Party councillor, let alone the deputy leader of Lambeth council, a borough whose population is 43 percent BAME?

SETTLING WITH WARE AND THE 'WHISTLEBLOWERS'

On July 22, 2020, only weeks after the *openDemocracy* brouhaha, the Labour Party announced that it had agreed to settle the libel claims of John Ware and the Labour Party 'whistleblowers' who appeared in his *Panorama* documentary 'Is Labour Anti-Semitic?' The full cost of the settlement has never been confirmed, although *The Guardian* estimated the settlement and associated fees at £600,000, including £180,000 paid in damages to the 'whistleblowers'.[9]

The party withdrew its 'defamatory and false allegations' against Ware and apologised 'unreservedly for the distress, embarrassment and hurt' its statements had caused. It reiterated that 'John Ware is a very experienced broadcast and print journalist, producer and author, and we have agreed to pay damages to him'.[10] The apology noted that 'if we are to restore the trust of the Jewish community, we must demonstrate a change of leadership. That means being open, transparent and respecting the rights of whistleblowers'.[11] Considering how the party was treating the authors of the Leaked Report at the same time—a matter addressed later in this book—this statement oozed hypocrisy.

The party issued a second and separate apology to Kat Buckingham, Mike Creighton, Sam Matthews, Dan Hogan, Louise Withers Green, Ben Westerman, and Martha Robinson. The party referred to them collectively as 'whistleblowers'. The apology confirmed that the party had also paid these 'whistleblowers' damages. Not only did the party statement 'withdraw all allegations of bad faith, malice and lying', it also issued another unreserved apology for any distress caused. The party further acknowledged 'the many years of dedicated and committed service that the whistleblowers have given to the Labour Party as members and staff. We appreciate their valuable contribution at all levels of the party'.[12] By then, the conduct of the likes of Matthews had been all-too-publicly revealed by the Leaked Report and shared widely on social media.

The apologies and settlements provoked widespread commentary, including upset responses from the Labour Party BAME Staff Network. The day before the settlement was announced, the BAME Staff Network wrote to Starmer as well as Deputy Leader Angela Rayner to caution that any apology 'to individuals named in the leaked report, whose conduct is under investigation by the Forde Inquiry and the EHRC, ahead of the investigations reporting, which we all understand to be imminent, risks prejudging and undermining the outcome of both investigations'.

When the BAME Staff Network made a joint submission to the Forde Inquiry in August 2020, particular ire was directed at the decision to settle with John Ware.

SLAPS ON THE WRIST

The Leaked Report alleged and compellingly documented serious misconduct. Yet the party took only the most limited and superficial disciplinary action in response. It brought disciplinary charges against seven former members of staff: Emilie Oldknow, Sarah Mulholland, Fiona Stanton, Neil Fleming, Tracey Allen, Julie Lawrence, and Patrick Heneghan. These charges were not brought against them in their capacity as former staffers, but instead with reference to their party membership. The harshest outcome of any disciplinary proceeding on this latter basis was expulsion from the party.

Notably, Labour made no attempt to bring disciplinary charges, either as a party or as an employer, against any individuals identified in the Leaked Report who were then still employed by the party, such as Simon Mills.

Six of the seven former members of staff were treated generously: three were let off entirely, two were issued reminders of conduct, and one received a punitive suspension that did not, however, result in any actual time out beyond the period of investigation.

News of the readmission of the six broke in the *HuffPost* on February 2, 2021, in a piece written by Rachel Wearmouth. The article soft-pedalled the charges against Oldknow and others and included a lengthy defence of Heneghan from an anonymous source.[13]

The only one of the seven former employees to be handed a lengthy suspension, and who potentially faced tougher censure, was Patrick Heneghan. Heneghan, like the others, had been administratively suspended on June 3. When the NEC finally met to consider his case, it decided that he would remain suspended while his case was referred up to the National Constitutional Committee (NCC). The NCC considered serious disciplinary cases and could recommend expulsion.

From there, the case languished without being heard for months. It is still not clear whether Heneghan's case has progressed—although, as shown below, documents strongly suggest that considerable pressure was being placed on the bureaucracy behind the scenes to come to a resolution.

But what emerges from the evidence is simple: the Starmer Project displayed little appetite for holding those exposed by the Leaked Report to account and moved swiftly to smooth the feathers of those embarrassed by having their obnoxious or worse conduct revealed. Indeed, the party failed to conduct any further internal inquiries and even elevated staff mentioned in the Leaked Report into senior positions in the party and, eventually, Number 10.

In July 2025, as this book was being finalised, *The Guardian* reported that the Labour Party had settled libel and privacy claims that had been brought by twenty individuals named in the Leaked Report.[14] The claims had been settled the previous year but not at that time publicly announced. Reporting estimated that it had cost the party £2 million to settle the claims, of which approximately £1 million was paid to the claimants. The remaining £1 million was paid to lawyers, including those of the claimants, whose costs had been covered by the party.

The party had simultaneously issued apologies to the claimants. Patrick Heneghan was among those who had received a payout; he had also received an apology for the 'false claim' that he had 'sabotaged' the 2017 general election via the Ergon House scheme. Another notable payout recipient was Joe Goldberg, a former Labour councillor, whose story is dealt with in Chapter 14.

The party's attitude to those it suspected of leaking the report—and thereby embarrassing the Starmer Project's factional allies—could not have been more different.

CHAPTER 10

NO, NOT THOSE WHISTLEBLOWERS

At the very same time that the Labour Party was apologising and paying off the *Panorama* 'whistleblowers' and either continuing to employ or doling out the most lenient of 'punishments' to those exposed in the Leaked Report, it was spending vast sums trying to identify who had leaked the report.

The publication of the Leaked Report had ensnared the party in three legal imbroglios. First, it was sued by Oldknow, Heneghan, and others, including for damages arising from the publication of the report. They were represented by Patron Law, the firm of Mark Lewis, who we met earlier as the advisor to LAAS and Rachel Riley's representative in libel cases. Second, and at much the same time, the party was sued by a second set of litigants who also claimed damages. The full list of litigants has not been disclosed—claimants have been anonymised in court filings—although they were revealed to be LAAS members.

The LAAS litigants were initially represented by Jonathan Turner, a founder of UK Lawyers for Israel who was appointed its chief executive in 2018.[1] Their case was then handed to 3D Solicitors and Daniel Berke. Berke was also a director of UKLFI, having been appointed in October 2019.[2] Mark Lewis, who represented the party bureaucrats, had been a director of UKLFI from September 2014 to 2017.

Third, the party had been placed under investigation by the Information Commissioner's Office (ICO). The ICO, a statutory body, can bring criminal charges where it believes that individuals have acted in breach of the Data Protection Act. It could make adverse findings against the Labour Party and levy substantial fines.

Sitting at the heart of all three of these cases were two simple questions: Who leaked the Leaked Report, and who should be held legally responsible? In order to indemnify it from any damages and avoid a hefty ICO fine, the Labour Party sought to escape responsibility for the leak. It also set out to find the leakers, whom it could then make legally responsible.

Alongside the Forde Inquiry, the party initiated an eye-wateringly expensive investigation into who had leaked the report, estimated to have cost over £1 million. As discussed above, the party chose not to hire a forensic auditor to help Forde establish the truth about the Ergon House scheme. The party's pursuit of those who leaked the Leaked Report appeared far more thorough. The party appointed a computer forensics firm called Stroz Friedberg, part of the Aon multinational conglomerate, and a private investigator named Morag Slater from CMP Resolutions. CMP Resolutions is a business relationship and conflict resolution firm that also conducts 'workplace investigations'.[3] Stroz Friedberg would examine the hard digital evidence while Slater would review documents and conduct interviews.

ROUGH TREATMENT

In parallel with the Stroz Friedberg and Morag Slater investigations, the party began exerting pressure on the authors of the Leaked Report, who included Harry Hayball, Georgie Robertson, Laura Murray, Karie Murphy, and Seumas Milne. The three junior members of staff—Hayball, Robertson, and Murray—were told to continue working from home during the Covid lockdown, but were then locked out of the Labour Party email servers that were essential for their work: a de facto suspension. The party would later admit that the only reason it did not issue these employees with formal suspensions was because of pushback from Unite, which was defending the three. Barros-Curtis led negotiations toward some sort of settlement. By May 2020, when negotiations were ongoing, he had been transferred from LOTO to the role of executive director of legal, a position he would hold for the next four years.

The party, via Barros-Curtis, offered to pay off Murray, Robertson, and Hayball to end their employment, with two caveats. First, it asked them to sign what they would allege amounted to Non-Disclosure Agreements (NDAs). This was particularly egregious as Murray and Robertson had both recently filed a sexual harassment claim, and NDAs would prevent them from speaking out publicly about this. Hayball also had an outstanding grievance against the party for bullying. When the BBC broke the story of the NDAs in 2022,[4] seven female members of Labour's NEC together with five female members of Labour's National Women's Committee wrote a letter of complaint to General Secretary David Evans that made its way into *The Guardian*. 'Trying to persuade women to sign NDAs to cover up abuse is a gross betrayal of Labour values', they protested.[5]

The second condition of the settlement was that the three staffers would need to indemnify the party against any damages arising from the Leaked Report. These could have amounted to potentially millions in claims. An agreement to indemnify would also have been a tacit admission that they had leaked the report, which they denied. The result was that Murray, Hayball, and Robertson decided to simply resign from their jobs in the party. They received no compensation.

One insider with knowledge of the negotiations recalled that McSweeney was also involved in these protracted discussions. The insider claimed that McSweeney had promised that

Murray, Hayball, and Robertson would receive some form of compensation regardless of whether they resigned or accepted a settlement: resignation leading to a three-month salary payment or a settlement leading to a six-month salary payment. Neither offer materialised.

The difference between the Labour Party's treatment of the *Panorama* 'whistleblowers', many of them long-time allies of the Labour Together Project, and the authors of the Leaked Report could not have been starker: the former got generous pay-outs and apologies, while the latter were forced to resign without compensation, despite the party having no hard evidence that they had leaked the report.

MAKING THE PERSONAL POLITICAL

Internal party documents show that senior party officials, including Alex Barros-Curtis, went to considerable lengths to try and bring a case against the authors of the Leaked Report. They oversaw the accessing of private emails and then arguably misled a statutory body, the ICO, about the process. Barros-Curtis was at the time the sole director of Starmer's leadership campaign vehicle, Movement for Another Future Limited. He now sits as an MP.

Staff who had worked on the Leaked Report were required to hand over their laptops for forensic analysis as part of investigations by the party and Stroz Friedberg. Party files show that, on at least one occasion, McSweeney was sent forensic evidence resulting from Stroz Friedberg's investigation of staff laptops. In a May 2020 email to McSweeney, Alex Barros-Curtis wrote, 'Forensics—best to keep to yourself', and attached a file named 'Forensics.zip'. McSweeney was thus being given detailed information from the laptops of the authors of the Leaked Report—a report that had undermined critical aspects of the 'antisemitism crisis' narrative McSweeney himself had been secretly promoting through his work with the Labour Together Project.

On May 19, 2020, the party's key contact at Stroz Friedberg/Aon—Jared Pallett—sent an update by email to Cassie Mathers, Tammi Robson (the Labour staffer in charge of IT issues), and Labour's external lawyer Nick Scott.

Pallett explained that, in the course of searching Karie Murphy's computer, Stroz Friedberg had discovered that she had maintained a personal iCloud email account. Murphy had added the account to her email programme, which meant that the emails were downloaded onto her laptop. They were contained in a single file called a PST—a Microsoft file that 'holds' all messages for a given email account.

Earlier exchanges on a different matter—searches of Hayball's laptop—show that the party was aware that it had only limited legal right to access personal emails; something it would also concede before the ICO, as discussed below. Murphy had also been given explicit assurances by the party that any forensic investigation would not access personal and private information.

These assurances and legal restrictions notwithstanding, an hour after Pallett's email was sent, somebody at Stroz Friedberg/Aon created an Excel spreadsheet that displayed a list of every single email sent and received in Murphy's private email account, along with the dates they were sent, recipients and senders, the subject line, and the names of any attached files (the full text of each email, however, was not sent). It listed 839 emails. Shortly thereafter, Nick Scott emailed Pallett, copying in Mathers, Robinson, and a second Stroz Friedberg/Aon employee. He attached an Excel spreadsheet (named 'KM_InboxList') identifying 136 emails of interest. Scott asked for these emails to be deposited in an online 'lockbox'.

Many of these emails appear to be unconnected to the Leaked Report; some were sent between Murphy and her lawyer Martin Howe and may well have been privileged.

Some weeks later, on June 12, 2020, Mathers wrote to Barros-Curtis with the subject line 'emails of note'. The email referenced Murphy's emails but warned that, 'it goes without saying, but we might need to be careful how these are used/ shared as they are from a personal account. Perhaps we could work out this kink next week if they need to be shared more widely'.

It is not clear precisely what happened behind the scenes, but within a few days, it appears that party officials became concerned about having accessed a personal email account in this way. On June 16, Stroz Friedberg shared its draft final report for comment and discussion. It appears that the party made a number of requests to amend this final report. On June 23, after a round of reviews, Mathers wrote to Pallett asking for certain amendments. She asked for the appendix to the Stroz Friedberg report to be revised to make it 'absolutely clear that we have not searched personal email accounts'. Further exchanges strongly suggest that the party and Aon, despite a desperate search, had not found copies of Murphy's emails on the party server.

In September 2020, the party submitted a lengthy report to the ICO in response to the latter's investigation. The report claimed that

> based on the materials that Stroz was able to access, it appears that there may be further relevant material stored in Ms Murphy's personal email inbox (as hosted on the party's servers). However, the party considered that it did not have a lawful basis under Article 6 GDPR [General Data Protection Regulation] to access Ms Murphy's personal email inbox.

The party coyly pointed out that the ICO had these powers and that it might want to exercise them.

This, of course, was false on two counts. First, the party *had* in fact accessed Murphy's emails, something it now conceded 'it did not have a lawful basis' to do. Second, the emails were *not* hosted on the party's servers, if Aon's investigation was to be believed. They were *only* found on Murphy's laptop.

This is extremely serious stuff. Not only did the party break into and view Murphy's private email inbox, it then appeared to mislead the ICO about what it had done.

CONSTRUCTING A CASE AGAINST THE CARTER RUCK FIVE

The party has never been able to definitively establish who leaked the Leaked Report—and nobody else has either.

In its September 2020 report to the ICO, the party admitted that it was 'probable that the source of the Leaked Report was a cloud account or system not owned by the Labour Party' and that Stroz Friedberg/Aon 'did not have access to, or visibility of, the contents of these third-party accounts'. Put more simply, the party found no email or phone exchange showing the Leaked Report being given to a journalist or third party.

Morag Slater came to much the same conclusion. The party's report to the ICO noted that Slater had provided a report on July 31 that had been further amended in August. After interviewing sixteen different people and reviewing documents given to her by the party, 'Ms Slater concluded that it was not possible to discern any prima facie case of wrongdoing on the part of any employee'. The party told the ICO that it rejected Slater's findings in part because she had failed to share materials with the party as her investigation was ongoing. The party neglected to acknowledge that Slater had put this protocol in place to ensure that her investigation was not tainted by rumours and leaks.

Now that two independent investigations had failed to come up with the desired result, the party told the ICO that it 'decided to place all the evidence in the hands of an internal officer, in the shape of Joseph Perry (head of human resources), with a view to him considering that evidence afresh'. Perry had already defended Simon Mills in relation to the *openDemocracy* letter, as described above. Perry's investigation reached a conclusion much more to the party's liking:

> Mr Perry has now considered these matters and has reached the firm view that: the evidence before the party established a good prima facie case sufficient to justify the commencement of disciplinary proceedings against Ms Robertson, Ms Murray and Mr Hayball. These individuals will now accordingly be charged.

Draft versions of the party's submission to the ICO show that one of the reasons it initiated disciplinary proceedings was in the hope that these would unearth evidence that could assist the party's ICO submission:

> As has been noted above, the party commenced a disciplinary process against Ms Robertson, Ms Murray and Mr Hayball. The party takes the view that further relevant evidence may be thrown up by this process. It intends to update the ICO as is appropriate in all the circumstances with respect to this process.

This text was deleted in the party's final submission to the ICO. Plausibly this was because it amounted to a plan to use an internal disciplinary process to squeeze out evidence the party could use to defend itself in the ICO's investigation. Questions would then certainly have had to be asked about whether this motive may have influenced the party's approach to the three young staffers.

The party subsequently argued that certain documents it had seen showed that people with access to the Leaked Report had also briefed the media. This claim was based almost entirely on evidence provided by Patrick Heneghan.

In June 2020, Heneghan had given the party a document called 'Two Groups', which he claimed had been circulated to the media. Heneghan claimed that 'Two Groups' had been given to a journalist who then passed it on to a person known to Heneghan. 'Two Groups' included text that also appeared in the Leaked Report. The inference was then drawn that the author of 'Two Groups' could only have been one of the authors of the Leaked Report, which then 'proved' that authors of the Leaked Report must have been behind its leaking.

The party's reliance on Heneghan's evidence was problematic for many reasons. One of the most notable was that, when Heneghan provided 'Two Groups' to the party, he identified two individuals as having given that document to the media. These two individuals were not among the five authors of the Leaked Report.

Equally notable was that the party itself had reached the view that Heneghan was an unreliable source and witness. In late 2020, the party bureaucracy composed a dossier and complaints report for consideration by the NEC, with a recommendation that Heneghan's case be referred up to the NCC. The report to the NEC, which integrated comments from an independent lawyer who reviewed the case, noted that 'serious concerns regarding the respondent's credibility as a witness have been raised due to various actions and statements from him that give an impression of opacity and contradiction, which may render his account somewhat unreliable'.

The Labour Party's inferential legal case, made in the absence of any compelling forensic or other evidence, thus rested almost entirely on a document—'Two Groups'—supplied by a witness whom the party itself considered 'unreliable'. Furthermore, the people identified by that witness as having distributed 'Two Groups' were not among the five individuals the party eventually tried to blame.

In late 2022, the party's case was dealt a further blow when the ICO informed Murray, Hayball, and Robertson that it was closing its investigation into the matter. The ICO had effectively determined that there was insufficient evidence to initiate proceedings. This determination meant that *three* investigations—Stroz Friedberg, Morag Slater, and the ICO—had independently tried and failed to identify who leaked the Leaked Report.

Alas, this consensus finding did not stop the party pursuing Hayball, Murray, Robertson, Milne, and Murphy, who, as noted, became collectively known as the 'Carter Ruck Five' after the law firm that represented them.

The Carter Ruck Five were put through two court cases. One (described above) was filed by LAAS members who argued that their identification in the Leaked Report had caused them harm for which they were due compensation.

In response, the party asserted that the Carter Ruck Five were responsible for the leak and that, if the Labour Party lost its case against LAAS, the Carter Ruck Five should be liable for the damages. This additional claim (known as a 'Part 20' application) followed the same narrative as set out in the ICO report, except this time it acknowledged that Karie Murphy's emails *had* been accessed from her computer. Regardless, the party failed to get an email it wanted to use admitted to proceedings, as it was legally privileged, having been exchanged between Murphy and her lawyer. The failed attempt to admit this document, conducted almost as a trial-within-a-trial, led to an adverse costs order of £90,000 against the party and murmured disquiet from unnamed NEC members to *The Guardian*.[6]

In September 2023, as public pressure mounted over the legal costs incurred by the party, it was announced that LAAS had withdrawn its case—it is not clear if some form of settlement was reached. 'We are grateful to have had the opportunity to have met with members of Labour Against Antisemitism to discuss their concerns and to thank them for all their work in challenging antisemitism', the party said in a statement.

The party made no comment about how LAAS had targeted left-wing Jews and been advised by a man convicted of 'harassing and bullying' behaviour toward a Palestinian activist, or about the tendency of the group's spokesperson, Euan Philipps, to cosplay as 'David Gordstein'. Philipps remains a spokesperson of LAAS as of August 2025, according to his 'X' profile.

But the settlement with LAAS did not end the proceedings. Instead, the party opted to continue its Part 20 claim, keeping the Carter Ruck Five in its legal crosshairs, presumably in an attempt to recoup the costs incurred by the party in the litigation to that point.

The case was eventually resolved in June 2024, soon after the general election was announced. The party stayed its case against the Carter Ruck Five, with both parties agreeing to swallow their legal bills.

It is not known precisely how much the party spent on this case, but it was likely in the millions—all to pursue individuals against whom it had no solid forensic evidence and even as it simultaneously spent vast sums paying off people identified in the Leaked Report as engaging in prima facie misconduct. As the party's head of legal affairs, Alex Barros-Curtis played an important role in these arguably calamitous decisions. What's more, as this book now reveals, Barros-Curtis' behaviour during the litigation process was positively outrageous.

On April 8, 2022, with the Carter Ruck Five case ongoing, Barros-Curtis wrote to the party's former general secretary Jennie Formby. He did not copy anyone else into the message. Barros-Curtis explained that he was writing to her in the context of the ICO's investigation into the party and the Part 20 application. He indicated that 'we are now required to gather witness statements from certain individuals, including yourself, given you were general secretary at the time'.

'The party, and the court, has now received the reply of the five former members of staff', Barros-Curtis wrote, referencing the Carter Ruck Five. 'You may be aware that within that reply, they allege that the leak of the report was in fact authorised by the party's leadership at the time, and that they were acting under those instructions'.

This was entirely false. The Carter Ruck Five had never claimed this in their defence—not least because their defence was that they had no idea who had leaked the report, never mind whether it was authorised by any other party.

This is extremely serious. Solicitors are held to a high standard and are expected to conduct themselves honestly in their dealings with all parties involved in litigation. Furthermore, Barros-Curtis now sits as a member of parliament. It is imperative that his conduct is properly investigated by the Solicitors Regulation Authority—not least because, as the next section shows, Barros-Curtis' conduct on another important and politically sensitive legal case also warrants serious scrutiny.

CHAPTER 11

TRAVESTY—THE EHRC REPORT AND THE STARMER PROJECT

On October 29, 2020, the Equality and Human Rights Commission published its report on antisemitism in the Labour Party. The report found the party responsible for unlawful harassment by two officials and also concluded that two of the party's policies or practices had amounted to unlawful indirect discrimination. These findings related to the period when Labour was led by Jeremy Corbyn. His successor, Keir Starmer, addressed the country in the wake of the report's publication. It was, he said, a 'day of shame'.[1]

Not one to be beaten in hyperbole, Jonathan Ashworth MP—the husband of senior McNicol staffer Emilie Oldknow, whose constituency had been selected to receive funds by the McNicol bureaucracy in the pre-Ergon House period—claimed that it was, in fact, the most shameful moment in Labour history: presumably even worse than the 2003 Iraq War and other crimes of the 'war on terror' that had ended hundreds of thousands of lives.[2]

Starmer announced that he accepted the EHRC report 'without qualification': 'We have failed Jewish people. Our members. Our supporters. And the British public. And so: on behalf of the Labour Party: I am truly sorry for all the pain that has been caused'.[3]

Within hours of Starmer's speech and the release of the EHRC report, the party would be thrown into crisis. Jeremy Corbyn would be suspended, triggering a Labour civil war. This eventually resulted in the decimation of the Labour left and the introduction of authoritarian rules that shackled debate and democracy in the party. Tens if not hundreds of thousands of party members left in disgust, while the party bureaucracy under the control of McSweeney, Evans, Barros-Curtis, and others made cynical use of the crisis to salt the earth and purge opponents.

But the Starmer Project was not merely happy to capitalise on the EHRC report—it did not simply exploit with typical opportunism an event not of its making. In fact, Starmer's bureaucracy had played an active and critical role in *creating* this political moment—by accepting the EHRC's patently incorrect findings and, at a critical juncture, withdrawing a key element of the (factually accurate) defence previously mounted by the Corbyn leadership.

POLITICISATION OF THE EHRC

The EHRC is a political animal. It is headed by a board of commissioners selected by the minister for women and equalities. Since 2010, that minister has been a Tory appointee.

As the EHRC was investigating antisemitism in Labour, the Muslim Council of Britain (MCB) submitted to the EHRC a dossier evidencing three hundred instances of alleged Islamophobia in the Conservative Party. The MCB's allegations closely mirrored those that had prompted the EHRC's investigation of Labour. But in May 2020, the EHRC announced that it would not open an inquiry into the Tories, who had committed to conduct their own investigation.[4] The Tory 'investigation' descended into farce when its report was ignored by the party leadership—without a single public word of criticism from the EHRC.

The EHRC has also been accused of discrimination itself. In October 2023, a former senior EHRC official, Preeti Kathrecha, sued the organisation, alleging unfair dismissal and racial discrimination.[5] Kathrecha, who left the EHRC in July 2021, further alleged in her witness statement that the regulator had become politicised as 'the board increasingly acted as an agent of the Conservative government and against parties or organisations which the government were opposed to . . . It is being used as a political weapon in a cultural race war'.[6]

This last reference to the EHRC's investigation into the Labour Party was oblique but obvious to anyone listening, not least because Kathrecha also alleged that she had been asked to sign off on the Executive Summary of the EHRC's Labour report without being shown any of the underlying evidence. She found that experience 'humiliating'.[7] Kathrecha would later withdraw her case.

Alasdair Henderson was the lead commissioner who oversaw the EHRC's investigation into the Labour Party. Henderson was appointed as a commissioner in April 2018 by Conservative minister Amber Rudd. He was reappointed in December 2022 by Kemi Badenoch (the Tory minister for women and equalities) and elevated to the position of joint deputy chair.

Henderson played an important role in the media reporting on the EHRC report. The EHRC report did not make a direct finding of unlawful conduct against Corbyn specifically, referring more broadly to alleged failings by Labour's 'leadership' (a phrase it never defined). But when the report was released, Henderson provided the quote that came to define the EHRC's findings: 'as the leader of the party at the time, and given the extent of the failings we found in the political interference within the leader of the opposition's office, Jeremy Corbyn is ultimately accountable and responsible for what happened at the time'.[8] This went substantially further than what the EHRC report actually said.

A month after the EHRC's report was released, *The Guardian* published embarrassing details of Henderson's social media conduct. Henderson was found to have 'liked' a range of unpleasant content on Twitter, including posts that dismissed 'homophobia' and 'Islamophobia' as 'propaganda terms'. He had also 'liked' content defending Roger Scruton, a controversial philosopher accused of antisemitism for his comments about George Soros and Hungary.[9] Henderson's Twitter account, since deleted, also showed that Henderson 'liked' and shared posts critical of Corbyn. The EHRC told *The Guardian* in response to this article that it would 'look into' Henderson's use of social media.[10] But in response to an FOI request submitted for this book, the EHRC refused to answer whether Henderson ever faced any disciplinary consequences.

Previously unreleased emails show that the Labour Party in the Corbyn period, and in particular its internal counsel Gordon Nardell, were taken aback by the EHRC's approach, which they found inexplicably aggressive.

In June 2019, for example, the EHRC asked the party for

> copies of any emails, WhatsApp or any other electronic communication relating to or referring to a complaint, whether made by official party emails, WhatsApp groups or otherwise. Electronic communications using personal, parliamentary or other emails or WhatsApp groups should also be included, e.g. those related to a union.

When the party responded with shock to this wide request, the EHRC refused to relent and instructed the party to contact specific individuals who would be ordered to preserve this sort of evidence. They listed thirteen names, amongst them Jeremy Corbyn and Gordon Nardell himself. Strikingly, the EHRC did *not* request any communications from the right-wing bureaucrats who had run the party for two years—*not even Iain McNicol, the party's general secretary for two of the four years that the EHRC was investigating.*

Perhaps unsurprisingly, and as shown below, the EHRC's zealous desire to pore through every WhatsApp group and delve into every nook and cranny of the Labour Party would suddenly evaporate when the Leaked Report identified evidence that threw into turmoil the established media narrative around the 'antisemitism crisis'—and with it, the EHRC's own investigation.

NONE SO BLIND

The EHRC is a strange and uniquely hybrid legal entity. Unlike a court of law, which adjudicates between parties, the EHRC is responsible for identifying whether there is suspicion of a crime, investigating it, and then coming to a judgment. In law enforcement terms, this effectively combines the roles of detective, prosecutor, and judge into one office. Such expansive authority confers a particular responsibility on the EHRC to conduct good faith inquiries that gather and examine all the evidence relevant to its proceedings.

In the case of its investigation into the Labour Party, however, the EHRC repeatedly blinded itself to crucial evidence. In its determination to ignore such evidence, the EHRC had an important ally: Starmer's Labour Party.

Two decisions encapsulate the EHRC's approach in this regard. The first related to the Leaked Report. The EHRC acknowledged the Leaked Report but claimed that 'it was not proportionate for us to require the Labour Party to provide the evidence underlying' it.[11] As a result, the EHRC never reviewed the substantial documentary evidence collected in support of the Leaked Report's allegations, many of which related directly to the EHRC's investigation.

Elsewhere in its report, the EHRC made a slightly different claim: 'the Labour Party informed us that it would be disproportionate and too onerous to provide this material to us'.[12] These variations were never reconciled; it was thus not clear from the

Commission's report whether the EHRC independently decided that it was not 'proportionate' to ask for the evidence underpinning the Leaked Report, or whether it simply agreed with the Labour Party's claim in this regard.

In fact, the Leaked Report was assiduously and comprehensively footnoted with evidence. Every footnoted source corresponded to an underlying electronic file. Each file had been meticulously placed in thematic folders and given a consistent naming convention. Providing this evidence to the Commission would not have been 'onerous'; it would have been extremely easy. In fact, it would have taken all of a few minutes to save the neatly tagged folders and carefully dated files onto a flash disk.

There are grave questions to ask as to why the EHRC determined it was not proportionate to ask Starmer's Labour Party for such manifestly pertinent material in the wake of the Leaked Report, when it had not long before made an extraordinarily wide discovery request to the Labour Party under Corbyn, which specifically singled out WhatsApp records as material of interest. Why the EHRC thought that it needed to see the WhatsApp messages of Corbyn-aligned staff, but none of the vast quantity of emails and WhatsApp messages sent by the likes of Matthews and McNicol and revealed in the Leaked Report, needs some serious explanation.

The EHRC's frustratingly ambiguous phrasing means that important questions about what role the Starmer leadership played in the EHRC's decision not to examine the evidence underpinning the Leaked Report remain unanswered. Whereas the EHRC said that the party had argued that it was not proportionate for it to provide the EHRC with such materials, the EHRC did not say *when* the party had communicated this. This was important: Recall that in June 2019 the party had baulked at the EHRC's wide request for all sorts of personal communications; the party specifically objected that it would not be proportionate to provide these. Was *this* communication what the EHRC was relying on when it said the party had taken this view?[13] Or did the EHRC reach out to the party subsequent to the Leaked Report, only to be rebuffed once again on the same grounds?

This might seem like fine-grained minutiae, but it has profound implications. If the EHRC was relying on Labour's June 2019 refusals, this would suggest that, in fact, the EHRC made no attempt to access materials referenced in the Leaked Report after its publication. It would also raise serious questions about the EHRC's attention to detail, as the materials appearing in the Leaked Report had not in fact been previously requested by the EHRC; the EHRC, remember, had remarkably decided *not* to ask for any personal communications from the likes of McNicol and Heneghan, whereas the Leaked Report quoted from these extensively. But if the EHRC relied instead on a letter of refusal dating from after the Leaked Report's publication, when Labour was led by Starmer rather than Corbyn, questions would have to be asked about why both the new Labour leadership and the EHRC were so keen to avoid new disclosures. My questions to the EHRC on this matter, asking for clarification, went unanswered.

In the end, the EHRC claimed that it had taken the Leaked Report 'into account where appropriate', even though 'we have not seen all of the evidence on which the conclusions in the leaked report were based'.[14] This was an astonishing admission: it would rely on a report whose evidence it had decided not to verify. On any version, this was slapdash and incomprehensible.

As it turned out, the EHRC appeared to refer to the Leaked Report primarily when it could effectively cherry-pick evidence that reflected poorly on the Labour Party under Corbyn. In total, the EHRC report made fourteen references to the Leaked Report, half of which were about why it had failed to access the underlying evidence. On the other occasions, it relied on fragments of the Leaked Report, choosing extracts that supported its findings and arguably neglecting crucial context.

One example was when the EHRC attempted to argue that Labour officials might have engaged in extensive informal discussions about the handling of individual complaints.

It could not point to any evidence it had seen that documented such discussions. Instead it observed that 'the Leaked Report referred to "thousands of messages exchanged on . . . an internal party messaging service" and 465,000 words in three WhatsApp groups'. If the Leaked Report was accurate on this point, then, the EHRC archly opined, 'it fundamentally undermines confidence in the fairness of the antisemitism complaint handling process'.

Alas, without further explanation or investigation, this inference drawn by the EHRC was virtually meaningless. What was the significance of 'thousands of messages' and '465,000 words' unless the EHRC knew what proportion of these, if any, had referred to complaints handling? Clearly, if the EHRC wanted to reach this finding in good faith, it should have made at least some attempt to find out what those alleged messages concerned.

In fact, the most cursory review of the two infamous WhatsApp chats would show that the vast bulk of the discussion had nothing whatsoever to do with antisemitism complaints. A search through the SMT group, for example, reveals that the word 'antisemitism' or a derivation thereof appeared precisely twice across many months. The same group made only two passing references to Jackie Walker, one of the more famous and controversial cases of alleged antisemitism. Ken Livingstone, another famous alleged case, was referred to seven times; most of these references consisted of quotes from news stories where he was mentioned.

The EHRC was also not minded to mention a crucial bit of context: the WhatsApp groups where these 'informal' discussions were assumed to have taken place (but which the EHRC did not bother to investigate) had been set up by the McNicol bureaucracy, which was not only hostile to LOTO but which spent much of its time actively ignoring and sneering at LOTO's suggestions.

This discussion was, as an aside, typical of the EHRC's approach to selectively naming and identifying officials. The report frequently notes that the Labour Party substantially improved the way it handled antisemitism complaints from 2018 onward, in effect confirming the primary underlying narrative of the Leaked Report. This improvement followed the dismissal of Iain McNicol as general secretary and his replacement by Formby, who was sympathetic to the Corbyn project and who radically shook up the party's inadequate complaints processes. But the EHRC made no attempt to recognise this fact or to acknowledge that the primary issues it tackled arose during the McNicol leadership. Indeed, even though McNicol was general secretary for fully half of the period the EHRC investigated, he was not mentioned once by name in the EHRC report. By contrast, Formby—his successor as general secretary, who by the EHRC's own account oversaw improvements in Labour's complaints system—was mentioned more than thirty times.

The EHRC's second decision to ignore evidence was perhaps even more egregious. Records show that on February 20, 2020, eight months prior to the EHRC concluding its investigation, ten Labour staff members had asked the party's lawyer, Gerald Shamash, to write to the EHRC. The ten staff members had not been interviewed by the EHRC and wanted to give evidence relevant to its inquiry. Some of these ten officials had direct experience handling antisemitism complaints and with the bureaucracy in general.

A week later, on February 27, 2020, Stephen Lodge, a senior principal lawyer in the Enforcement Team of the EHRC, responded to the request. 'You indicate your clients, 10 named Labour Party staff, may have useful evidence for the investigation and enquire whether we intend to approach them collectively or individually', Lodge wrote. 'We thank your clients for their willingness to assist the investigation. However, we do not consider it necessary to request information, documents or evidence in your client's possession'.

This letter is, without hyperbole, an outrage. Ten staff working with or near to the complaints processes in the Labour Party had requested to give evidence to the EHRC. The EHRC made no attempt to establish what evidence these ten individuals might have had and whether it might have been relevant to its investigation. The EHRC just rejected the request out of hand, as it refused point-blank to gather the evidence.

TRAVESTY

The EHRC's investigation looked at three issues: how the party handled complaints; whether the party's training was adequate to enable party staff to handle complaints effectively; and whether any 'agents' of the party had made its Jewish members uncomfortable or threatened their dignity, in a manner that could be construed as harassment.

The EHRC found that the party had committed unlawful 'indirect discrimination' through its 'policy' of political interference by LOTO in complaints and by neglecting to adequately train staff responsible for complaints handling. The EHRC also accused the party of unlawful 'harassment' because two party 'agents' had made statements that were detrimental to the dignity and comfort of people of 'Jewish ethnicity'. Specifically, the two 'agents'—NEC member Ken Livingstone and a local councillor named Pam Bromley—had committed harassment because they had articulated 'antisemitic tropes' and had suggested that allegations of antisemitism were 'fake or smears'.

Importantly, Bromley's case had already attracted McSweeney's attention back in 2019. Complaints against her had been reported in the press, with much coverage focused on how long it was taking the party to deal with them. According to Pogrund and Maguire, McSweeney had 'helped to orchestrate' reporting on this issue in *The Sunday Times*.[15] The precise reporting that McSweeney 'helped to orchestrate' is not disclosed, nor is the manner of the orchestration. A review of the *Times* and *Sunday Times* archive shows that the papers reported twice on Bromley's case: once in April 2018 when it noted that LAAS had complained about her, and again in April 2019 when it reported that she had returned to the party after serving a suspension.[16]

The latter article was jointly written by Richard Kerbaj and one Gabriel Pogrund, both of whom had worked on the 'hate factory' article that McSweeney and Ahmed had helped place in *The Sunday Times* in April 2018.

Bromley would formally complain about the April 2019 article—written jointly by Kerbaj and Pogrund—to the media regulator IPSO. That article reported that Bromley had accused Prime Minister Theresa May of having orchestrated the Manchester Arena bombing as a 'handy excuse to squash Jeremy Corbyn's support'. Bromley denied that her words could be used to draw that implication. IPSO agreed to mediate the dispute. Although *The Sunday Times* did not admit wrongdoing to IPSO, a resolution was eventually reached after *The Sunday Times* published a 'correction': 'Ms Bromley did not allege that May plotted the bombing, only that it provided her with a "convenient excuse" to deploy troops. We apologise for the error'.[17] We saw above that Stop Funding Fake News had cited the successful resolution of an Impress investigation into *The Canary* as evidence that *The Canary* was 'fake news'. One wonders what SFFN would have to say about the resolution of Bromley's complaint against *The Sunday Times*, regarding an article that McSweeney had helped to orchestrate, also resolved through mediation with a media regulator.

Returning to the EHRC: its findings in respect of the Labour Party were riddled with legal contortions and factual errors. The party was held responsible for unlawful harassment because of statements made by Livingstone and Bromley that constituted 'unwanted conduct related to Jewish ethnicity' and had 'the purpose or effect of violating the dignity of one or more Labour Party members, or creat[ing] an intimidating, hostile, degrading, humiliating or offensive environment for them'.[18] The EHRC held Labour responsible for these statements because it found that Livingstone and Bromley were 'agents' of the party.

The idea of an 'agent' did heavy lifting in the EHRC's investigation. An agent was defined by the EHRC as 'someone who has authorised functions or duties on behalf of an association, but is not a worker employed by it, even if there is no formal contract between them'.[19] The EHRC clarified that a person was an 'agent' of the Labour Party if they 'carried out authorised functions' and had 'some authority to represent the Labour Party in relation to third parties'.[20]

The EHRC confirmed that there is no 'reasonable steps' defence for agents. In simple terms, this meant that the party could not avoid a finding of harassment on the grounds that it had, for example, made antisemitism an expellable offence and repeatedly issued statements condemning antisemitism. The party, in short, could mount no defence *at all* against the charge that it was legally responsible for statements by Livingstone and Bromley. This was because of a quirk in the law, which one judge has called an 'anomaly', that permitted a 'reasonable steps' defence to be used in relation to employees but not to agents.[21] The result was that, if Livingstone and Bromley had been employed by the party, the party could have mounted a defence; their lack of remuneration erased this possibility. This application of the law skirted close to violating principles of natural justice, finding the party guilty on a charge against which it could offer no defence (other than by arguing that the conduct was not antisemitic), and which it was accused of implicitly authorising even though the party's rule book made it clear that people could be expelled for conduct that was grossly detrimental to the party, and that the party was opposed to racism and discrimination of all kinds.

The EHRC report was held up by many commentators as vindicating claims that antisemitism had become widespread in the Labour Party under Corbyn. The EHRC report did not make this finding. On the contrary, one interesting implication of the EHRC's approach was that its findings actually revealed how *little* antisemitism there was. The EHRC took an enormously broad approach to identifying agents; it was also happy to find people guilty of antisemitism on the basis of implicit 'trope'-based discourse and, in the case of Bromley, questioning the scale of antisemitism in the party. And yet, despite its wide definition of party 'agents' and its expansive understanding of the term 'antisemitism', the EHRC's multi-year investigation was only able to unearth just *two* supposed agents who allegedly breached this very low threshold of offence. The point bears repeating: national media coverage suggested that the party was riddled with antisemitic officials, councillors, and representatives, and yet the EHRC, after an exhaustive trawl, turned up a handful of supposedly unlawful statements by all of two individuals.

But the problems don't end there. The EHRC's findings were not just based on a questionable application of the law. In the case of Bromley, the findings were also factually incorrect.

The EHRC found Bromley guilty based on statements she had posted online between April 8, 2018, and December 15, 2019. Almost all of her comments quoted by the EHRC (bar one) were to the effect that the Labour 'antisemitism crisis' was exaggerated or politically motivated—a claim that was at least arguable and which our new knowledge of the Labour Together Project's undisclosed work has further strengthened, not least because it was McSweeney, running his covert projects to destroy Corbynism with his pot of unlawfully undeclared funds, who had 'helped to orchestrate' the reporting on Bromley in *The Sunday Times*.

Bromley had been suspended from the Labour Party on April 4, 2018, and expelled in February 2020.[22] This means that at the time Bromley made the posts referenced by the EHRC, she was suspended from the Labour Party. The EHRC's report recognised this fact and also acknowledged that '[i]f a member is suspended while they are under investigation, they cannot stand as a candidate in any election or represent the Party in any position while the suspension is in place'.[23]

The conclusion is inescapable: Bromley was *not* an 'agent' of the party at the time she made the relevant comments because she was suspended. This means the EHRC found the Labour Party guilty of unlawful harassment because of the conduct of an alleged 'agent' who the EHRC itself acknowledged could not in fact 'represent the party in any position'.

Media coverage of the EHRC report was silent on the potentially profound and far-reaching implications of its findings on all aspects of British public life. The EHRC had determined that organisations could be held legally responsible for the conduct of their 'agents' and that organisations could mount no defence. It also construed 'agents' extremely broadly. This had enormous legal implications for a huge range of organisations, from rotary clubs or church hall associations to the Tory party—if the EHRC ever bothered to mount an investigation.

It is hard to overstate the importance of this finding to Labour and, in turn, national politics. As we will see in future chapters, the party would cite the EHRC's findings to argue that it needed to aggressively vet candidates for office because the implication of these findings was that the Labour Party would be liable if any of its elected representatives ever said anything that breached equalities law, and that the party could not mount any 'reasonable steps' defence.

The EHRC's finding that Bromley had committed unlawful harassment by disputing the scale of antisemitism in the party was a clear warning: no scepticism towards the mainstream narrative about an 'antisemitism crisis' would be permitted. This despite abundant evidence that such scepticism was warranted—like, for example, the role played by Labour Together and SFFN in inflaming the 'antisemitism crisis' through secret astroturf fronts, or non-Jewish campaigners' repeated complaints of antisemitism against left-wing Jews (in one case while using a Jewish-sounding pseudonym). The EHRC attempted, in effect, to codify into law the crime of 'denialism': a concept introduced in this context by the wretched and politically slanted work of the Labour Together Project and SFFN.

The party would apply the EHRC's findings with a characteristic factional bias, almost exclusively targeting left-wing members while ignoring problematic statements from the right. But it was the EHRC that gave the Starmer Project what amounted to a factional weapon in the first place: a tool that would inevitably be used to insulate the party's factionally motivated selections from legal or even political challenge and to justify its purge of left-wing and even soft-left party members.

Serious questions must be asked about why the Labour Party under Starmer accepted the EHRC's findings, especially in relation to Bromley. They were obviously nonsense. The Labour Party could only have accepted the findings if it did not apply its mind to the report or else decided that accepting incorrect findings was politically opportune. Or perhaps it was a combination of both: the party's inattention to detail arose because the findings drove another nail in the coffin of Corbynism.

POLITICAL INTERFERENCE

Just like its finding of unlawful harassment, the EHRC's conclusion that 'political interference' in complaints handling by Corbyn's leadership office had indirectly discriminated against Jews was riddled with logical inconsistencies and factual errors. The Starmer bureaucracy should have rejected and challenged this finding but endorsed it instead.

The EHRC defined political interference in complaints handling as 'people influencing the decision-making process or taking decisions outside of established processes'.[24] Under this definition, the very same action either would or would not breach the law depending on what a party's rule book provided. If the Labour Party rule book had only *permitted* LOTO to directly decide all complaints, then, according to the EHRC's definition, such intervention would no longer breach the Equality Act. Indeed, the Tory rule book *does* allow the political leadership to intervene in complaints handling, and so Boris Johnson or Rishi Sunak becoming involved to discipline a rival would not constitute unlawful 'political interference', according to the EHRC. The EHRC's definition clearly muddled up form, function, and content to produce an absurd result.

The EHRC then reviewed the party's complaints handling processes and rules. These were described in granular detail in

Chapter Four of the EHRC's report. The EHRC determined that 'LOTO staff do not have a role in complaint handling under the Labour Party's published complaints process'.

Next, the EHRC determined that Corbyn's LOTO had intervened in antisemitism complaints. It claimed to have found twenty-three examples of LOTO interference. It placed particular emphasis on the period between March and April 2018, when LOTO staff frequently gave opinions on individual cases.

As the Leaked Report, the Forde Report, and other evidence has made clear, where LOTO did intervene in antisemitism complaints, it did so largely in order to *speed up* the processing of complaints or to urge that members be investigated. LOTO involvement was *not*, as has been frequently implied, primarily directed at defending allies of Corbyn's leadership. When the EHRC discussed this period in its critique of Corbyn's leadership, it cited two examples when LOTO had 'interfered' in antisemitism complaints involving left-wing members. In both cases, including that of Ken Livingstone, LOTO staff had advised either the immediate suspension of the accused or for the disciplinary process to proceed apace.[25]

But for the EHRC, the reason, intent, and effect of 'political interference' was immaterial. The very act of interference, the EHRC found, would make Jewish members who complained to the party uncertain as to whether the process was unfair or tainted in some way. And because Jewish members were proportionately more likely to complain about antisemitism, 'political interference in antisemitism complaints, and in "politically sensitive" complaints generally, put Jewish members at a particular disadvantage compared to non-Jewish members'.[26] This was considered to be a form of indirect discrimination, an unlawful act.

What the EHRC had found was that Jewish people had been indirectly discriminated against when LOTO had intervened to *speed up* the suspension, expulsion, or disciplining of people accused of antisemitism.

This finding is particularly striking in light of an email that has never previously seen the light of day. On January 20, 2017,

Philip Rosenberg wrote to Jayne Fisher and Laura Parker. Parker and Fisher worked in LOTO: Fisher as stakeholder manager and Parker as Corbyn's personal political secretary. Rosenberg was director of public affairs at the Board of Deputies of British Jews. His email was sent from a Board of Deputies address and featured his Board of Deputies email signature. He was also a Labour Party councillor in Hampstead and Kilburn. He is, at the time of writing, the president of the Board of Deputies of British Jews, which has repeatedly defended Israel's conduct in Gaza, as discussed in Chapter 23.

Rosenberg wrote that, in light of other cases, 'there is now growing concern in Jewish and wider circles that this might lead to Ken Livingstone and Jackie Walker being readmitted. This would be of course be [*sic*] really damaging, and anything that the Leader's Office can do to prevent this would be very helpful'.

Rosenberg did not ask for any specific intervention. But per the reasoning adopted in the EHRC report, *anything* that LOTO could have done to act on Rosenberg's request would have been considered political interference. With this email in mind, the EHRC's findings against the party can be helpfully refined: the Labour Party was found guilty of unlawfully discriminating against Jews because LOTO had 'interfered' in disciplinary cases—a course of action that had implicitly been requested from LOTO by the Board of Deputies of British Jews.

There is a further irony to the Rosenberg story. Rosenberg was one of the 'talking heads' who appeared in John Ware's *Panorama* documentary, which had also made the allegation that LOTO had unduly interfered in antisemitism complaints. There is no evidence that Ware knew of Rosenberg's email, but it did mean that Ware's documentary alleging interference by LOTO in complaints included a man who, on behalf of the Board of Deputies, had directly asked LOTO to interfere. In yet another twist, Rosenberg had come to believe that party staff had mishandled his own complaint of antisemitism against a member who allegedly compared him to a Nazi. Who was the investigating officer in his case, guilty of this purported mishandling? None other than heroic 'whistleblower' Ben Westerman—another of Ware's key witnesses.

The logical errors in the EHRC's finding of political interference were glaring, but the most important problem was that the EHRC's determination was factually incorrect. It was incorrect because, despite the EHRC's statements to the contrary, the party rule book made it abundantly clear that the leader's office had a wide remit to investigate and formulate charges in individual complaints. This is established at Clause I, Paragraph A of Chapter Six, helpfully titled 'Disciplinary Rules'. This clause appeared in every party rule book between 2016 and 2020, spanning the entire period of the EHRC's investigation. It provided that:

> In relation to any alleged breach of the constitution, rules or standing orders of the party by an individual member or members of the party, the NEC may, pending the final outcome of any investigation and charges (if any), suspend that individual or individuals from office or representation of the party notwithstanding the fact that the individual concerned has been or may be eligible to be selected as a candidate in any election or by-election. The general secretary **or other national officer** shall investigate and report to the NEC on such investigation. Upon such report being submitted, the NEC may instruct the general secretary **or other national officer** to formulate charges against the individual or individuals concerned and present such charges to the NCC for determination in accordance with their applicable procedures. *(emphases mine)*

Translated from legalese, the initial part of this clause provides that the NEC 'may' suspend somebody while an investigation into an alleged rule breach takes place. This is what is often referred to as an 'administrative suspension'. But the wording here is key: the text says the NEC 'may' do this, not that it 'must' do so. The NEC can exercise its discretion about whether it suspends somebody in this manner or not. Importantly, the NEC can decide whether to suspend while an investigation takes place, the result being that somebody doesn't have to be suspended in order to be investigated.

The second part of this clause, however, is not permissive but prescriptive. It provides not that something *may* be done, but that something *must* be done: 'The general secretary or other national officer shall investigate and report to the NEC on such investigation'. The word 'shall' in that sentence means the specified action is required, not discretionary. If there is a rule breach, therefore, the only thing that *must* follow is an investigation whose findings are reported to the NEC.

This investigation in turn *must* ('shall') be performed by the general secretary or any other 'national officer'. Importantly, the rule book does not say the alleged rule breach must be referred to the general secretary or other 'national officer' by any other person; simply that, once the party or its officers learn of it (through some undefined and undisclosed way, including, presumably, learning about it through the media), the party *must* investigate, and that investigation *must* be undertaken by either the general secretary or some other 'national officer'.

Who qualifies as a 'national officer'? Chapter Four of the party rule book (in particular Clause II, Paragraph 2) stipulates that the party has a number of 'national officers'. One of those 'national officers' is the 'leader' of Labour Party.

So once the party learns that somebody may have broken the party's rules, the NEC can decide whether to suspend that person, pending the results of an investigation. However, that person *must* be investigated, and that investigation *must* be undertaken by a party officer, such as the general secretary or *the party leader.*

In other words, not only does Labour's rule book not *prohibit* LOTO involvement in complaints, but on the contrary, it *demands* that the party leader or other national officer investigate them. Involvement by the party leader in disciplinary investigations is therefore entirely in line with what the party rule book does not merely permit but mandates—and cannot be considered 'political interference' according to the EHRC's own definition.

This provision of the rule book makes a good deal of practical sense. It ensures that an allegation of wrongdoing must be investigated and not ignored. The results of this investigation must then be reported to the NEC, so that it cannot die with the first officer who investigates it. During this entire period, the NEC can decide whether it wants to suspend the member accused. Again, this is sensible: some allegations may be patently absurd or prima facie trivial, and thus not worth suspending a party member over.

The EHRC's failure to identify and discuss this issue is frankly inexplicable. The party rule book is the apex law of the Labour Party. It forms the binding contract between the party and its members. Everything the party does, and is empowered to do, flows from the rule book. The party rule book provides explicit and detailed rules for handling disciplinary cases and puts them in a separate chapter dedicated to this topic.

But at no stage is this chapter—Chapter Six—of the party rule book on 'Disciplinary Rules' mentioned or referenced by the EHRC. This is astonishing. The EHRC's investigation was, at heart, an investigation of how the party applied its disciplinary rules to the handling of antisemitism complaints, and yet the EHRC made *no reference* to the foundational text that established what those rules were. Not only that, it then *misconstrued* the party's rules in order to ground a finding of unlawful discrimination.

It gets worse. What has not been properly understood or acknowledged is that the EHRC's finding on this point relied on an unforgivable intervention on the part of Starmer's Labour

Party. In its chapter on 'political interference', the EHRC noted that the Labour Party had initially defended LOTO's involvement in complaints. The party argued that LOTO was allowed to be involved and informed of complaints involving MPs, NEC members or where there was 'high reputational risk to the party'. It defended this position by citing the party rule book, noting that this required the leader to 'uphold and enforce the constitution, rules and standing orders of the party and ensure the maintenance and development of an effective political Labour Party in parliament and the country'. This was, in essence, the defence mounted by Corbyn's Labour Party against the charge of political interference.

The EHRC, however, noted that in subsequent 'representations' to it,

> the Labour Party clarified its position. It accepted that the leadership must have no role in determining disciplinary outcomes. It clarified that the leader's duty to 'uphold and enforce the constitution [and] rules . . . of the Party' means that 'the Leader is entitled to involve himself with the disciplinary procedure generally, to ensure it adequately upholds the values of the party, and is effective in its operation'.

Numerous insiders confirmed that at no stage did the Corbyn party machinery ever issue this 'clarification'. It was, in fact, issued by *Starmer's* leadership. This clarification, and the party's acceptance of the report, would almost certainly have been signed off on by David Evans, McSweeney's close personal ally, and Starmer himself.

Corbyn's Labour Party had mounted a defence to the EHRC's findings that was factually accurate. When Starmer took over the reins, the party decided to withdraw this valid defence and substituted, in its place, an effective admission of guilt—for an offence that Corbyn's team did not in fact commit.

CHAPTER 12

THE PURGE LISTS

The EHRC mangled the law and misrepresented the facts to falsely tar the Corbyn movement as antisemitic, with the collaboration of the Starmer leadership. But the role played by Starmer and his team was still more disgraceful in light of their own conduct prior to the EHRC report and what they went on to do only hours after the EHRC report was released—namely, to materially, directly, and repeatedly interfere in the handling of antisemitism complaints.

THE PURGE LISTS

In the early days of Starmer's leadership bid, he went on the BBC to sell his vision for the party. During the show, Starmer was asked about the antisemitism crisis. 'What I would do is I would lead from the top and say it's my responsibility to deal with it', Starmer assured. 'I wouldn't say it's for someone else. I want the files, I want to know the numbers on my desk so that I can monitor this'. His firm conclusion: 'there has to be leadership from the top and a personal involvement in this'.[1] Or, to apply the reasoning of the EHRC, Starmer risked unlawfully discriminating against Jews by politically interfering in antisemitism complaints.

It was plainly a risk he was willing to take.

Files show that, a month after Starmer became leader, both he and his office became personally involved in handling anti-semitism complaints, along with Deputy Leader Angela Rayner and, after his appointment as general secretary, David Evans. Their initial focus was on ensuring that individuals appearing on what were effectively two purge lists were punished and expelled from the party.

The first purge list was sent into the party on May 13, 2020, by none other than Steve Reed MP, a central player in the Labour Together Project. Reed emailed Thomas Gardiner (then head of Labour's Governance and Legal Unit) and Alex Barros-Curtis (then in LOTO), attaching a dossier of evidence against ten individuals. Reed explained that he had received the dossier from an unstated source in his role as shadow secretary for communities and local government. Reed was unambiguous in his request, invoking 'commitments' made by Starmer and Rayner as a source of authority:

> As you will see, the allegations are profoundly worrying and appear highly credible. Given the commitments made by the Leader and Deputy Leader of the Labour Party to act swiftly to eradicate anti-semitism from our party, I trust you will immediately suspend these individuals and institute a formal investigation.

Reed's email acknowledged that he had not generated the evidence himself but that he was forwarding information gathered by others. As GLU began processing the dossier of complaints, GLU staff noticed that the metadata on one of the complaints listed Dave Rich of Community Security Trust as the person who had modified it last. Rich refused to speak to me for this book.

Among the ten individuals on Reed's list were Jenny Manson, David Miller, Ken Loach, Jonathan Rosenhead, Pete Willsman, Glyn Secker, and Mike Cushman. It was a remarkable collection. Four out of the ten individuals accused of antisemitism were Jewish: Jenny Manson, Jonathan Rosenhead, Mike Cushman, and Glyn Secker. All four were also prominent members of Jewish Voice for Labour.

Within an hour, Barros-Curtis was following up on the email with Gardiner and ensuring that the complaints were forwarded immediately to GLU. Barros-Curtis' email emphasised the 'seriousness of what some are saying' and asked, 'what can be done about them?' Gardiner forwarded the complaints to Laura Murray (the head of complaints in GLU, who reported to Gardiner) and asked that the cases be 'prioritised' to determine if the dossiers contained new evidence and whether new action should be taken. Murray, who received the list just before 5:00 p.m., promised to have a response by the next morning.

On May 14, 2020, the day after Reed submitted his purge list, the party received another list of suspects, this time numbering eleven individuals. This list was sent by Phil Rosenberg, public affairs director for the Board of Deputies. Rosenberg, too, had appeared in Ware's *Panorama* documentary as one of its unidentified talking heads—and, as noted above, had written to Corbyn's office in 2017 requesting action to achieve desired outcomes in relation to the Jackie Walker and Ken Livingstone cases.

This time, Rosenberg sent his list of complaints directly to Ellie Robinson, the deputy political director in LOTO. Emails suggest that Rosenberg or somebody else with access to the list had given it to Robinson verbally the day prior to the email—the same day that Reed was submitting his list—and that Robinson had made hand-written notes that misspelled several names. Rosenberg's email acknowledged an earlier discussion and then requested further ongoing updates: 'I would appreciate a conversation with you about when and how we might go about seeing whether and how these cases had been resolved'.

The Board of Deputies briefing demanded nearly instantaneous action. The briefing claimed that all eleven cases listed were 'clear-cut cases of antisemitism' that 'require swift conclusion'. In the Board of Deputies' view, the proper outcomes of the cases wasn't even up for discussion: the cases were 'among the most serious we have seen, and all require permanent expulsion from the party'. The briefing asked for an update by the end of May on all cases, 'the resolution of which will signal a significant step towards healing the Labour Party's relationship with our community'.

An external lobby group thus gave the Labour Party leadership office less than three weeks to expel eleven party members or make significant progress in that direction, lest the party be considered insufficiently committed to 'healing' its 'relationship' with the Jewish 'community'.

Rosenberg's briefing expressed gratitude 'for the input of online activists Labour Against Antisemitism, who have been tracking a number of these cases'. The Board of Deputies' purge list was, in effect, a LAAS purge list. The party was being all-but-instructed to summarily expel eleven members who had attracted the attention of LAAS, an online group whose problematic approach to left-wing Jews has been documented above and whose most prominent spokesperson at the time was none other than Euan 'David Gordstein' Philips.

Five days later, the Board of Deputies issued a public statement announcing that they had submitted the list, though without identifying the individuals involved. This would have doubtless added to the political pressure being placed on the party behind the scenes.[2] The Board reiterated that the cases had to be settled quickly and that the party's reputation was at stake. But evidently something had been taking place behind the scenes that met with the Board's approval in the days between the original list and the release of the public statement. In a comment rich in irony, the Board expressed its pleasure that Starmer had been 'moving forward with his commitment to make Labour's disciplinary processes independent'.

This, of course, was at the precise moment when the Board was directly demanding that LOTO staff achieve specific disciplinary outcomes and inform the Board of case developments—even though the disciplinary process was supposed to be guided by principles of privacy and data protection laws. How this qualified as 'independent' is anyone's guess.

Indeed, party emails show that GLU staff were hyper-aware that they needed to deliver results—that is, suspensions and expulsions—and that they believed they had to do so because of political pressure from the Board of Deputies. In one update, shared with Barros-Curtis, a GLU staffer responded to one of the Board of Deputies cases by noting that allegations levelled in the LAAS dossier were not only old but had already been dealt with by the party: the member had explained a Facebook-related mistake, which had previously been accepted in mitigation. The GLU staffer's update on the case noted that 'the evidence [provided by the Board of Deputies] is not new', but that 'the reputation of the party is a factor in decision-making, and given the interest of the BoD, we have searched her social media again and put the evidence and proposal through sign-off'.

Emails show that the Board of Deputies' briefing document was forwarded by Ellie Robinson, in Starmer's office, to Barros-Curtis, Gardiner, and Morgan McSweeney. At the time, Barros-Curtis still worked in LOTO; he would be transitioned into his role as acting legal director a week later. The Board of Deputies list was thus forwarded by the deputy political director in LOTO to Starmer's chief of staff and to the lawyer, still in LOTO, who was the sole director of Starmer's leadership campaign vehicle—a position he still held as of early 2025. This email, moreover, directed the head of GLU to look at the cases. GLU staffers, in particular Gardiner and Murray, used the same email thread to respond and give updates, copying in, again, Robinson, McSweeney, and Barros-Curtis.

Emails show that GLU staffers understood that Barros-Curtis was based in LOTO or—following his appointment as acting executive director of legal—that the updates being sent to him were for the benefit of LOTO. For example, on Friday, May 15—one day after the Board submitted its purge list—Murray sent an email to Gardiner and other staffers. She attached updates on the Board's cases and referred to 'the questions *Alex from LOTO* put to us about these complaints' (emphasis mine). In another exchange about the progress of a specific complaint, the subject line read 'For LOTO'. A lengthy email in late May 2020 from Murray to other GLU staffers provided a detailed update on the Board of Deputies and Steve Reed cases. Its subject line read: 'Update for ABC/LOTO'—'ABC' denoting Barros-Curtis. Murray asked Hayball, copied into the email, to 'please update the below case information for ABC/LOTO'.

At just past midnight on Monday, May 18, Barros-Curtis wrote a lengthy response to a file that had been sent the previous Friday with details about specific cases. Barros-Curtis issued a series of direct instructions. He directed that David Miller, on Reed's list, be immediately expelled based on evidence he had supported the campaign of former Labour MP Chris Williamson, who ran as an independent in 2019. Barros-Curtis also identified two other people on the Board of Deputies list to be suspended. He again copied in Morgan McSweeney and Ellie Robinson from LOTO.

In late June 2020, Thomas Gardiner resigned from his position as head of GLU; emails show that Gardiner had bumped heads with Barros-Curtis in mid-May 2020 over their respective roles and responsibilities. Barros-Curtis was appointed as executive director of legal in late June 2020. For the month prior—while the purge lists were being processed—he had been on secondment to GLU from LOTO as Labour's acting head of legal.

GLU staff members were also made powerfully aware that Barros-Curtis was acting with Starmer's personal authority and backing. This was conveyed in typical Labour form (via the press) in a *Jewish Chronicle* article of June 18, 2020, that revealed 'Starmer's blueprint to reform Labour'.[3]

'Meanwhile, in move [*sic*] designed to help speed up the backlog of complaints, a trusted ally of the Labour leader has been moved into the party's Southside headquarters in central London as a "management enforcer" to ensure that allegations of anti-Jewish racism are properly dealt with', *Jewish Chronicle* reporter Lee Harpin wrote. 'Labour's compliance unit are now being closely managed', one party insider told the paper. 'For anyone seeking to stay in their jobs it would not be sensible to disobey their new manager's requests. The manager has also been given the power to step in and make decisions himself if need be'.

GLU staff were thus being warned, via the media, that they would lose their jobs unless they slavishly followed the instructions of an 'ally' of Starmer dropped into Southside.

The 'enforcer' went unnamed for two weeks before being confirmed as Alex Barros-Curtis by Lee Harpin in a follow-up article on June 29, 2020.[4] This time, the *Chronicle* confirmed that Barros-Curtis had already been 'at the centre' of multiple 'high-profile' suspensions of Labour members and councillors. It also repeated the threat to GLU staff to follow his orders on pain of dismissal. If there was any doubt as to whom Barros-Curtis answered, and from whom he drew his authority, it was dispelled by the summary headline shouting from the front page of the *Chronicle*'s website: 'Revealed: Starmer's Antisemitism Complaints Enforcer'.[5]

All of this was precisely the sort of behaviour that the EHRC would determine as unlawful. The EHRC found the party guilty of having breached equalities law because LOTO had gotten involved in complaints. Complaints were supposed to be handled exclusively by staff in GLU, operating independently of political influence exercised by LOTO, according to the EHRC. But Starmer's office was repeatedly and directly involved in managing the complaints submitted by the Board of Deputies and Steve Reed. Furthermore, there was arguably no effective distance between the official who oversaw the complaints team—Barros-Curtis—and Starmer's office, not least because Barros-Curtis served simultaneously as the party's head of legal, the sole director of Starmer's leadership campaign vehicle, and—according to media reporting—Starmer's personal 'antisemitism complaints enforcer'.

Starmer was regularly updated on the progress of the two purge lists. These updates took the form of neatly formatted reports titled, 'Labour Party: Outstanding Antisemitism Disciplinary Cases'. The reports were addressed 'To: Keir Starmer QC MP, Leader of the Labour Party' and marked 'From: Alex Barros-Curtis, Acting Executive Director of Legal Affairs for the Labour Party'. They were also sent and addressed to Rayner and Evans. When Barros-Curtis sent these reports to Starmer, he copied in Morgan McSweeney. On at least two occasions, Barros-Curtis sent his updates to Starmer's *personal* email address rather than to his Labour Party account.

Barros-Curtis prepared four such reports, dated May 23, June 7, June 14, and June 21, 2020. These all fell within the period when Barros-Curtis was on secondment from LOTO as acting executive director of legal affairs. Barros-Curtis supplemented his reports with detailed updates from GLU, also compiled weekly. The reports from GLU, from June 7 onward, provided detailed updates on the Board of Deputies/LAAS and Steve Reed lists. The updates were provided for each individual named on those lists.

On June 26, 2020, Barros-Curtis sent an email supplying all these personalised briefings for Starmer to solicitors from the law firm Fieldfisher, which was then providing secretariat services for the Forde Inquiry. However, this was the last-ever mention of these personalised case-by-case updates. After this point, the reports appear to stop entirely.

The reason is never explicitly addressed in any source reviewed for this book. But the timing is strongly suggestive. On July 10, 2020, David Evans confirmed to Labour MPs that the party had received a draft copy of the EHRC's investigation. While the draft EHRC report has never been released, the final EHRC report confirms that the EHRC had already made draft findings on political interference. Indeed, it was in response to these draft findings that Starmer's machinery issued its 'clarification' that withdrew the defence mounted by Corbyn's team and replaced it with an admission of guilt—based on an acceptance of the EHRC's contention that LOTO had no proper role in the handling or outcome of any specific disciplinary cases.

One plausible inference to draw is that the detailed case-by-case reporting to Starmer halted in response to the EHRC draft findings. These findings would have made it clear that LOTO's handling of the Reed and Board of Deputies cases were the essence of political interference. In fact, Starmer had overseen a far more aggressive, purposeful and *proactive* intervention by LOTO in complaints handling than had ever occurred under Corbyn.

This makes the 'clarification' issued by Starmer's machinery to the EHRC all the more hypocritical. At the very time the party signed on to the EHRC's factually incorrect finding on political interference, in order to help indict the Corbyn leadership, the party's most senior bureaucrats and indeed its new leader had been engaged in precisely this sort of 'political interference' for weeks beforehand.

Importantly, if one accepted the EHRC's findings as the Labour Party under Starmer did, this type of political interference would strongly suggest that Starmer's party was guilty of the type of unlawful indirect discrimination against Jewish people that Starmer had so piously addressed on the release of the EHRC report and for which Corbyn's party was condemned.

There is strong circumstantial evidence that the party was well aware of how its handling of the Board of Deputies/LAAS and Reed lists would look in light of the EHRC's findings. One of the individuals identified in the Board of Deputies/LAAS list was Rebecca Massey. As discussed below, she was expelled by the party for supporting Chris Williamson, a former Labour Party MP. Williamson left the party in late 2019 after being suspended for opining that the party's approach to the 'antisemitism crisis' had been 'too apologetic'.[6] Following her expulsion, Massey submitted a Subject Access Request (SAR), which compelled the party to disclose all the material it held on her.

Data provided under a SAR can be redacted if it might reveal personal information about another individual or individuals. But in Massey's case, the redactions appear to go substantially beyond this. Numerous emails were sent about her case with the subject line 'For LOTO: Rebecca Massey'. This subject line was repeatedly redacted, presumably to hide the fact that LOTO was directly involved. The redactors, however, forgot to redact this in one instance; a report in *The Electronic Intifada* about the involvement of LOTO in her case soon followed, but was largely ignored.[7] I reviewed an unredacted copy of her SAR report for this book; it shows that *mention of LOTO was repeatedly removed* from both the body of the emails and their subject lines.

BY ANY MEANS NECESSARY

The evidence of alleged antisemitism contained in the Reed purge lists was for the most part disputable. Of the ten individuals Reed complained about, three complaints were rejected out of hand, including those against Jenny Manson and Ken Loach. In the case of Manson and Loach, GLU commented that no investigation had been opened because 'no complaint was received which was a rule breach'; in a third case, it noted that it had already been heard and resolved.

The case against Ken Loach was, to judge by what can be reconstituted from GLU files, farcical. The complaint was that Loach had argued that the Labour Party was not institutionally antisemitic. GLU staff pointed out that this was the position of the Labour Party itself. But that did not mean the complaint would go nowhere. In the GLU update on his case, which was copied to Starmer, GLU staff noted that 'discussion of proscribed groups and Labour Against the Witchhunt is relevant here'. In the Labour Party context, membership of or support for a group classified as 'proscribed' is grounds for automatic expulsion.

Emails show that, at the same time as these complaints were being dealt with, a GLU staffer had drafted an opinion explaining how the NEC could proscribe Labour Against the Witchhunt. Labour Against the Witchhunt had been established to fight against what it saw as the unfair weaponisation of antisemitism allegations to kick people out of the party. It included a number of Jewish figures amongst its prominent supporters. The staffer believed that Labour Against the Witchhunt's conduct amounted to antisemitism—for the crime of denialism. They advised that proscribing the group would be 'transformative' for GLU as it could then rapidly process cases of people who associated with the group. 'This would eliminate a huge amount of work for GLU'. The staffer prefaced their briefing by noting that they were not a lawyer and that this couldn't be considered legal advice.

Labour Against the Witchhunt would be proscribed in 2021 and Loach would be duly expelled for associating with the group. Serious questions need to be asked about whether groups like Labour Against the Witchhunt were proscribed merely to furnish Labour bureaucrats with a pretext to expel members who had otherwise not breached any rules and whose membership was politically uncomfortable.

Emails show that GLU staff scrabbled around to find any sort of offence that would allow people on the lists to be suspended and expelled, even if it wasn't for antisemitism. Two of the individuals on the Board of Deputies/LAAS list were thus ultimately expelled because they had retweeted a statement in support of Chris Williamson, which GLU considered supporting a non-Labour candidate: an auto-exclusion offence. Professor David Miller, on the Reed list, was auto-excluded because he had assisted Chris Williamson's campaign to stand as an independent MP. In all of these cases, the offences had been proactively sought out by GLU staff—with the support of managers—rather than flowing from the original complaints.

In his first update to Starmer, Barros-Curtis explained the virtue of taking this approach in frank terms. 'I take the view that it is preferable to immediately suspend—and, where possible, move to automatically exclude—antisemitic members by whatever means possible', Barros-Curtis explained to Starmer, taking it upon himself to personally determine whether members were antisemites without any due process. 'Rather than spend time and effort taking them through a disciplinary process for a specified antisemitism offence, if we are able to remove that same member much more quickly by another permissible means, we should do so'.

The same update to Starmer shows that Barros-Curtis had some unique advice for GLU about those cases where the evidence already supplied wasn't sufficient to uphold an antisemitism complaint. After explaining that GLU had rejected certain complaints due to the weakness of the evidence, Barros-Curtis noted that 'I have instructed the team to consider if they require other evidence, then they should reach out to Steve Reed and/or the Board of Deputies to identify whether the authors of the dossiers might be able to assist in this regard'. Barros-Curtis was, in effect, telling GLU staff to ask LAAS, via the Board of Deputies, for additional evidence that could be made to stick.

At one stage, Barros-Curtis' endorsement of the whatever-sticks approach directly targeted left-wing Jews. As noted above, on May 18, Barros-Curtis had written a series of instructions to GLU on individual cases. In that same discussion, under the heading 'JVL' for Jewish Voice for Labour, he wrote that he had reviewed JVL's registration with Companies House. 'Based on what Companies House says, it would appear to me that the nine directors of JVL should be automatically excluded for breaching Clause I.4.A.B of Chapter 2 of the Rule Book', he explained. 'Can you please review and confirm because if this is the case, all nine should be auto-excluded immediately'. GLU staff had to explain that Barros-Curtis' reasoning was problematic; if the approach suggested by him was adopted, all other Labour Party pressure groups and factions (like Progress and, indeed, Labour Together) would have to be banned as well.

It is a reflection of the upside-down nature of the Labour Party 'antisemitism crisis' that the party's most senior legal figure—the sole director of Starmer's campaign vehicle and Starmer's own 'antisemitism complaints enforcer'—sought to summarily expel a raft of Jewish people.

Indeed, if Barros-Curtis' approach had been adopted, it would have allowed the party to immediately exclude the four Jewish members on Reed's list, all of whom were members of JVL. As it was, none of the four were expelled or suspended for any length of time based on the evidence supplied by Reed; although, in the case of Professor Rosenhead, he found the experience of being investigated and briefly suspended so offensive that he chose to resign. Some, however, were later investigated or expelled when the party proscribed certain groups, including Labour Against the Witchhunt. Again, this raises serious questions about whether proscriptions were imposed simply to furnish a pretext to expel individuals not otherwise guilty of offences but who pressure groups had demanded be punished.

A number of individuals on the Board of Deputies/LAAS list had a long history of online social media spats with LAAS and its advisor Jonathan Hoffman. In these cases, the party was being asked to immediately expel people who had long-running political disputes with Hoffman and LAAS, based on evidence that LAAS itself was submitting.

Barros-Curtis' updates to Starmer were striking for their implicit recognition of the political dimension to complaints processing. Barros-Curtis accordingly discussed how the party's disciplinary decisions might make their way to the ears of interested stakeholders when the party was constrained, under data protection rules, from publicly announcing specific disciplinary outcomes. As noted above, when the Board of Deputies submitted its list, it asked to be updated on a regular basis. Gardiner pushed back when queried on this, pointing out that data protection rules prohibited it.

In the event, once the suspensions began to flow from the lists, they became public knowledge soon enough, usually because they were reported with indignation by the individuals themselves or in sympathetic media. In two updates, Barros-Curtis happily shared screenshots of this happening. He piously introduced one screenshot by noting that, 'whilst the party does not comment publicly on disciplinary cases, we know that it is inevitable that the information becomes public (given so many of these individuals cannot help complain about it on social media once they are confronted with the consequences of their actions)'. This was 'doing our work for us', he added.

In a later update, Barros-Curtis cited the case of Rebecca Massey announcing her expulsion—Massey's SARs, recall, would later be edited to remove email subject lines that included the phrase 'for LOTO'. 'Whilst the party does not comment publicly on disciplinary cases, the individuals we are acting on continue to spread the word on our behalf', Barros-Curtis again noted with satisfaction. 'Otherwise, there continues to be a positive reaction online and from stakeholders reaching out to us', Barros-Curtis informed Starmer directly thereafter.

CHAPTER 13

THE SUSPENSION OF JEREMY CORBYN

In his portentous address following the release of the Equality and Human Rights Commission report, Sir Keir Starmer pledged to end political interference in the party's disciplinary process: 'We will ensure that neither the Leader, the Deputy Leader nor our offices will have any involvement in the outcome of complaints initiated under Labour Party processes'.[1]

Starmer broke this promise within hours of its utterance.

A half-hour before Starmer's speech, Jeremy Corbyn had published on Facebook his response to the EHRC report.[2] Corbyn did not accept all of the findings of the EHRC report but hoped its recommendations would be 'swiftly implemented to help move on from this period'. Corbyn also reiterated that there was some antisemitism in the Labour Party, said it was 'wrong' to deny this, and expressed regret that his attempts to reform Labour's complaints processes had been 'stalled' by an 'obstructive bureaucracy'. What ignited controversy was his assertion that '[o]ne antisemite is one too many, but the scale of the problem was also dramatically overstated for political reasons by our opponents inside and outside the party, as well as by much of the media'.

Corbyn's statement was arguably ill-advised. But what Corbyn said was also true. Both the Leaked Report and the EHRC itself confirmed that the party had improved complaints handling in the years that Formby served as general secretary. There was ample evidence showing that the media did, indeed, give an unwarranted sense that the party was irredeemably riddled with antisemitism and that Corbyn himself endorsed this; there are so many examples that it is hard to choose one, but perhaps the most hyperbolic was the allegation made on LBC Radio by Simon Heffer, a *Sunday Telegraph* journalist, that Corbyn was 'a man that wants to reopen Auschwitz'.[3]

Most importantly, Corbyn was arguably describing exactly the sort of political work that Morgan McSweeney and his collaborators like Imran Ahmed had been doing in secret—with their pot of undeclared funding—as they were working to destroy Corbyn and Corbynism. As set out extensively above, it was McSweeney and Ahmed's undeclared briefing that had led to the incendiary 'hate factory' articles in *The Sunday Times* that mixed real and serious accusations of antisemitism with allegations that were prima facie absurd (like simply having seen a Facebook post from a Jewish anti-Zionist). It was also McSweeney and Ahmed who launched the astroturf Stop Funding Fake News campaign, which stimulated much consequential coverage and led to the Community Security Trust's alarmist *Engines of Hate* report, itself a source of national media headlines.

Within two hours of Corbyn's statement being posted, the party was making moves to suspend him. These unfolded entirely outside of the proper complaints handling process that the EHRC had elaborated on—albeit inaccurately—in its report.

At 12:30 p.m., Patrick Smith, the party's head of disputes, emailed Alex Barros-Curtis and Andrew Whyte, the head of external governance. Barros-Curtis oversaw GLU as executive director, while Smith and Whyte served as heads of units within GLU. Smith had attached a draft suspension letter. By 12:58 p.m., he had edited the suspension letter, informing those copied in that it was 'tweaked and ready to send'. The suspension letter informed Corbyn that General Secretary David Evans had decided to invoke his powers, as delegated to him by the National Executive Committee, to place Corbyn under administrative suspension pending an investigation by the NEC. Barros-Curtis had by then moved out of the leader's office, but he was still the sole director of the company that had run Starmer's leadership campaign.

The party's handling of the case reeked of media management. The email attaching Corbyn's letter of suspension was sent at 1:03 p.m. from the Labour Party disputes account; *LabourList*'s Sienna Rodgers tweeted out news of Corbyn's suspension at literally the same minute, 1:03 p.m.

The party made no attempt to establish whether Corbyn had received his notice of suspension until the following day, when Barros-Curtis left a voice message on Corbyn's parliamentary phone. Corbyn only learned of his suspension when he was doorstepped outside his house by an Associated Press photographer at 2:00 p.m., an hour after his letter had been sent.

Much as he had repeatedly done prior to the publication of the EHRC report, Barros-Curtis ensured that LOTO was fully informed of what had transpired. Thus, at 1:33 p.m., Barros-Curtis emailed a copy of Corbyn's suspension letter to McSweeney, Jenny Chapman, Ellie Robinson, Luke Sullivan, and Ben Nunn, all of whom were in LOTO. Also copied in was Nick Parrott in Deputy Leader Angela Rayner's office. Barros-Curtis urged the recipients to 'please keep this confidential'. LOTO staffers were therefore provided with Corbyn's suspension letter before Corbyn himself had been made aware of its existence.

Emails show that GLU staff were furious that Barros-Curtis and others had not bothered to inform let alone consult them about the suspension. GLU's staff, rather than department heads, would usually have been expected to log, investigate, and report on complaints. At 3:10 p.m., two hours after Corbyn's suspension, acting GLU director Andrew Whyte emailed his staff to inform them of developments. 'It is unacceptable for the team to learn these things from the media before being formally told as employees. This is several hours after the event', one staffer immediately responded. Another concurred:

> This is no environment to conduct fair and *independent* investigations on this issue or any other. That somebody has spoken to *LabourList* about this ahead of GLU staff is an indication of the low regard [in which] staff and members are held. I appreciate the difficulty in reacting to live events, but it seems time was made quick enough to brief Sienna Rogers [*sic*]. [first emphasis mine]

Rodgers was the first journalist to tweet news of the suspension. It was remarkable that, within a few hours of the EHRC's report, GLU staffers were complaining about an 'environment' that precluded 'independent' investigations.

'The highly reactive manner in which some of our investigations are conducted undermines the process and allows those who have previously been investigated to dismiss findings. Any genuine concern in tackling racism is eroded by such action', a third GLU staff member wrote.

Barros-Curtis intervened to stop the flood of comments. He informed the staffers that they could raise issues with him and Whyte personally, but 'sending them in this forum is not appropriate'.

In the media frenzy that ensued, Starmer himself could not manage to get the story straight about who had actually suspended Corbyn. In one BBC interview, Starmer claimed that the decision had been taken entirely by Evans, although Starmer couldn't help noting that it was a decision he 'fully support[ed]'.[4] But this contradicted what Starmer had said during a different interview on the BBC that same day. After confirming that the leader had no role in complaints handling, Starmer then responded to a comment that 'this might define your time in the Labour Party' with a terrific chest thump that suggested he had taken the decision himself. 'I'm not going to shy away from difficult decisions', he declared. 'That's what leadership is, difficult decisions. We made a very difficult decision yesterday, we've made other difficult decisions in the last six months'.[5]

Not much later, media reporters tried to untangle the matter based on frenetic briefings from party officials. Thus, on the same day, the BBC's Nick Watt reported on *Newsnight* that 'what allies of Keir Starmer are saying is that he was consulted on the suspension of Jeremy Corbyn from the party and the removal of the whip, but that those decisions were made by the general secretary David Evans and Chief Whip Nick Brown'.[6]

But the EHRC had, in addition to ruling that LOTO had no role in complaints, also found that 'GLU considered opinions from the [general secretary's office] to be "outside views" on disciplinary cases'.[7] Indeed, the EHRC's detailed presentation of how the party's complaints system was supposed to function permitted no role for the general secretary or their office.[8] Citing Evans' involvement was, as a result, effectively admitting to what the EHRC had characterised as political interference, and it is striking that 'allies of Keir Starmer' did not seem aware of this in light of the EHRC's findings. It must certainly raise questions about how well Starmer's 'allies', maybe even Starmer himself, understood the report Starmer had just accepted in full and without reservation.

As multiple accounts now confirm, Starmer was in the room where it happened.[9] Immediately following his address to the media announcing the EHRC's findings and his solemn promise that 'neither the Leader, the Deputy Leader nor our offices will have any involvement in the outcome of complaints', Starmer ascended to the eighth floor of party headquarters, where he discussed what to do about Corbyn. He was joined by Evans, McSweeney, Barros-Curtis, and Rayner. Barros-Curtis was asked to give his opinion on an appropriate sanction; he suggested suspension as expulsion would be vulnerable to legal challenge. All attendees agreed, the letter of suspension was dispatched to Corbyn's email address, and *LabourList* was given the go-ahead to post about it the minute the letter had left the party's outbox.

Another first-hand account is offered by Len McCluskey, the leader of Unite. McCluskey recalls that he received a telephone call from Starmer to inform him that Corbyn had been suspended. 'I had to pinch myself to make sure I wasn't in a bad dream', McCluskey writes. McCluskey claims that Starmer took personal responsibility for the decision: 'He put me in an impossible position and I had no choice', Starmer reportedly told McCluskey. McCluskey is adamant that this conversation happened and says his testimony can be corroborated by 'a member of my staff [who] was with me in my office as I listened to the phone on the loudspeaker'.[10]

McCluskey says Starmer told him that he was 'beyond angry' with Corbyn because he felt Corbyn had 'gone out of his way to directly contradict that line in my [Starmer's] speech'. Starmer was referring to his warning that '[i]f there are still those who think there's no problem with antisemitism in the Labour Party, that it's all exaggerated, or a factional attack, then, frankly, you are part of the problem too. And you should be nowhere near the Labour Party either'.[11]

Another source interviewed for this book recounted how Evans often told the war story of Corbyn's suspension. The source claimed that Evans bragged of 'taking the fall' for Starmer by claiming publicly to have made the decision himself, even as it was clear that Starmer played a meaningful role in the decision. The source was astonished at the candidness of this boast, not least for its ignorance of what the EHRC said about the involvement of the general secretary's office in complaints.

Remarkably, the party's letter suspending Corbyn specified that it was doing so under Clause I(a) of Chapter 6 of the party rule book. This is precisely the clause quoted extensively above, which showed that any 'national officer' of the Labour Party—including the party leader—had broad authority to investigate complaints. This was precisely the clause that disproved the EHRC's finding that Labour had committed unlawful 'political interference'. The letter helpfully provided, in a footnote, the text of the first half of the clause. But it was careful to excise the second half, which would have confirmed that any 'national officer' could investigate any rule breach, thereby totally invalidating the EHRC's findings and, crucially, the Starmer leadership's acceptance thereof. In the technical and rule-bound culture of Labour Party bureaucracy, this amounted to a brazen slap in the face: Corbyn was informed he was being suspended after having disputed elements of the EHRC report, under a clause of the rule book that itself cleared him of the EHRC's false accusation.

It is hard not to feel a degree of appalled awe at the political moment that McSweeney had orchestrated—and would ruthlessly exploit.

We now know that McSweeney played a central, undisclosed role in seeding the 'antisemitism crisis' narrative for years. We now know that he was secretly involved in 'engineer[ing]'[12] the EHRC's investigation into Corbyn's Labour Party. We now know that he then guided Starmer to the leadership of the party and installed loyalists throughout the party bureaucracy. We now know that the Starmer Project then withdrew Corbyn's legally sound defence against the EHRC's critical findings and replaced it with an admission of guilt for offences Corbyn's leadership team did not in fact commit. We now know that McSweeney personally attended the meeting that decided to suspend Corbyn for arguably describing precisely what McSweeney had been doing for years in the shadows. We now know that the party suspended Corbyn using the very clause in Labour's rule book that invalidated the EHRC's findings and proved that Corbyn's office was not guilty of 'political interference' as defined by the EHRC. We now know that McSweeney, Starmer, and their associates met to suspend Corbyn less than an hour after Starmer promised the country that precisely this sort of thing would never happen again. Perhaps we now know that Corbyn, and the popular movement he had invigorated, never stood a chance.

If there is any thread of natural justice running through this sorry story, it is impossible to discern.

Corbyn's suspension from the party and from parliament immediately unleashed a wave of angry protest. It was the last straw for many of the left-wingers who had joined Starmer's team expecting him to act in good faith. One senior member of the Starmer team remembers speaking to Morgan McSweeney on the afternoon Corbyn's suspension was announced. 'I told him this was going to split the party', he recalled. 'I know', McSweeney calmly answered, without any further elaboration. 'What can you say? At this point, I knew that everything had been a lie'.

Almost immediately after the suspension was announced, attempts were initiated behind the scenes to negotiate a way out of the crisis. On the afternoon of the suspension, just as Starmer was busy big-manning his 'tough decisions' in the media, McSweeney called Jon Trickett, an MP close to Corbyn and the Unite leadership. McSweeney explained that LOTO was willing to negotiate a way out of the impasse and to find a way to bring Corbyn back into the fold. When Starmer was called directly, he confirmed that he was personally interested in finding a way to de-escalate and resolve the issue. Trickett and McCluskey, the erstwhile leader of Unite, were dispatched to lead the negotiations.

Trickett and McCluskey met the next day with Starmer, McSweeney, and Angela Rayner. After initial soundings, Starmer noted that he would be satisfied with a statement from Corbyn clarifying his statement on the EHRC report. McCluskey recalls that he had carefully confirmed with Starmer that, if an agreement on Corbyn's clarifying words could be reached, Starmer would be happy with the suspension being lifted. So much for an 'independent' complaints process! McSweeney indicated that he had already roped in Simon Fletcher, who worked with LOTO and had been close to the Corbyn project, to help draft a statement. McCluskey and Trickett approved their collaboration.

By the next day, a draft text had been agreed by all parties. McCluskey claims that he explicitly confirmed with McSweeney that Corbyn's suspension would be lifted, that 'Jeremy would be back to normal', and that this arrangement had Starmer's personal backing. Starmer's team pushed for Corbyn to publish the statement immediately, but Corbyn himself hesitated, wary of being betrayed.

Text messages between Fletcher, Trickett, and McSweeney showed that McSweeney was intimately involved in stage-managing the entire disciplinary process. At one stage, McSweeney asked whether he needed to get the NEC to delay hearing Corbyn's case when there was a wobble about when Corbyn would release his statement. In another exchange, McSweeney explained the disciplinary outcomes that would come to fruition depending on when and how Corbyn released his statement.

All of this was, of course, the height of 'political interference' and illustrated that McSweeney was confident that he could pre-determine the result of the NEC disciplinary proceedings before the NEC panel had even met. Applying the reasoning of the EHRC report, which Starmer accepted, such interference arguably constituted unlawful discrimination against Jews.

In the end, it was only when the NEC met to discuss his case on November 17, 2020, that Corbyn published his clarifying statement. Corbyn confirmed that 'concerns about antisemitism are neither "exaggerated" nor "overstated". The point I wished to make was that the vast majority of Labour Party members were and remain committed anti-racists deeply opposed to antisemitism'. The NEC considered his statement and, on this basis, agreed to readmit Corbyn with a simple reminder of conduct.

Corbyn's readmission provoked yet another furore, this time from his critics. A spokesperson for the Jewish Labour Movement claimed it was 'extraordinary that just weeks after the EHRC found that the Labour Party had discriminated against Jewish members through political manipulation of the disciplinary process, it appears that the party expedited this case for hearing by a factionally aligned political committee'.[13] One wonders what the JLM might have said had they known that it was their own Adam Langleben's long-time collaborator McSweeney who helped engineer the EHRC investigation, and who was now practicing the political interference they claimed to oppose. And what of the fact that Starmer's *suspension* of Corbyn *also* flew in the face of those same EHRC findings? That went by unremarked.

The chair of the Board of Deputies of British Jews, Marie van der Zyl, also decried Corbyn's return as a 'retrograde step' in Labour's 'relations with the Jewish community'. She protested the selective expediting of Corbyn's case by his 'allies on the NEC' and said that Corbyn's 'confected non-apology' had added 'insult to injury'.[14] She apparently forgot to mention that the Board of Deputies itself had urged Starmer's office to expedite cases of *its* choosing.

The response from Dame Margaret Hodge is widely believed to have been decisive. A grandee of the party's Blairite wing, Hodge—Jewish herself—had been one of the most strident voices criticising Corbyn during the 'antisemitism crisis'. In one infamous scene, Hodge had confronted Corbyn in the House of Commons and shouted that he was an 'antisemitic racist'.[15] Hodge tweeted that Corbyn's readmission was a 'broken outcome from a broken system . . . This is exactly why the EHRC instructed Labour to set up an independent process!'[16] It was widely reported that Hodge had threatened to resign from the party if Starmer didn't act.

And so Starmer, within hours of the NEC readmitting Corbyn on the basis of a text that had been agreed with Starmer's office, announced that he had decided that the Labour whip would not be returned to Corbyn—the effect being that, while Corbyn would be readmitted as a member of the Labour Party, he would not be able to sit as a Labour MP in parliament. 'The disciplinary process does not have the confidence of the Jewish community', Starmer explained on Twitter.[17]

Starmer's outriders soon began denying that Starmer's office had reached any sort of agreement with Corbyn, in direct contradiction with multiple first-hand accounts and the text message exchanges between McSweeney, Fletcher, and Trickett. One unnamed source within Starmer's office told *The Guardian* that 'there was no deal'. Any discussions between Corbyn's allies and Starmer's people simply amounted to 'lobbying' on Corbyn's behalf, they said.[18]

Corbyn would never have the Labour whip returned. He would eventually return to parliament in 2024 as an independent MP, almost certainly ensuring that his exile from the Labour Party would be permanent.

The entire affair was a sorry microcosm of Starmer and the project he fronted. As ever, Starmer could not resist a macho brag about his 'tough decisions' in media appearances, but immediately wilted when people expressed their anger at him personally. Deals and promises made and accepted in good faith were broken, and then a media programme was rolled out to baldly deny the facts staring everyone in the face.

CHAPTER 14

THE PRINCIPLES OF NATURAL (IN)JUSTICE

The Equality and Human Rights Commission report, the suspension of Jeremy Corbyn, and the decision to permanently strip Corbyn of the Labour whip together had three important consequences for British politics.

The first was civil war. By November 2020, the left in the Labour Party was increasingly convinced that Starmer's leadership campaign had been a con, and that he represented a lurch toward the ugly factionalism he had claimed to oppose.

The second was the Labour leadership's adoption of an authoritarian approach to internal dissent, which has come to define the party ever since. Rules were introduced to prohibit expressions of solidarity with Corbyn and criticism of certain aspects of Starmer's conduct. In the face of this crackdown, left-wing members abandoned the party in droves, further consolidating Starmer's power.

The last outcome was perverse, especially in the context of a political scandal ostensibly centred on the fairness and objectivity with which the party handled disciplinary matters. Bluntly, the EHRC's findings and recommendations triggered a process that has deeply politicised how complaints in the party are handled, a politicisation that found its ultimate expression in the mistreatment of left-wing Jews under the guise of fighting antisemitism. At the same time, the party quite literally eschewed principles of natural justice in its treatment of disciplinary cases. On top of all this, the party bureaucracy also facilitated the creation of a virtual 'VIP Lane' that allowed politically important complainants—like the right-wing NEC member and campaigner Luke Akehurst—to submit complaints directly to the party's senior bureaucrats and receive updates on confidential matters.

CENSORSHIP AND EXODUS

On the day after the EHRC report was released, Labour's general secretary David Evans codified guidance to party members and officers. It warned that the 'country is watching us' and advised party members in control of Facebook and social media group accounts that 'close moderation will be essential'. Evans suggested that 'you may wish to consider temporarily restricting the ability of other members or individuals to post'. Most notably, Evans instructed that whereas Constituency Labour Parties could pass motions related to the EHRC report, any 'motions that seek to question the competence of the EHRC to conduct an investigation in any way, or repudiate or reject the report or any of its recommendations must be ruled out of order'.[1] Considering the raft of basic factual errors in the EHRC report, and the clearly political nature of its appointments, this ruling was particularly draconian.

Matters became farcical after Jeremy Corbyn's suspension and the decision to not return to him the whip. In the week following Corbyn's suspension, Evans issued guidance to CLPs and branches that any motion discussing *any* 'disciplinary matter' would be ruled out of order.[2] When Corbyn was readmitted to the party but denied the whip, Evans issued fresh guidance that prohibited any motion touching on the whip decision.[3] This included any expression of solidarity with Corbyn and, most comically, any motions that expressed no confidence in Starmer or Evans. Evans explained that the restrictions, including those that prohibited any criticism of Starmer's and Evans' handling of the Corbyn case, were necessary because 'motions . . . are providing a flashpoint for the expression of views that undermine the Labour Party's ability to provide a safe and welcoming space for all members, in particular our Jewish members'.[4]

Many CLPs refused to abide by the directions. According to Labour Party files, the party identified at least forty-seven separate CLPs that passed motions in breach of Evans' instructions. An Excel spreadsheet compiled in February 2021 by Patrick Smith, the party's head of disputes, recorded the name and position of every CLP or branch officer suspended from the party for allowing 'non-competent' motions. It illustrated a diligent commitment to monitoring the party membership and policing its conduct. The party was assisted in this effort by Luke Akehurst, who became something of a clearing house for people to send information about potentially out-of-order motions, which he would forward directly to the party's top bureaucrats.

Smith's Excel spreadsheet indicated that ninety-five CLP or branch officers were suspended from November 12, 2020, onward. Just under a third of those suspended were CLP chairs. The spreadsheet included a handy list of the topics addressed by each incriminating motion, which, together, made for enlightening reading. On twelve occasions, the topic and reason for suspension were listed as a variation of 'solidarity' (doubtless with Corbyn); thirty-four mentioned 'whip' or some derivation thereof; eight were listed as 'Freedom of Expression/No Confidence'.

The hardline stance taken by Evans was reinforced by public comments from the likes of Deputy Leader Angela Rayner, whose intervention particularly appalled left-wing members who had previously viewed her as the left candidate for deputy leadership. Addressing a Jewish Labour Movement meeting in which a JLM member complained that a motion in solidarity with Corbyn had made them feel uncomfortable, Rayner promised that 'if we have to suspend thousands of members, we will do that'. Like Evans, she confirmed that 'there's no debating what the EHRC said'.[5] Rayner's unqualified backing of the EHRC report, to the point of delegitimising any scepticism toward it, is especially hard to stomach seeing as she, along with McSweeney and Starmer, had already violated its findings on political interference by directly involving herself in Corbyn's suspension—less than an hour after Starmer had promised that both his and her offices would never do such a thing again.

The suspensions meted out by GLU were ultimately heard by the NEC Disputes Sub-Committee. In January 2021, Shabana Mahmood, the Parliamentary Labour Party's representative on the NEC, was elected as sub-committee chair. This meant that a prominent player in Labour Together would be reviewing disciplinary charges brought against members who had criticised the conduct of the party's leader and general secretary, both of whom owed their positions to the Labour Together Project. Such was the reality of Starmer's 'independent' complaints process.

Although many other factors no doubt came into play, the combined responses of Starmer, Evans, and Rayner confirmed to many members that the party had fallen under the control of a faction that had no interest in party unity, democracy or free speech. Corbyn's suspension triggered a substantial exodus of party members. Whereas membership remained relatively stable between the end of the December 2019 election and the end of 2020, it plummeted thereafter. Labour lost over 90,000 members between December 2020 and December 2021 alone, followed by more than 36,000 members between the end of December 2021 and May 2023.

The downward trajectory in membership numbers appears to have accelerated further in response to the party's policy toward Israel's destruction of Gaza, discussed later. Between January and April 2024, Labour membership fell by over 24,000. This meant that the party shrunk by fully 165,000 members between December 2019 and April 2024. This is a net figure; given that some people also joined the party over the same period, the gross number of members choosing to leave the party was even higher.

Put otherwise, under Starmer's leadership, the Labour Party membership declined by a nearly one-third. (See Table 3.) The total number of people leaving the party was almost equal to the entire Tory party membership, which was estimated at 175,000 in 2022. If those leaving Labour had formed their own party, it would have been tied for the second biggest political party in the country by membership.

TABLE 3. Labour Party Membership, 2019–24

Date	Members (including those in arrears)
December 2019[6]	532,046
December 2020[7]	523,332
December 2021[8]	432,213
May 2023[9]	395,811
March 2024[10]	366,604

Leading party officials have not just acknowledged this collapse in membership but celebrated it. In January 2022, for example, Rachel Reeves was ebullient about how many of the members in her own patch had left the party. 'Membership in my constituency is falling and that's a good thing', she commented. The people who had left 'should never have joined the Labour party. They never shared our values'.[11]

But by 2025, as membership continued to drop even after Labour's 2024 election landslide, this confidence in the virtue of losing members appeared to evaporate. In May 2025, after reports that the party was losing a member every ten minutes[12], *LabourList* reported that Labour would no longer provide regular briefings on membership numbers to NEC members.[13] Typically, NEC members would expect to receive updates every two months; by mid-2025, and presumably because the figures would start to look anaemic next to the burgeoning membership of Reform, it was briefed that the party would only publish membership data once a year when it sent an annual report to the Electoral Commission.

THE 'VIP LANE'

The Starmer leadership's pious grandstanding aside, little was actually done to improve the party's system for handling disciplinary complaints or insulate it from political pressure. Under the leadership of Starmer and Evans, for example, politically important or well-connected individuals were able to receive favourable treatment through a de facto complaints 'VIP Lane'.

One of the people who made extensive use of this VIP Lane was right-wing NEC operative Luke Akehurst. He used it to either push for the expedited resolution of cases he felt strongly about or to get updates on how select disciplinary cases had progressed.

In November 2020, for example, amid the spate of 'non-competent' CLP resolutions, Akehurst forwarded a complaint about a CLP motion directly to Alex Barros-Curtis. Barros-Curtis had, by then, moved from LOTO to take up the role of executive director of legal affairs—in effect, as Starmer's 'enforcer' overseeing the complaints team.[14] As previously noted, Barros-Curtis retained his simultaneous position as the sole director of Starmer's leadership campaign vehicle throughout this period.

Akehurst flagged the presence of a 'very obvious antisemitic conspiracy theory' in the CLP motion, which had raised 'the related issue of a donation of £50k to Keir Starmer's leadership campaign from Israel lobbyists via Trevor Chinn that was not declared until a month after Starmer was elected. Is he now compromised by accepting that money?' In under ten minutes, Barros-Curtis had forwarded the email to the heads of GLU and Disputes with the comment: 'clearly, this is totally unacceptable'.

Akehurst was thus able to secure direct access to the most senior complaints staff and achieve almost instantaneous results: to silence criticism of one of the key funders of Labour Together, Trevor Chinn, who was also a board member of the Jewish Leadership Council, itself affiliated with an Israel lobby group (BICOM) that worked closely with Akehurst. Until his election as an MP in July 2024, Akehurst was employed as the director of We Believe in Israel, which had developed out of a conference hosted by BICOM. Thus was a committed Labour right-winger and paid Israel lobbyist able to almost instantly trigger the Labour Party into recoding the most reasonable of questions about the influence of donations on a candidate's policies—the elementary stuff of politics—as antisemitic hate-speech requiring disciplinary sanction.

A month later, in December 2020, Akehurst wrote to Barros-Curtis about former Labour staff member Patrick Heneghan. Recall that, at the time, Heneghan's case was one of only two stemming from the Leaked Report that had not yet been resolved. Akehurst had been elected to the NEC just over a month previously.

On December 23, 2020, Heneghan wrote to Akehurst to complain of his treatment by the party and about the failure of Barros-Curtis to reply to his repeated emails. Within fifteen minutes, Akehurst had forwarded Heneghan's email to Barros-Curtis and General Secretary David Evans. Despite Akehurst admitting that the case was 'sensitive' because of the Forde Inquiry, he asked for an update about the case 'in so far as possible'. 'As an NEC member I am seeking reassurance that Mr Heneghan's case and that of his other former colleagues are all being expedited and resolved'. Akehurst was using his position on the NEC to push for an 'expedited' resolution of the disciplinary cases of right-wing officials implicated in serious wrongdoing by the Leaked Report.

Barros-Curtis responded to Akehurst in under eight minutes, copying in Evans. 'I can give you that reassurance', Barros-Curtis informed Akehurst. 'Confidentially, I can say to you that I will shortly have an update for Patrick (and other members of staff) . . . I only say to reassure you—and Patrick—that I am looking to make progress on this'.

On February 26, 2021, Akehurst again wrote directly to Evans and Barros-Curtis. This time he was advocating on behalf of Joe Goldberg, national vice chair of the JLM.

In mid-2018, Goldberg had tweeted about a Muslim councillor in Haringey, Emina Ibrahim. He had criticised the fact that she had blocked him on Twitter, ending his comment with '#jezbollahpoliticsinaction'. Ibrahim complained, saying that she found the tweet 'highly offensive' because it played 'on the name Hezbollah a terrorist organisation—directed at a Muslim woman'. She also fretted that people who did not know her might conclude that she had links to Hezbollah, putting her in danger of confrontation from the far right.

In February 2019, Goldberg resigned from the party prior to an investigation taking place. But later that year, in September, the party investigated the matter and decided it was sufficiently problematic to issue a notice of investigation. Since Goldberg was no longer a party member, a note was placed against his name, recording the allegation. When Goldberg tried to rejoin the party in 2020 to vote in the leadership election, his application was denied on this basis.

Despite Goldberg's later claim to be totally unaware of the investigation, it had actually featured in the highly publicised Leaked Report.[15] Importantly, it was also mentioned in a report written by the Labour Muslim Network (LMN) and published in 2020. The LMN report argued that Muslims in the Labour Party experienced widespread Islamophobia and feared that the party did not take this seriously. It cited the Goldberg incident (albeit not by name) as an example, criticising the length of time the party had taken to initiate an investigation into his case.[16]

When Goldberg's attempt to rejoin the party was rebuffed, Akehurst forwarded Goldberg's response—which appealed that decision—to Evans and Barros-Curtis, copying in the JLM's chair Mike Katz. Akehurst asked Evans and Barros-Curtis directly to 'look at the appeal . . . He resigned from the party over antisemitism and it would send a very important signal to JLM and the Jewish Community if he was able to join'.

Put otherwise, in order to send a 'signal' to 'JLM and the Jewish Community', the party needed to immediately review its decision to exclude a JLM higher-up against whom there was an outstanding complaint of Islamophobia. Akehurst sent this email after both the Leaked Report and the LMN report had been published.

Goldberg was ultimately readmitted in August 2021. He announced his readmission on Twitter. Ibrahim, noting the post and tagging Starmer as well as Rayner, responded with incredulity: 'Taking Islamophobia seriously?'[17]

The Labour Together Project's Steve Reed MP was an equally prolific user of the 'VIP Lane', having pioneered this approach when submitting his purge list in May 2020.

On December 4, 2020, little over five weeks after the EHRC report was published, Reed wrote directly to Barros-Curtis and Evans to complain about a local constituent, Katie Wilson-Downie. Reed had written to Evans' private, Proton Mail email account rather than to his official Labour Party inbox. Proton Mail is a privacy-focused email provider often used by journalists and activists because it encrypts messages such that it cannot fulfil law enforcement requests. Serious questions need to be asked about how extensively Evans used this non-Labour address for Labour business.

Wilson-Downie was a well-known local activist who devoted considerable time to fighting for justice in relation to the Windrush scandal. She did so alongside her father, Conroy Downie, a former soldier who had fallen victim to the scandal. The two were reported to have advised thousands of former Windrush victims as part of a long-term campaign.[18]

Reed's email to Barros-Curtis and Evans attached a document containing two screenshots from local constituency WhatsApp conversations. The conversations show that Wilson-Downie had tried to make the argument that antisemitism was not the same as racism because Jewishness is not a race;

antisemitism was a different form of oppression, but oppression nonetheless. She also pointed out that many Jewish people presented as Caucasian and that they thus formed part of the 'white supremacy hierarchy'. She further argued that 'you cannot be racist to someone unless you are attacking their race . . . We need to apply political correctness to the overused term anti-Semitism'.

Reed appears to have misunderstood the point of this last sentence, which he construed as 'deny[ing] the fact of anti-Semitism in the Labour Party'. In fact, Wilson-Downie was asking that terms like antisemitism and racism be used carefully and correctly in line with their actual meaning. Contrary to Reed's suggestion, she had made no comment on whether there was antisemitism in the party. Reed, as he had done previously, concluded: 'I trust you will be able to suspend her membership pending further investigation on these comments'.

Eleven days later, on December 15, Barros-Curtis forwarded the complaint to Andrew Whyte and Patrick Smith, noting that it had been sent by Reed. Barros-Curtis also forwarded another set of complaints from Reed (discussed below) but asked that they look into this one in particular. The following day, Wilson-Downie was suspended from the party and asked to respond to the allegation that her conduct was antisemitic. 'This is institutional racism', she complained within hours, simultaneously announcing her resignation from the party.

A month later, she asked the party to confirm her resignation was duly processed, using the correspondence to complain that she had been suspended for correctly pointing out that Jewishness is not a race, 'hence why you have black, white and arab [*sic*] Jews'.

Barros-Curtis diligently updated Reed on this case. On the seventeenth, the day after Wilson-Downie's suspension, Barros-Curtis wrote to Reed 'to confirm, confidentially, that [she] has been suspended pending further investigation'. Reed, of course, had no right to be updated directly, and this exchange completely fell outside the approved complaints handling process as detailed by the EHRC. It was arguably the sort of conduct the EHRC had determined constituted unlawful discrimination against the Jewish community.

Reed had used the same channels only days earlier to send a dossier of complaints about other members in his constituency—all participants in the local CLP's 'political education' WhatsApp group. The complaints were sent directly to Barros-Curtis and to Evans' private Proton Mail address. As with Reed's original purge list, the evidentiary basis for these complaints was so slim as to cast a disturbing light on his judgment.

In one case, Reed complained about somebody sharing an article by the journalist Jonathan Cook that mounted a critique of the EHRC report.[19] Reed's dossier declared the article and Cook himself antisemitic. Cook's article was, in fact, a reasoned and forensic exploration of the manifest and obvious flaws and errors in the EHRC's report, some of which have been explored above. An edited version of the essay had appeared on the respected news website *Middle East Eye*.[20] In another case, the dossier complained about an individual questioning the legitimacy of the EHRC—even though their offending post made no mention of the EHRC at all.

The majority of Reed's complaints concerned the anger expressed by members of Reed's CLP over the treatment of Marc Wadsworth, a well-known Black anti-racist campaigner with strong connections to south London. The hounding of Wadsworth was one of the most egregious incidents in the entire 'antisemitism crisis'.

During the launch event for Labour's 2018 Chakrabarti Report, which looked into claims of antisemitism in the party, Wadsworth addressed the crowd. He had seen Labour's anti-Corbyn Ruth Smeeth MP and a *Daily Telegraph* journalist share a document. Wadsworth commented that Smeeth was working 'hand in hand' with hostile media. Smeeth stormed out of the event, and Wadsworth was accused of peddling an antisemitic conspiracy theory. Wadsworth was most surprised: he'd had no idea Smeeth was Jewish.

Wadsworth was eventually expelled from the party for bringing it into disrepute. The incident became a defining moment in the Labour 'antisemitism crisis'. When Smeeth eventually gave evidence before a party disciplinary panel, she walked to Labour Party headquarters in Southside 'protected' by a phalanx of supportive MPs—Wes Streeting prominent amongst them. This provided a visual accusation that Smeeth needed a cohort of MPs to protect her from violence by the antisemitic Corbynista mob. What she actually 'needed' protection from was a handful of campaigners who protested Wadsworth's mistreatment, a good number of whom were both elderly and Jewish. As mentioned previously, it was Wadsworth's treatment that led the Jewish councillor Jo Bird to suggest the party adopt 'Jew process' so that it could embody the principles of fairness and justice she believed were inherent in the best parts of the Jewish cultural tradition—a joke for which she was herself accused of antisemitism.

Reed's dossier lingered on the anger expressed by members of his CLP over Wadsworth's mistreatment, which they speculated may have been the result of racial discrimination. One post compared the harsh response to Wadsworth with the leniency shown to Reed himself, who had been accused of antisemitism when he referred to a Jewish businessman as a 'puppet master'. Reed was instantly absolved of his crime when he asserted that he had no idea that the person he was referring to was Jewish. But when Wadsworth put forward the same defence, on grounds no weaker, it cut no ice. One of the complaints included a screenshot of a member drawing this precise comparison, alongside a mild critique of the EHRC report's limited sample size—submitted by Reed himself as a sanctionable offence!

Another entry in Reed's dossier accused a CLP member of 'attacking' Margaret Hodge using 'antisemitic tropes'. The presumed 'antisemitic trope' was to refer to how Hodge had profited from her family's business. This, in turn, related to an investigation in South Africa alleging that the Hodge family company had run a joint enterprise that traded steel in apartheid South Africa in the 1980s, for which it was criticised by Britain's anti-apartheid movement.

A spokesperson for Hodge admitted that her family had run the subsidiary but claimed that Hodge had donated her earnings from it—although they were not able to recall the recipient charity, the amount she donated, or how she had calculated her earnings; or to answer whether Hodge had benefitted from an increase in the value of her shares. The article referred to Hodge as 'a very British apartheid profiteer'.[21]

'INDEPENDENT' COMPLAINTS HANDLING

In the aftermath of the EHRC report, the party developed an 'action plan' to begin introducing an 'independent complaints mechanism'. This included creating and appointing an antisemitism advisory board and a reference group; the former a group of individuals that would offer guidance on dealing with antisemitism in the party, and the latter a series of organisations that would act as institutional advisors. In effect, these bodies were given the power to steer the party on what conduct constituted antisemitism.

The advisory board was appointed in February 2021 by General Secretary David Evans. Emails show that Evans and the party had rejected recommendations from John McDonnell MP for potential left-wing Jewish members who might serve on the Board. These recommendations had been compiled in consultation with JVL and included recognised authorities on antisemitism such as Brian Klug and Antony Lerman. Klug was a senior research fellow at the University of Oxford, while Lerman had founded and directed the Institute for Jewish Policy Research. The advisory board instead included individuals like Mike Katz of the JLM; Marie van der Zyl, the president of the Board of Deputies; and Margaret Hodge.

The appointed 'reference group' comprised the Jewish Leadership Council, the Jewish Labour Movement, the Board of Deputies of British Jews, and the Community Security Trust. Two of these groups (the JLC and the CST) had advised Labour Together on the creation of the Center for Countering Digital Hate, which spawned the Stop Funding Fake News astroturf campaign, while McSweeney had worked with the JLM on its submissions to the EHRC's investigation into the Labour Party.

All of these organisations were highly political and endorsed views on Israeli policies and Zionism that could be considered to have a constraining impact on pro-Palestinian activism. The Board of Deputies and JLC, for example, have opposed the Boycott, Divestment, and Sanctions (BDS) campaign targeting Israel, which had been inspired by the successful sanctions campaign against apartheid South Africa. Many pro-Palestinian activists consider the BDS campaign one of the most effective ways to force peaceful change in Israel and the Occupied Palestinian Territory. In evidence to parliament in September 2023, the Board of Deputies testified that it had worked to 'combat the antisemitic threat that the BDS campaign poses to . . . Jewish constituents'.[22] For its part, the JLC called BDS 'a pernicious effort to single out the world's only Jewish state for unique treatment' and argued that '[p]ublic bodies which adopt or promote BDS policies undermine their relationship with Jewish communities'.[23] As shown in the penultimate chapter of this book, the JLC and the Board of Deputies would repeatedly defend Israel even as it carried out a 'plausible' genocide in Gaza. Whatever one makes of these statements and arguments, it stretches credulity to claim they are not political or do not reflect a partisan perspective on a contested debate.

Israel advocacy groups conveyed their position on BDS directly to the party in December 2020, in a meeting between Steve Reed and representatives from the Board of Deputies, the JLC, the CST, and the JLM. The CST was represented by Dave Rich; the JLC was represented by Trevor Chinn, among others; and the Board of Deputies was represented, inter alia, by its vice president Amanda Bowman. At the time, the party was still composing its EHRC 'action plan', which envisaged creating the advisory board and reference group.

The content of the meeting is recorded in a set of minutes that were distributed by Reed's assistant, Owain Mumford, and copied to Ellie Robinson, Andrew Whyte, and Barros-Curtis. These minutes were mentioned in the first part of this book as they included comments made by both Chinn and Rich endorsing the work of Labour Together in 'fighting antisemitism'.

There was much discussion about the problematic nature of the Labour Party's grassroots and the need to 'vet' local candidates. But the most explicitly political topic was raised by Bowman and concerned BDS. She acknowledged that Labour might 'hesitate to support' the anti-BDS legislation that was being pushed by the Tories, but 'advise[d]' that the party 'would be unwise to do anything to oppose' it. 'There is still a long way to go to build trust with Labour', the minutes record her saying. 'Community support has been dwindling but don't need unnecessary own goals on Israel-Palestine'.

Bowman further stressed that the Board of Deputies was

> keen to counter suppositions from Labour MPs that because they're nominally committed to combatting antisemitism, that it gives them carte blanche to say what they like about Israel. Criticism should reflect the IHRA definition and be like any other country.

The last sentence referred to a controversial document that cast the application of 'double standards' to Israel as antisemitic.

This, of course, ignored that no other country in the world had been accused of breaching the anti-apartheid convention by such respected human rights authorities as Amnesty International and Human Rights Watch. 'Whilst views within the community differ on Israel', Bowman claimed, 'the overwhelming majority of British Jews oppose these boycotts'.

Reed was obsequious in his response: 'Steve will never accept attempts to exceptionalise [*sic*] and delegitimise Israel', the minutes recorded. 'Steve's visit to Israel as an MP helped him understand the security and political situation in the middle [*sic*] East'. Reed agreed to talk with LOTO and party whips about the anti-BDS legislation and suggested that efforts be made to help councillors and others visit Israel to help them understand the situation as he did.

The entire exchange was a powerful illustration of the blurring of lines between antisemitism and anti-Zionism; it also provides disturbing insight into how members of the reference group felt comfortable using their enhanced access to the Labour Party to push a broader political agenda. Labour members were now expected to accept that the integration of pro-Israel advocacy groups into the party's complaints handling process amounted to making that process independent of political influence.

NATURAL (IN)JUSTICE: PROSCRIPTIONS AND THE EXPULSION OF LEFT-WING JEWS

In July 2021, the NEC approved a plan to 'proscribe' four groups; the effect was to make membership or support of the groups an immediately expellable offence. The notion of what constituted 'support' was extremely elastic. It could stretch to simply attending a meeting or online gathering of the groups, liking a single social media post, or giving an interview to an affiliated newspaper.

The four groups proscribed in 2021 were Labour Against the Witchhunt, Socialist Appeal, Labour in Exile Network, and Resist. Resist had been co-founded by former Labour MP Chris Williamson as a vehicle to mobilise grassroots democratic socialist initiatives after his expulsion. Socialist Appeal was the British extension of the International Marxist Tendency; it is best known for its fortnightly newspaper of the same name, which is a mainstay at progressive rallies and marches. Labour in Exile was established to resist what it saw as the unfair disciplinary treatment of socialist members of the Labour Party. Labour Against the Witchhunt was formed to oppose what it saw as the political weaponisation of the Labour 'antisemitism crisis'. In 2022, Labour in Exile and Labour Against the Witchhunt merged to form the Socialist Labour Network.

In March 2022, the party proscribed three additional left-wing groups: the Alliance for Workers Liberty, the Labour Left Alliance, and the Socialist Labour Network; the latter, as noted above, a merger of two previously proscribed groups.

Proscriptions were applied retrospectively. Any member who had ever indicated any of the broad forms of 'support' for any of the proscribed organisations, even if they had done so before that group was proscribed, now faced automatic exclusion. This was the essence of unfairness and abundantly vulnerable to legal challenge. To safeguard against this, the party rule book was quietly amended.

It had long contained a clause guaranteeing that 'members have the right to dignity and respect, and to be treated fairly by the Labour Party. Party officers at every level shall exercise their powers in good faith and use their best endeavours to ensure procedural fairness for members'. The 2022 rule book included a new provision stating that 'neither the principles of natural justice nor the provisions of fairness' stipulated by this long-standing clause would apply to proscription cases. It was, perhaps, the bluntest possible expression of the party's authoritarian bent under Starmer's leadership and of the perverse outcomes generated by a political crisis ostensibly centred on the fairness of how the party handled complaints.

The proscription of these groups allowed the party to swiftly expel people the Starmer regime found politically unpalatable but who were not otherwise guilty of any offence. The proscription of Labour Against the Witchhunt, in particular, was used to expel left-wing Jews and their allies who had questioned various claims relating to the 'antisemitism crisis' but who could not be found guilty of antisemitism.

In September 2022, for example, Naomi Wimborne-Idrissi, a co-founder of Jewish Voice for Labour and a lifelong pro-Palestinian activist, was elected to the party's NEC, becoming the only Jewish member of the body at the time. Her election provoked a furious response from the Board of Deputies, JLM, and others, who demanded action. Within three weeks of her election as the NEC's only Jewish member, the party issued Wimborne-Idrissi with a suspension for having once addressed a Labour Against the Witchhunt meeting. By December 2022, she had been expelled. In the same month, the party expelled two more Jewish JVL members on similar grounds: Heather Mendick, who had previously worked in Corbyn's leadership office, and Stephen Marks.

Most notoriously, proscription allowed the party to expel the renowned filmmaker Ken Loach, who had publicly associated with Labour Against the Witchhunt. Loach confirmed that he had been kicked out of the party in August 2021, the month after the proscriptions came into effect. For Loach, this was confirmation that there was 'indeed a witchhunt'. It is hard not to see Loach's expulsion via proscription as the culmination of a plan hatched a year prior to ensure that he was expelled at the insistence of Steve Reed.

Other cases were less well-known but no less disgraceful. In November 2021, the party expelled the well-regarded Harrow councillor Pamela Fitzpatrick. Fitzpatrick had a long history in local activism, including as director of the Harrow Law Centre. The centre provides Harrow residents with free legal advice on asylum, housing access, and other issues. Fitzpatrick's sole offence was that she had given an interview to the Socialist Appeal's newspaper in May 2020, prior to the group's proscription. Party files show that Fitzpatrick had complained to the party that she had previously been the victim of serious harassment by a well-connected, right-wing party member (an allegation that this member denied). 'The expulsion of Pam Fitzpatrick is the culmination of a campaign of harassment that should never be accepted in any organisation, let alone the Labour Party', John McDonnell MP said in response.[24]

In February 2023, JVL felt moved to describe the party under Starmer as a hostile place for left-wing Jews who had dared to question received wisdom on the 'antisemitism crisis' or criticised Israel in terms considered unacceptable by party mandarins. In a letter sent to the EHRC, JVL provided a raft of damning statistics. It was aware of at least sixty Jewish members who had been 'targeted' for investigation on accusations of antisemitism by the party. It estimated that Jewish Labour Party members were 5.8 times more likely to be investigated for alleged antisemitism than non-Jewish members. JVL members were 37 times more likely than an average party member to be investigated, and JVL executive members were fully 248 times more likely to be investigated on the same grounds.[25]

Proscription was also disproportionately applied to Jewish members. In total, JVL counted seventeen Jewish Labour Party members expelled from the party for 'supporting' proscribed groups. All but one of these were JVL members; four were members of the JVL executive committee. JVL members were thus an estimated sixty-three times more likely to be expelled for proscription offences than the average non-Jewish member of the Labour Party.[26]

'Jewish members investigated or sanctioned over antisemitism find the experience profoundly oppressive', JVL observed. 'Indeed, it feels like antisemitism itself; we feel hated'.

'PROCESSED AND PROUD'

Few victims of the Starmer Project were as undeserving as Riva Joffe, an elderly Jewish woman. Her cruel treatment exemplified the way in which Starmer's Labour Party showed callous disregard for decent people and illustrated the perverse outcomes produced by an 'antisemitism crisis' driven by questionable actors.

On September 27, 2020, the Labour Party received three complaints about Joffe. They all attached the exact same report accusing Joffe of posting antisemitic comments, including 'demonising Israel by inaccurately describing it as an apartheid state'. Two of the complaints were submitted by individuals with unusual names; both were sent from Proton Mail addresses. Extensive searches have been unable to confirm if these were real people. The third email was sent by 'David Gordstein', the Jewish-sounding nom de plume of LAAS' non-Jewish spokesperson Euan Philipps.

The complaint attached two pieces of evidence. The first was a screenshot of Joffe sharing a poster for the sixteenth Israeli Apartheid Week, an annual protest associated with the global BDS campaign. The second was the text of a lengthy Facebook post that Joffe had made in the JVL Facebook group. She lamented Richard Burgon MP's expression of regret for having said that 'the enemy of peace is not the Jewish people but Zionism'. She speculated that Burgon had relented because he 'felt the hot breath of Labour Friends of Israel' and that a similar fear of the 'Zionist lobby . . . makes Jeremy [Corbyn] wilt under their gimlet glare'.

Joffe's family had a long pedigree in fleeing and fighting injustice. Her Jewish grandparents fled from Lithuania to South Africa in the face of antisemitic persecution by the Russian empire. In South Africa, her parents became active members of the socialist resistance against the racial segregation that eventually crystallised as apartheid. During World War II, Joffe's father was imprisoned as a seditious communist in an internment camp, where he faced oppressive treatment from Afrikaner guards and Nazi sympathisers who were interned at the same location. Joffe's family were close friends with Joe Slovo, the legendary Jewish South African activist against apartheid.

Joffe's family left South Africa after the war to settle in the UK. They became stalwarts of the London anti-apartheid movement. Their home became a locus of fundraising and a safe base for comrades, including such luminaries of the resistance as Elinor Sisulu and Paul Robeson. Joffe, steeped in the internationalism of her parents and informed by their political views, became a firm opponent of Zionism, which she believed had led to the oppression of Palestinians.

Joffe combined a lifetime of activism with a career as a respected psychoanalyst. She had rejoined the Labour Party after Corbyn's election, becoming a well-known and active member of her local Cantelowes branch in Starmer's constituency of Holborn and St Pancras. In this role, she had contact with Starmer, who knew her personally.

Joffe's son, Stefan, told me that joining the Labour Party under Corbyn had been a lifeline for his mother. 'For ages she struggled to even get out of bed' following her partner's death, he told me. 'But joining a party she associated with hope, which got her meeting all sorts of comrades, gave her a sense of real happiness'.

In September 2021, Joffe received a notice of investigation from the Labour Party in response to the complaints submitted by 'David Gordstein' and two unidentified complainants. Joffe was unwell at the time and receiving ongoing treatment that was keeping her alive.

'The complaint really, really knocked her', Stefan told me. 'She was really upset. She couldn't believe this thing that had previously brought her so much joy could now cause her so much hurt'.

Joffe responded with a heartfelt defence of her views. Donning her psychoanalytic hat, she speculated on why the party under Starmer pursued Jews like her so aggressively:

> Honestly—a therapist would say, 'this frenzy of purging you are driven to—it's not the behaviour of mature adults. It smacks of desperation, fear and panic'. Is it really us—a quite reasonable group of democratic socialist citizens—that cause you such deep-seated and even pathological insecurity?

Joffe shared her response to the Labour Party with left-wing groups in Starmer's constituency. Not long after, Joffe told her friends and allies that she had decided to stop the treatment that was keeping her alive. She had lived an amazing and fulfilling life, she said, and she was reconciled to death. She passed away on September 21, 2021.

Joffe died while still under investigation by the Labour Party for antisemitism. In response to a complaint submitted by the Jewish-sounding pseudonym of a non-Jewish man, her life's last political act: explaining why she, an elderly Jewish woman with extensive personal and family experience of antisemitic persecution and a proud record of fighting apartheid and discrimination, was not guilty of antisemitism.

Joffe's son Stefan was horrified at the party's treatment of his mother. He was particularly aggrieved that her case would be left unresolved by the party after her death. He wrote repeatedly to the party, telling them that his mother had died and asking them to confirm that the case had been closed. When he did not get a response, Stefan reached out to Andrew Feinstein, a friend of Joffe's in the constituency. Feinstein wrote to Starmer personally, asking him to resolve the matter. Feinstein and Stefan believed that Starmer might be willing to reply because he had known Riva Joffe personally. But Starmer did not respond. Stefan still does not know what became of his mother's case.

'Now, in my eighties, and on a somewhat smaller scale certainly—I face becoming a "political exile" from a party that for a few hopeful years was my political home', Joffe had ended her response to the party. 'Meanwhile, I will be joining a well-respected group of comrades and friends, all "processed and proud"'.

PART FOUR

A LAWLESS AND 'RACIST' PARTY

CHAPTER 15

THE HIERARCHY

By early 2021, the Starmer Project had taken near total control of the Labour Party bureaucracy, now firmly under the thumb of General Secretary David Evans and Alex Barros-Curtis, the executive director of legal. The Equality and Human Rights Commission report and the response to Corbyn's sacking had legitimised the bureaucracy's intervention in the politics of the party at all levels, precipitating a mass exodus of members that still further empowered the project.

This internal control was further consolidated by National Executive Committee elections in November 2020 and the election of new subcommittee chairs in January 2021. These allowed key Starmer Project allies to take up positions of influence over important NEC matters. As noted previously, Shabana Mahmood, a long-time Labour Together insider, was elected chair of the NEC's disciplinary subcommittee in January 2021. In effect, the Starmer Project's bureaucratic allies would work within the party to discipline dissident left-wing members revolting against Evans' authoritarian tendencies, while all disciplinary cases would be heard and overseen at the NEC level by one of Labour Together's eight 'brave' MPs. It was a slick machine. Another key development was the election of UNISON's Wendy Nichols as head of the NEC's Organisational Sub-Committee, which was in charge of key governance matters. She would become a key player in many of the case studies discussed below.

This centralisation of control enabled and encouraged disturbing behaviour. Across three illustrative episodes examined in this chapter, the party machinery used every trick in the book to undermine the basic tenets of democracy, malign and discredit opponents, and even collude in an attack on a media outlet that was reporting accurately on serious local governance failures.

These case studies are discussed here for two reasons:

The first is that they act as a corrective to a lamentable media tendency to breezily state that Starmer 'changed' the party. This rendering has often implied that Starmer's 'changes' were an admirable democratic exercise, achieved by winning arguments and votes in party forums. This impression is reinforced by the media's general failure to acknowledge the victims of this process of 'change'. By telling their stories in full, these episodes confirm how contentious and bloody Starmer's 'changes' really were.

Second, these case studies illustrate the nature and style of the political machine created by the Labour Together and Starmer projects. They reveal decisions that frequently skirted the limits of the law and certainly violated principles of natural justice. In addition, the episodes examined arguably reveal an underlying racism or Islamophobia that excluded and marginalised BAME constituencies.

The case studies show how, under the Starmer Project's control, the Labour Party could credibly be accused of becoming both lawless and racist.

THE LEAKED REPORT (AGAIN)

Almost from the outset of Starmer's leadership, many party members and staff expressed unease over its approach to racism. This first expressed itself in relation to the Leaked Report. Its revelations of party official's alleged racism and seeming indifference to Islamophobia had alarmed BAME staff.

Internal party emails show that BAME party members were equally distressed—and that this distress was not considered a priority by party higher-ups. On June 2, 2020, in the midst of the historic Black Lives Matter (BLM) protests, the *HuffPost* ran a feature about Black voters leaving the Labour Party. The article quoted many leavers who cited the revelations in the Leaked Report as confirmation of what they had long suspected—that the party, from its machinery to its MPs, harboured disdain for Black members and MPs.[1]

On the same day, in response to the article, a staffer in the party's membership unit circulated a question to their colleagues in the same unit. They asked if the party held any statistics on BAME members leaving and suggested a meeting to discuss the situation. Another official in the membership team confirmed that in the period between the Leaked Report being made public (on April 12) and June 2, 2020, fully 6 percent of the party's entire BAME membership had formally resigned, while a further 4.5 percent had effectively quit by cancelling their debit orders—a loss of one out of ten BAME members in less than two months.

'That seems pretty bad to me', the first staff member commented. This time, however, the staff member copied in two more senior members of the party: Nick Parrott (Angela Rayner's chief of staff) and Anneliese Midgley. Midgley, recall, had originally been selected by Starmer for the position of general secretary but was appointed an advisor in LOTO after her candidacy was spiked.

Parrott appeared concerned by the data and asked for further information. The following day, however, everyone was told by a senior official in the membership team that staff were too busy, 'so unless it's mission critical then they don't really have the time to pull this together at the moment'.

Three weeks later, on the twenty-sixth, the staff member who had raised the concern originally approached the membership team again. They asked for more details, as it 'would be really useful info particularly in terms of how we communicate to BAME members going forward and in light of the salience of the BLM movement'. While they were told that the information was important, the team was 'extremely busy' and the data not 'easily accessible'. Finding out how many BAME members had left the party would have to be deferred to another time.

The exchange clearly upset the staff member who had started the conversation, because the email chain was shortly thereafter forwarded to a member of the BAME Staff Network. They, in turn, wrote to Nick Parrott and Helene Reardon-Bond (recently drafted into LOTO), expressing concern and confusion. 'I've just been sent this email chain which has naturally concerned me', they explained. 'Am I missing something? I can imagine the membership team are extremely busy at the moment. But it does seem as though BAME members are not a priority for their team'.

BLACK LIVES DON'T MATTER ENOUGH

On May 25, 2020, George Floyd was killed in Minneapolis, asphyxiated when a police officer knelt on his back and neck for nine minutes and twenty-nine seconds. Floyd's death was recorded, along with his final, plaintive pleas. 'I can't breathe', he told the assembled police squad. Derek Chauvin, the police officer who killed Floyd, was convicted and sent to prison for twenty-two years.

The awful video of Floyd's death spread like wildfire on the internet and catalysed the BLM movement. The protests extended to the UK (albeit somewhat constrained by Covid lockdown) and culminated in the toppling of a statue of Edward Colston into the Bristol Harbour. Colston's company had transported one hundred thousand slaves from West Africa in the years 1672 to 1689, making Colston and his family oligarch-level wealthy. The plinth to Colston's statue had declared him 'one of the most virtuous and wise sons' of the city.[2]

The Starmer leadership's response to this outpouring of rage and grief was inept and tone-deaf. As global protests raged on June 29, five days prior to the Bristol incident, Starmer gave a deeply unfortunate interview to the BBC.[3] He referred to BLM as a 'moment' rather than a movement, adopted a cringe-inducing machismo while setting out how he had worked with the police, and dismissed calls for radical reform as wrong-headed.

This was a view that would not survive much scrutiny: in 2021, the Metropolitan Police (Met) appointed Louise Casey to conduct an internal review in light of the abduction and murder of Sarah Everard by a police officer that same year. Her report, published in 2023, found that the Met was 'guilty of institutional racism, misogyny and homophobia'.[4] Casey found that the Met was losing public consent for its operations and recommended 'radical, structural options' like dividing the Met into multiple sections.[5]

Starmer expressed regret for his dismissive comment on BLM. But only days later, speaking to LBC, Starmer said it was 'completely wrong' to pull down Colston's statue; instead, the statue, long subject to complaints from local residents, should have been 'brought down properly, with consent'.[6]

Starmer's version did not age well. Four individuals who were charged with criminal damage for toppling the statue were cleared in a jury trial in 2022. The Irish barrister Blinne Ní Grálaigh, who represented one defendant and would be part of South Africa's legal challenge when it accused Israel of genocide at the ICJ, commented that the jury 'determined that a conviction for the removal of his statue—that glorified a slave trader involved in the enslavement of 84,000 black men, women and children as a "most virtuous and wise man"—would not be proportionate'.[7]

The following day, as criticism erupted over his Colston comments, Starmer used Twitter to post a picture of himself and Angela Rayner 'taking the knee' in an empty office—a gesture signalling support for BLM. It was the day of George Floyd's funeral. This photo was striking for its total lack of political nous. For right-wing audiences, it provided a neat visual confirmation that Starmer was a 'woke' BLM warrior; for many on the left, including staff in the Labour Party, it was offensive gesture politics belied by Starmer's previous statements.

That afternoon, the BAME Staff Network dispatched a stinging letter to Nick Parrott and Helene Reardon-Bond, among others, explaining how the party leadership had let down BAME staff and members:

> The brutal murder of George Floyd has shocked the world, but for Black people everywhere, including in the UK, many speak of events igniting a trauma. A trauma that has uprooted all our own experiences of racism and oppression, both covert and overt, to the forefront . . . Many members of staff expected the Labour Leadership to find a way to answer questions about the protests and protestors that avoided, absolutely, any hint that their action was unjustified. Taking the lead from Black Labour politicians would have achieved exactly that. Instead, the top line briefed was that Keir Starmer, leader of the Labour Party, condemns the 'completely wrong' tearing down of the statue of slave trader Edward Colston in Bristol at the weekend.

The letter urged the party to consider the matter in the round, foregrounding questions as to why the statue had not previously been removed despite long-term anger at its presence and reminding the party that many great acts of anti-racist activism were illegal, citing the likes of Rosa Parks and Nelson Mandela as examples.

The BAME Staff Network pushed the party to put Black voices, in particular its Black MPs, at the forefront of the discussion and asked for assurances that the party still backed the policies set out in its popular 2019 Race and Faith Manifesto. But, reduced to its essence, the letter was an emotional plea as much as it was political: 'Black members of staff need to know that the Leadership of our party understands the pain and trauma. We need a leadership that is quick to listen to this pain, and does not condemn how it manifests'.

The Network received a sympathetic response from Reardon-Bond, who copied in Morgan McSweeney and the deputy political director in Starmer's office, Ellie Robinson. Reardon-Bond would be effectively delegated by LOTO to oversee the handling of issues arising from BLM inside the party.

Within two days, the BAME staff letter had been all but dismissed. On June 12, 2020, Robinson sent a 'black community engagement plan' to other LOTO staffers, including McSweeney, Ben Nunn, Jenny Chapman, and Claire Ainsley. Despite the BAME Staff Network's plea for Black staff members and MPs to be brought into the discussion, the email chain included only one Black person out of thirteen recipients. The remaining twelve were white.

Perhaps that is why the plan was so tone-deaf and sat so awkwardly with the version of events put forward by the BAME Staff Network. Completely overlooking the anger and hurt in the Network's letter, the plan opened on a self-congratulatory note: 'We have managed to walk a delicate line over the past two weeks—for example, our positioning on the statue made clear we are a proudly anti-racist party campaigning for race equality while being able to bring the majority of the public (who did not think the statue should have been brought down in that way) with us'. This self-confidence is difficult to understand given the dissatisfaction among BAME staff.

More concerning was the plan's desire to frame the party's response to racism to avoid alienating voters in Labour's traditional northern heartlands—the so-called 'red wall'—who had increasingly defected to other parties. 'Publicly we have landed in a clear, widely acceptable and morally defensible position', Robinson wrote. 'However it has raised bigger strategic questions that we need to keep sight of. These questions hinge on choices about which voters we are trying to win in which seats—and therefore on the character of the argument that we want to prosecute in 2024'.

The party's response to BLM and issues of racism would thus be driven by electoral calculation, not ethical principle. 'No matter how serious the economic situation gets, the liberal-authoritarian axis is still going to be a key driver of voter's behaviour over the next 4 years', Robinson explained. 'Johnson is attempting to get us back into a position on the "culture war" that divides our "red wall" voters from our liberal urban voters'. A reasonable reader might well interpret this to mean that the party could not adopt a full-throated anti-racism for fear of alienating imagined racists in the 'red wall'.

Robinson's plan acknowledged the anger of BAME staff but ended on another problematic note that would powerfully illustrate the findings of Martin Forde KC (discussed later) that the party had failed to get its own house in order on issues of racism: 'we mustn't lose sight of other communities that are a strategic priority for us to engage with (in particular Hindu and Jewish communities)'.

Even at the height of BLM, it seems, the party fretted that prioritising the concerns of Black stakeholders would absorb too much time. More to the point, it illustrated that the party understood anti-racism and community engagement to be a zero-sum game, in which heeding the concerns of one community would alienate another. Arguably, this was a function of the party's refusal to adopt a principled and, most importantly, consistent anti-racism that could unite all its disparate constituencies.

ACTIONS AND NOT WORDS

As Starmer's political biographer Oliver Eagleton has astutely noted,[8] the party's approach to BLM was two-fold. While it triangulated its public positions for fear of angering target voters in 'red wall' seats, it attempted to mollify staff by proffering a series of internal party reforms designed to take their concerns into account—or at least enact the performance of doing so.

There are strong indications that these internal reforms were not being proposed out of principle but instead as a form of damage limitation. The party's 'black community engagement plan' had noted that

> internally, we have a prominent group in the PLP [Parliamentary Labour Party], staff and membership that feel we should have gone further to unequivocally support BLM . . . Therefore, a lot of next steps listed below focus on internal management to prevent an escalation and a consequential undermining of our public positions.

The party's internal reforms, in short, were designed to prevent angry BAME staff from becoming a public relations problem.

What thus transpired was an elaborate performance of 'listening' and soothing words whose sincerity was undermined by the party's real-world actions. Those actions revealed a disregard for the careers of BAME staff and a propensity to police their expression even in this fraught moment. Nowhere was this clearer than in the treatment of Louis Mendee (a prominent member of the BAME staff network), revealed by party files.

Mendee, patently smart and well qualified, had worked since 2019 in the general secretary's office. In the first week of July 2020, during Covid lockdown, Mendee was instructed out of the blue to take an 'informal leave of absence'. It took weeks for Mendee to discover what prompted this: two strongly worded tweets criticising Starmer and Rayner for their responses to BLM. In one tweet, Mendee criticised Starmer for engaging in gesture politics by taking the knee. Mendee was eventually shown screenshots of the tweets taken within an hour or so after they'd been posted, suggesting a close monitoring operation.

After getting Human Resources involved, Mendee was allowed to return to the party but shunted on secondment into a laborious role redacting Subject Access Requests. Following months of arduous administrative work, Mendee was supposed to move to a new role better suited to their skill set. But the day before their secondment was supposed to end, it was suddenly extended. Mendee would not, as a result, be allowed to take up their new role, and would instead be required to do months more of redacting work. Remarkably, Mendee was not consulted about the decision to extend the secondment but instead informed about it as a done deal.

Mendee raised the issue with party headquarters, which agreed that they would eventually be allowed to move into another role. But before Mendee could do so, they were suspended and then investigated because the party suspected Mendee of leaking materials related to the disciplinary case of Sir Trevor Phillips—to which we return later.

This treatment was clearly insensitive and arguably ugly. Certainly, it is easy to see how Mendee would draw the inference that they were being punished because of their pained, authentic reaction to the killing of George Floyd and their concern—shared by large numbers of other BAME staff—that the response of the party leadership had been tone-deaf and insincere.

'AUTHENTIC VALUES ALIGNMENT'

A similar fate befell the Community Organising Unit (COU). The COU was established in June 2018 and was largely seen, at least by the party's right wing, as an irredeemable product of Corbynite decadence. The journalist Gabriel Pogrund reported on Twitter that COU staff were also distrusted by the party bureaucracy as 'indelibly' linked to Corbyn's chief of staff, Karie Murphy: '[I]ts staff are seen as her personal allies'.[9]

The COU was also the most diverse unit in the party in terms of race, gender, and age. One notable graduate of the COU programme was Zarah Sultana, who was subsequently elected as an MP.

Growing to twenty-nine staff by 2019, the COU sought to reverse the party's weakening presence in wider communities, itself caused by a long-term decline in trade union membership. COU staff would join forces with local campaigns and campaigners, identify and train up-and-coming community figures, and host regular community events. One of the most celebrated COU initiatives was the establishment of a Labour-affiliated community hub in Broxtowe. It provided advice to residents and became a de facto clothing and food bank. The hub was eventually closed in August 2023, after party headquarters took control of the hub's bank account and neglected to pay rent.[10] In January 2025, twenty Labour councillors in Broxtowe left the Labour Party to form the Broxtowe Independents, citing widespread anger at welfare cuts brought in by Starmer's incoming government. The mass defection led to Labour losing control of the council.

In the aftermath of Labour's 2019 election drubbing, attempts were made to highlight the role of the COU in limiting the scale and damage caused by the collapse in popular support for the party over Brexit. In a post-election briefing, the COU recorded how it had dramatically increased the number of in-person contacts and appeared to soften the decline in support, especially in the thirty marginal seats to which COU members were deployed. It pointed to the example of Yorkshire, where seats serviced by the COU saw a mere 3 percent swing away from Labour as opposed to a 10 percent swing regionally.[11]

Labour Together's 2019 election review had also considered the role of community organising. While it chuntered that the COU had not been properly integrated into the broader national campaign, the review forcefully recommended that the party should '[m]ake community organising central to what we do . . . This work needs to become a permanent and integrated part of our structure from top to bottom'.[12]

The COU's fate was evidence that, despite public pronouncements to the contrary, few in the Starmer Project took the election review seriously, regardless of its Labour Together provenance.

The COU unit was shut down with little ceremony in February 2021. Just after noon on February 3, Pogrund tweeted out that 'Labour has told its community organising unit, introduced under Corbyn, that their contracts will not be renewed from May. Another key moment in Keir Starmer's battle to transform the party and remove Corbynistas from HQ'.[13]

Pogrund's tweet was truly a scoop: he had been briefed about the unit's closure before COU staff had been told the bad news directly. COU staff, many of whom were members of the BAME staff network, were thus informed of their imminent retrenchment, in the middle of the pandemic, via a journalist's tweet. The pill was particularly bitter because COU staff were not given any serious undertakings that the party would seek to redeploy or re-employ them elsewhere.

The timing of the announcement was especially unfortunate because, one day prior, *The Guardian* had published a story quoting from extracts of a branding and strategy review conducted by outside consultants hired by the party.[14] The strategy suggested that the party needed to embrace and express more open and symbolic displays of patriotism: 'The use of the flag, veterans, dressing smartly at the war memorial etc. give voters a sense of authentic values alignment', the strategy explained. This review partially explained why the party had shoehorned the Union Jack into every publicity shot or speech by Starmer.

Whether fairly or not, these overt performances of symbolic nationalism bore resemblance to the British far right, which fetishizes the flag. 'I was just sat there replaying in my mind the storming of the Capitol [in Washington the previous month] and thinking: are you really so blind to what happens when you start pandering to the language and concerns of the right?' an anonymous party employee told *The Guardian*.[15]

Unsurprisingly, the BAME Staff Network was deeply upset by the decision to disband the COU. On February 8, 2021, the Network sent a letter addressed to Starmer personally. 'It is regrettable that after months of collaboration in good faith, we are now seeing policy decisions made by the party in how we treat staff are in contradiction to our policies and aims as an organisation', the letter pointedly noted. 'In light of recent events, the network is concerned the party is not taking adequate steps to protect BAME staff during this difficult period, and as above, may in fact be actively briefing against them'.

As with many of the BAME Staff Network letters during the first year of Starmer's leadership, the pain and sense of betrayal is palpable. The letter pointed out that BAME staff had both embraced and empowered the party's entire diversity and inclusion strategy that had been implemented in the wake of BLM. More importantly, the Network believed that they were responsible for its achievements, including the creation of a Diversity and Inclusion Board and unconscious bias training. 'Yet, we are the same people who are being pushed out after dedicating our lives to improving the organisation so that we are electable as a government', the letter pointed out, noting, just in case the party didn't get it, that 'given the diverse nature of the Community Organising Unit, many of our members, our committee, and even representatives on the Diversity and Inclusion board would be affected by this decision'.

IMPUNITY

The sensitivity of BAME staff to the party's adoption of flag-and-country rhetoric did not come out of nowhere. There was important context in the party's failure, throughout 2020, to oppose two draconian pieces of Tory legislation.

The first was the Overseas Operations Bill. The Bill, first introduced into the House in March 2020, put in place a 'triple lock' of mechanisms purportedly designed to prevent former serving members of the military from 'frivolous' investigations for crimes committed abroad—including war crimes, torture, murder, and crimes against humanity. The 'triple lock' effectively made it nigh-on-impossible for offences to be prosecuted five years or more after they had been committed.

The Bill was widely criticised for granting effective impunity to British combatants abroad and undermining the UK's commitment to international human rights law. Opposition to the bill on the left of the party was fierce and culminated in a mini-rebellion in September 2020. Starmer's team pushed for Labour MPs to abstain on the bill, a compromise position designed to foreclose Tory attacks on Labour as insufficiently patriotic. Eighteen MPs from Labour's Socialist Campaign Group, including three junior shadow cabinet ministers, broke a one-line whip in order to vote against.

Starmer's heavy-handed response was to fire a number of parliamentary private secretaries (an MP appointed by a minister to be their assistant), including the young BAME MP Nadia Whittome—an arguably severe reaction to breaking a one-line whip, which is considered the least prescriptive. But it was the way these firings took place that really rankled staff. Whittome, clearly caught off guard, was effectively informed that she had been sacked live on air. It was typical of the Starmer machine's penchant for humiliating opponents as part of an effort to look decisive. This modus operandi did not escape the attention of junior party staffers. One explained that Whittome's firing was the moment they formed the opinion that the Starmer leadership was hyper-factional and cruel, particularly towards BAME figures.

The second Tory initiative was the Covert Human Intelligence Sources Bill, more commonly referred to as the 'Spy Cops Bill'. The Spy Cops Bill sought to establish immunity for undercover police officers who committed crimes while performing their duties. The Bill would have effectively made it legal for undercover police officers to commit serious crimes, including murder and torture.

The Spy Cops Bill was part of a latticework of legislation put forward by the Tories from 2020 onward that massively constrained the rights to protest and dissent, while freeing the hand of the state, military, and security services to act with near impunity. It was also proposed in the wake of the imminent opening of an inquiry into Spy Cops abuses, which, as mentioned previously, flowed from revelations of how undercover police had infiltrated environmentalist, left-wing, and anti-racist groups. Starmer, of course, had been heavily criticised by victims of the Spy Cops scandal for refusing to properly investigate the matter while he was director of public prosecutions.

The Spy Cops Bill was opposed by a panoply of human rights organisations. Amnesty International argued that it threatened basic democratic freedoms while increasing the scope for abuse and warned, 'there is a grave danger that this Bill could end up providing informers and agents with a license to kill'.[16]

It does not take a genius to see how backing—or even just refusing to oppose—the Spy Cops Bill would have aggravated people upset by the party's response to BLM. That movement took aim at both institutional racism and the excesses of unrestrained police forces. Certainly, the complaints about police racism that were being voiced in the US also resonated with many in the UK; one poll published in November 2020 found that 'the vast majority (85 percent) of Black people in the UK are not confident that they would be treated the same as a white person by police'.[17]

Left-wing MPs made clear that the Spy Cops Bill would disproportionately impact the BAME community. In an impassioned parliamentary speech, Zarah Sultana pointed out that previous Spy Cops infiltrations had 'overwhelmingly' targeted left-wing, anti-racist, and climate justice groups, noting that only three far-right groups—out of over a thousand—were monitored in the same way.[18] 'It is argued that the bill is all about preventing terror atrocities, but we know that such powers will also be used on low-level criminality and will disproportionally affect BAME communities', Kate Osborne MP wrote in *Tribune*.[19]

But Starmer's team had other concerns: they fretted about how the triumphal Tories might accuse Labour of a patriotism deficit and so chose not to oppose the bill. Instead, in October 2020, Starmer imposed a one-line whip on Labour MPs to abstain. In the end, thirty-four Labour MPs defied the whip by voting against the bill—nearly double the previous rebellion. Seven were frontbenchers.

Bruised by the previous rebellion, Starmer opted not to fire or punish the frontbenchers for this round of infractions. But he remained unrepentant about the decision to acquiesce in the bill.

ISLAMOPHOBIA AND THE PARTY LEADERSHIP

In July 2020, only three months after Starmer's election as party leader, the Labour Muslim Network announced that it was undertaking what it would eventually call 'the largest Islamophobia consultation of Muslim Labour Members in history'.[20] The result of that consultation, which included extensive polling, was set out in an excoriating report published in November 2020.[21] The survey found that 29 percent of Muslim members had directly experienced Islamophobia in the party, 37 percent had witnessed Islamophobia in the party, and 48 percent of Muslim Labour members did not believe that the Labour Party took Islamophobia seriously.

Importantly, the consultation revealed that Muslim Labour members held a particularly dim view of the party leadership, which they considered was even less responsive to issues of Islamophobia than the party as a whole. Over 59 percent of Muslim members stated that they did not feel 'well-represented by the leadership of the Labour Party', while 55 percent did not 'trust the leadership of the Labour Party to tackle Islamophobia effectively'.

Two interesting trends were identified when it came to explaining why so few Muslim members believed the party took Islamophobia seriously. The first—prefiguring what Martin Forde KC would highlight in his long-delayed report—was that many members surveyed believed there was a hierarchy of racism in the Labour Party such that 'the Muslim experience with racism sat at the very bottom of the party's priorities'.

The second was that the release of the Leaked Report had had a significant impact on Muslim members, because it presented evidence that allegations of Islamophobia had not been properly dealt with by the party. The report highlighted the case of Joe Goldberg and Emina Ibrahim, which, as seen in the previous section, ended with Goldberg being readmitted into the party despite the allegations of Islamophobia against him. His readmission came after prompting by the right-wing NEC member Luke Akehurst. The LMN found that the Leaked Report 'was prevalent and influential in responses' to questions about whether the Labour Party took Islamophobia seriously.

The LMN's report was acknowledged with sonorous gravity by Starmer, Rayner, and Evans. In an official statement, Starmer and Rayner 'thanked the Labour Muslim Network for this important report', confirmed that 'Islamophobia has no place in our party and society', and committed to 'rooting it out of the party'.[22]

General Secretary David Evans, for his part, sent a party-wide email to staff on the day preceding the report's publication. Evans reiterated, along with Starmer and Rayner, that Islamophobia was terrible and they would do all they could to stamp it out. Evans noted that even though progress had been made, 'there was still work to be done', which 'will be led by Keir, Angela, and I'.

In fact, as would become increasingly clear in 2021, the party was only too willing to repeatedly downplay the seriousness of the issue, or, alternatively, to actively embrace Islamophobia as part of its war against the left.

CHAPTER 16

THE NEWHAM DOSSIER

On March 12, 2021, the Labour Party wrote to members of the East Ham and West Ham Constituency Labour Parties to inform them that both had been put into 'special measures'. As of February 2025, the CLPs remained suspended. The effect of this suspension was that branch and CLP meetings could no longer be held, and that the CLPs would no longer choose their own candidates to run as Labour MPs and councillors. Total control over this would be exercised by party headquarters.

The CLPs were in Newham, one of the most deprived boroughs in the country and one of the staunchest Labour strongholds. The party had won all of the council's sixty seats in each of the three local elections held since 2010, most recently in 2018. For historical reasons and because of the first-past-the-post system, any local politics that mattered happened within the Labour Party. The real-life impact was that the Labour Party had suspended local democracy for over three hundred thousand people in the midst of a global health crisis.

To justify the CLPs' suspensions, the Labour Party explained that it had 'recently been in receipt of a significant number of serious allegations regarding the conduct of Labour Party members and membership recruitment practices in Newham. The allegations are wide ranging and supported by a considerable amount of evidence'.[1] Alleged irregularities included issues with new member sign-ups over a 'significant period'.

Underscoring the gravity of alleged wrongdoing, the party claimed to 'also understand that allegations of electoral fraud are being separately investigated by the Metropolitan Police'. In fact, the Met confirmed to journalist Henry Zeffman that 'an assessment was completed which concluded that no police investigation was required' after receiving a report the previous August that alleged electoral fraud.[2]

The officers and members of both CLPs say the party did not provide them with any underlying evidence to justify the claims. But as it turned out, the CLPs' suspension was based on a dossier and subsequent materials submitted by a local Labour Party member, David Gilles.

The contents of the Gilles dossier should have rung alarm bells with Labour Party officials and prompted them to investigate its production. Instead, the party seems to have taken the dossier at face value and used it as the rationale for suspending two CLPs. That the suspension remains in force *four years later*, while there appears to be no current investigation into either the dossier or the allegations it makes, is a matter of grave democratic concern. It is effectively an indefinite suspension of local democracy while allegations hang over members of these CLPs without an indication of when they may be resolved.

RECENT REMINDERS

At the time Gilles submitted his dossier to the Labour Party—first in February 2021 and then again with an update the following month—the party bureaucracy should have been operating with a heightened awareness of the issue of Islamophobia in the party and in Newham especially.

As noted previously, the Labour Muslim Network's report about Islamophobia in the party had prompted rueful and apologetic statements from Keir Starmer and Angela Rayner, with promises to do better. In October 2020, a grouping in Newham called the London Muslim Community Forum addressed concerned and indignant letters to Starmer, David Evans, and Newham Council Chief Executive Althea Loderick. The Forum brought together local mosques (including the East London Mosque and the Finsbury Park Mosque) and Muslim organisations (like the Newham branch of MEND). The letters set out complaints of Islamophobia against three Newham councillors. They also called for an immediate 'Independent Inquiry' to investigate whether a 'culture of Islamophobia' had come to pervade Newham's Labour-run council.

Party emails show that details of the complaints were forwarded to Labour's disciplinary staff in the Governance and Legal Unit to be processed, and that at least one councillor was disciplined for sharing a video by a far-right commentator, Anne Marie Waters, that made derogatory comments about Muslims. But no direct response was made to the Forum, which created the impression that the complaints had not been taken seriously. Party records show that there was still no response by mid-2021, despite the Forum seeking an update in January 2021.

INFILTRATION AND CONSPIRACY

David Gilles' dossier ran to over a hundred pages. It alleged that a group of left-wingers—some white but many Muslim—were plotting to 'take over' both of Newham's CLPs.

The origin of the purported conspiracy 'was the election of a new party Leader in 2015'. Corbyn's election spurred 'a small number of party members', designated the 'Core Group', to 'use illegitimate methods and communal divisions in an attempt to take power'.

Underpinning Gilles' account, but never fully acknowledged, was the fact that the Core Group and the local left were to be feared because they were successful. In his narrative, it appeared as if long-silent local members had transmogrified into the worst type of Labour member: an active one with an opinion. 'While many of the Core Group are long standing

Labour Party members they have not traditionally been interested or involved in national Labour Party politics', Gilles commented. '[T]his changed with the election of Corbyn since when they have become "more Corbynite than Corbyn"'.

The power of the newly energised local left was exerted most forcefully in 2018. Newham mayor Sir Robin Wales—revealed by internal party emails to be a friend of the Labour Party's right-wing bureaucracy—was deselected and replaced as Labour's mayoral candidate by Rokhsana Fiaz, a local councillor backed by Momentum. Wales had either headed the local council or served as mayor for an uninterrupted twenty-three-year period. Fiaz had run on a platform calling for the party to 'unite' and be 'truly radical again'.[3] According to Gilles, the Core Group had coalesced 'around what they saw as the failure of Robin Wales, then mayor, to address the needs of the South Asian communities of Newham as they defined them'.

Gilles provided details of what was described as the behaviour of the Core Group. He presented accounts of how motions were passed or meetings were convened in a manner that he claimed breached the party rules, and complained at length about how certain Core Group members moderated comments in Facebook groups unfairly.

But some of Gilles' complaints went beyond procedural gripes. They were characterised by a tendency to construe humdrum, day-to-day political activity as a malign conspiracy that Gilles claimed should be investigated for 'bringing the party into disrepute'.

In one extended section, for example, Gilles complained that the Core Group had decided to organise outside of party structures as well as existing council initiatives to deliver community aid while also criticising certain council policies. Whereas Gilles allowed that 'members are free to challenge and disagree with party policies', he contended that the Core Group were engaged in activity that went 'beyond these democratic norms and looks more like an organised attempt to undermine the Council'. He claimed that 'instead of using a coherent political critique', the Core Group 'look[ed] for populist issues to attack the Council by whipping up dissatisfaction through front campaigns, lies and the use of social media'.

One example Gilles cited in this regard was the role of the Core Group in setting up Covid relief programmes. He said that one member, Obaid Khan, was gathering personal data in order to provide direct relief to those impacted by Covid. It was the height of irony, considering that Gilles' own dossier was, as discussed below, based on membership data he had no right to access.

Gilles found fault with another two organisations formed to provide humanitarian and food assistance to the local community: Voice for Newham and The Humanitarian and Saving Lives Trust. Both, according to Gilles, were 'largely run by members of the Core Group'. This, too, was criticised, because it took place outside of the council's initiatives and did not work directly with other community organisations like the Newham Food Alliance.

Gilles conceded that 'no doubt many involved in the initiatives described here did so for the best of reasons, and there is no suggestion that the people who benefitted from assistance were anything other than in need of help'. But he did not accept that altruism could explain the participation of the Core Group.

Another observer might interpret this group's activities as an attempt to fill gaps in local provision in a borough known for its high levels of poverty and its peripatetic immigrant communities. But for Gilles, these initiatives were part of 'a concerted and deliberate pattern of building separate sectarian initiatives to undermine Council supported and existing community groups they could not control and gain access to the contact details of vulnerable individuals'.

The 'sectarian' methods identified by Gilles cross-pollinated with his concern that local citizens were being subjected to undue political pressure by members of the Core Group. Gilles thus listed, in detail, the property holdings of three members of the Core Group. Using local membership data to which Gilles was not entitled, Gilles tracked how many of these properties also hosted additional registered Labour Party members—a good deal.

Gilles saw this as highly suspicious. There was no evidence put forward to suggest that party members living in the houses of Core Group members had been forced to join under pressure. Gilles nevertheless urged that this 'all suggests that there is a need for additional safeguards to ensure that Newham Labour Politics [*sic*] does not become adversely influenced/tainted by conflicts of interest involving property ownership and any associated abuse of the tenants living in private sector rented homes or other regulatory infringements in the future'.

There is a strong argument to be made that Gilles' 'concern' about the abuse of power on the part of Muslim landlords was an expression of Islamophobic tropes about 'Big Man' patronage politics.

'WEAPONISING' RACE AND FAITH

Gilles acknowledged that his focus on wrongdoing by mostly Muslim members might be seen as problematic. But Gilles protested that such an accusation was nothing more than a red herring that should be dismissed: 'The Core group use faith and race as a weapon', he explained. 'They will doubtless answer the charges in this Report by calling them racist and Islamophobic'.

Gilles then set out how faith and race were, in his words, 'weaponised'—a claim that, if applied to Jewish people, could have seen him expelled from the party. The evidence included a badly worded text from an unidentified person about how the new mayor was not a 'good Muslim', which Gilles placed at the door of the Core Group without explaining why. Other evidence included the fact that the council was criticised by party members for 'failing to govern in the interests of the South Asian community in Newham re matters such as planning consents for places of worship/community centres and parking issues generally'.

This argument by Gilles barely entertained the possibility that the South Asian community was indeed badly served by the council, that Muslim and South Asian councillors as well as party members were raising in good faith issues that emerged in their communities, or that even their contentious claims nevertheless constituted perfectly legitimate political opinions.

Gilles then set out further purported evidence that race and faith were being weaponised. This included a number of cases where Muslim and South Asian Labour members accused white members of Islamophobia and racism. In one revealing example, Gilles referred to himself in the third person to complain that 'David Gilles' and another white member 'were both accused of racist behaviour' after they challenged two Core Group members' 'poor chairing' of a meeting.

So, while Gilles conceded that 'debate can be robust in the Labour Party and from time to time tempers will flare', the fact that non-white members of the Core Group had made allegations of Islamophobia 'add[ed] up' in his view 'to a consistent pattern of harassment well outside the party's traditions and rules, and one designed to deter participation in public life'.

It was, at the very least, a remarkably tone-deaf criticism to appear in a report based on the in-person surveillance of Muslim party members.

SURVEILLANCE

Gilles' two central concerns were that prominent local Core Group members (or their supporters) did not really live in the constituencies in which they registered and that some form of unidentified behaviour had led to the inflation of CLP membership in an allegedly suspicious manner. The latter, in particular, formed the heart of Gilles' demand for both CLPs to be immediately suspended.

Gilles attempted to prove that key members of the Core Group were living in different wards or constituencies than those to which they were registered with the party. Gilles focused primarily on Muslim members. He used the membership data held by the local party to establish the contact details, including the addresses, of Core Group members. Gilles was not a CLP officer and thus had no right to access this information.

Gilles compared this membership data against evidence from in-person surveillance of Core Group members. He disclosed the car license plate numbers of Core Group members, noting where these cars had been seen parked. One person and his family were accused of living in a different ward (but in the same CLP) than the one to which they were registered, which Gilles claimed to have proved because the member's 'car [license number] has been observed on several occasions in late 2020, including after the 2020 December lockdown,' in the other ward.

Mehmood Mirza, another CLP member who Gilles cast as central to the activities of his 'Core Group', was also accused of misstating his residential address to the Labour Party. This, it was claimed, was proven by the fact that 'he has been seen taking his children to school' at two separate schools (an academy and a primary school). Gilles disclosed both the schools to which Mirza was alleged to have sent his children. Mirza's car was also tracked. 'His car, [license plate], has been seen parked on several occasions near to' an address different to the one he had registered with.

Perhaps the most disturbing example of surveillance was directed at a CLP official Gilles accused of having moved out of Newham and into Slough. Through some unknown mechanism, Gilles had secured private data to support his argument. This included referencing an application form that had been submitted by the CLP official for her child to attend a school in Slough. How Gilles had secured access to a private application form submitted in a different borough—dealing with a child—was not disclosed in his dossier.

The experience of being spied on in this way was deeply upsetting for Mirza, who was presented with a copy of the dossier by Al Jazeera for its documentary series on the Labour Party. 'It looks like somebody is constantly monitoring me', he said.

> They've got all the information about me, what I do, where I go, where my children go . . . I'm surprised and I'm gutted . . . I'm scared, more scared after seeing this. The level where they can go to . . . Somebody following your children to school, it's not normal is it?[4]

The surveillance of members was particularly alarming to Halima Khan, the only Muslim staff member in Labour's GLU. 'The members in Newham were essentially stalked and for me it posed a significant safety risk because in the dossier was mentioned where members had parked their cars, their car registration numbers, where their children went to school', Khan explained. 'That's a serious safeguarding issue, and the fact that the party didn't see it as one was of concern'.[5]

JUST A LITTLE BIT OF RACIAL AND ETHNIC PROFILING USING STOLEN DATA

Gilles' next substantive complaint was that, using membership data he had no right to access, he had picked up potential membership irregularities because, bluntly, too many people from certain majority-Muslim ethnicities and nationalities were joining. Gilles identified the problems in the membership lists of the East Ham CLP, one of the two CLPs in Newham.

Labour Party membership lists do not record the race, ethnicity, or language groupings of its members. Gilles, too, would not have personally known the many thousands of local party members.

Instead, Gilles worked with unidentified 'South Asian activists' who examined the membership lists for East Ham

CLP and inferred individuals' ethnicities from their names. Gilles then extracted the numbers of party members of different ethnicities over time and tracked their relative increase and decrease. Besides the obvious risk of classification errors, it was just an appalling thing to imagine: people combing through a membership list and then using their best guess to assign ethnic identity against a set of names.

Gilles used the data to slice the local party membership into eight ethnic, racial, and national categories: Bengali, 'Gujerati' [*sic*], Hindu, 'MuslimOther', 'OtherWhite/BAC [British Afro-Caribbean]', Pakistani, Sikh, and Tamil. Both the raw numbers and the proportions of party members falling into each category were traced over time, from the 2015 general election to a period following Starmer's election in 2020.

The key data point Gilles wanted to highlight was neatly visualised in a line graph. This graph tracked four figures: total CLP membership (a black line); 'white/BAC' membership (a purple line); 'other' (a red line); and—most importantly—a category labelled 'Bengali, Gujarati & Pakistani', represented by a green line—in effect, a Muslim-majority line. The graph purported to show that 'Bengali, Gujarati & Pakistani' membership had increased substantially as a portion of the local party membership.

Gilles also raised issues with how many new members were listed as unwaged, and he flagged concerns that multiple sign-ups were registered against the same email address or phone number (hardly surprising in a highly mobile community that shared resources or where there would be uneven comfort with English, the language of party membership forms and the like). These figures were then compared, again, against the supposed ethnicity of party members.

Gilles argued that the figures pointed to a specific and unexplained irregularity: that 'recent new members are disproportionately drawn from the Bengali and Pakistani communities and latterly the Gujarati community'.

Imagine, if you will, that a party member had gained access to CLP data (to which they had no legal entitlement) and used people's names to determine whether they were Jewish. Imagine if a party member in an area with a large Haredi Jewish population, like London's Stamford Hill or Newcastle's Gateshead, identified every person named Goldstein or Cohen or Levi, assigned them a 'Jewish' tag, tallied up just how many had joined over time, and then plotted the result on a graph. Imagine that the party member then used confidential contact details and sign-up information to check how many newly registered Jews were saying they were in work and whether they were using the same email addresses. Imagine that, when said party member discovered that a 'disproportionate' number of Jews were joining, that party member alleged some nebulous irregularity that meant the CLP had to be shut down.

As it was, Gilles had no ready explanation for the increase in members from the 'Bengali, Gujarati & Pakistani' communities, nor any explicit theory as to why this might be problematic. He even acknowledged that 'the picture shown is not *evidence* in itself of malpractice'. But he argued nevertheless that 'it does provide strong circumstantial information warranting a much closer look by the party nationally' to ensure that the membership lists had not been somehow 'corrupted' or that there had been no 'electoral fraud'.

What this corruption might amount to was not fully explained; nor was it explained how these perceived issues, gleaned from an analysis of inappropriately held membership data in the East Ham CLP, should also be used as evidence of potential membership issues in a wholly separate CLP (West Ham) for which Gilles had no membership data. The only explanation that Gilles was willing to hazard was that 'anecdote suggests that heads of households had encouraged to sign up members of their families, possibly without their knowledge, on reduced or youth rates'.

How Gilles could have possibly determined that people were being enrolled without their knowledge is not clear and he provided no evidence to prove the assertion. Nor did he explain why it would be problematic for CLP members to encourage their relatives to join their political party, or whether the level of people being signed up on unwaged rates might be unusual during a pandemic in which vast numbers of people employed outside of formal contracts lost their cash jobs.

In fact, Gilles' dossier amounts to very little by way of concrete evidence or even cogency, instead comprising a scattergun collection of disconnected acts of presumed or implied perfidy. The membership data issue, in particular, sat as a free-floating allegation that seemed to have little or no concrete connection to any other concerns raised in the report—certainly Gilles provided no evidence, and would probably be unlikely to discover any, that his notorious 'Core Group' was colluding to sign up members from specific communities in ways that violated the law.

This is where the picture of generalized wrongdoing that Gilles attempted to paint—be it questions about registered addresses or the competence of CLP motions or nefarious claims of Islamophobia—was supposed to have additional explanatory power: some indeterminate and unusual growth in membership was not to be accounted for in a simple or benign way but, instead, as the function of a vague but pervasive malevolence that was supposed to define the politics of 'sectarian' people with whom Gilles disagreed, many of them Muslim.

TRAVESTY

Gilles first provided his report to the Labour Party on February 3, 2021, addressing it directly to General Secretary David Evans. His covering letter recorded that he also provided a copy of the report and its appendices to Newham Mayor Rokhsana Fiaz; Newham's two Labour MPs Lyn Brown and Stephen Timms; and Chief Superintendent Richard Tucker, the Newham borough commander of the Metropolitan Police.

The Labour Party should have immediately submitted Gilles' dodgy dossier to the Information Commissioner's Office

(ICO), given the clear risks it raised that data had been misused. The Metropolitan Police, for its part, should have immediately initiated an inquiry into Gilles' surveillance of Newham residents. At the very least, the accessing of protected personal data such as school application forms warranted investigation.

The report should arguably also have been submitted to the Equality and Human Rights Commission, given the obvious risks it represented in terms of unlawful discrimination and harassment.

However, far from investigating Gilles and taking steps to protect the targets of his improper surveillance, Gilles instead appears to have been *encouraged* by the Labour Party, and in particular by General Secretary Evans, to keep the goods coming. On May 31, 2021, Gilles compiled an update of his report, which he sent with a covering letter to Evans and Barros-Curtis. The covering letter confirmed that Gilles had, in addition to his February correspondence, sent a first update of his report to Evans on March 9, 2021. The same letter confirmed that Evans responded to Gilles on March 10, 2021, to which Gilles also wrote a response, the content of which was undisclosed.

The timing of these exchanges is all-important. On March 11, 2021, the NEC held its monthly meeting. The NEC's Organisational Sub-Committee convened after the general meeting. It was at this meeting that the decision was made to suspend the CLPs. Thus, only two days after Gilles had sent his update, and one day after Evans had responded to him, Gilles' 'evidence' was used to shut down two huge CLPs, both of which remain suspended to this day. The NEC's Organisational Sub-Committee meeting was chaired by none other than Wendy Nichols—who would play a major role in the Rothery affair, discussed next.[6]

Gilles' report, which should have sent alarm bells ringing in party headquarters for the in-person surveillance of Muslims and ethnic profiling of members on which it was explicitly based, was instead embraced and used to shut down local party democracy in Newham indefinitely.

But this was not the end of the matter. Halima Khan, who would become a courageous whistleblower on racism and Islamophobia in the Labour Party, told Al Jazeera that she had seen the dossier as it came into the party and had raised concerns about its content. Khan worked in GLU at the time and was overseeing complaints related to Newham. She was also the only Muslim staffer working in GLU. She told Al Jazeera that not long after she raised her concerns about the dossier, she was taken off the Newham brief.

The main details of this outrageous story were covered by Al Jazeera in its series *The Labour Files*. Many people either know about it or should know about it, including the party's leadership. But despite this, there has been no outrage, no media scandal, and no real consequence: an indifference bordering on omertà that is hard not to contrast with the media furore and aggressive regulatory enforcement that marked the alleged 'antisemitism crisis' under Jeremy Corbyn.

CHAPTER 17

WHEN ANNA ROTHERY MET THE STARMER MACHINE

On February 1, 2021, the Labour Party announced its three-person, all-women shortlist for the upcoming mayoral election in Liverpool. The three Labour candidates were Wendy Simon, Ann O'Byrne, and Anna Rothery. Rothery was the lord mayor of Liverpool. Along with the other candidates, she had already passed a due diligence test and suitability interview, which had taken place in the days before.

Rothery was a popular two-term lord mayor and the first Black holder of the role in the city's history. She also had the virtue of being far removed from historical allegations of corruption that swirled around the former mayor, Joe Anderson. The allegations against Anderson's administration were sufficiently serious that the Tory government announced plans to take Liverpool Council under central government control only a month after Labour announced Rothery's place on the shortlist.

Rothery's primary selection should have meant a swift transition to party hustings, a brief campaign, and a vote by the Labour Party membership that she had every chance of winning.

Instead, within three weeks, Rothery's mayoral candidacy was effectively scrapped. The party announced that the entire shortlist announced in February 2021 had been dumped, and that Rothery along with her two competitors would be barred from any further participation in the election. The party was swiftly accused of racism and political skulduggery.[1]

The accusation was truer than anybody could have known.

'NOT IDEAL'

On February 3, the *Liverpool Echo* ran a lengthy interview with Rothery in anticipation of the selection contest being put to members. Rothery voiced respect for the Corbyn project and called for Corbyn himself to be restored as a Labour MP in good standing: 'I'd like to see the whip returned to Jeremy and the CLP officers who have faced arbitrary suspension to be reinstated. Everyone should have a voice in our party, in an atmosphere of mutual respect and inclusivity'. Rothery further explained that 'Jeremy brought a new generation to our cause—young, diverse, hopeful. We need to ensure our city values and hears the voices of many'.[2] Five days later, Rothery reiterated her call.

Rothery's comments quickly attracted the attention of party bureaucrats, who sent multiple emails raising issues with Rothery's comments, social media posts, and performance at party hustings. The emails were sent between some of the party's most senior bureaucrats, including Barros-Curtis, Evans, Fraser Welsh (head of internal governance), and Andy Smith (a regional higher-up). In one email sent by Evans to National Executive Committee member Ann Black, he confirmed that 'we are actively looking at the process due to other complaints'.

By the sixteenth, a decision had been made. Andy Smith drafted letters sent to the candidates, which announced that the selection process would be reopened. Emails show that Welsh wrote the draft letter before getting approval from the NEC and the selection panel; it was only later that afternoon that he got written confirmation from the chair of the panel,

Wendy Nichols, approving the halt to balloting and a new set of interviews.

Nichols was then head of the NEC's Organisational Sub-Committee and chair of the Liverpool mayoral shortlist selection panel; as discussed above, she had led the NEC sub-committee that received and acted on Gilles' Newham dossier. Another key player in this imbroglio was Anna Hutchinson, a senior party bureaucrat, then serving as executive director of elections and field delivery. While she was not on the selection panel, Hutchinson provided assistance in their meetings. A long-time party employee, she was a member of one of the WhatsApp groups revealed by the Leaked Report—although her own contributions to them were generally anodyne.

Emails show that the bureaucracy went into overdrive to gather as much 'evidence' of wrongdoing as possible to be put to Rothery, with Evans the most prolific. On February 19, 2021, the same day the re-interview was to take place, Evans sent an email to Barros-Curtis, Hutchinson, and Smith titled 'Panel Material'. The email showed, beyond doubt, that Evans was personally directing how the panel should go about interviewing candidates.

One attachment to this email was a letter sent as a Word document directly to Evans by Alan Dean. Dean had been Labour's chief whip on the Liverpool city council during Rothery's prior tenure as a councillor. Dean lost his council seat in 2018, which his allies blamed on the Corbyn and Momentum surge.[3] Dean's letter would be central to the decision to remove Rothery from the ballot.

Dean opened by noting that he had 'been asked to contact you in relation to Councillor Anna Rothery and her (un)suitability to stand as Labour's candidate'. His letter then worked its way through a generalised character assassination that drew on arguably racist and sexist tropes. Rothery was attacked as an 'untrustworthy, dishonest person who is solely motivated by her ego, status and financial gain'. Dean claimed she had a 'Jeckill [*sic*] and Hyde' character in that she could 'be quite rational and then in a few seconds turns into a screaming banshee'.

The most consequential element was Dean's account of an incident in 2011 involving Rothery and another Liverpool councillor, Nick Small. Small was seen as an opponent of the Liverpool left; he had played a key role in amplifying claims of widespread left-wing antisemitism in the Liverpool Riverside CLP and had frequent arguments with well-known left-wing figures.

One of those figures was Audrey White, who in 2022 would famously confront Starmer in a Liverpool café. White's questioning and Starmer's manifest discomfort ensured the video went viral on left-wing social media. White was known for having led a huge protest against sexual harassment in the 1980s, which led to her immortalisation in the film *Business as Usual*. White was played by the Oscar-winning actress and future Labour MP Glenda Jackson.

One interaction between White and Small typified his petty political methodology and reveals how problematic it would be to take at face value his version of events. According to evidence submitted by White to the Labour Party, she had submitted a Subject Access Request to the Liverpool council Labour Group Office in March 2017 asking for information held on her. Small wrote back to White from his official Liverpool government address, explaining that 'I have the information you have requested'. However, in order for him to supply the information, he instructed White to 'send me a cheque for £10 to the Labour Group Office'. Alternatively, she could send him 'two cheques each for £5 made payable to Progress Limited and Jewish Labour Movement or one cheque made out to N M Small and I will donate £5 to these two organisations on your behalf'.

Small, of course, would have known that White did not support either group and that this would be seen as an insult. White unsurprisingly baulked at the request and referred the matter to a caseworker at the ICO. That caseworker found that Small had violated the Data Protection Act by asking for donations to specific entities as a condition for White to access data to which she was legally entitled.

The document sent by Dean to Evans also enclosed three emails that Dean had received in 2011 from Small, Rothery, and another councillor. They all related to an incident that had taken place in March of that year. Briefly: Small wrote to Dean alleging that, in the course of a social event, Rothery had caused a ruckus when she claimed that the Labour group in Liverpool was racist, pointing out that she was its lone Black councillor.

Small claimed that he had denied the racism charge and emphasised that efforts were being made to increase diversity. However, according to Small's 2011 account, Rothery then became angry, calling him racist and a 'fat, pompous twat'. He further claimed that, shortly thereafter, Rothery 'struck me on two separate occasions'. He admitted he had not seen what she did 'but it felt like she poked me in the back of my head with a fingernail'. At the time, the incident had been described by an article in the *Liverpool Echo*, which alleged that Rothery had 'prodded [Small] in the head after a heated exchange about institutional racism'.[4]

After Evans sent around Dean's letter, Small emailed Andy Smith. 'I have been asked to provide a statement about an incident', Small wrote, prefacing his new version of events. He now claimed that, back in 2011, he had agreed there was an issue with institutional racism but denied that any Labour councillors were racist. He also now claimed that Rothery had thrown two punches at his head and that both had 'connected'. In the intervening decade between the event and his recollection, the position on structural racism that he remembered articulating became more subtle and reasonable, while his account of Rothery's conduct became more egregious.

The day after Evans circulated Dean's email, Rothery submitted her own written account of the incident. Rothery asserted that it was she who had been harmed, by a 'verbal racial attack'. She simultaneously submitted a statement from Joe Anderson, the mayor at the time. Anderson stated that he had read Rothery's statement, found it to be accurate, and confirmed that it was Small's behaviour that was unacceptable. He also stated that the situation had been resolved when Small apologised to Rothery for the incident.

All of the accounts make for uncomfortable reading. Shorn of the drama, the incident involved the lone Black councillor on the Liverpool council raising issues of structural and systematic racism in the Labour Party. These claims were rejected by a group of all-white councillors, which led to an escalation of tensions sufficient to seriously upset Rothery. How she dealt with this experience is contested, although Small's own version of the event suffers from being recalled so differently in 2021 compared to 2011. But it doesn't take an act of enormous imagination or empathy to see how Rothery could easily have experienced the entire incident as an expression of the very structural racism she complained about.

'UNFAIR, ARBITRARY AND CAPRICIOUS'

Rothery's re-interview took place at 2:30 in the afternoon of the nineteenth. Emails show that Evans, Barros-Curtis, and others were feverishly putting together information for the panel to use in the interviews. So, at just past noon, Barros-Curtis forwarded the material distributed earlier that day by Evans, but with the name of Alan Dean redacted. Twenty minutes later, Barros-Curtis distributed a detailed list of questions specifically for Rothery.

On the twentieth, one day after the re-interview took place, Rothery's lawyer Martin Howe emailed the party. He explained that 'we have serious reservations' about how Rothery's interview was conducted. Howe's letter claimed that Wendy Nichols, who chaired the meeting, made a number of 'biased' interventions, particularly around the Nick Small incident. The letter alleged that Rothery was asked if she had engaged in any past behaviour that could embarrass the party. When Rothery said no, Nichols allegedly intervened to state that the answer 'must' be 'yes' on three occasions, pointing to the Small incident. 'This was an extraordinarily hostile position for the Chair to take', the letter alleged.

There is strong evidence to suggest that the factual recounting of the meeting was accurate, even if the interpretation of whether it was hostile was up for debate. Party emails show that staff were concerned that Rothery had recorded the interview (conducted remotely) or had somebody watch it simultaneously, presumably because of the fidelity of Howe's account.

Howe explained that Rothery intended to challenge the matter in court to demand that her name be included in any ballots released by the party. Howe asked that the party respond by the following Monday, February 22, confirming that her name would be included on the ballot. If this confirmation was not forthcoming, she would issue proceedings, including an emergency injunction to halt any decisions being made.

What subsequently transpired was astonishing. Barros-Curtis responded the following day, February 21, to Howe's letter. He rejected the idea that the matter was urgent and sought to dissuade Howe from issuing injunctive proceedings as this would be

> premature and misconceived . . . The Labour Party will provide you and your client with a substantive response to your letter by no later than 5:00 p.m. on Wednesday February 24, 2021. My understanding is that there will not be any substantive decisions taken in relation to the Liverpool mayoral election selection process until then at the earliest, in any event. If that were to change, we will be happy to advise.

Barros-Curtis concluded the email by repeatedly urging Howe not to take any action, at least in part because no decision would be made, he claimed, before February 24.

Barros-Curtis' promise that no substantive decisions would be made before February 24 was plainly misleading. In fact, on the very day that Barros-Curtis sent that email, the twenty-first, the selection panel had reconvened and decided they would reopen the nominations process. The panel was slated to meet again the following day to decide whether Rothery or the two other candidates would be allowed to be included in the nominations. Contrary to Barros-Curtis' written commitment, Howe was not informed.

While it is not clear if Barros-Curtis was aware of this meeting on the twenty-first, he certainly knew that a meeting on the subject was imminently in the works. Emails show Barros-Curtis contemplating what might occur at a soon-to-be-convened meeting. Indeed, remarkably, the emails show that Barros-Curtis was talking about an imminent meeting just before he emailed Howe promising that nothing would happen until the twenty-fourth.

In fact, correspondence shows that Barros-Curtis was eager for a decision to be made as soon as possible. Importantly, Barros-Curtis explained that the urgency was due to the need to issue ballots quickly so as to ensure that the Labour Party would have a candidate in place with sufficient time to contest the mayoral election.

Recall that in Howe's original letter to the party, he had emphasised that Rothery needed a reply by February 22 as the case was urgent, given the imminence of the mayoral election. Barros-Curtis, in his original response to Howe, argued that 'we do not accept this matter is urgent' because there was 'substantially more than a month . . . for the Labour Party to shortlist and select its candidate'. So Barros-Curtis was telling Howe that the matter was not urgent because the party had ample time to run the ballot, as part of correspondence in which he was also telling Howe that no decision would be taken prior to the twenty-fourth. Yet at the very same time, Barros-Curtis was telling others that a decision on Rothery and others should be taken urgently because the party was under serious time pressure to run the ballot.

It is clear that Barros-Curtis was eager for a decision to be made on February 21, knew a decision would be made on the twenty-second or twenty-third, but had nevertheless told Howe that no decision would be made before the twenty-fourth.

The panel did indeed meet on the evening of the twenty-second, as Barros-Curtis had been predicting. He attended to assist the panel, literally sitting in on and contributing to discussions where a decision was made—yet still neglected to inform Howe that a decision was forthcoming. Why Barros-Curtis did not do so is not discussed explicitly anywhere, but one plausible reason is that Barros-Curtis was allowing a situation to develop that would furnish the party with a set of minutes that could withstand a legal challenge (as explained below).

The panel decided that none of the candidates, including Rothery, would be allowed to stand. Howe and Rothery were not informed until the following day, February 23, one day before Barros-Curtis had promised to respond to Howe's opening salvo.

The party announced the decision the same day in public. It claimed it was concerned, primarily, with the need for candidates to act with the 'highest levels of integrity and honesty'—the unstated but unmistakable inference being that Rothery had failed this test.

A MATTER OF MINUTES

On February 25, two days after the decision was announced, Howe pulled the trigger, informing the party by letter that Rothery intended to take the matter to court. Howe instructed the party to retain all records related to the decision, which had to be provided to him by 2 p.m. on the twenty-sixth.

Emails show that frantic efforts followed to produce a set of minutes that could be disclosed to Howe by February 26. In the early evening on the twenty-fifth, Anna Hutchinson emailed Barros-Curtis. Hutchinson had sat in on the selection meeting alongside Barros-Curtis to provide assistance, including by taking notes. Hutchinson attached a copy of her minutes. The minutes show that the panel had decided on Sunday, February 21 to reopen the nominations process, although it appears this discussion was not minuted. Howe, of course, had not been informed of this important development.

The minutes record that the panel was 'unsettled and unhappy' with the discussion about the '2011 dinner'—the incident involving Small and Rothery. Hutchinson commented, in summarising the panel's views the previous day, that 'there are two completely contrasting versions of events', which appears to have been sufficient to count against Rothery.

The panel also lingered on the 'behaviour of Rothery on 2 separate occasions by 2 separate unions on behalf of their members in the last 2 years regarding her behaviour'. This discussion was complicated and is not delved into here, except to note that emails show the party was unable to find any hard evidence to back up the allegations, which in the end were entirely apocryphal. Rothery was nevertheless damned by the unsubstantiated claims.

The most important part of Hutchinson's minutes was that they put on record a lengthy intervention from Barros-Curtis. Barros-Curtis explained that there were 'legal points that need to be raised, it will inevitably rile people up'. He disclosed to the panel that an unnamed candidate had threatened an injunction 'if the party did not act by midday today to restart the process'. He confirmed that the candidate had complained that this was 'a biased process' and that 'conversations were hostile'.

On this basis, he said, it was 'important that we minute' the decision, as they had seemingly failed to do the previous day. He further told the panel that this was a 'crucial decision', that 'the honesty and integrity of our candidates' was vital in light of the EHRC's findings on the party's liability for the conduct of its agents, and that it was 'critical that the highest standards of probity are expected and demanded of our candidates'. Indeed, he said, the idea that candidates act with 'honesty and integrity' was at the 'cornerstone of our democracy'.

At just past midnight on February 26, Barros-Curtis replied to Hutchinson with an edited version of her minutes. He asked Hutchinson to send the revised minutes to the panel members to get them to confirm that they were a 'faithful reflection' of what was discussed. Hutchinson duly did so a few hours later. There is no indication that Hutchinson disclosed to the panel members that Barros-Curtis had substantially edited the minutes.

Barros-Curtis' edited minutes differed in substantial respects from Hutchinson's original. The Barros-Curtis minutes did not reflect himself addressing the meeting. His interventions were recast as discussions by the panel; in his revised account, it was the *panel* that now 'discussed' the importance of the issue, and 'unanimously agreed' on the 'honesty and integrity of the candidates', and accepted that certain events might flow from the decision.

Barros-Curtis also removed all reference to the discussion about the threatened injunction. All that was left was an anodyne comment that 'the panel also accepted that there might be a legal challenge' to their decision. The court, when it would later review these minutes, was thus being deprived of key information about what was being said in the meeting and by whom.

Why did Barros-Curtis make these edits? Did he edit them because a judge might be swayed by the argument that the threat of an injunction on the basis of bias might have unduly influenced the decision of the panel? And were Barros-Curtis' edits sufficiently material as to mislead the court by omitting key information about who said what and when?

I don't know the answer to these questions. But they would certainly make for a spicy line of inquiry if Barros-Curtis were forced to answer them before the Solicitor's Regulation Authority, which I believe should give serious consideration to probing Barros-Curtis' conduct on this and other matters.

Barros-Curtis' minutes would be central to the litigation that followed; his minutes were submitted to the court to prove the probity of the party's decision. The judge, who decided in favour of the Labour Party, quoted extensively from the minutes, placing emphasis on the quote Barros-Curtis had injected into the proceedings (but placed into the mouths of 'the panel') about how the 'honesty and integrity' of the party's candidates was 'a cornerstone' of 'our democracy'.[5]

Barros-Curtis wrote to David Evans, Anneliese Midgley, Andy Smith, Anna Hutchinson, Andrew Whyte, Fraser Welsh, and Matt Pound (then still in LOTO) on the day the party won its case against the candidate who had once hoped to become the first Black mayor of Liverpool. Barros-Curtis noted in celebratory terms that 'I am pleased to say that the Claimant has been ordered to repay the party's (substantial) costs on this matter in full, thereby meaning our members' monies will not have been wasted on this'. Evans wrote: 'Alex. Thoroughly well done. Please pass on our thanks to the team. Your contract has been agreed, we will not be including a win bonus'.

This sorry affair had important consequences. Firstly, the entire process was plainly damaging to Rothery's career and reputation. It stopped Rothery just as she looked like she had a good chance to win the election for the Liverpool mayoralty, a position of considerable prestige. Moreover, the party explained the scrapping of its original shortlist on the basis that it needed to be confident it was selecting candidates with the 'highest levels of integrity and honesty'. The strong implication was that Rothery had failed to meet this standard, a statement that had serious reputational implications in light of ongoing corruption scandals then inflicting the city.

Furthermore, Rothery's case would create important legal precedent. Cutting to the quick of a very long judgment, when the court found in favour of the Labour Party, it thereby confirmed that the party had extremely wide discretion to select its candidates and that the courts would be most reluctant to become involved in the details of selection processes. The judgment also affirmed that the party (and the NEC in particular) was entitled to select those candidates it believed had the best chance of winning elections.

These findings would underpin and inform the party's later decision to prevent Corbyn from ever standing as a Labour candidate again. As I describe below, the precedent created by the NEC blocking Corbyn as a candidate would have profoundly anti-democratic implications.

CHAPTER 18

HACKING *INSIDE CROYDON*

On February 17, 2021, a hacker broke into the email and the Twitter account of *Inside Croydon*, a local independent media outlet edited by an old-school, pound-the-pavement reporter named Steven Downes. Croydon is the stomping ground for three central Labour Together figures: Steve Reed (the MP for Croydon North; the constituency became Streatham and Croydon North in 2024), David Evans (who ran his polling and political advisory outfit, The Campaign Company, from the borough), and Morgan McSweeney.

When Downes reported the hack to the Information Commissioner's Office (ICO), he was told that the most likely explanation was that someone had bought a copy of Downes' email and Twitter passwords from the dark web, effectively purchasing them from international cybercrime syndicates.

The intent of the hack was obvious: to identify the sources used by the outlet in reporting on local matters and, by revealing them, to discredit those sources as well as the outlet that had failed to protect them. The hackers used *Inside Croydon*'s Twitter account to post a single message, outing three of *Inside Croydon*'s confidential sources: Stephen Mann, Robert Canning, and Andrew Pelling. All three were local Labour councillors who had criticised the council leadership run by local allies of Steve Reed.

While Downes was almost immediately able to regain control of his Twitter account, his entire email server, including all of the correspondence shared with local confidential sources, was downloaded. Within days, the hacked contents of Downes' email account were injected directly into the Labour Party bureaucracy. Some of the party's most powerful bureaucratic figures, as well as Steve Reed, were not only aware of this astonishing fact but decided that the unlawfully obtained data should be used to target their factional opponents in the party.

THE AUDACITY OF ACCOUNTABILITY

Inside Croydon launched its local reporting in 2010. Downes, who is politically on the left, was sympathetic to Corbyn and the possibility of a left revival in the party. He also had a long history of reporting critically on Reed and other political figures close to him, who ran Croydon's local government. Croydon council was forced to declare effective bankruptcy in November 2020.

As well as covering alleged incompetence and mismanagement in Croydon council, *Inside Croydon* had also broken stories about David Evans' political consultancy firm, The Campaign Company. In July 2018, Downes reported that The Campaign Company had been awarded £200,000 in contracts by local Croydon government officials over a period of four years.[1] He also reported that Evans had played a key role in overseeing Labour's 2014 local electioneering that saw it take control of Croydon council. That newly elected council then awarded Evans' firm four contracts over the next four years.

A key figure in the local Croydon government over these years was Alison Butler, who was both a local councillor and the deputy leader of Croydon council. Butler was also the former partner of David Evans, with whom she had a daughter. Butler failed to declare her conflict of interest regarding Evans or The Campaign Company, *Inside Croydon* reported, in relation to a

£16,000 contract awarded to The Campaign Company.[2] Butler did not respond to *Inside Croydon*'s request for comment prior to the article being published.

Downes' local knowledge meant he closely followed the careers of Reed, Evans, and McSweeney. Following the withdrawal of the Labour whip from Jeremy Corbyn and the crackdown on local parties after the EHRC report, *Inside Croydon* reported extensively on the multiple votes of no confidence in Evans around the country.[3]

Inside Croydon's focus on Reed and McSweeney meant that it occupied a unique place in the UK media landscape. This was most powerfully illustrated in February 2021, when the Electoral Commission announced its investigation into Labour Together's failure to declare donations. *Inside Croydon* was one of only two outlets in the entire country that reported on the matter. The only other UK publication to cover the Commission's announcement was *The Canary*—the target of Stop Funding Fake News.[4]

This means that *both* of the British media outlets that reported on Labour Together's run-ins with the Electoral Commission were targeted by Steve Reed, either directly or through SFFN, the astroturf campaign he helped create as part of the Labour Together Project.

GETTING RID OF DOWNES

Internal Labour Party emails show that Steve Reed and his reputed ally Tony Newman, the leader of Croydon council, had long harboured an antipathy toward Downes.

On October 10, 2016, Newman sent an email to Dan Simpson, a regional Labour official. Newman noted that Downes had recently joined the Labour Party and wanted to find some way to prevent this from happening. 'Ahead of meeting up this week I want to send you some "articles" from a guy called Steven Downes who writes a very bitter local blog site called *Inside Croydon*—Key issue [is that] Downes is now back as a party member—[and has published] constant attacks on Steve Reed, Councillors and unelected officials', Newman wrote. 'Both myself and Steve R[eed] of the view he needs to go in terms of party membership, but we can't risk him being reinstated and the subsequent martyrdom that will follow . . . Is this an OK email to send you some of his "work" to?'

'Yeah, send it to this address and I'll have a look', Simpson replied. Simpson forwarded Newman's email to another Labour Party official two weeks later, indicating that they had spoken about the issues raised by Newman. It is not clear what became of the complaint. Downes remained a party member.

However, the Labour Party bureaucracy, prompted by Reed and Newman, would play an important role in derailing Downes' nascent party career after he had been selected by members to stand as a Labour councillor in July 2017. Ironically, Downes had decided to stand primarily for journalistic reasons: to test the allegation from local party members that the party bureaucracy was interfering in selection processes. His own experience confirmed the accuracy of the claim.

On July 31, 2017, Reed wrote to Newman. He attached a dossier setting out Downes' perceived wrongdoing. The document, Reed wrote, 'was sufficient as a submission to the Local Government Forum', which selected candidates, 'to have him removed as a potential candidate, but also grounds for a complaint to have him expelled from the Labour Party'. Reed was effectively attempting to get an independent media editor expelled from the party, based in part on the editor's negative *but accurate* reporting on him.

Reed's dossier amounted to very little besides an amusing list of all the occasions when Downes had dunked on him. The dossier listed a number of articles in which *Inside Croydon* had criticised Reed personally or commented on the dysfunction of Croydon council. Reed was particularly aggrieved because *Inside Croydon* often used a satirical photo of him featuring a photoshopped Tory rosette.

Newman forwarded Reed's dossier to the local regional organiser, Martin Tiedemann. Newman's critique was even more strident, accusing *Inside Croydon* of peddling scurrilous misinformation. 'Steven Downes uses his website, *Inside Croydon*, to run a consistent campaign of hostility, distortion and abuse against Croydon North Labour MP Steve Reed and Croydon's Labour Council', Newman alleged. Downes' reporting, the dossier claimed, 'extends way beyond critical but legitimate commentary about elected Labour representatives. It is a conscious, active and occasionally libellous attempt to distort and misrepresent facts to undermine confidence and support in the Labour Party, the Labour Council, and the Labour MP'. Downes has never been sued for libel with respect to the articles listed.

But Downes was not just a misinformation merchant, according to Newman's email to Tiedemann; he was also a sexist bully:

> His personal & often sexist attacks on our Deputy Leader Cllr Alison Butler & senior female council officials, are bullying and intimidation of the worst kind, and any public message he had been panelled [selected as a potential council candidate], would rightly be greeted with outrage and horror, from both party members and many local residents.

Butler, as noted, would go on to feature in Downes' reporting on the awarding of contracts to The Campaign Company. 'As Leader I absolutely share Steve Reed MP's view, that the author of this often anti Labour [*sic*] hate site should have no place in the Labour Party', Newman told Tiedemann.

Emails show that Tiedemann was receptive to the approach and reached out to GLU complaints official Sam Matthews for advice. Matthews advised Tiedemann on the various mechanisms that could be used to deal with Downes, even raising the possibility that the party (via GLU) could suspend Downes and use that as a basis for a 'change of circumstances' interview: an effective re-interview that could be called if the local body choosing councillors came across relevant new information. Despite lengthy exchanges, Matthews' help was eventually not needed.

By December 2017, Downes' candidacy was finally ended for good. The reasons for his removal were parochial and silly, as befits this era of internal bureaucratic wrangling. Downes had responded to his nomination in another ward by sending an email to the local ward email list, refusing the nomination because of the hostility of that ward's local party toward him and his blog. The party found that Downes' email was inappropriate as it looked like he was using the Labour Party's local email list to promote his blog.

The person central to this complaint and Downes' eventual removal as a candidate was a local Labour councillor named Clive Fraser, himself an ally of Tony Newman. When *Inside Croydon*'s email was hacked in early 2021, Fraser was one of the party representatives who somehow received a copy of the hacked material and, with the permission of a party official, used it to launch complaints against his local party enemies.

FACTIONAL WEAPONISATION OF THE INSIDE CROYDON HACK

On February 23, 2021, a local Labour figure in a nearby borough, Ruth Bannister, wrote to the Labour Party. She copied in Fraser, Reed, and senior Croydon local government figures including Hamida Ali, the leader of Croydon council.

Bannister informed Reed and others that an unidentified person had approached her with the contents of the hacked emails, which she had started to review. It appears that she had already raised the matter with some of the email recipients, although the extent of this disclosure is not clear. Bannister explained that she had come into possession of over two hundred files, which she had spent the previous week reading. Considering the date of her email to the party, this suggests that Bannister must have received the hacked emails shortly after the date of the illegal intrusion.

Bannister uploaded a zip file containing seventy-seven megabytes of hacked emails and shared the link with her interlocutors. She claimed that she had identified documents showing that four prominent local Labour members—Pelling, Mann, Canning, and a fourth left-wing member named David White—had been sharing information with *Inside Croydon*. Bannister said that the contacts between the site and White 'look to me to be a breach of party rules'. The other three were guilty, according to Bannister, of sending 'emails providing *Inside Croydon* with quotes, tips, opinions, and full-blown copy of articles subsequently published'. These three, Bannister claimed, 'have been the source of leaks to/authors of articles for *Inside Croydon*, and . . . they have been actively and consistently breaching party policy'.

There was no acknowledgment that the councillors could legitimately be seen as whistleblowers about a Labour council that was allegedly driving Croydon into financial ruin. Nor was there any acknowledgment that the information had been obtained unlawfully such that reading and sharing it posed ethical as well as legal questions.

Outsiders may have expected that the Labour Party, its most senior bureaucrats, and Steve Reed himself would have baulked at handling material obtained through the illegal hacking of an independent media website. Arguably, everybody who came into contact with the material should have contacted the appropriate authorities, as well as *Inside Croydon*, to inform them of the situation.

Instead, party officials decided to spread the hacked information far and wide. Shortly after receiving the hacked material, Clive Fraser forwarded it on to a regional Labour Party official, Oliver Davis, copying in Hamida Ali and one other person. Fraser asked Davis whether he could legally use the documentation to start disciplinary proceedings. Davis, who himself forwarded the information to another regional organiser, wrote back saying that it was fine to use the material. 'Essentially, there is a legal obligation to investigate into potentially criminal conduct, alongside a wider public interest argument that this matter requires investigation in order to mitigate potential harm to the wider public', Davis explained. It is surprising that Davis and those who received the hacked data apparently saw no legal issue with the use to which this data was put.

Between February 28 and March 1, 2021, about two weeks after the hack, Bannister submitted formal complaints to the Labour Party about Pelling, Canning, White, and Downes himself, using as evidence the emails hacked from Downes' server. Ten days later, on March 10, 2021, Fraser launched disciplinary proceedings against Pelling, Canning, and White, two of whom refused to participate in the process because it was based on stolen data.

When the councillors received the disciplinary charges, they swiftly informed Downes. Downes wrote to the leader of Croydon council informing her that it was a potential criminal offence to handle the material and citing the case reference number he had been given by the Metropolitan Police. He says he did not receive a reply. Fraser also submitted a complaint about White to the party bureaucracy. He attached four documents, all taken from the hacked material, as the basis of his complaint. Fraser forwarded his complaint to Oliver Davis, who immediately forwarded it on to General Secretary Evans, copying in Reed and another regional organiser. Davis' email indicated that Reed was aware of its contents and wanted action: 'Hi David', Davis wrote, 'Steve Reed has asked us to forward this to you—if you need any more info just let us know'. Within a minute of receiving the email, Evans forwarded it on to Barros-Curtis.

To recap: hacked data, taken from an independent local news site, was used to identify the site's confidential informants, who were providing the public with details of Croydon's poor governance. This stolen information was then used to launch Labour Party disciplinary proceedings against the site's sources. Some of the most powerful people in the Labour Party bureaucracy were aware of all this—including Evans and Barros-Curtis, who were copied in, allegedly with the approval of Steve Reed.

The kicker: at the time, Reed was serving as the party's shadow justice minister.

PART FIVE

CRISIS AND CONSOLIDATION

CHAPTER 19

BATLEY AND SPEN AND THE BATTLE FOR SURVIVAL

On February 18, 2021, about three months after he had stripped Jeremy Corbyn of the Labour whip, Keir Starmer delivered a speech that heralded a 'New Chapter for Britain'.[1]

Despite having been party leader for ten months, Starmer had yet to outline any substantive, specific policy proposals. His outriders in the media swatted aside requests for the same on the basis that any policy articulated by Starmer would be stolen by the Tories. Starmer's 'New Chapter' speech was accordingly briefed breathlessly by Starmer's office as the moment all discretion would be cast aside and Starmer's true vision for the country revealed. One LOTO insider recalled that Starmer's speech was sold to the media as an intervention of the same magnitude as the Gettysburg Address.

The flagship policy that Starmer introduced, following a lengthy disquisition on Tory elitism and Starmer's inherent fairness, was the introduction of 'British Recovery Bonds'. Although only the sketchiest of details were provided, the essence of the policy was that the government would issue bonds that middle class and wealthy people could buy and which would attract favourable interest rates. The bond sales would fund a National Infrastructure Bank that would finance the rebuilding of infrastructure. It was a barely comprehensible technocratic headline policy that, at its core and shorn of grand verbiage, offered well-to-do people the boon of favourable credit interest rates at a time when the government could borrow funds on the open market at rock-bottom prices.

Within two days, the British Recovery Bonds—the heart of Starmer's 'New Chapter for Britain'—all but disappeared. Starmer has never referred to them subsequently, nor has any substantial media coverage examined the proposal beyond a polite and bemused assessment the following day. Its death was signalled when journalist Robert Peston unpicked the policy in a single, damning tweet. He pointed out that Starmer's grand plan was really a way to 'pay an interest rate well above the near zero [*sic*] gilts rate, in which case its [*sic*] government redistributing income to the middle classes and those with more savings and higher earnings'.[2]

Starmer's failed Gettysburg Address was typical of his first year in office. Admittedly navigating the tough terrain of a lopsided Tory majority, Covid lockdowns, and a vaccine rollout that massively boosted support for the Tories, Starmer nevertheless cut a tetchy and shallow figure. His lauded 'forensic' approach to the parliamentary jousting of Prime Minister's Questions never materialised; instead, and in spite of the government's mishandling of the pandemic that led Britain to the highest death toll in Europe, Starmer frequently found himself congratulating Prime Minister Boris Johnson and his party on their leadership. His erratic complaints and oppositional stances were inconsistent and largely seen as opportunistic; he was quickly slapped with the nickname, 'Captain Hindsight'.

The suspension of Corbyn and the subsequent eruption of intra-party warfare, while reported on with approving nods from the UK's mainstream press, arguably softened Labour Party support and made it harder for Starmer to articulate any message beyond, 'I'm not Corbyn'. Conventional wisdom holds that the public, more than anything, recoils from a party embroiled in internal conflict.

The first half of 2021 saw Labour's polling fall off a cliff after a brief rebound at the end of 2020. By the middle of April 2021, the party polled at 29 percent according to YouGov—down 3 percent on Labour's 2019 election result. According to YouGov, it was the lowest Labour had been in the polls since Starmer took office and three points lower than the first poll after Starmer won the leadership election. After a year of Starmer's leadership, Labour's position in national polling had gone backwards.

THE HARTLEPOOL FIASCO AND THE 'LABOUR TOGETHER RESHUFFLE'

It was against this background that the country went to the polls in May 2021 for local elections as well as a by-election in Hartlepool.

Hartlepool had been held by the Labour Party ever since the constituency was created in 1974. Labour had performed particularly well in 2017, increasing its vote share by 16.9 percent to win 52 percent of all votes cast. Although Labour held the seat in 2019, it suffered a negative swing of 14.8 percent, reducing its vote share to 37.7 percent and halving its numerical majority. Labour's 2019 victory was also heavily contingent on the fact that the Brexit Party stood a candidate, which split the pro-Brexit vote. In 2016, the constituency had voted overwhelmingly to leave the EU.

The Brexit Party factor would no longer be in play in 2021, not least because the Tories had negotiated and passed a Brexit package at the end of 2020. Starmer had whipped his MPs to support the deal. It was a poke in the eye to Labour supporters who believed that Starmer's anti-Brexit positioning prior to 2019 had stemmed from a principled cosmopolitan commitment to European integration, a belief no doubt based on his leadership pledge to defend freedom of movement. Labour's subsequent approach to the issue was, quite transparently, designed to insulate Labour and Starmer himself from justified criticism that they had worked to stop Brexit ever since 2016.

Despite Hartlepool's strong pro-Brexit leanings, Starmer's office nevertheless picked as its Hartlepool candidate a vocal Remainer, the local NHS doctor Paul Williams. Williams was a close friend of Jenny Chapman, the founding member of the Arlington Group, who was then still working within LOTO. Williams was effectively forced on the constituency by LOTO, with Chapman said to have played a prominent role. In a preview of how the party would rigorously control candidate selection in the years that followed, the local party was given a shortlist . . . of a single candidate.

The 2019 general election had seen Williams lose his North Yorkshire seat of Stockton South, which he had won by the narrowest of margins (and after a huge positive swing toward Labour under Corbyn) in 2017. As an MP, he had angered his constituents by taking a strong Remainer position, becoming a notable figure in the anti-Brexit People's Vote campaign, despite 58 percent of his constituency voting for Brexit in 2016.

It also did not take long for embarrassing information to emerge about Williams, indicating how little due diligence work was done to vet him before this prominent by-election. The media reported, within days of his selection, that he had posted arguably sexist comments on his Twitter account about Tory politicians. 'Do you have a favourite Tory MILF [Mother I'd Like to Fuck]?' he asked. The public was then swiftly reminded that he had taken over £8,700 from the Saudi government to tour their kingdom in 2018 while he was trying to undo the British electorate's democratic vote for Brexit. Williams determined, based on his visit, that a country that regularly beheaded dissidents and was reducing Yemen to rubble was 'modern and progressive'.[3]

As a candidate, Williams leaned heavily on his NHS pedigree; the strongest element of his campaign was his support for returning services to the local university hospital that had been slashed due to austerity. But it then emerged in late April 2021 that Williams was the lead commissioner on a report that had argued for those very services to be removed, a recommendation that was then implemented in full by the Tory government. His attempt to argue that this intervention was designed to ameliorate Tory cuts floundered in bureaucratese, while the co-chair of the Tory party could delightedly brand him a 'hospital hypocrite'.[4]

Labour's Hartlepool campaign frequently took on a ghostly air. Covid-related physical distancing requirements meant that Starmer, who travelled up to canvass, was frequently photographed standing at an awkward distance from residents. Left-wing social media boggled at the number of times Starmer, Williams, and National Campaign Coordinator Angela Rayner chose to take refuge in pubs to be pictured with pints, in the style of Nigel Farage.

Equally macabre was the resurrection of Peter Mandelson, Hartlepool's former MP, who materialised on the campaign trail. This gave social media critics a perfect opportunity to repeatedly post an infamous picture of Mandelson hanging out with the since-deceased serial abuser Jeffrey Epstein. Mandelson was close to Morgan McSweeney, and his presence on the doorstep served as a visual reminder of the Blair circle's continued influence at the highest level of the party.

Unsurprisingly, the party was annihilated, both in Hartlepool and the local elections. In Hartlepool, the Tories got 15,529 votes to the Labour Party's 8,589. At 28.7 percent, Labour's share of the Hartlepool vote was the lowest the party had ever achieved in the constituency. Labour also lost 327 local council seats against the Tories' gain of 235, losing control of eight councils. The Labour Party was the only one of the three major parties to lose seats; the Lib Dems had gained a modest eight. The Green Party gained an impressive eighty-eight, more than doubling their number of local councillors.

Starmer's political ineptness was brutally exposed by Hartlepool and by his flustered response. Giving an interview in the aftermath of the defeat, he famously gabbled, with an air of panic, that in response to the defeat he would 'change the things that need changing and that is the change I will bring about'.[5] Clips of his sweating response were shared with derision on social media. It is now widely reported that Starmer teetered on the brink of resigning but was talked out of his despondency by McSweeney, who urged the need for even further 'change' across the party.

The party and its allies bravely attempted to spin the loss as a hangover from the previous leadership—a form of 'long-Corbyn'. Mandelson was wheeled out for the cameras to deliver one of the more comical variants of the wretched 'on the doorstep' arguments that are deployed with dispiriting regularity in the Labour Party to assert the public's belief in the unbelievable. Appearing on TV to diagnose Labour's defeat, Mandelson claimed that people on the doorstep were not just disgusted by Corbyn but by the party's selection of the centre-left Ed Miliband over his Blairite brother David more than a decade earlier. 'One person said to me, "sort yourselves out, sort yourselves out. You picked the wrong brother and you ended up with Corbyn and so that's goodbye to you"', Mandelson asserted.[6]

One insider recalled the dismal morale of party staffers close to LOTO, which was exacerbated by an angry intervention from McSweeney. Addressing staff in the wake of the loss, McSweeney chastised them for being too 'inwardly focused' on Labour Party issues and posited the need for Labour to move much further right to align itself with the population. 'The staff just needed a bit of love, a bit of care, in that moment', one insider recalled. 'Instead they got blamed for the failures of their superiors'.

Labour's defeat, however, was also an opportunity for those with historical links to Labour Together. In late April 2021, Steve Reed's personal assistant emailed McSweeney, Jenny Chapman MP, Shabana Mahmood MP, and Jim McMahon MP to set up a dinner with Trevor Chinn in mid-May (after the Hartlepool by-election). Reed's assistant indicated that the dinner would be used to 'discuss Labour Together and how to drive the agenda forward'. What that 'agenda' might be was not disclosed, but participants were informed that 'Trevor has kindly agreed to foot the bill'.

The Hartlepool defeat provided the scope for a reshaping of the shadow cabinet in a way that benefitted Labour Together grandees. Starmer, who had been uninterested in a reshuffle his advisors had been pushing since January, was suddenly prompted into action. It appears that, in his moment of doubt, Starmer was strong-armed into a reshuffle that had the effect of consolidating the power of the Labour Together contingent. Andrew Grice, former political editor of *The Independent*, noted that 'Starmer's shake-up has been dubbed the "Labour Together reshuffle"'.[7]

Deputy Leader Angela Rayner was blamed in pre-emptive leaks for the party's failures in Hartlepool. Intensive shuttle diplomacy was then required to keep Rayner onside—achieved by offering her a glittering array of party titles—as she mulled a leadership challenge. But Rayner was also removed from her influential position as national campaign coordinator on May 10, 2021, and replaced by Labour Together's Shabana Mahmood. Lucy Powell, another MP from the Labour Together stable, was simultaneously appointed shadow minister for housing.

But the real seismic change was the firing of the soft-left Anneliese Dodds as shadow chancellor and her redeployment as party chair. Dodds was replaced by Rachel Reeves, one of Labour Together's eight 'brave' MPs, who, after 2020, was the recipient of generous donations from Sir Trevor Chinn and who, after 2023, would rely on Labour Together to launch and herald her imminent rise to the chancellorship.

The impact and importance of Reeves' appointment cannot be overstated. For the first time in over half a decade, Labour's shadow chancellor would be a dyed-in-the-wool respecter of economic orthodoxy. Reeves had embraced and argued for austerity and, especially from 2023, would set out her stall through publications and briefings for Labour Together. Her appointment as shadow chancellor was, after Corbyn's suspension, the most profound defeat of Corbynism yet—and a total and uncompromising repudiation of the progressive and redistributive economics that Starmer had promised the membership in 2020.

BATLEY AND SPEN

The Hartlepool disaster left the Starmer Project in its weakest position since Starmer took office, and arguably thereafter, the cabinet shake-up notwithstanding. Even natural allies began to fret about Starmer's lack of charisma and electability. Lord Andrew Adonis, a Blair-era cabinet minister, wrote a lengthy take-down in *The Times*. 'Unfortunately, he turns out to be a transitional figure—a nice man and good human rights lawyer, but without political skills or antennae at the highest level', Adonis wrote.[8] The next by-election battle on Labour's agenda—Batley and Spen in July 2021—was Starmer's make-or-break moment.

Another electorally crucial 'red wall' constituency, Batley and Spen had much in common with Hartlepool. It had been held by Labour since 1997, and the party's majority had increased substantially in 2017: it received 55 percent of the vote in that election, up from 41 percent in 2010 and 43 percent in 2015. In 2019, however, the constituency had returned a Labour win only because the Tories lost six thousand votes to the Heavy Woollen District Independents, which had been established by a former UKIP candidate. Like Hartlepool, Batley and Spen had voted to leave the EU, although by a smaller margin than in Hartlepool.

Three factors, however, made Batley and Spen unique. The first was that Batley and Spen had been the constituency of the Labour MP Jo Cox. Cox, considered to be a Remainer, was murdered in 2016 by Thomas Mair, a far-right constituent reportedly obsessed with Nazis. A witness at Mair's trial would recount that Mair had shouted, 'This is for Britain. Britain will always come first'. The murder of Cox had a profound impact on the area: in the following by-election, the Tories and Lib Dems withdrew from the contest, leaving the way open for Labour's Tracy Brabin to win virtually unopposed. It was Brabin's election as mayor in the May 2021 local elections, and her subsequent resignation as an MP, that triggered the by-election.

The Labour Party would choose Kim Leadbeater, Jo Cox's younger sister, as its candidate. Leadbeater was selected almost immediately after the by-election was called; her local Constituency Labour Party agreed to waive the usual requirement that she hold party membership for at least a year prior to her selection. Leadbeater could draw on both the emotional pull of her relationship to her sister and a long and well-regarded history of local activism. Unlike Paul Williams, who was seen purely as a Starmerite plant, Leadbeater inspired genuine cross-factional support in the party, which encouraged a flood of volunteers to assist her campaign. The Get Out the Vote Campaign, in particular, was seen as decisive in turning out the few hundred votes by which the party would eventually win.[9]

The second distinct factor was that Batley and Spen had a large South Asian population, much of which was Muslim and of Pakistani descent. Under previous leaders, especially Corbyn, this community was reported to have largely voted in favour of the Labour Party, following national trends. But, as has been discussed above in relation to the Labour Muslim Network report, Starmer's leadership was viewed with particular concern by Muslim Labour members, the majority of whom believed that Starmer and his project failed to properly represent Muslims or care about their concerns.

It was not an unjustified belief. In April 2021, for example, Starmer pulled out of a planned virtual Ramadan iftar dinner that had been organised with the Ramadan Tent Project. Starmer withdrew at the last minute after the party had been approached by *The Jewish Chronicle* with evidence that the CEO of the Ramadan Tent Project, Omar Salha, had advocated for a boycott of Israeli dates during Ramadan. A large part of the

Israeli date crop is grown in the illegally occupied West Bank. A pro-Palestinian NGO circulated an angry petition, which quickly secured two thousand signatures, claiming that 'in this selective disengagement, the Labour leader is discriminating against Muslims, which feeds into the systemic Islamophobia that is rife within the Labour Party'.[10] The chair of the same organisation told *Middle East Eye* that 'the sentiment the leadership has ostracised the Muslim community is widespread'.[11]

This fostered precisely the sort of dissatisfaction that could be exploited by George Galloway, the former leader of the Respect Party. Galloway's record as a fierce opponent of the Iraq War and the wider War on Terror had earned him considerable political cachet among British Muslims. Galloway entered the race almost as soon as it was called and made clear he was doing so in order to catalyse the end of Starmer's leadership. 'If Keir Starmer loses this byelection, it's curtains', Galloway reportedly enthused.[12]

There was thus a real chance that the entire Starmer Project would falter as a consequence of its seeming embrace of a hierarchy of racism, leading many to believe that Starmer's Labour Party did not prioritise issues of Islamophobia.

One LOTO insider claimed that Starmer was apparently convinced that the party's reputational collapse in the Muslim community could be placed at the feet of the left-wing commentator Owen Jones. Two days before polls opened, Jones had published an interview with Galloway that Starmer believed had boosted Galloway's reach and local popularity. This was a strange conviction, not least because Jones—who loathed Galloway—was neither the only journalist to give Galloway an opportunity to express his views nor the only one to slam them. The insider saw Starmer's fixation on the interview as reflective of his blindness to how profoundly he had alienated BAME communities over the preceding eighteen months.

To be sure, Jones was not the only culprit identified by the Starmer team for the growing Muslim alienation from Labour. 'We're haemorrhaging votes among Muslim voters', a senior but unnamed Labour official briefed *The Mail on Sunday*, 'and the reason for that is what Keir [Starmer] has been doing on antisemitism. Nobody really wants to talk about it, but that's the main factor', the source claimed.[13] Muslims, in other words, were antisemitic and therefore angry at Starmer's approach to the issue. A few days after the election, another senior source claimed that the party had lost 'conservative Muslims' over 'gay rights and Palestine'.[14] Thus, within the space of two weeks, senior party sources had claimed that the Muslim community of Batley and Spen was both homophobic and antisemitic.

The Labour Muslim Network called this briefing 'patently vile' while David Evans personally committed to investigating it.[15] Evans, at the time, was not just general secretary; he was also the head of the party's Diversity and Inclusion Board established in the wake of BLM, as a sop to BAME staffers distressed by structural racism in the party. However, an insider then working in Evans' office confirmed that Evans made little progress with the investigation.

SAVED BY THE GUARDIAN

On July 1, 2021, Batley and Spen constituents finally voted, returning a tiny Labour majority of 323 votes. Galloway picked up over eight thousand votes. Starmer and the party were cock-a-hoop. 'It is a start. Labour is back. Labour is coming home', Starmer told celebrating party activists.[16]

There were various reasons why Labour managed to scrape a victory. But one hitherto unexplored factor was that the campaign benefitted from a decision made by *The Guardian* to publish a damaging story only after voting had finished—despite being tipped off three weeks prior to election day.

On July 6, 2021, five days *after* the Batley and Spen vote, the paper broke the story that the party had lifted the administrative suspension then in place against Sir Trevor Phillips.[17] Phillips, the former head of the Equality and Human Rights

Commission who picked Peter Mandelson as the best man at his wedding, was readmitted without the matter being heard by the National Executive Committee.

Phillips was suspended in March 2020, having faced persistent allegations of Islamophobia from the likes of the Muslim Council of Britain. For example, Phillips had characterised British Muslims as a 'nation within a nation' in a discussion about how few Muslims wore Remembrance Day poppies, and opined that placing a Christian girl into foster care with a Muslim family was 'akin to child abuse'.[18]

Phillips was embraced by the likes of the right-wing think-tank Policy Exchange, which published a lengthy report (that included Phillips' suspension letter) about how allegations of Islamophobia were being used to stifle free speech.[19] Phillips claimed that he was the victim of a witchhunt and criticised the party's adoption of the All-Party Parliamentary Group on British Muslims definition of Islamophobia.

The response was maddening for anyone who had followed the 'antisemitism crisis', in which similar arguments—that claims of anti-Jewish racism were being used to stifle debate—were treated as themselves antisemitic and deserving of punishment. By contrast, Phillips' suspension was lifted soon after he was hired to present a high-profile political talk show on Sky News. The divergent treatment of Phillips as compared to similarly high-profile figures accused of antisemitism revealed a stark hierarchy of racism in the party and in society at large.

The Labour Muslim Network said of Phillips' readmission to the party: 'Trevor Phillips' case is one of the most high-profile recent examples of Islamophobia within the Labour Party and quietly readmitting him behind closed doors, without apology or acknowledgment, will only cause further anxiety and hurt among Muslims'.[20]

The Guardian was informed of Phillips' readmission in mid-June 2021, right in the middle of the Batley and Spen campaign. *The Guardian* was satisfied enough to send a right of reply to the Labour Party on June 18, 2021, to which the party offered a 'no comment' response. But it would report the story on July 6, 2021, five days after the polls closed, and a full three weeks after it had been told of the issue and approached the party for comment. This is not to suggest that there was some vast *Guardian* conspiracy pulling strings behind the scenes. Certainly, putting together stories, especially source-based, can be difficult, and it would have taken at least a few days to confirm the matter with the party and seek quotes.

But it is hard to believe that *The Guardian* would have been so slow in reporting the story had it concerned Corbyn or antisemitism, and certainly not if it had had the potential to undermine or end Corbyn's leadership. When the Ken Livingstone furore broke out in 2016, for example, *The Guardian* almost instantaneously set up a rolling news feed of denunciations and outrage. The newspaper would run dozens of articles on the issue. With Trevor Phillips, it took three weeks to publish a short (but otherwise decent) article, which received no follow-up.

In a very real sense, Starmer's campaign, facing the potential electoral consequences of its own hierarchy of racism, was saved, at least in part, because this same hierarchy was reflected and reproduced in the media.

Immediately after the Phillips story leaked, the party undertook an investigation to identify the leak's source. It ended up blaming Halima Khan, the GLU's only Muslim member, who had previously been in charge of the Phillips case. Khan, recall, had raised issues with Gilles' Newham dossier, and this led to her removal from the Newham file. Also blamed was Louis Mendee, Khan's close colleague, who had been suspended for criticising Starmer's response to BLM. Both were effectively dismissed. In a case where the party was embarrassed because it became public that it had readmitted a man accused of Islamophobia, its response was to remove BAME staff members it considered responsible for the leak.

Khan brought a claim for unfair dismissal and 'direct race discrimination' against the party; an unemployment tribunal found against her in August 2024. The tribunal was nevertheless critical of the Labour Party's conduct in the case—and of how Barros-Curtis, the party's head of legal, had comported himself on the stand. The tribunal said it was 'concerned that the [Labour Party's] disclosure of relevant material has not been as conscientious or thorough as it should have been'. Notably, the party had not disclosed an email that had been 'an important feature' in the decision to suspend Khan. That email, from a 'media organisation', had asked the party for a response on the Phillips controversy on June 18, 2021. The tribunal judge noted that when Barros-Curtis was questioned in court about this issue by Khan (who had no legal representation), he had 'proceeded to look it up on his laptop, despite being in the middle of giving sworn evidence, astonishing behaviour for a practising solicitor'.[21] Barros-Curtis thus had ready access to a document that was central to the proceedings—evidence that should have been disclosed to Khan, but was not.

The tribunal proceedings also established that Barros-Curtis had been central to the processes that led to the Phillips case being dropped. In October 2020, only weeks before the party would formally adopt the EHRC report, Barros-Curtis wrote to Khan asking her for details on the Phillips case, 'as we're getting a few chases on it'. When Khan updated him, Barros-Curtis asked to be kept abreast going forward so 'I can manage the stakeholders who keep chasing me'. He did not identify who these 'stakeholders' were.

The case then stalled with no progress being made. In May 2021, Barros-Curtis, the employment tribunal found, 'was being chased once more' about the case. Barros-Curtis accordingly sought an update and, finding that the case had not progressed, held a meeting with one of Khan's colleagues. The tribunal found that this meeting resulted in 'a decision to lift the administrative suspension' while a different staff member would continue with the investigation.[22] This confirms that Barros-Curtis was directly involved in the decision to lift Phillips' suspension. As noted above, Barros-Curtis was the sole director of Starmer's campaign vehicle and had been introduced to the media as

Starmer's ally and 'enforcer'. Did his role in the Phillips complaint amount to what the EHRC had characterised as 'political interference'?

It is striking how differently Phillips was treated as compared with others who had been processed by the party's complaints machinery. As discussed below, many Jewish members, like Andrew Feinstein, had found themselves in endless disciplinary limbo seeking the resolution of cases that never progressed.

No less striking was the lack of interest in Khan's case from the British media, which had assiduously reported on allegations of interference in disciplinary cases by Corbyn's staff. *The Guardian* initially covered the Khan story but did not report on the tribunal judgment or the confirmation of Barros-Curtis' involvement in lifting Phillips' suspension. Only Lee Harpin—the journalist who had reported Barros-Curtis' role as Starmer's 'enforcer' back in 2020—covered the resolution of Khan's case, in one lone article for the *Jewish News*.[23] This article did not mention Barros-Curtis by name, despite the tribunal's strong criticism of the recently elected MP.

CHAPTER 20

IN THE ASCENDANCY

Survival in Batley and Spen gave the Starmer Project breathing room to tighten their grip on the party, with sights set on the September 2021 annual conference.

Starmer's team went into the conference unbuoyed by any great enthusiasm amongst the party membership, despite having cleared the Batley and Spen hurdle. Starmer's war on the left enjoyed tacit support from most broadsheets but was seen by large swathes of the membership as self-destructive, petty, and dishonest. In early September 2021, Laura Parker, the former Momentum director who had publicly supported Starmer during the leadership election, finally spoke out to *The Guardian*. 'There are 40% of the membership who voted for Jeremy twice and then for Keir. They were united around his pledges', she claimed. 'Now any efforts towards party unity are absolutely blown up, it is dead in the water. I can't believe there's a single one of that 40% who doesn't feel like me, totally totally despairing and actually quite angry'.

Parker's comments chimed with those of Tom Kibasi, who had been involved in incubating Starmer's leadership bid. In February 2021, just as the party bureaucracy was to launch its attacks on democracy in Liverpool and Newham, Kibasi wrote in *The Guardian* that in Starmer's 'first year as leader, he has provoked a completely unnecessary war with the left . . . A full-frontal assault on the membership was both unnecessary and avoidable'.[1]

Starmer was still accused of failing to outline any specific policies and identify concretely what he stood for—warning signs that the promises of his leadership bid were sure to be broken. Where Starmer did venture into substantive terrain, his forays fell flat, as shown by the tepid-to-mocking reception given to the fourteen-thousand-word pamphlet he published with the Fabians in September 2021. Portentously titled 'The Road Ahead', it was seen as another attempt to define Starmerism in the minds of the public. John McDonnell dismissed it as a 'Sermon on the Mount written by a focus group'.[2] Even commentators one would expect to support Starmer's centrist revival, like Rafael Behr, were unimpressed. Attacking the 'boilerplate' that served to 'suffocate decent ideas', Behr commented that 'if the reason for extrapolating a point across a vast pamphlet is to appear heavyweight, this one achieves the opposite'.[3]

The pamphlet, truly a vacuous concatenation of conventional wisdom and homilies, had no discernible impact on Starmer's leadership, except to provide still further indication of the shallowness of Starmer's politics. One aspect of the pamphlet, however, was worth noting, not least in light of Starmer's previously radical mood music: across over fourteen thousand words, Starmer didn't mention socialism once.

NEVER AGAIN

Starmer claimed he was turning 'outwards' by promising voters a new 'contract' for a 'contribution society'. In fact, the Starmer Project remained ruthlessly focused on the party's internal, factional reconstitution. As such, the primary goal of the project heading into conference was to massively curtail internal party democracy.

In the weeks leading up to conference, Starmer informed his shadow cabinet that he wanted to end the party's 'one member, one vote' model for choosing the leadership. His maximalist offer was to restore the party to the Electoral College model, scrapped in 2014 by Ed Miliband. Under that system, the party was split into three sections, whose votes were given equal weighting: the Parliamentary Labour Party (i.e. Labour MPs), the membership, and the unions. This massively diluted the voting power of the membership and boosted the power of the PLP, which experience had proven was instinctively hostile to any leadership challenge from the left.

Starmer also proposed to limit the number of motions heard at conference—at which Labour Party policy was supposed to be made and agreed through democratic votes—along with changes to help incumbent MPs get reselected with fewer pesky membership challenges. These were all part of a project to put the Labour membership back in its box after a period of unacceptable democratic effervescence.

As with nearly anything of importance under Starmer's leadership, the real driving force behind the changes was McSweeney. Months before the conference, he had set up a secretive WhatsApp group codenamed 'Project Ex' to plan this moment of decisive rupture. A key member of the group was Luke Akehurst of We Believe in Israel and Labour to Win. Akehurst was indefatigable in producing a comprehensive picture of the politics of the potential delegate attendees and how their votes might fall. Conference was the moment that the long-germinating Labour Together Project would cap its years of misdirection and political subterfuge with a victory that would secure its ultimate aim: to insulate the party's right-leaning bureaucracy, MPs, and leadership—in short, its managerial elite—from the democratic will of the party's left-leaning membership.

Starmer finally met union leaders in the week before conference. Union figures presented the meeting to the media as a humbling dressing-down for Starmer, who had been grilled on proposals for an electoral college. Starmer eventually relented on the electoral college issue. But he would stick with a plan to change the rules so that any new leadership contenders would need the backing of least 20 percent of the PLP in order to stand. It was swiftly pointed out that this rule change would have meant that in the 2020 leadership election, Starmer would have been the only qualifying candidate. He also continued to push for changes that scrapped the registered supporter programme, by which supporters could pay a one-off fee to vote in any future leadership election.

The conference promised increased tension and a potential left-wing fightback, not least because there was an outside chance that, with enough support, conference might refuse to ratify David Evans' appointment as general secretary. But Evans ultimately prevailed. There were certainly flashpoints, not least during Starmer's own conference speech, which was enlivened by heckling from the crowd. 'Changing lives or chanting slogans?' was Starmer's pre-prepared response, delivered with the scolding attitude of a high-school headmaster.

The left could claim some victories at conference, especially around the adoption of left-wing resolutions.[4] Members passed a 'Green New Deal' motion that endorsed the public ownership of energy, as well as a motion to back renationalising the internet fibre network and the Royal Mail. Arguably the most contentious resolution dealt with Israel: a successful motion condemned 'Israel's continuing illegal actions' and declared that 'Israel is intent on eliminating any prospects of Palestinian self-determination'. It promised to stop arms sales to Israel and introduce sanctions to block trade with 'illegal' Israeli settlements.[5]

The motions were a powerful indication that the party membership was still more left-wing than the Starmer Project. Meanwhile, the response of the party leadership showed how comfortable it felt in overriding member opinion. Almost as soon as the motion on Palestine was passed, for example, Shadow Foreign Secretary Lisa Nandy told *Jewish News* that the leadership 'cannot support this motion' as the motion 'does not address issues in the Israeli-Palestinian conflict in a comprehensive or balanced way'.[6] Starmer reportedly supported

Nandy's statement. Nandy was a director of Labour Together at the time.

The defining issue was how Labour would choose its representatives and leader going forward. Here the Starmer Project achieved a crowning victory. Its proposed reforms required any aspiring leadership candidate to gather endorsements from at least 20 percent of the PLP to run, made it harder for local party structures to initiate proceedings to replace their parliamentary candidates, ended the registered supporters programme, and prevented people from voting if they did not already have six months of membership under their belt. On September 26, this reform package was narrowly passed by 54 to 46 percent.

Leftists looking for comfort could take satisfaction in how the unions successfully resisted Starmer's opening maximalist position: the reintroduction of an electoral college. But the rule changes that did pass were sufficient to substantially eliminate the possibility of any left-wing Labour leadership candidate in the near future. In particular, the increased threshold of required MP support was devastating: as set out in the next chapter, the party bureaucracy would insert itself repeatedly into the parliamentary candidate selection process, freezing out left-wing contenders on flimsy grounds and thereby ensuring that the incoming cohort of MPs would be both highly loyal to the Starmer regime and markedly right-wing. The rule changes and the Starmer Project's systematic rigging of parliamentary selections were all patently designed to preclude the prospect of another Corbyn moment, which the right wing had long blamed on the surge of new members who had joined in anticipation of voting for Corbyn.

In this tight contest where every vote counted, the Starmer Project's war on the membership likely made the difference. As noted previously, in the wake of Batley and Spen, the NEC passed rules that proscribed organisations like Socialist Appeal and Labour Against the Witchhunt, with all charges applied retrospectively. In conjunction with the mass exodus of disillusioned or disgusted left-wing members and the disciplinary measures meted out to CLPs that opposed the party's treatment of Corbyn, this ensured that a large number of potential conference delegates were taken out of the picture—disproportionately from the party's left wing.

In the days leading up to conference the party's disciplinary unit went into overdrive, issuing notices of investigation and suspension to left-wing delegates. The notices were timed so that, even if the delegates survived the allegations, they would only be able to resume their functions after conference was over. 'Reports coming in of several constituency delegates to conference receiving last-minute notices from Labour HQ threatening disciplinary action and barring them from attending Labour Party conference', John McDonnell tweeted. 'It's opening up the party bureaucracy to accusations of vote fixing. Beyond farce'.[7]

One notable case illustrating this process concerned David White. White had been one of the individuals the party had attempted to target based on the materials hacked from *Inside Croydon*. He was a left-wing member of forty years' standing, a solicitor, and a former councillor. He had been selected by his CLP Croydon Central, near to Steve Reed's patch, as one of five delegates to attend party conference. But just days prior to the event, White was issued with an administrative suspension. He was accused of antisemitism over two tweets posted in 2014[8] for which he had already been investigated by the party in 2016.[9] White was eventually expelled from the party in 2022 for these tweets—but then readmitted three years later when the party's newly created Independent Review Board found fault with how the original NEC panel overseeing his expulsion had approached his evidence.[10] The process was, indeed, a farce.

This is how the Starmer Project completed its hostile takeover of the party. Having tricked its way in with false promises of unity and radical policies, the project's operatives then seized control of the bureaucracy and used its prerogatives to ensure that it would be virtually impossible for another left-leaning leader to be elected by the party again, whatever the changing views of the membership. Even if Starmer had not gone on to defeat the Tories, he'd have already achieved something that, for Britain's political and economic elite, was arguably even more vital: there would never be another 'Corbyn moment'. Never again would ordinary Labour members so freely choose who would lead their party.

PART SIX

A GOVERNMENT-IN-WAITING

CHAPTER 21

TORY IMPLOSION AND THE ACCELERATION OF THE STARMER PROJECT

From late 2021 onward, the Conservative Party imploded in spectacular fashion. Labour simply had to watch as it all fell apart. Prime Minister Boris Johnson was unravelled by 'Partygate', the scandal in which Johnson and his colleagues were photographed enjoying social gatherings as the rest of the nation hunkered in Covid lockdown. Once Starmer just about survived 'Currygate'—his own Covid-era scandal—Johnson was in a death spiral.

A cost-of-living crisis, driven by the war in Ukraine as well as rapacious corporate profiteering, was then exacerbated by the baroque idiocy of Johnson's short-lived successor, Liz Truss, and her chancellor, Kwasi Kwarteng. Kwarteng's mini-budget collapsed the British pound, famously ending Truss' premiership in less time than it took a lettuce to decompose, and forced the Tories into a panicked and ham-fisted coronation of Rishi Sunak.

The Conservatives never recovered. Voters were unwilling to reward a party that delivered three leaders in a single parliamentary term alongside a collapse in living standards usually associated with historic calamities on the order of the Great Depression or the world wars.

Tory favourability ratings plummeted to barely conceivable levels, sending Labour's numbers soaring. On December 10, 2021, YouGov polling showed support for the Tories down to 32 percent, just as stories of Johnson's Covid cavorting came to light. For the first time in a year, Labour overtook the Tories. They did not trade places again. On October 21, 2022, YouGov reported that a mere 19 percent of the population intended to vote Conservative. Multiple seat projections suggested the Tories would struggle to reach a hundred seats; some, because of the vagaries of first-past-the-post, suggested they would struggle to get in the teens. The Labour Party rocketed to 56 percent support in the polls. Within a few weeks, polls normalised slightly, but from November 2022 onward, the Labour Party regularly polled in the mid- to upper -forties, while the Tories languished at about 24 percent.

There is a debate to be had about whether these poll numbers were due to a genuine increase in support for Labour or merely reflected a total collapse of public trust in the Tories. Despite a stream of articles that effectively anointed him the next prime minister, there was no uptick in popular support for Starmer himself. Indeed, YouGov's monthly tracker showed that, as the Tory poll lead evaporated, increasing numbers of voters counter-intuitively came to *disapprove* of Starmer.

Although experiencing a brief bounce in the immediate post-Truss period, from December 2022 onward more people disapproved of Starmer than approved of him. Between December 2022 and May 2024, Starmer's average net approval rating was -11. At the end of February 2024, in the wake of his Gaza ceasefire debacle (discussed later), his net approval rating fell to -19, its lowest point in eighteen months (Figure B).

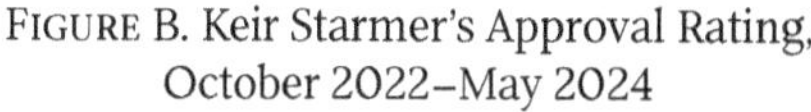

FIGURE B. Keir Starmer's Approval Rating, October 2022–May 2024

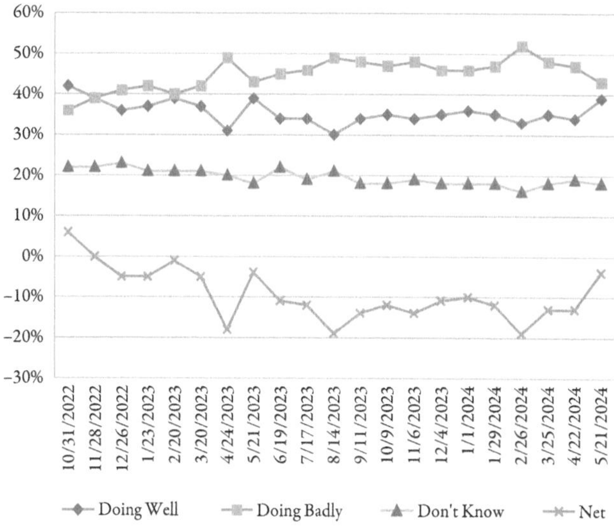

Meanwhile, Prime Minister Sunak could only dream of such lofty heights as minus-eleven. Between December 2022 and October 2023, Sunak averaged a 29 percent approval rate for his work as prime minister against a 55 percent disapproval rate: an astonishing -26 percent on average. Importantly, Sunak's polling grew consistently worse over time. In December 2022, 50 percent of the population disapproved of his performance; his net approval ratings dropped to -40 by October 2023 and -42 by April 2024.[1] By the time he called the election in June 2024, Sunak was the most unpopular sitting prime minister entering into a UK general election since modern polling records began.

There is no gainsaying that the Labour Party turned positive polling into real results, winning a series of key by-elections in 2022 and 2023. In June 2022, it gained Wakefield from the Tories. A year later, in July 2023, Labour took Selby and Ainsty, returning the cherubic Keir Mather to the Labour benches. In

October 2023, the party won three out of three by-elections, including in Central Scotland's Rutherglen and Hamilton West, where it took advantage of the Scottish National Party's own Tory-like implosion. Many of these by-elections were marked by low turnout that saw a relatively static Labour vote prevail over a Tory opponent in freefall. Where Labour lost, as in Uxbridge, it did so only narrowly.

A similar albeit slightly less impressive trend materialised during the 2023 local elections. The Tories were smashed, losing over a thousand council seats as the country continued to punish the Conservatives' inability to govern with even a modicum of competence. The Labour Party picked up five hundred seats—nothing to sniff at but not quite the surge many expected. The biggest achievers in that election were the generally smaller and less well-funded Liberal Democrats, who increased their seats by over four hundred, and the Greens, who almost doubled their tally from 241 to 481.[2]

Labour's sizeable poll lead from late 2021 onward, together with its by-election and local election wins, empowered the Starmer Project to accelerate its remaking and reshaping of the party. This top-down reconstruction was further emboldened by the emergence of a de facto alliance—always lurking but expressed with increasing confidence over time—between the Starmer Project and the party's right-wing Labour to Win faction (itself an umbrella organisation combining the right-wing organisations Labour First and Progress). In practice, a division of labour crystallised: Labour Together's associated MPs and officials like McSweeney and Reeves would control overall election strategy and policy as well as the shadow cabinet, while Labour to Win foot soldiers in the National Executive Committee and at the local level worked to marginalise the left and also moderate soft-left candidates and representatives.

The result was that, between 2022 and mid-2024, the party's already depleted internal democracy virtually ceased to exist as selections were fixed and the leadership engineered total and complete fealty. As this process accelerated, many of the themes that had dominated the first two years of the Starmer Project began to assert themselves without significant restraint, including the continuation of a de facto hierarchy of racism and a marked lurch to the right on policy, the latter a function of a wholehearted embrace of corporate lobbying and the generosity of a politically-minded wealthy donor class.

FORDE IGNORED

In mid-July 2022, the Forde Report was finally released. This inquiry examined both the unauthorised disclosure of the Leaked Report and substance of its allegations. Chaired by the respected barrister Martin Forde KC, the report was also endorsed and supported by his fellow panel members Baroness Lister, Baroness Wilcox, and Lord Whitty. Many have tended to forget that, while the report bore Forde's name, he was one of four authors, the other three a panel of hardly radical lords and baronesses.

Forde's report did not opine on the identity of the leakers because of the ongoing investigation by the Information Commissioner's Office. But it did make findings on the general accuracy of the Leaked Report's underlying allegations. It also offered a number of broader observations about the conduct and character of the Labour Party subsequent to the publication of the Leaked Report.

Forde's investigation was widely seen as credible. It is evidently written with an open mind and a sensitive appreciation for detail. In general terms, and with many caveats, Forde's report confirmed some of the key thrusts of the Leaked Report. It thereby undermined mainstream narratives around the antisemitism crisis—narratives that McSweeney's undisclosed projects had once seeded and that the party under Starmer would use as a justification to exclude the left. It is therefore perhaps unsurprising that the party, now firmly under McSweeney's control, would respond so outrageously to Forde's findings.

The Forde Report found evidence of extraordinary factionalism within the Labour Party bureaucracy, and was damning of the WhatsApp group chats between Labour officials that had been quoted in the Leaked Report. Forde found that the Leaked Report had, with just a few exceptions, accurately reflected the tone and content of these group chats.[3] Forde was also clear that the Leaked Report's allegations of racism and sexism, again revealed by the WhatsApp group chats, were credible. Forde agreed that right-wing staffers had used the membership 'validation' process to go 'trot hunting' and remove left-wing members during leadership elections.[4] Most importantly, Forde also found that the issue of antisemitism had become unhelpfully caught up in the war between the party's factions: 'rather than confront the paramount need to deal with the profoundly serious issue of antisemitism in the party, both factions treated it as a factional weapon'.[5]

Arguably, this latter sentence appears to have been somewhat misread by commentators looking to rehabilitate the more unsustainable aspects of the 'crisis'. In particular, some have interpreted it to mean that the Labour left was also somehow instrumentalising the issue of antisemitism for factional ends. In the context of the rest of the report, however, Forde's observation more likely referenced the fact that some on the left came to believe that the issue of antisemitism was *only* a factional issue—that *all* accusations of antisemitism were made in bad faith and should be treated as such, a reflex that may have prevented some in the party from tackling the matter where accusations were better-founded.

When discussing antisemitism education, Forde acknowledged the key role of the Jewish Labour Movement—but then committed the cardinal sin of pluralism:

> [W]e do recognise that there are other Jewish voices amongst Jewish communities and Jewish members of the party. Hence we are disappointed that there has been a refusal to engage at all with Jewish Voice

> for Labour's proposals for antisemitism training and that CLPs are, we are told, not even allowed to enlist their help.[6]

Forde's recognition that non-Zionist Jews were due fair treatment and inclusion would lead to the rejection of his report by many of those invested in hyping up the Labour Party 'antisemitism crisis'.

The Forde Report also found that the Ergon House scheme was 'wrong', although it fell short of arguing (as this book has) that Ergon House had a material impact on the 2017 general election.[7] As noted previously, Forde also refrained from passing an opinion on the legality of the expenditure in the Ergon House scheme insofar as it related to national versus local spending, which the report said was beyond its investigative remit. I still harbour doubts that Forde's team was provided with everything relevant to the Ergon House scheme that the party held in its server.

Forde's report was implicitly damning of Ware's *Panorama* documentary as well as a good deal of media coverage of the 'antisemitism crisis'. This focused on the period between March and April 2018, when LOTO staff were asked for their advice by GLU staff on individual cases. The emails this process generated, Forde argued, were leaked and 'subsequently used to form the basis of wholly misleading media reports which suggested that LOTO staff had aggressively imposed themselves on the process against HQ's wishes'.[8]

Arguably the most important element of Forde's report was its evaluation of the party's culture as a whole. In particular, Forde's report was damning about the party's treatment of BAME staff and members. With lawyerly restraint, it noted that

> many individuals supplied evidence of discrimination and a perceived hierarchy of protected characteristics. To be clear, the evidence received pointed to a perception that some protected characteristics

> were regarded, by the Party, more highly than others. Equally, this meant that some were less highly regarded.[9]

It was an opinion that Forde appeared to share, leading him to argue that 'outrage' directed towards antisemitism in the party 'should be matched by equally strong measures against all forms of discrimination, within Party workplaces as well as within the membership. This is the least we could expect from a party committed to anti-discrimination'.[10]

The Forde Report provided ample illustration of how widely this perceived complacency in the face of certain kinds of racism was felt, including a dedicated annex setting out verbatim extracts of people's experience of racism in the party (staff in particular). It was here that the now well-worn phrase 'hierarchy of racism' was recorded.[11] Forde's inclusion of these quotes was a hard-to-miss suggestion—a plea even—that these issues be taken seriously by the party at all levels.

This aspect of the Forde Report echoed earlier letters from the BAME Staff Network (discussed above) about the party's response to Black Lives Matter. In both instances, the sincerity of the plea and its relatively unassuming nature are striking. The plea was to take issues of racism seriously and listen to a variety of voices. It speaks volumes that the party leadership could not reach this low bar.

Forde was explicit that problems of racism in the party were not a mere historical concern but a live issue that extended into the Starmer period. '[T]he party's more recent steps to address the problems with antisemitism . . . have not been matched by a commitment to tackle other forms of racism, nor by a full-scale effort to get its house in order as an employer', Forde made clear.

Many of the loudest voices in the controversy over Labour's 'antisemitism crisis' responded with fury to Forde's report. Euan 'David Gordstein' Philipps of LAAS complained that the recommendation for JVL training on antisemitism amounted to 'gaslighting the Jewish community' and that the Forde Report was a 'whitewash'.[12] A non-Jew criticising a recommendation to include a wider range of Jewish views in the Labour Party's conversations was certainly a creative take on diversity. Philipps and LAAS, as shown earlier, had played a key role in amplifying the wretched Stop Funding Fake News astroturf campaign that had been secretly incubated by McSweeney and Imran Ahmed.

Adam Langleben, national secretary of the Jewish Labour Movement, also condemned the report's openness towards JVL.[13] In a column for the *Jewish News*, Langleben politely acknowledged that Forde was respected and independent, but also implied that the barrister should stay in his lane: '[h]e understands racism more broadly without being an expert in antisemitism'.

Langleben also criticised Forde for having 'gone beyond' a 'narrow remit' that excluded any examination of antisemitism. Forde's role, Langleben argued, was 'not to investigate antisemitism—that job was done by the EHRC'. Langleben characterised Forde's remit as 'narrow' even as the panel's terms of reference gave the inquiry the discretion to investigate and report on the 'truth or otherwise of the main allegations in the [Leaked] Report' and to 'determine which are the most significant allegations'. This surely included the issue of antisemitism and the party's treatment of it, which, after all, was what the Leaked Report was fundamentally about. Langleben also dismissed Forde's recommendation that the party engage with JVL as 'preposterous', criticising him for wandering into an issue (antisemitism training) that Langleben asserted lay beyond Forde's jurisdiction.

Langleben's haste in responding to Forde seems to have precluded him from engaging fully with the report. In one passage, Langleben claimed that Forde's report confirmed the findings of the BBC *Panorama* documentary—a laughable proposition, as would soon became clear. Langleben was also keen to make it clear that 'Forde's findings are not Labour Party policy' and flatly asserted that Labour 'won't' adopt some of his recommendations.

Langleben, of course, had worked closely with McSweeney during the Corbyn years, when McSweeney was operating in secret to undermine the Corbyn project. Together, they had identified councillors and party staffers who might have been prepared to contribute to the JLM's submissions to the EHRC. Langleben had also appeared as one of the unidentified 'talking heads' in the BBC *Panorama* documentary. Forde's findings had at the very least complicated the narratives that had been created by the JLM's leaked final submission to the EHRC, the *Panorama* documentary, and even the findings of the EHRC itself.

Stephen Pollard, a former editor of the *Jewish Chronicle*, also called the Forde Report a 'political whitewash'.[14] He attacked its claim that opponents as well as supporters of the Corbyn leadership had 'weaponised' antisemitism, claiming that Forde had thereby equated 'those perpetuating racism with those fighting it'. But what really provoked Pollard's rage was Forde's recognition that there were a 'number of legitimate approaches' in the Jewish community to the vexed issue of what constituted antisemitism and how to tackle it, and Forde's acknowledgment in this respect of the legitimate existence of JVL. 'With just that one sentence, the entirety of the report is rendered unfit for purpose, because it shows that Mr. Forde has not grasped even the most basic parts of the issue'.[15] Pollard concluded that Starmer should, in effect, ignore the report: 'Sir Keir Starmer will and should be judged on how he deals with antisemitism, not on what QCs he appoints tell him'.

In my opinion, the responses of the likes of LAAS, Langleben, and Pollard arguably encapsulated the hierarchy of racism at the heart of the 'antisemitism crisis' and illustrated the very point Forde was making. None of them appeared to give significant weight to the report's lengthy discussion of racism or Forde's plea for the party to tackle all forms of racism and other forms of discrimination. Instead, for Pollard and LAAS in particular, Forde's single sentence recognising the heterogeneity of views in the Jewish community and dignifying JVL meant that all of Forde's work was to be rejected and dismissed—including, one would assume, the detailed recommendations Forde provided to direct the party on the path to dealing with the racism in its ranks.

The party's own response to the Forde Report was an outrage. Starmer was almost disdainful, claiming that the report had nothing to do with him. 'What the Forde Report shows is how dysfunctional the party was under Jeremy Corbyn, because it was a report on what the situation was two years ago', he explained to the BBC, misrepresenting and diminishing the report in doing so. 'I didn't need the report to tell me we needed to take action', he added, effectively implying that Forde's hard work had been a waste of time as it merely explored the obvious.[16] It was a remarkably disrespectful thing to say about the work of a fellow Queen's Counsel, never mind a Black colleague who was raising concerns about racism in Starmer's party.

Figures close to the party also immediately briefed the press that, contrary to the Forde Report's advice, they would make no attempt to engage JVL in the delivery of antisemitism training. A week after the report was published, a JLM source was quoted as saying that the party's NEC would not discuss the issue and that 'senior figures in Keir Starmer [*sic*] were well aware that JVL represented a "minority" and "much criticised viewpoint" that conflicted with mainstream UK Jewry'.[17] Forde and others would no doubt have been aware of the extent to which such briefing undermined the report as a whole.

Black Labour MPs registered and objected to this wholesale dismissal of Forde's endeavour. A week after the report was released, Kate Osamor said she felt

> let down by Keir Starmer's dismissal of findings of racism in the party . . . Rather than acknowledging the findings, issuing an apology to those affected, sanctioning the individuals involved, and publishing a plan to rid the party of racism, Starmer took to the radio to disregard the report altogether.[18]

Diane Abbott told *The Guardian* that she had not received any apology from the party for the comments made by staff against her, which Forde found to be drawn from 'racist tropes' that 'bear little resemblance to the criticisms of white male MPs'. Abbott complained that '[i]n a private sector organisation, people who were as blatantly racist as this would be disciplined, if not sacked'.[19]

Perhaps the most important aspect of the party's response to Forde was to appoint an NEC working group to assess his recommendations. Forde was keen to speak to this group. At least one NEC member briefed the press that some participants in the working group felt the same way. But the request was overruled and the NEC working group was barred from speaking directly to Forde. The result was that the party, in effect, prevented Forde from having any role or input in the implementation of his own report.

One of Forde's most significant recommendations was for the party's permanent machinery to become neutral with respect to internal political disputes, akin to a civil service. The rationale went to the heart of Forde's findings: factionalism among Labour Party staff, and the conduct it inspired, had done untold damage to the party. Here was yet another opportunity to confront a toxic political culture and rectify it; and another time that any suggestion of meaningful change was spurned.

So on this matter, the party and Starmer himself were clear:

> The recommendation that HQ/regional staff should regard their roles in the Party as akin to civil service roles and remain neutral have [*sic*] been considered by the General Secretary's Office and the Leaders' [*sic*] Office and given the political judgements required at all levels of the Party, are rejected. Staff are expected to take a steer from the leadership of the organisation in all their dealings and as such cannot also remain neutral. They are expected to act politically and develop their political skills in a

> professional environment. The expectation that all staff should be politically impartial is an unrealistic one in the view of the Leader and General Secretary and would undermine the Party's ability to recruit, retain and develop the best political operators (skills that are needed both to win a general election and if the Labour Party were to win power).[20]

Put otherwise, the party and Starmer's response to the overwhelming evidence of factionalism in the Leaked Report and Forde Report was to embrace the mechanism by which factionalism could be expressed. Party staff would never be neutral but instead were 'expected to take a steer from the leadership in all their dealings'. This expectation would certainly have surprised Corbyn's leadership team, which many party staff did their best to 'steer'—off a cliff. It must also fly close to breaching the EHRC's strictures against political interference: if every aspect of the bureaucracy was required to take direction from the political leadership, then how could this fail to affect the handling of complaints, too? Regardless, it was a candid admission that the Starmer Project understood the party as a vehicle to manifest and implement its will, and not as a body designed to serve the party's members or fairly implement the party rule book to manage healthy democratic contestation.

One wonders whether, following Labour's general election success in 2024, the Starmer Project believed the same of the British state.

SILENCING FORDE

In late February 2023, and in the absence of any meaningful engagement from the party with his report, Forde gave an interview to Al Jazeera.[21]

His decision to speak to Al Jazeera was notable. In October 2022, Al Jazeera had released a four-part documentary series,

The Labour Files, based on what it called 'the largest leak in British political history'. The series addressed some of the stories detailed in this book, such as the Newham dossier. Two of its four programmes delved into topics considered by Forde, namely, the 'antisemitism crisis' and racism in the party, the latter through an episode called 'The Hierarchy'. The series contained extraordinary material but was almost universally ignored by the British media; veteran journalist Peter Oborne claimed that there was a media omertà on the topic.[22]

The documentary series would have been closely scrutinised by Labour headquarters, which likely sighed in relief at the absence of any British media coverage. Forde's agreement to talk to Al Jazeera could be seen as a tacit acknowledgment of Al Jazeera's work and would doubtless have drawn fresh attention to it. In his interview, Forde noted that he had watched *The Labour Files* and concluded that Al Jazeera must have had access to even more material than him.

Forde claimed that he had heard virtually nothing from the party since his report had come out. Apart from discussing some housekeeping issues with General Secretary David Evans and meeting a caucus of Black MPs, he said he had 'not spoken to anybody within the party machine'. He suggested that this response was hardly sufficient to address the perception, which his report had diagnosed, that Labour operated a hierarchy of racism.

Forde was also struck by the extent to which he was completely ignored by the media. He said he had been approached by just a *single* media outlet on the day of the report's publication—and even that reporter admitted they hadn't read it.

It is, indeed, striking just how little mainstream media attention was paid to the Forde Report at the time, not least given the vast amount of ink spilt on the 'antisemitism crisis' about which he made important findings. Could this systematic incuriosity reflect the fact that Forde's findings disrupted a mainstream media narrative that nobody in power was particularly minded to revisit? It is also concerning that the Forde

Report has largely been ignored in contemporary retellings of Labour Party history. It is notable, in light of the gravity of Forde's findings and the political implications of his subsequent treatment, that he barely features in Pogrund and Maguire's book on this period, *Get In*. Indeed, Forde is given just a single mention across 480 pages, and then only to note his appointment. Forde's findings, the release of the report, and the party's response are not discussed at all.

Extraordinarily, Forde also claimed that he had come under direct pressure from the BBC to alter the report's findings. 'I would be grateful if you would consider amending your report in respect of your references to Panorama so that it more fairly reflects what the programme said', the editor of *Panorama*, Karen Wightman, had written to Forde in relation to his comments about how LOTO intervention had been reported in the media.

Forde also received an email from *Panorama* journalist John Ware, who claimed that Forde's report 'has done significant damage to my reputation and to that of the Corporation for journalistic integrity'. Ware demanded a response by the following day and copied in the editor of the *Jewish Chronicle*, Jake Wallis Simons. Forde was 'taken aback' and felt that Ware's letter was akin to a 'letter before action'. Forde diplomatically noted that, while Ware had 'followed the evidence', Forde's investigation was, in effect, more complete. This was because, unlike Ware, 'I also interviewed some of those who hadn't participated in [*Panorama*] from the alternative faction . . . and I would like to think as a Barrister now for thirty-eight years, I have a degree of forensic skill in determining the credibility of witnesses'.

Forde was also critical of the party's approach to the Carter Ruck Five, noting that he and his team had not been able to identify the source of the Leaked Report's disclosure. 'Isn't it just a terrible shame that that's taking the focus away from what I would've thought would be the main objective of a political party which is campaigning and winning an election', he commented.

In the wake of Forde's interview, the party reiterated a belated and non-specific apology to anyone who had experienced ill-treatment as reported in the Forde Report—a patent exercise in panicked damage-limitation.[23] The apology failed to name or apologise directly to Diane Abbott, despite Forde's clear findings about her treatment. Internal files show that the party also went to extraordinary lengths to try to shut Forde up and to prevent him from speaking to Al Jazeera altogether.

In early February 2023, Forde wrote to General Secretary Evans, noting that he had heard nothing from the working group despite his desire to meet with them, and highlighting that he had not given any media interviews up until that point. Forde said he was now minded to give an interview to Al Jazeera: 'I do not feel I can avoid interaction with the media altogether, without it looking as if I am not truly independent', he explained.

Evans took two weeks to respond—something of a slap in the face considering the work and effort Forde had given to the party. Evans first breezily dismissed Forde's desire to meet with the working group then pondering Forde's own recommendations. 'I think they have moved onto implementation, and I believe as you suggest that the prospect of them wishing to meet is now probably not on the agenda', Evans explained.

Next, Evans explained that it would be 'inappropriate' for Forde to be interviewed by Al Jazeera. 'With their production of the Labour Files, they demonstrated their political partiality and are not considered a reputable news outlet following multiple scandals, including producing and distributing holocaust denial videos on their online platform'. One reasonable reading of Evans' letter, or an implication that might be drawn, was that Forde might be tainted with the allegation of antisemitism if he decided to speak to Al Jazeera.

The comments about Al Jazeera were scurrilous. In this case, Evans referenced a video that had been posted on Al Jazeera's social media feed in 2019 and quickly deleted when issues were raised; Al Jazeera had said it 'completely disown[ed]' the video. The primary producers of the content were suspended and forced to attend 'mandatory bias training'.[24] Evans used this one incident to smear all of Al Jazeera's content. But perhaps it was only to be expected that the party would respond negatively to *The Labour Files*, given that the series had, amongst other things, revealed Evans' role in handling the Newham dossier.

In fact, Al Jazeera English was well-regarded internationally, and from 2023, its reputation would be enhanced further by its coverage of Israel's 'plausible' genocide in Gaza. This coverage was remarkable for its bravery and rigour amidst the Israeli onslaught, which killed numerous Al Jazeera journalists and their families.

Forde gave the interview despite Evans' objection. On February 28, Al Jazeera sent a right of reply to the party seeking comment; this was five days after Evans had responded to Forde's original courtesy letter. The right of reply noted that Forde had made comments critical of the party, surveyed above.

Two days later, Forde received a severe letter from the Labour Party, sent via its solicitors Norton Rose Fulbright. It is striking that the party went straight for the legal route, rather than reaching out to Forde directly. The letter focused on two primary grievances: that Forde had given 'extensive negative and highly prejudicial commentary on the party's conduct' following the report's publication, and that he had commented on the Carter Ruck Five case, which was 'entirely outside of the remit of the [Forde] Report and raises issues about which you plainly are not able to comment'. A careful reading of the letter shows that the party's anger tended to hover around the matter of the Carter Ruck Five case, suggesting that Forde's comments had struck a particularly sensitive nerve.

The letter construed Forde's courtesy email to Evans (informing him of the decision to speak to Al Jazeera) as amounting to a series of hard-and-fast commitments, which the party then claimed had been breached. 'When you gave these assurances . . . you can be taken to be aware that the party would have had no reason to second-guess these assurances given that they were provided: (a) by a senior barrister directly to that barrister's client; and, further, (b) against the backdrop of the client having made explicit its views as to the inappropriateness' of Forde speaking to Al Jazeera. In fact, the party claimed, Forde had not been 'true' to his 'word', as he had spoken about issues not raised in the Evans letter. The implication that Forde had lied in his 'assurances' to the party was a grave accusation and stepped remarkably close to alleging serious professional misconduct.

In fact, the party did allege this explicitly. The party's position was that 'you have seriously misconducted yourself by doing the very things you explicitly assured the party you would not do', and that Forde's comments were 'seriously prejudicial' to the party and 'otherwise entirely inappropriate'. 'That such conduct has been committed by a senior barrister who can be taken to well understand the importance of dealing with his client honestly, straightforwardly and in good faith is all the more concerning', it continued. 'Still further, such conduct raises serious questions as to whether, despite your claims to independence and impartiality, you are in fact seeking to pursue your own political agenda, irrespective of the harm which such conduct may cause the party'.

Without overstatement, this was an extraordinary letter. Forde, a well-respected Black KC, having dedicated considerable time to diligently investigating issues of racism for the Labour Party, was now being told that he would be misconducting himself if he spoke in public about his findings as well as the party's (lacklustre) response.

In mid-2024, I provided copies of this correspondence to *The Independent*, which reported on the matter in the wake of the humiliating treatment of Diane Abbott and Faiza Shaheen (discussed later). Forde commented to *The Independent* that 'I am sure that people will definitely see it [the correspondence] as a collateral attack on a Black professional'.[25]

Party files show that Forde appointed BDB Pitmans as his legal representatives; they had provided secretariat services for his inquiry. Their response to the party was an exercise in cutting brevity. It noted that Forde had made no undertakings to Evans, having sent him a letter as a courtesy, and argued that the party was trying to weave a tale out of leavings. 'It appears you cannot make a genuine complaint and so are seeking to rely on purported assurances given in an email'.

It also recorded that Forde had been appointed by the party as an 'independent' (emphasis in original) chair of the investigation, and that

> he is not, and has never been, in a usual barrister-client relationship with the party. It was not and is not Mr Forde KC's role to promote or protect the party's interests generally or in relation to matters contained within the party's report . . . We note your generalised threat that the party is 'considering all of its options'. We consider the party's complaints to be baseless.

The party did not pursue that matter further—until it discovered that Forde planned to speak in public again about his own report, at an event hosted by Compass.[26] Once again, party lawyers attempted to deter Forde from speaking. This time, Forde does not appear to have bothered to respond, and the party's attempt to muzzle him again came to nothing.

But the whole exchange typified the Starmer Project's abject response to the Leaked Report, which illustrated both the project's hyper-factional nature as well as its tone-deaf and arguably dismissive approach to issues of racism.

To recap: in response to the Leaked Report, which identified a highly dysfunctional political culture riven with racism and sexism that undermined the party's ability to function as an electoral force, the party had sought to manage the fallout by appointing a well-respected Black KC to lead a thorough investigation. While that investigation was ongoing, the party subtly undermined its work and made clear that it cared little about the contents of the Leaked Report by issuing public statements that prejudged Forde's findings, hiring and promoting individuals whose conduct featured critically in the Leaked Report, and paying off the bureaucrats whose poor conduct had been exposed in the Leaked Report—many of whom were McSweeney and Imran Ahmed's political allies. The tiny handful of former staffers who were disciplined were handed only the mildest of slaps on the wrist.

Internal party files show that officials were largely unconcerned with how the Leaked Report's evidence of racism and Islamophobia had alienated sections of the membership, and that the party did not even consider investigating the reported exodus of BAME members. Instead, all significant party resources were directed towards suing the authors of the Leaked Report (the Carter Ruck Five) on the charge of having leaked the report, despite having no hard forensic evidence of this. Millions of pounds were expended on this fruitless endeavour, with all sorts of shenanigans—like cracking open Karie Murphy's private email inbox—dogging the party's panicked search for evidence. It was during this process that Barros-Curtis, Starmer's hand-picked 'management enforcer', sent his outrageous and entirely misleading email to Jennie Formby that misrepresented the Carter Ruck Five's defence.

Then, when Forde's sober and mild report was released, the party and Starmer responded dismissively, with Forde's suggestion that the party accept a plurality of views on matters of antisemitism used as a reason to undermine the report's credibility. After Forde gave a typically measured interview to Al Jazeera to raise concerns about how the party was ignoring his findings, the party sent him aggressive lawyers' letters accusing him of misconduct and demanding his future silence.

REMAKING THE PLP

From late 2021 to 2024, the Starmer Project accelerated its process of remaking the party in its image. Throughout this period, the party's higher echelons assiduously ensured that Labour representatives at all levels of the party were drawn from a narrow, right-wing faction loyal to the project.

At the national level, the Tories' multi-year implosion, Labour's poor showing in the 2019 general election, and its strong polling numbers gifted the Starmer Project a unique opportunity to remake the Parliamentary Labour Party. Labour's landslide election victory in 2024 saw it add two hundred new MPs, all selected by a Starmer Project that disdained party democracy and valued loyalty above all else. The leadership had been brutally efficient and deeply unfair in shaping the process for choosing these new potential MPs.

The enduring significance of this transformation should not be underplayed. 'This is the most fundamental attempt to change the DNA of the Labour Party in its entire history', one unnamed Labour MP told *openDemocracy* in April 2023.[27]

The process of selecting candidates for parliament ahead of the 2024 general election was closely overseen by Morgan McSweeney, who was responsible for getting Labour election-ready. He worked with Labour First's Matt Pound and Matt Faulding. Faulding was appointed by Starmer's office, in late 2021 or early 2022, to take charge of the day-to-day management of the selection process. Faulding had previously served as the deputy director of Progress, a pressure group formed in 1996 to support Tony Blair. Luke Akehurst was often chosen as the NEC representative overseeing selection panels or participating in them. The result, bluntly, was that four white, middle-aged men, all linked to the party's most aggressively right-wing minority factions, unilaterally reshaped Labour's parliamentary presence in this unique period of flux.

The stitch-ups were straightforward affairs. The NEC representatives overseeing parliamentary candidate selections worked alongside the party's regional bureaucrats to filter who could and couldn't make it onto each selection longlist. Key to this process was the introduction of a 'due diligence' exercise overseen by the right-dominated NEC, which scoured the histories of left-wing candidates to find any marginally credible reason (sometimes making do with not even that) to exclude them. Once the NEC had purged selection longlists of political impurities, the lists were given to local parties as the basis for developing a final shortlist to go to the membership. If local parties got uppity and tried to cultivate a non-factional shortlist, the NEC simply suspended the local committees and took over the selection process—or pushed through their choices after head office interference caused entire CLP executives to resign, as happened in Wakefield in 2022[28] and in both Broxtowe and Copeland in 2023.[29]

By 2024, however, even this sham performance of democracy was jettisoned. In March 2024, it was reported that the NEC's Ann Black had sent a message to CLP WhatsApp groups stating that the remaining candidate selection processes would not involve local voting. Instead, candidates would simply be appointed by the NEC.[30] As we will see in the final chapter of this book, the process took on a farcical air after Prime Minister Sunak called the general election, with the NEC parachuting its own members, like Luke Akehurst, into safe Labour seats, without so much as a passing nod towards democracy.

Starmer had, of course, promised the Labour Party membership during his leadership campaign that he would bring this sort of thing to an end. As part of his 'reform and unite' platform announced in early February 2020, Starmer declared that 'local party members should select their candidates for every election. The NEC should not impose candidates on local parties'.[31]

Opposition to Starmer's dictatorial party management was not just the griping of a disaffected left wing. The only journalist who kept tabs on the Labour selection process in any depth was Michael Crick, the former political editor of the BBC's flagship political programme, *Newsnight*. His damning conclusion: 'Labour's selection processes are unfair, and verge on corrupt'.[32]

Crick observed that selection procedures were systematically skewed in order to bring about the 'utter annihilat[ion]' of the left, as virtually every candidate with a left-wing or strong trade union background was stitched up or prevented from standing. One common method was the 'heir and a spare' approach, whereby Labour headquarters ensured its favoured candidate would stand against one other person who, while not the leadership's first choice, would still toe the line.[33]

Two examples show how the selection process was distorted in ways that undemocratically precluded the selection of candidates identified with the party's left.

Emma Dent Coad, a long-time local councillor, had defied expectations to become the MP for Kensington in 2017 on the back of the Corbyn surge, winning by just fifty votes. She was the first Labour MP to ever win the constituency. In 2019, she lost by another tiny margin—150 votes out of 43,762 cast—to a Brexit-related Liberal Democrat surge. Dent Coad had built a solid local reputation for her sensitive and hard-working response to the Grenfell disaster, which happened in her constituency the week after she was elected. Dent Coad failed to make it onto the NEC-curated longlist, despite being the sitting Labour leader on the council. The reasons for her exclusion were not clarified but, as ever, unnamed Labour sources briefed the media: she was reportedly removed because she had spoken at demonstrations organised by the Stop the War Coalition.[34] Starmer, of course, had used footage from Stop the War marches in the promotional video used to launch his leadership bid, implying his support of the organisation and its anti-war politics.

Dent Coad eventually resigned from the party in April 2023. She explained that she was disgusted that Starmer had recently taken a £1,000 gratuity in the form of football tickets from the building firm Mulalley & Co—a matter discussed in the next chapter. Suffice to note, for now, that the firm had only recently been fined over £10 million for having installed ill-performing cladding on five tower blocks in 2005.[35]

Another example of party manipulation was its failure to longlist the renowned anti-racist campaigner and Labour councillor Maurice Mcleod for the seat of Camberwell and Peckham. Mcleod was well known as the former political editor of *The*

Voice, which focuses on the UK's Black communities, and was identified with the party's left. 'As a black, working-class Londoner, who has lived his whole life on council estates, I felt like I was exactly the kind of person who my fellow constituents might want to see represent them in parliament', Mcleod wrote, explaining why he tried to run.[36]

Mcleod was blocked from the longlist, falling at the NEC's dreaded due diligence stage. Mcleod was told that there were four problems arising from the due diligence test. One, he had once liked a tweet by the Green MP Caroline Lucas before he was even a Labour councillor. Two, he had once, long ago, criticised the Labour council online. Three, he had once given a quote in a media interview in which he said he backed the IHRA working definition of antisemitism (that the party had adopted in 2019) but was concerned about some of its supporting examples. Several of these examples were widely criticised, as they appeared to conflate antisemitism with legitimate, accurate criticism of Israel. Fourth, he had mistakenly failed to cast a vote in the council chamber on the adoption of the IHRA definition, which was spun by Tory councillors as him walking out. Even his Tory opponents later came to believe this was a genuine mistake, and the council chamber was instructed not to raise it again.[37]

Mcleod's exclusion provoked a furious reaction. Three participants in the constituency selection process resigned, posting a statement explaining that they refused to 'sign off on a fraudulent process' that had been 'fixed to exclude socialists and anti-racism campaigners'.[38] Mcleod's exclusion was also criticised by a host of BAME MPs, including Diane Abbott and Bell Ribeiro-Addy, and messages of solidarity were sent by Zarah Sultana, Florence Eshalomi, and Fleur Anderson.

Labour Black Socialists condemned the move and said they were left 'breathless' by the decision.[39] One of the most biting comments, reported in *The Voice*, came from the renowned *Guardian* journalist Gary Younge. Labour's 'message to the black community: those who work tirelessly in your interests over decades, representing the party at a local level, should not apply for parliament. We want your votes but not your voice', he posted to Twitter.[40]

Mcleod's exclusion was particularly shocking given that the Forde Report had only recently been published, to the Labour Party's near-total indifference. *The Voice* criticised the party's failure to take Forde seriously and its failure to respond to Al Jazeera's *The Labour Files* documentaries, which it accused party leaders of 'trying to ignore'.[41]

In March 2019, the Labour Party had launched the Bernie Grant Leadership Programme, named after one of the country's first Black MPs. The programme was established to increase the number of BAME candidates for parliament and offered training for aspiring MPs.[42] By 2023, not a single graduate of the programme had been selected as an MP candidate. Maurice Mcleod had been a graduate, as had Mish Rahman, a well-known left-wing campaigner. Rahman failed to make the longlist for Wolverhampton West in 2023 despite being an elected member of the party's NEC. In effect, his own NEC colleagues had determined him unsuited for an MP role, indicative of how factional the body had become.[43] Those same NEC members would then select themselves for safe parliamentary seats, with no local party involvement, during the general election.

In July 2023, Bernie Grant's widow Sharon Grant told *The Guardian* that she feared the lack of proper progress for Black MPs and aspiring candidates meant that the entire leadership programme may not be 'worthy of bearing Bernie's name', while also raising the real likelihood that 'black and brown voters may choose to stay at home or cast their vote elsewhere'.[44]

The same *Guardian* article carried multiple quotes from graduates of the programme, all of whom remained anonymous. The graduates' patent fear of reprisal for putting their names to their experiences lurks powerfully as an unstated theme of the article. In one disturbing paragraph, *The Guardian* noted that 'some BGLP graduates, who have asked to remain anonymous, fear they will not ever be able to reach a Labour leadership role because they have worked or campaigned on behalf of migrant rights, against the hostile environment, or on issues of structural racism, which puts them "in conflict" with party officials'.[45]

One unnamed Asian graduate of the programme gave *The Guardian* one of the most succinct and powerful deconstructions of how the party's factionalism cut across issues of race and identity. 'I don't think the party has conscious bias and is actively seeking to block people of colour', the graduate of the programme explained. 'But sadly, there's a higher propensity of ethnic minorities to be blocked from selections as we are inherently in tune with fighting for equality, worse as many ethnic minorities tend to sit on the left'.[46] The war on the left, on this version, disproportionately targeted ethnic minorities because there were more representatives of ethnic minorities on the left of the party.

Instead, the vast majority of selected candidates were drawn from a tiny demographic: white, middle-class, with backgrounds in 'respectable' professions and the third sector—and, as it would later emerge, with careers in lobbying.

Faced with criticism of rigged selection processes, the party's stock response was that the process had been designed to ensure the selection of only the best-quality candidates who had no skeletons in the closet. This just added salt to the wound inflicted by the exclusion of BAME candidates. It was also demonstrably false.

Indeed, despite an alleged commitment to quality, all sorts of candidates from the right made the cut. Dominic Beck, for example, resigned soon after his selection as the MP candidate for Rother Valley was announced. The local press reacted with consternation to his selection, as Beck had been part of a Labour council that resigned en masse after a 2015 report slammed their conduct around the sexual exploitation of 1,400 children in Rotherham over a period of twelve years. The report found that the council had been more concerned with protecting its reputation than with safeguarding constituents.[47]

In late 2023, allegations of potential fraud began circulating in respect of the selection process for the seat of Croydon East, next door to Steve Reed. *Inside Croydon* reported on concerns that somebody had tampered with membership lists in a way that could affect the online voting process. The allegations of fraud were serious enough for the Labour Party to pause the constituency's selection process while it mounted an investigation.

In 2024, the party confirmed that there had been widespread tampering with members' data. *Inside Croydon* reported that the matter was being investigated by the police.[48] The alleged fraud had apparently been conducted via the Anonyvoter system: vote-handling software brought into the party by Evans and created by Croydonites who were viewed as being close to him. According to a report by Crick, based on a Labour source, the party's investigation established that the personal details of 120 individuals had been changed and that thirty potentially fraudulent electronic votes had been cast.[49]

As I noted in the preface, Anonyvoter had been of particular interest to the unknown individual who called me in 2024 pretending to be an *openDemocracy* journalist in an attempt to find out what I knew about various Labour-related scandals.

Days after the Croydon East story broke, Sam Tarry decided to speak out in the media. Tarry, a well-known left-winger, was sacked from Labour's front bench after joining a union picket in 2022. This decision was criticised by many, as he was an MP for a party representing organised labour through formal union affiliations. Tarry lost the local vote to be re-selected as the Labour MP for Ilford South a few months later in October 2022, when he was beaten by Jas Athwal. Party files show that Athwal was a close ally of Labour Together's Wes Streeting, who represents the constituency next door. Tarry alleged that he only lost to Athwal because of Anonyvoter manipulation. 'I want to be absolutely clear—the Anonyvoter system was used to deselect me, rigged to change the result against [the] wishes of my local party'.[50]

In August 2024, only a month after Athwal's election as an MP, the BBC would run a damning investigation into the state of a flat that he rented out to local tenants.[51] Athwal owned fifteen rental flats, making him parliament's biggest landlord. He explained that the flat's poor condition was due to failings by his property manager—an explanation that failed to address Athwal's own responsibility for ensuring that his tenants were not living in squalor.

Another deselected left-wing MP, Beth Winter, also believed that she had lost her bid to be reselected as Labour MP because of Anonyvoter.[52] The Labour Party denied wrong-doing in both cases and emphasised that it had confidence in the systems used.

NURSING A GRUDGE

The Starmer Project's attack on party democracy would encompass all levels of representation, including directly elected mayors. In 2023, the sitting mayor of the North of Tyne Combined Authority, Jamie Driscoll, became the party's next high-profile factional victim.

In 2018, Driscoll had been elected as a councillor in the Newcastle ward of Monument. Driscoll was the co-chair of Newcastle Momentum.[53] In February 2019, he was selected by local Labour members as the party's candidate in the inaugural mayoral election for the newly created North of Tyne position. Driscoll bested Nick Forbes, the right-wing candidate who had led Newcastle city council since 2011, and proceeded to comfortably win the mayoral vote.

Driscoll intended to run for re-election in 2024 as the Mayor of the newly expanded seat of North East Combined Authority, but party mandarins had other ideas. In June 2023, shortly before members were due to vote on their preferred candidate, party officials intervened to remove Driscoll from the Labour longlist. It was a bold move: the party had effectively nobbled a sitting mayor. Even normally quiescent media were astonished by the decision, not least because Driscoll, a well-regarded and effective administrator, was held in high esteem even by those across the aisle, like Tory minister Nadhim Zahawi. Many had been impressed by Driscoll's deft negotiation of a multi-billion-pound devolution deal for the North as well as his management of the Covid crisis.

Driscoll's 'crime' was that he had shared a platform with the famed socialist film director Ken Loach in March 2023. Driscoll had hosted a discussion of Loach's work, much of which is set in and explores issues specific to the North of England. By this point, Loach had been expelled from the party over his support for proscribed groups; an expulsion that, per Labour Party rules, Loach was not permitted to appeal. As noted above, the proscriptions plainly offended natural justice as people could be expelled for being associated with proscribed groups before they had been banned by the party. Days before Driscoll was deselected, Loach was given a standing ovation at the Cannes Film Festival upon screening his latest and last film, *The Old Oak*.

Because Loach was not technically expelled for antisemitism, party officials could not directly allege that Driscoll was deselected because he had associated with an antisemite. Instead, the public was informed that Driscoll had broken an unwritten and non-existent rule about speaking on a platform alongside somebody expelled for an offence that amounted to guilt by association. Driscoll was thus expelled for guilt-by-association with a person guilty by association: guilt by association squared, perhaps, or once removed.

The accusations against both Loach and Driscoll nevertheless dripped with unstated implications of antisemitism, even if party officials could not say this outright. For example, when *The Guardian*'s Simon Hattenstone (himself Jewish) interviewed Rachel Reeves, and Driscoll was discussed, Hattenstone pushed back on the claim that Loach was antisemitic. 'You don't think Loach is antisemitic? OK. Well we have to agree to differ', Reeves responded.[54] When Hattenstone asked for hard evidence, Reeves equivocated: 'Look, I'm not on the bodies that make those decisions, but I think it's right we have a zero-tolerance approach', she repeated twice, failing to answer the question. It is not clear which bodies Reeves was talking about or what decisions they supposedly made, considering that Loach has never been found guilty of antisemitism by the Labour Party.

As this book has revealed, Loach was one of the names on Steve Reed's 2020 'purge list'. When Loach could not be found guilty of antisemitism, the party machinery under Starmer then explored how proscribing groups could enable it to expel people against whom it had little or no evidence of wrongdoing. Driscoll's deselection was thus arguably a long-term consequence of the Labour Together Project's 'secret planning' to 'seize control' of the Labour Party, in part by covertly inserting itself into the Labour Party 'antisemitism crisis'.

There was another aspect of Driscoll's deselection related to Labour Together. Recall that in 2019, Driscoll had beaten out Nick Forbes to become Newcastle mayor. Forbes was particularly close to Morgan McSweeney. In 2010, McSweeney had taken up a position as the head of the Labour Group Office at the Local Government Association, which the *New Statesman*'s Rachel Wearmouth has described as 'something of a priest hole for moderates during the Corbyn era'.[55] Forbes was the leader of the Labour group at the time, working closely with McSweeney. As noted previously, when Wearmouth penned her portrait of McSweeney in November 2022, Forbes provided multiple approving quotes about McSweeney's intolerance for the left. Was Driscoll's card forever marked because he had once bested McSweeney's ally?

Driscoll eventually resigned from the party in anger and launched a crowdfunding campaign to run as an independent. The funding drive reached its target of £25,000 in just two hours. By October 2023, it had raised over £130,000.[56]

Driscoll's resignation letter was one of the more notable entries in what had by then become something of a literary genre: the indignant denunciations of those betrayed by Starmer. 'In 2020 you told me to my face that you would "inspire people to come together . . . disciplining people to be united is going nowhere"', Driscoll wrote. 'You've broken that promise'.[57]

In May 2024, despite running a popular and innovative campaign, Driscoll was beaten by Labour's Kim McGuinness, who became mayor of the North East Combined Authority. Driscoll had stood as an independent; his campaign was a stark reminder of the difficulties of challenging dominant party structures with their access to voter data and substantial resources.

Ironically, considering the reasons for Driscoll's defenestration, McGuinness' selection was criticised by national charity The Traveller Movement after news emerged that she had used a 'racial slur' on Twitter in 2011, for which she later apologised. It was the sort of infraction that would likely have proven fatal to her candidacy had she been on the party's left wing. '[F]uck off! I am not a gypsy!' she had tweeted.[58]

IDEOLOGICAL PURITY

By mid-2023, and following Driscoll's deselection, the Starmer Project began to extend its control-freakery and public humiliations beyond the Labour left as it increasingly targeted the so-called 'soft left' of the party. In doing so, the children of this project started to eat their fathers and former friends.

The target chosen by the Starmer Project to signal its unwillingness to compromise with even the soft left was Neal Lawson. Lawson, a member of the party for forty years, was no Corbynite. He had advised Gordon Brown in the 1980s and been a strategist for Tony Blair in the 1997 general election. Following a stint in PR, Lawson established Compass, a centre/soft-left pressure group, in 2003. He has served as its executive director ever since.

In many ways, Compass is what Labour Together had misleadingly professed to be. Compass' unique selling point is to act as a node through which people from all political parties and factions can come together to achieve the 'Good Society'. 'We are founded on the belief that no single issue, organisation or political party can make a Good Society a reality by themselves so we have to work together to make it happen', it explains on its website.

In late June 2023, Lawson received, seemingly out of the blue, a Labour Party notice of investigation. Lawson was told that he was being investigated for a tweet he had published in 2021. In line with Compass' big-tent approach, Lawson had retweeted a post from a Lib Dem MP suggesting that it would make sense for some voters to back Green Party candidates in local elections to achieve the best progressive (and anti-Tory) outcome. Lawson commented that this was 'grown-up, progressive politics'.[59] Lawson was told in 2023 that he was under investigation for supporting another political party—an auto-exclusion offence that could end his four-decade membership. His case would only be resolved two years later, in 2025, when the charges were dropped with no explanation as to why it had taken so long to process an obviously absurd charge against him.

Lawson's investigation appeared to come out of nowhere. But Labour Party emails show that Lawson was the subject of a complaint as early as 2021, filed by none other than Luke Akehurst, complaining about this 2021 tweet. Party emails show that in May 2021, Akehurst used the 'VIP Lane' to directly email General Secretary David Evans and the party's head of legal Alex Barros-Curtis. Akehurst sent Lawson's tweet with the facetious comment, 'I think Neal Lawson is a Labour Party member . . . He appears to be endorsing Green candidates for the Osney and St Thomas ward of Oxford City in his tweet'.

Akehurst had unsuccessfully run as a Labour councillor candidate in the nearby St Mary's ward in Oxford in May 2021. He was thumped by the two winning Green Party candidates, who received over a thousand votes each to his six hundred-odd, perhaps giving an additionally bitter flavour to his complaint against Lawson.

As would happen on other occasions, Akehurst's complaint was fed into the party bureaucracy by Evans. The complaint eventually wended its way, via Barros-Curtis, to the GLU staffer who handled auto-exclusion cases. It is not clear what that GLU staffer eventually found, but what is known is that Akehurst's complaint was shortly moved into a folder on the Labour Party server called 'Auto-Exclusion Complaints/AUTO EXCLUSION NOT REQUIRED—NARB'. The complaint was filed as such by July 2021 at the latest. This would strongly suggest that Akehurst's complaint was dismissed at the time, which would also explain why a case being dealt with at the highest levels of the party bureaucracy, at the prodding of Akehurst, did not progress for two years.

Why the complaint against Lawson was seemingly reactivated in 2023 is not clear, although it is easy to see how Compass' commentary on developments in the party could have rubbed party officials the wrong way. In November 2022, Compass had issued a public call for people to sign an open letter to Evans condemning the way that Labour Party headquarters was controlling MP selections. If the '[v]ice-like control' being exerted by party officials did not end, Compass warned, 'Labour will become a narrow clique with no authentic claim or ability to build the new democratic and political settlement our country desperately needs'.[60] In February 2023, Lawson wrote an impassioned article criticising Starmer's 'purge of the left' after Corbyn had been banned from standing as an MP (discussed below).[61] When Driscoll was deselected in June 2023, Lawson told the media that the decision was a 'democratic disgrace'.[62]

But perhaps most importantly, it was in March 2023 that Compass hosted its lengthy webinar with Martin Forde KC who, only days earlier, had spilled the beans about his rough treatment by the Labour Party to Al Jazeera. As revealed above, the party had been extremely aggressive towards Forde prior to his appearance at the Compass event, sending him legal letters protesting his decision to explain his findings and recommendations to the public.

In a commentary for *The Guardian*, Lawson almost certainly correctly explained the investigation into him as a consequence of the party's effective capture:

> The reason is that the party machine is no longer run in this long and rich spirit of pluralism. It has been captured by a clique who see only true believers or sworn enemies. They are behaving like playground bullies, using people's desperation to get rid of Tories and the limitations of the voting system to enforce discipline internally and externally.[63]

Lawson wrote movingly of his consternation at seeing long-time friends and MPs terrified of somehow offending the party's bureaucrats.

Lawson's close collaborator Jon Cruddas MP was equally angry. He, too, explained Lawson's treatment as resulting from the party's capture by a narrow and repressive faction. '[W]hat we are witnessing is not just an attack on Neal or Compass or the soft left', Cruddas warned.

> It is an attack on a liberal and pluralist tradition of justice pursued through democratic, constitutional and political reform and the pursuit of individual and human rights. The right-wing faction who appear to be running the party, singling out Neal and deciding who is and is not a candidate or member come from a very different tradition—colder, more authoritarian and utilitarian, in which politics is all about state capture and factional control.[64]

Recall that it was Cruddas who had actually set up Labour Together back in 2015. After Lawson's mistreatment, Cruddas agreed to speak with me, in a discussion that took on a tragic air more poignant for the fact that the exigencies of investigative reporting meant that he could not be told the full picture of the Labour Together Project at the time. What emerged was that Cruddas, clearly a decent man with integrity, was a true believer in Labour Together. He, like his comrades at Compass, genuinely wanted to find a way to bring the party together, even if he did not always instinctively align with the Corbynite left.

What also emerged was how little Cruddas really knew. He was ignorant of the Center for Countering Digital Hate, for example, expressing a surprised consternation that it was even being brought up in relation to Labour Together. He was astonished and dismissive of Labour Together's more recent statements that it was behind Starmer's election. It appears that Cruddas, despite being a director of Labour Together, had no idea of what it was really doing or the true nature of a project he ostensibly started. It was painful to see how little he knew about his long-term colleagues in Labour Together—how they were, in fact, the very same 'cold, authoritarian and utilitarian' figures who, in his own words, pursued politics to achieve 'state capture and factional control'.

The tragedy was not limited to Cruddas because Lawson himself was also a long-time collaborator and friend of Labour Together. Prior to the 2020 Labour leadership election, Lawson had travelled to various Labour Together stay-aways where party unity was discussed. He appeared in the July 2019 video described above, in which McSweeney waxed poetic on the need for party reconciliation and unity—at the very same time he was running undeclared projects to destroy the party's left. Lawson had spent considerable time giving his insights to McSweeney, often in Lawson's own kitchen on the banks of the Thames. Arguably, Labour Together's previous public face was an elaborate act of mimicking the language and philosophy of Compass; Lawson would eventually declare in 2025 that McSweeney had 'ransacked' Compass for 'content and connections', writing vituperatively about how Labour Together under McSweeney was a 'modern-day version of the Militant Tendency, a party within a party, masquerading as something it was not, lying to people about its purpose and then biting the hand that fed it'.[65] The Labour Together Project and the Starmer Project that succeeded it repaid Lawson's generosity in their typical style: betrayal.

PUBLIC HUMILIATION

The repeated targeting of left-wing members, MP candidates, and councillors became so systematic under the Starmer Project that it took on a ritualistic quality: a performance in which allies and officers of the Starmer Project used their platforms and the media to humiliate and exclude high-profile members of the left—inside and outside the party. Cold political calculus determined who could and couldn't be targeted at any one time. But once the calculation was made, the rite was enacted with spite and obvious schadenfreude.

No enemies have animated the Starmer Project like Jeremy Corbyn and Diane Abbott, both of whom were subjected to this vindictive ritual.

In March 2023, Keir Starmer proposed a motion to the NEC that was seconded by Labour Together's Shabana Mahmood. The motion had the effect of ensuring that Corbyn, still a Labour member, would be barred from standing as a Labour MP candidate ever again after forty years in the role. The motion read:

> The Labour Party's standing with the electorate in the country, and its electoral prospects in seats it is required to win in order to secure a parliamentary majority and/or win the next general election, are both significantly diminished should Mr Corbyn be endorsed by the Labour Party as one of its candidates for the next general election.[66]

Members of Corbyn's CLP in Islington North were clear that they wanted the chance to select their own candidate, but they were ignored, no doubt because the membership firmly supported Corbyn.

Starmer's motion passed by twenty-two votes to twelve. A senior Labour source briefed the media that 'Keir Starmer has made clear that Jeremy Corbyn won't be a Labour candidate at the next general election. The Labour Party now is unrecognisable from the one that lost in 2019',[67] confirmation again that Starmer's leadership pitch to not 'trash' the Corbyn period had been abandoned.

Media coverage focused on Corbyn's humiliation but failed to note two important features of the NEC motion that excluded him. The motion first set out the NEC's responsibility to maintain a Parliamentary Labour Party and act in the party's best interests. It then determined that the NEC had the authority to judge what was in the party's best interests, and this included deciding who could and couldn't stand as an MP.

This reasoning and language was clearly taken from the Anna Rothery case, her unsuccessful legal case having established a precedent that the party could exploit to seize almost unfettered control of the selection of candidates. To pass legal muster, party officials would merely have to avoid a level of arbitrariness that was undefined and hard to prove. The Corbyn motion confirmed just how important the Rothery case had been in empowering the party bureaucracy to accelerate its factional control over the party's composition.

Starmer's resolution itself established an important precedent as well. The motion baldly asserted that the NEC had virtually untrammelled power to do whatever it wanted, provided it could argue that failing to do so would harm the party's electoral chances—a criterion that was wholly subjective. The NEC and party leader thus arrogated to themselves a near limitless power to determine who could and couldn't represent the party in parliament. It was a radically anti-democratic move that effectively stripped British citizens of their right to select Labour's candidates for office. Instead, this critical function was made the exclusive privilege of just thirty-four people. It was a coup.

The clique's next target was Diane Abbott, the country's first Black woman MP. On April 23, 2023, *The Observer* published a two-paragraph letter Abbott had written in response to an earlier piece published in the paper. Abbott's letter tried, clumsily, to distinguish between racism and other forms of prejudice. 'Tomiwa Owolade claims that Irish, Jewish and Traveller people all suffer from "racism" . . . They undoubtedly experience prejudice. This is similar to racism and the two words are often used as if they are interchangeable', she wrote.

> It is true that many types of white people with points of difference, such as redheads, can experience this prejudice. But they are not all their lives subject to racism. In pre-civil rights America, Irish people, Jewish people and Travellers were not required to sit at the back of the bus. In apartheid South Africa, these groups were allowed to vote. And at the height of slavery, there were no white-seeming people manacled on the slave ships.[68]

The letter was slammed for allegedly erasing Jewish experiences of racism. Abbott had the whip withdrawn on the same day the letter was published, while an investigation was undertaken.

Abbott apologised and withdrew her letter with a statement on Twitter only hours after it was first published. 'I wish to wholly and unreservedly withdraw my remarks and disassociate myself from them . . . Racism takes many forms, and it is completely undeniable that Jewish people have suffered its monstrous effects, as have Irish people, Travellers and many others. Once again, I would like to apologise publicly for the remarks and any distress caused as a result of them'.[69]

The party has never issued a personal apology to Abbott for the way she was treated as detailed in the Leaked Report and confirmed in the Forde Report.

The party's response to Abbott's letter stood in stark contrast to its handling of cases involving a range of other MPs who had made similarly offensive statements, but whose apologies were accepted so that they could retain the whip.

Steve Reed, as noted previously, had caused offence when he called a Jewish businessman, Richard Desmond, a 'puppet master', which was deemed an antisemitic trope. His apology was accepted on the basis that he had been unaware that Desmond was Jewish.

Barry Sheerman, writing about two Jewish businessmen—Richard Desmond and Philip Green—noted that they were on an original list for seats in the House of Lords, but were subsequently withdrawn. 'Apparently there has been a run on silver shekels', Sheerman joked, referring to Israel's currency.[70] He, too, apologised, and was absolved. At no stage did he lose the whip.

Rachel Reeves, for her part, delivered paeans to Britain's first woman MP,[71] Nancy Astor, failing to even acknowledge that Astor had a well-documented history of antisemitism. Reeves has never apologised.

Then there is Neil Coyle, who had the whip withdrawn in February 2022 but returned in May 2023. Coyle was accused of abusive behaviour while drunk in the Strangers' Bar. This included shouting anti-Asian comments at the British-Chinese journalist Henry Dyer. Coyle admitted he had a drinking problem and, after a period of recovery, was readmitted to the party. It may be debated whether this was the right call, but his readmission came in any case as a slap in the face only two months after Corbyn had been blocked from standing and a month after Abbott had the whip withdrawn. Some apologies clearly carried more weight than others.

At around this time, *The Voice* backed a petition by Labour Black Socialists and the Campaign Against Anti-Black Racism in the Labour Party. 'As a lifelong campaigner for equality and justice, Diane Abbott has been at the forefront of anti-racism campaigns, giving voice to the voiceless and lending her support to communities and families who have been victims of racist policing, school exclusions, deaths in custody, racist attacks, murders and the hostile environment policies of successive Tory governments', the petition read.[72]

In September 2023, Abbott claimed that the entire disciplinary process, by then five months old, was not just 'fraudulent' but did not even exist.[73] She had been told, strangely, that the investigation no longer sat with the Labour whips but was being investigated by Labour headquarters, after which she had heard nothing more.

The party's treatment of Abbott became a hot-button issue in March 2024, when *The Guardian* reported on leaked recordings of the Tories' single biggest donor, the businessman Frank Hester. Hester had said that Abbott 'should be shot' and that looking at Abbott makes you 'want to hate all black women'.[74] The comments were awful, and the Tories were rightly pilloried for trying to deflect from and defend Hester's conduct.

Starmer's party sought to make political hay out of the situation, even while Abbott remained suspended from the whip. The party released fundraising emails decrying the comments (but failing to mention Abbott by name), while the likes of Anneliese Dodds declared that a 'trailblazing' Abbott deserved some respect. It was a wretched performance in light of Abbott's ongoing suspension, the party's dismissive response to the Forde Report, and the fact that the party has still, many years later, not bothered to apologise directly to Abbott for the comments detailed in the Leaked Report. How the party will now respond to senior Number 10 advisor Paul Ovenden's comments about Abbott, revealed here for the first time, remains to be seen.

This cynical political theatre soon played out in parliament. In a packed session in the Commons, where Hester's comments were addressed by Sunak and Starmer, each looking to score political points, Abbott, wearing a distinctive red dress, repeatedly rose as she sought to make a comment about her own mistreatment. Sky News calculated that she rose over fifty times in the session looking to speak. She was entirely ignored by the speaker of the House Lindsay Hoyle, the Labour MP for Chorley prior to his election as speaker. As shown below, Hoyle had only weeks prior plunged the Commons into chaos when he violated decades of parliamentary convention to allow Starmer to wriggle out of a corner on a motion about the need for a ceasefire in Gaza.

Immediately after the session, Starmer would approach Abbott in parliament. 'I saw that Diane Abbott was in the chamber so instinctively I went over to her to check she was alright', he would later recall to the journalist Lewis Goodall. In fact, according to Abbott, the interaction was the height of absurdity: 'Let me know if there is anything I can do', Starmer told her. 'You could restore the whip', she replied. 'I understand, just let me know if there is anything . . . ', he replied. 'Restore the whip', Abbott reiterated. 'I understand'.[75]

CHAPTER 22

MARCH TO THE RIGHT

In July 2023, the Labour Party narrowly lost a by-election in Uxbridge and South Ruislip, called after the humiliating resignation of its MP, the former prime minister Boris Johnson. The constituency had been a Tory safe seat before Johnson's premiership. Had the Labour Party won this election, as some polling had suggested was a real possibility, it would have been a huge result.

In the event, Labour lost by just 495 votes, or 1.6 percent. Figures around Starmer immediately blamed the loss on ULEZ ('Ultra Low Emission Zone'), the policy whereby heavily polluting cars are charged a daily rate to drive in London. ULEZ was introduced under Labour's London mayor Sadiq Khan and was thus popularly associated with the Labour Party, even if it had been first conceptualised and put into motion by the Tories.

Three days after the loss, Starmer addressed his party at the ongoing National Policy Forum that was ostensibly deciding Labour's platform for the next general election. Starmer insisted that Uxbridge was a 'reminder [that] in an election, policy matters. And we are doing something very wrong if policies put forward by the Labour Party end up on each and every Tory leaflet'.[1]

Starmer's contribution was both inane and profoundly revealing. He effectively argued that the Labour Party should refrain from adopting any policy that the Tories could try to turn to their electoral advantage. It was the first open reference to the practice of 'shadowing' that he had used so effectively to erase the difference between himself and Rebecca Long-Bailey during the Labour leadership election. The smart politics, Starmer effectively confirmed, was to simply copy the Tories so they could have no way of attacking Labour.

The intervention spoke to two interlinked and mutually reinforcing developments, both of which were contingent on the total control the Starmer Project had imposed on the Labour Party and the increasing certainty that it would form the next government in the wake of a Tory collapse.

First, from 2023, the party started putting itself explicitly on a general election footing, underpinned by an electoral strategy developed by Labour Together and adopted by the party with gusto. The strategy sought to move the party rightward on key policy issues so as to deny Tory strategists their traditional anti-Labour attack lines.

Second, and in conjunction, the party opened its doors to big business, wealthy billionaire donors (many of whom had previously donated to the Tories), and corporate lobbyists. A veritable revolving door now connected party staffers linked to the Starmer Project with major lobbying firms representing the full range of multinational corporate profiteering. These corporate interests were increasingly being invited into the party to help draft its future platform—securing their interests just as they had done under the Tories.

THE RE-EMERGENCE OF LABOUR TOGETHER

Labour Together was at the forefront of both these developments, facilitated by its effective relaunch and retooling.

In early 2023, Steve Reed, Lisa Nandy, and Jon Cruddas stepped down from the board of Labour Together. Insiders explained that the departure of Cruddas was not a happy affair. Cruddas was apparently concerned that Labour Together was being turned into a de facto 'adjunct of the Leader's Office', although this perhaps underestimates the importance of Labour Together in providing an institutional policy home for shadow chancellor Rachel Reeves, too. Not long after it published *Red Shift*, Labour Together would launch Reeves' grand policy pitch: 'securonomics'.

Sir Trevor Chinn retained his position on the board and was joined from October 2022 by Josh Simons as a director. Simons is a specialist in artificial intelligence who became a vocal public advocate for Labour Together's electoral strategy. He had previously worked as a policy advisor to Corbyn but left the party in 2016, writing a stinging piece in *The Guardian*. 'In the eyes of the leaders of the British far left, Israel's occupation—for some, even Israel's existence—offers a firm moral basis for antipathy towards Jews in Israel or, more ambitiously, towards Jews everywhere', he alleged.[2]

Simons would become Labour Together's assertive public face, defending the right-wing approaches that were increasingly being adopted by the Starmer Project. By 2024, Simons was describing the organisation he fronted as 'Keir Starmer's provisional wing'.[3] Simons was parachuted into a safe Labour seat in the first weeks of the July 2024 general election and now sits as an MP, his salary paid by taxpayers instead of Labour Together's mega-rich donors. As discussed in the preface to this book, he was copied in to correspondence with the agency that Labour Together had hired that looked into me, my colleagues, and my family following the 2023 *Sunday Times* article raising issues with Labour Together's undeclared donations.

In May 2023, Lord Jonathan Kestenbaum was appointed the third director of Labour Together. Kestenbaum, a successful businessman, was one of sixty-seven peers who signed a public letter attacking Corbyn over alleged antisemitism in July 2019.[4] He had previously served as the chief executive in the office of Chief Rabbi Jonathan Sacks (a fierce Corbyn critic) and as a board member of pro-Israel lobby group BICOM.[5]

By 2024, Labour Together boasted an impressive roster of staff made possible by generous donations, which increased dramatically from the beginning of 2023. In the eighteen months to May 2024, Labour Together's staff complement grew from one to thirty-four; adding in the advisory board and fellows brought its employee count to seventy.[6] Throughout 2022, Labour Together survived on just over £100,000 donated by Chinn and Taylor, the only two reported donors. But it then began to be lavished with gifts. Between January 24, 2023, and July 8, 2024, Labour Together received more than £4 million in donations, many from new donors—although Taylor remained the most generous, donating £2.1 million between January 2023 and July 2024. (See Table 4.)

The scale of Labour Together's resources, in the context of the UK's broader political funding environment, is hard to overstate. An analysis by Scottish paper *The National* in June 2024 showed that the £1.92 million donated to Labour Together in 2024 was equal to 56.5 percent 'of all political donations to regulated donees, as in those not made directly to parties' in the same period.[7]

Transparency International UK (TI-UK), the British arm of the global anti-corruption organisation, has sounded the alarm about the impact of such huge political donations on the health of British democracy. 'These sorts of giant amounts so far removed from most of the public's disposable incomes risk further undermining public trust in the system, as it looks like democracy for sale'.[8] TI-UK has sensibly proposed upper limits on the political donations that can be made by individuals.

TABLE 4. Donations to Labour Together, January 2023–July 2024[9]

Donor	Amount Donated
Martin Taylor	£2,102,000
Gary Lubner	£663,900
Lord Sainsbury	£313,000
Francesca Perrin	£210,000

(continued)

Donor	Amount Donated
Ecotricity Group	£150,000
Ian Laming	£100,000
Sir Trevor Chinn	£86,500
Nick Marple	£75,000
Daniel Luhde-Thompson	£50,000
Fiona Mactaggart	£50,000
William Perrin	£50,000
William Reeves	£50,000
Joseph Rowntree Reform Trust	£40,000
Lionel Cooke Memorial Fund	£30,000
Phillip Chambers	£20,000
Labour Climate and Environment Forum	£20,000
Mike Craven	£10,000

Labour Together stalwarts Chinn and Taylor were joined by some notable new contributors. One was Fran Perrin, philanthropist and daughter of the billionaire Lord Sainsbury, alongside her husband. Her father was the organisation's third-biggest donor over the period. Lord Sainsbury had been a prominent supporter of Tony Blair.

The most generous new donor was Gary Lubner (£663,900), the inheritor of the PG Group, which had made its original fortune in apartheid South Africa. Lubner was a donor to the United Jewish Israel Appeal,[10] a charity in which Chinn and Kestenbaum had played important roles and which aims to 'invest in young people and education in Israel and the UK Jewish Community, and the connection between the two communities'.[11] Lubner's son, Jack, is now a prominent member of the Jewish Labour Movement and was elected the chair of Young Labour in April 2024.

Gary Lubner only started making sizeable donations to Labour causes in 2022, after announcing his support for a

Starmer government. Beginning in April 2022 and ending with a whopping £900,000 donation made in June 2024 to boost the party's general election war chest, Lubner donated £5,930,000 to the Labour Party and a further £288,000 to the associated Co-operative Party. In 2023, he also made four donations valued at £125,000 to Labour to Win, the body used by Luke Akehurst to out-organise the left in the party. Lubner's choice of recipients was a powerful recognition of the importance of both Labour Together and Labour to Win for the Starmer Project.

By early 2024, Labour Together was reported to be so well staffed and funded that it had placed large numbers of its own employees into the Labour Party. By May 2024, the *Financial Times* reported that the organisation was paying the salaries of staff working with nine separate shadow ministers.[12] Recipients of the largesse included the offices of some of Labour Together's 'brave band' of eight MPs who were credited with defeating Corbynism and securing the rise of Starmer, such as Wes Streeting and Rachel Reeves.

From late 2023 onward, Labour Together thus effectively became a hybrid entity: although formally existing outside of the Labour Party, it directed substantial resources to staffing the party, with a no doubt commensurate impact on policy. Electoral Commission figures show that Labour Together gave cash and non-cash donations valued at £607,914 to the Labour Party from October 2023 to July 2024, including over £75,000 in cash and non-cash donations during the 2024 general election.

Josh Simons was clear that Labour Together effectively coordinated its work with the most influential people in the party, also confirming the continued importance of Morgan McSweeney to its work. 'Everything we do is co-ordinated closely with Morgan McSweeney and Sue Gray and with Deborah Mattinson',[13] Simons told the *Financial Times* in May 2024, illustrating how the lines between the party leadership and Labour Together had become difficult to distinguish. Gray was Starmer's chief of staff; Mattinson his director of strategy.

Labour Together's growing influence has been hard to ignore. But most media outlets have only warily noted its impact on Labour Party policy without drawing critical inferences or raising questions about the policies it promoted and the interests it served. Not so Solomon Hughes, who has an excellent muckraking record tracking the influence of corporate lobbying in politics. Writing in *Jacobin*, Hughes noted that Labour Together 'looks . . . like a scheme for a band of high-net-worth individuals to shape Labour's leadership, fixing them to the low-tax, pro-market policies they and their bank balances prefer'.[14]

In six short years, the Labour Together Project had gone from running a secret campaign to destroy the Corbyn movement by secretly fuelling an 'antisemitism crisis' that demoralised and disorientated the Labour left, to serving as a vehicle for wealthy donors to influence Labour government policy. A political-media class that refuses to at least acknowledge these remarkable facts and begin to consider their implications is doing us all a disservice.

RED SHIFT AND LABOUR TOGETHER'S FABULOUS COMING-OUT PARTY

Starmer's shift towards a more right-leaning electoral strategy began in 2022 at the reported instigation of Morgan McSweeney.

One left-wing NEC member recalled that, in 2022, McSweeney gave a presentation to the NEC on the party's electoral strategy. McSweeney drew on other elections to plot a path to power, focusing in particular on the success of Olaf Scholz's Social Democratic Party (SPD), which won more seats than any other party in the September 2021 German federal election. Scholz became German chancellor after protracted coalition negotiations in December 2021.

McSweeney reportedly travelled to Germany to meet with the SPD and learn from their electoral strategy. His takeaway, bluntly, was that Scholz had won by being uninteresting and uncontroversial. Scholz was criticised for being leaden, earning the nickname 'Boring Olaf'. But he did and said absolutely nothing to indicate that he would challenge the status quo and leaned heavily into the idea of 'respect' rather than redistribution. Some media even speculated that he was purposefully copying the body language of his predecessor Chancellor Angela Merkel, the long-time leader of the conservative CDU. This was 'shadowing' at its most extreme, and when opposition leaders made missteps or became embroiled in scandal, Scholz was well placed to benefit handsomely by default.

In a striking prefiguration of the Starmer government's first year, Scholz's popularity tanked not long after his election. In 2025, his party would be annihilated in the German federal elections, receiving its lowest vote share since 1887 at the same time that the far-right AfD party surged in the polls. One wonders whether the Starmer government will learn any lessons from Scholz's technocratic premiership and the consequences of failing to materially deliver for voters in the context of a resurgent global far right.

This approach—shadowing the opposition while avoiding all controversy—was given purported intellectual heft in April 2023 when Labour Together published its first substantive piece of research since the 2020 electoral review—*Red Shift: Labour's Path to Power*. Much of what this work set out concerning Labour's electoral strategy would be reflected in the party's 2024 general election pitch.

Labour Together used *Red Shift* to relaunch the organisation in the public consciousness. It was also the moment in which, as noted above, Labour Together finally came clean about aspects of its past. It was during the public announcement of *Red Shift* that Labour Together first acknowledged that it was responsible for Starmer's leadership campaign, which had been denied at the time.

Red Shift was written when Labour was riding high in the polls. It was an assertive, even cocky guide to how Labour could translate its relative popularity into power. As ever with Labour Together, it was based on extensive public opinion surveys. Rhetorically, *Red Shift* made half-hearted attempts to argue that the party would improve the lives of ordinary people, but it was fundamentally an expression of the 'politics as advertising' school of thought that sees citizens as consumers and parties as changeable brand propositions.

Red Shift's polling allowed it to 'segment' the British electorate into six groups. In order to win the election, *Red Shift* claimed, the party would need to win over four out of these six segments: the Activist Left, the Patriotic Left, Centrist Liberals, and Disillusioned Suburbans. It paid particular attention to the Disillusioned Suburbans, who it identified as the most important segment, personified as an imagined 'Stevenage Woman'. Stevenage Woman was not particularly politically engaged, leaned a bit to the right on social issues and a bit to the left on the economy, thought things were unfair but needed only limited reforms, and didn't mind immigrants who appeared on *Bake Off* but also didn't think that just any old foreigner should be let in.

Red Shift was clear that neither the Activist Left nor the Centrist Liberals were in play. They would vote Labour regardless and were in any case concentrated in safe Labour seats. The central strategic question was thus: 'who wins the Patriotic Left and the Disillusioned Suburbans?' These were the two demographics that Labour needed to target to win a majority, even if their views were incommensurate with those of the Activist Left and Centrist Liberals. This was a slap in the face for Centrist Liberals, who arguably formed Starmer's natural cultural constituency but were now being told that their loyalty to Labour would be rewarded with irrelevance.

But *Red Shift* went beyond just suggesting that the Activist Left should not be targeted. It argued that, in fact, Labour's core 2019 voter base should be actively *repudiated*, along with the party's membership and even some Labour MPs. '[T]he vast majority of voters that Britain [*sic*—Labour] needs to win are more socially conservative than Labour members, politicians, and activists', *Red Shift* argued. 'The one group . . . who backed Labour in 2019 was the Activist Left. They are the segment most out of kilter with the rest of the UK electorate on social and cultural issues'.[15] In pursuit of more conservative voters, Labour should tack right on social policy.

The concern that 'taking positions like these might imperil the Labour Party's core support' was brushed aside; it wasn't even contemplated that the party might attempt to reflect its own left-leaning membership and persuade others. 'We found no electoral case whatsoever that this is a concern that should worry the Labour Party'.[16] Simply, the left and even the centre would be ignored, and with nowhere else to go, they would have to suck it up.

After three years of pushing the heads of left-wingers into school toilets, Labour Together was evidently confident that the left was vanquished, both within the party and in society at large. As seen later, this premise would be seriously tested by the party's response to the crisis in Gaza, which accelerated a process in which the Activist Left began seeking political representation through other parties or independents.

Labour Together's contemptuous discounting of the Activist Left meant it felt at liberty to abandon any pretence of desiring party unity or showing respect for the past. Instead, Labour Together now embraced a completely different tone, language, and message than those which had defined Starmer's leadership campaign. Whereas Starmer had positioned himself as a Corbyn continuity candidate, *Red Shift* now celebrated 'how significantly the Labour Party has changed since it ejected Jeremy Corbyn and elected Keir Starmer'.[17]

Labour Together now highlighted as the most important lesson of the 2019 election that the 'vast majority of British people agreed on one thing: that Jeremy Corbyn could, should and would never be their Prime Minister'.[18] How Labour secured 32.1 percent of the total vote share under these conditions in 2019 was not worth explaining, it seemed, even if Corbyn's personal ratings were indeed very poor leading up to that election. But at least Labour Together acknowledged that the 2019 election *existed*; the 2017 election was not mentioned once. In fact, the entire year 2017 was not mentioned a single time in the report. Apparently, there were no lessons to be learned from how Labour had secured 40 percent of the national vote and its highest vote share since 2001.

In historical terms, this was an extraordinary lapse. Since 1974, the Labour Party has won 40 percent or more of the national vote only three times: twice under Blair (1997 and 2001) and once under Corbyn (2017). But it was only the wisdom of Blair, who was referred to warmly throughout, that required rapt attention. One might not agree with Corbynism, but it is another thing to simply wipe from the record Labour's best vote in four elections.

This failure to acknowledge that 2017 happened took on a farcical quality precisely because *Red Shift* focused on Stevenage as the ultimate bellwether seat, and 'Stevenage Woman' as its personified expression. In 2017, the Labour Party secured 43.4 percent of the vote in Stevenage, up from 34.2 percent in 2015 and 33.4 percent in 2010. In fact, the party's Stevenage result in 2017 was its best in terms of vote share since 2001. Yet the project that achieved these gains was, in *Red Shift*'s account, actually anathema to the very people who voted for it.

Red Shift manfully tried to claim its clear factional thinking was based on the scientific realities of its polling. But when the data was examined, it was revealed to be a typical example of pollsters guiding answers and then interpreting them in line with their preconceived ideas.

Cat Hobbs, the founder of a group pushing for nationalisation, was surprised to find that two of Labour Together's target demographics, and particularly 'Stevenage Woman', didn't support nationalisation. This was not the trend picked up in most national polling on the topic over a number of years. When she was given the underlying polling data, she discovered this was largely based on one question. It asked people to rate themselves on a spectrum from 1 to 7. Choosing '1' would indicate total support for the proposition that 'government should nationalise as many major industries and services as possible, bringing them into public ownership'. Choosing '7' would indicate support for the idea that 'government should privatise as many major industries and services as possible, letting private companies provide them'.

The effect was to ask people whether they wanted to move to a command economy where every major industry and service (not just energy, water, rail, and mail) was nationalised, or whether they wanted Elon Musk to tower over a global anarcho-capitalism. Despite this, a surprisingly large number of people actually put '1' as their answer, but only 7 percent of the voters who *Red Shift* cared most about—the 'Disillusioned Suburbans'—wanted to 'nationalise a swathe of industries'.[19]

The result, in Labour Together's mind, was that because 'Stevenage Woman' didn't want the government to nationalise her hairdresser and supermarket, this meant she didn't want to nationalise anything. And because 'Stevenage Woman' was, according to *Red Shift*, the demographic that mattered most, a broadly popular plan to nationalise mail, energy, and water would not be introduced.

The upshot of *Red Shift*'s analysis was that Labour's policy platform should have two planks. First, it must 'hold the line on social and cultural issues'. Who it was holding the line against was not made clear; by implication, it was all those suckers who voted for the party in 2019. The views of the only two segments that mattered had to be foregrounded. 'These voters believe that we should not increase immigration numbers. They believe Britain should be proud of its past. They believe that young people do not respect British values. They believe that certain places should be made safe by restricting entry by biological sex', *Red Shift* proclaimed. On crime, 'our target voters think prisons should, primarily, punish criminals'.

It so happened that the party leadership that Labour Together retrospectively claimed to have helped elect—a role it did not disclose playing at the time—already reflected these values:

> Since 2020, the Labour Party has significantly changed its course on social and cultural issues. With a former Director of Public Prosecutions at the helm, Labour is tough on crime, once more, and it believes in exerting a firm grip over migration. It supports robust military support for Ukraine against Russian aggression, is comfortable with the Union Jack, and sings the national anthem at its conference.[20]

One wonders how 2020 Labour Party members would have voted if this was the version of Starmer they'd been presented with, and not the radical eco-socialist trans ally who wanted to review all arms sales and pass new laws to constrain the war-making powers of the government.

To be sure, *Red Shift* caveated that the party should not swing too far on these issues as they were the terrain on which the Tories would try to run their election. There was always a 'balanced and principled position' to be taken, it argued. But an enumeration of these 'balanced' positions showed how much ground *Red Shift* had already ceded to Tory arguments:

> You must be tough on crime, not just its causes. You must control Britain's borders, not just create a safe route for immigrants. You must address inequalities that are geographic and class-based, not just those that are based on protected characteristics.

It does not take a genius to deconstruct this language: *Red Shift* was advocating a 'war on woke'. The proposition that one must not just focus on 'protected characteristics' seemed to imply that ordinary working folk were being left behind because in politically correct Britain, too much attention was being paid to disabled Black lesbians. Many might have interpreted such language as calling for the Labour Party to do less to combat discrimination based on race. The language on immigration was also revealing, referring to 'immigrants' and 'safe routes' at the very time the Tory party was shouting about migrant boats and threatening to relocate refugees to Rwanda. *Red Shift*'s language effectively conflated refugees with migrants, subtly conceding the heart of the Tory argument.

By February 2024, Labour Together was following this logic and beginning to openly espouse Faragist views, especially on immigration. On February 14, 2024, Josh Simons, now Labour Together's leading public spokesperson, appeared as part of a panel on Iain Dale's LBC radio show. As his fellow commentators beat their chests about all sorts of right-wing talking points, Simons, not to be outdone, doubled down on some properly worrying discourse.

In response to a lurid segment in which a journalist on the panel lamented how asylum seekers were cutting a swathe of violence through the country, Simons explained that his 'main concern' with the policy of sending asylum seekers to Rwanda

> is not actually the human rights implications of it . . . My main concern is that this is a complete waste of money and it won't work, it won't stop the boats . . . My problem with Rwanda is that it won't work, so the question is, what are you going to do instead? I think while the Conservatives say they are being tough on the borders and beefing up policing and so on, I've seen no real evidence that's in fact what they are doing with the commitment and clarity they need to . . . Why don't you send the smuggler gangs and put them on the barge that has been set aside for the asylum seekers, and then ship the barge up to the north of Scotland for all I—you know, who cares?[21]

Perish the thought that 'human rights implications' might be a factor.

But the really important point was that Labour Together understood Labour Party policy on these issues as relational. It sought to find a 'balanced position' in light of the Tories' focus on these matters, which recognised that the concerns the Tories were articulating were 'legitimate' but criticised their solutions as unworkable. This relational strategy inevitably meant that, as the Tories moved increasingly rightwards on social and cultural issues, Labour would track them, seeking only to 'balance' them out, finding 'sensible' alternative solutions to the social hysterias contrived by the most right-wing Tory government in memory.

The second plank of *Red Shift*'s analysis was that Labour should adopt a 'bold economic programme focused on economic security'. No detailed economic framework was actually outlined (this would be set out in future Labour Together publications, discussed below), but the policy proposal was built on the dual recognition that Labour's target voters were all economically insecure but sceptical about how much the government should intervene in the economy to right this situation. After much boilerplate about centring the issue of 'security', the only clear recommendation was that the UK should try to copy the Biden administration. Within a month, Reeves would publish her own Labour Together monograph, making precisely the same argument.

SHADOWING: THE POLITICS OF HOPELESSNESS

Red Shift was a candid admission of a central argument of this book, namely, that for years the Labour Together Project worked systematically and ruthlessly behind the scenes to erase the left from the Labour Party and assert top-down control over the party membership. Having crushed the left and disempowered the membership, the Labour Together and Starmer projects were then free to lurch to the right on policy.

In practical terms, this meant shadowing the Tories as they moved closer toward the talking points of the far right, especially from 2023 onward. In so doing, Starmer embraced policies and positions that directly contradicted pledges he had made to the membership in 2020 as well as commitments he made after becoming party leader.

For example, Starmer told LBC in October 2022 that there was 'not a great deal between the major parties on immigration'.[22] To be fair, Starmer was talking specifically about the issue of points-based immigration, but his claim applied more broadly than that. In the lead-up to Labour's annual conference in October 2023, Labour's shadow home secretary Yvette Cooper told *The Telegraph* that immigration was too high and the country should be aiming to issue fewer work visas;[23] it chimed with statements made in 2022 by Starmer, previously Mr. Freedom of Movement, that the NHS was employing too many foreign staff.[24]

In September 2023, Starmer and Cooper visited Europe to outflank Tory fearmongering over migrant boats—from the right. Starmer and Cooper announced that they would treat 'people smugglers' as terrorists.[25] This was a stupid policy that policed symptoms without addressing causes[26] and used ugly language to boot: if people smugglers were terrorists, then asylum seekers were a weapon.

Under Steve Reed's oversight as shadow minister for justice, to which position he was appointed in September 2021, the party remixed the Blairite 'tough on crime' mantra by declaring that it now sought to 'prevent crime, punish criminals, protect the public'.[27] In late 2022, Reed announced that the parents of children found to have committed antisocial behaviour offences would be forced into parenting contracts that would teach them how to get their kids in line. A threat of a £1,000 fine would hang over parents who did not cooperate.[28] In 2023, Reed backed an advertising campaign that accused Prime Minister Rishi Sunak of disagreeing that 'adults convicted of sexually assaulting children should go to prison'. This was an arguably reckless allegation to level against Britain's first South Asian prime minister, given that inflammatory right-wing tropes were in circulation that highlighted the prominence of 'Asian grooming gangs' in the UK. Reed and the party refused to recant in the face of widespread disgust, and Labour's Twitter posts featuring this attack line remain live as of August 2025.[29] Reed had helped found the Center for Countering Digital Hate, whose ostensible mission was to fight exactly the sort of incendiary misinformation Reed was now peddling.

On welfare, Starmer prepared to make 'tough choices' that would hurt poor people. In July 2023, he announced that the Labour Party would not scrap the two-child benefit cap introduced by the Tories in 2015. This was a screeching U-turn on a policy that almost the full breadth of Labour MPs and supporters considered appalling. Just a month prior, for example, the shadow work and pensions secretary Jonathan Ashworth had told *The Mirror* that the cap was among the 'most heinous elements of the system which is pushing children and families into poverty today'.[30]

In a moment laden with symbolism, Starmer defended this decision in front of a well-heeled audience at the Tony Blair Institute for Global Change. Starmer complained to Blair that, '[w]e keep saying collectively as a party [that] we have to take decisions, and in the abstract everyone says, "yes, that is right". . . . But when we get [to] a tough decision, . . . they say, "well I don't like that"'.[31]

In 2024, the party confirmed that it had no intention of reversing a Tory decision to remove limits on bankers' bonuses, and further that it would not increase corporation tax during the lifetime of the next parliament. Britain's corporate tax rate, at 25 percent, is the lowest in the entire G7; it was increased from 19 percent by the Tories in 2023, meaning that Labour's policy was, in effect, to simply keep what the Tories had already implemented. In the space of less than a year, between mid-2023 and early 2024, Starmer's party had thus stated that they intended to keep taxes on corporations and the rich low, and allow bankers to be paid the sorts of bonuses that were widely viewed as having contributed to the 2008 financial crash—all while claiming that there was not enough money to end the two-child benefit cap.

Labour tracked the Tories on civil liberties, too, which was striking considering the Tories' unusually authoritarian legislative agenda. In May 2023, in the midst of the much-criticised preventive arrest of anti-royalist demonstrators, Starmer said that the party had no intention of repealing the Tories' Public Order Act passed that month. The Act massively expanded the scope of police powers to disrupt and stop any protest considered disruptive, and even gave police the power to issue protest-banning orders that would prevent individuals from attending events.[32] Starmer assured critics that there simply hadn't been enough time for an act that erased fundamental rights to 'bed in', and that any defects could be resolved by case law and fresh guidance.[33]

It was under the powers granted by this Act that five Just Stop Oil protestors would be sentenced to five years in prison in July 2024—much longer than the average sentences for assault or robbery. Their offence was planning to disrupt a motorway, in order to bring attention to the climate crisis that threatens the foundations of modern life.

Amnesty International has argued that the Act's other consequence—the introduction of stop-and-search powers that police may deploy against protestors without any cause for suspicion—would be counterproductive and 'likely to increase racial discrimination'.[34]

Party policy on the NHS was equally concerning. Despite repeatedly pointing out the near collapse of the service, the party refused to commit to any increased funding after a lengthy period of austerity and a devastating cut in real-term wages for NHS staff. Instead, the party promised reform, holding out that the NHS' many problems would be resolved by artificial intelligence, while the shadow health minister Wes Streeting explained that Labour would look to bring in private sector contractors to expand NHS capacity in the short run.

On climate change, arguably the most consequential policy, the party's rhetoric remained more progressive than the Tories. But when real choices had to be made, Labour backed Tory plans. In 2023, for example, the Conservative government announced approvals for a raft of new oil and gas drilling licences in the North Sea's Rosebank oil field; when operational, the field would obliterate the UK's chances of meeting its carbon emission targets.[35] Starmer explained that he would refuse to rescind the licences, on the basis that it would threaten the 'stability' so required by investors, apparently failing to see that investor certainty could be achieved just as well by saying that such developments *wouldn't* happen under him. It was also another clear repudiation of his previously stated belief that anything 'bad for the environment is bad for the economy'.

The heart of Labour's environmental policy was its 'Green Prosperity Fund'. In May 2023, Rachel Reeves launched her brand as shadow chancellor on a glitzy trip to the US, supported by the publication of a thirty-page Labour Together monograph with the depressingly dull title, *A New Business Model for Britain*.[36]

Reeves' great economic plan was to adopt what has become known in the US as 'modern supply-side economics', or, more often, 'Bidenomics'. Despite its slightly misleading name, the policy is not just a cold rehash of neoliberal supply-side economics, instead envisaging a more active economic role for the state than the neoliberal norm. In essence, it seeks to enable or support private enterprise by using state spending and industrial policy to direct private spending at specific industries.

While more promising than strict neoliberalism, this approach nevertheless precludes state ownership of productive capacities; it also envisages that state funds will, ultimately, be used to drive profitability for the private sector, albeit in industries that are hopefully slightly less destructive than, say, coal mining. It also specifically disavows the possibility of nationalisation. For her part, Reeves was adamant that Labour had no intention of bringing water, energy or mail into public ownership. More mixed signals were given on rail, likely because the rail industry's repeated failures meant that swathes of the network had already come under national control.

What Reeves never sufficiently explained is how the party would deliver Bidenomics without one of the key prerequisites for its enactment in the US: a massive state spending spree, designed in part to create the conditions for these private-public partnerships to flourish. Between 2021 and 2022, Biden's administration introduced three pieces of legislation, including the Inflation Reduction Act and the Bipartisan Infrastructure Law. The US government predicted at the time that these would lead to close to $2 trillion in federal spending over ten years—nearly $200 billion per year.

But in February 2024, all Reeves' fancy footwork was undermined by the announcement that the party would no longer commit to spending £28 billion a year on its Green Recovery Plan, apparently for fear of Tory attack lines. Starmer confirmed on February 8, 2024, that the party would only commit to spending £23.7 billion on Green Recovery Plan policies over the entire life of the next parliament, equal to a paltry £4.74 billion a year—about 10 percent of the 2023 defence budget.

One of the biggest cuts was to a planned housing insulation scheme that Reeves admitted in pained interviews would no longer be rolled out—quite literally leaving average people colder and poorer as they paid gas and electricity bills that had rocketed in previous years. On the same day that Labour announced that the plan had been dumped, it was confirmed that the world had passed 1.5 degrees of warming over an entire calendar year for the first time.[37]

Media reporting strongly suggested that there was a key player behind the scrapping of the pledge: Morgan McSweeney.[38]

The decision to scrap the £28 billion-a-year pledge also drove a coach and horses through the party's economic offer. Starmer and Reeves had repeatedly stated that their primary mission was 'growth', and that any increase in public expenditure would be predicated on achieving it. The Green Recovery

Plan sat at the heart of this growth plan. Scrapping the £28 billion thus amounted to a de facto junking of Reeves' grand industrial policy, shredding her 'securonomics' less than a year after it had been introduced.

Labour's abandonment of these spending plans and its commitment not to raise corporation tax were music to millionaire and billionaire ears. In January 2024, Starmer was filmed walking around a branch of the supermarket chain Iceland with the firm's boss, Richard Walker.[39] Walker had only recently tried to become a Tory MP[40] and publicly defended the Tory plan to send asylum seekers to Rwanda.[41] Now he heartily endorsed Starmer.[42] Another new convert was Iain Anderson, founder of the H/Advisors Cicero communications consultancy (read: lobbying firm), who endorsed Starmer and Labour in 2023.[43] In August 2022, he had backed Liz Truss for Conservative party leader. 'I've been a Conservative for almost 4 decades—I've known @trussliz almost half that time. I've worked with Liz on economic reform and boosting opportunity. She has fresh ideas and real energy . . . that's why I'm backing #lizforleader', Anderson had posted alongside a photo of himself and Truss on Twitter.[44]

In December 2024, six months after Labour's election landslide, Anderson was made a non-executive director in the Department for Business and Trade while still simultaneously serving as chair of H/Advisors Cicero. His appointment was criticised as 'cronyism' by the Tories but subsequently defended on the basis that his role at H/Advisors Cicero was now simply 'ambassadorial'. However, one lobbyist told the *Financial Times* that Anderson's appointment was 'absolutely ridiculous' and 'shocking', explaining that 'the conflict of interests is so blindingly obvious, it just shows appalling political judgment'.[45]

The only remnant of the party's growth plan was an ambition, aired at its 2023 annual conference, to build 1.5 million houses. This would be achieved by 'cutting red tape' and 'reforming planning'. This idea was implausible given that big housing conglomerates already sat on hundreds of thousands of properties that had received planning approval but which they had opted not to develop, at least in part to protect the value of already-built housing stock. The policy also uncomfortably evoked the spectre of Grenfell Tower, where 'cutting red tape' and deregulating in the interests of housing companies had led to the deaths of seventy-two people in a tragically avoidable inferno.

On foreign policy and national security, the difference between the Tories and the Labour Party became literally non-existent. Under Starmer, the party backed a post-9/11-style increase in defence spending in response to the Ukraine crisis, estimated at some £10 billion a year.[46] Both Labour and the Tories have enthusiastically intervened in the Ukraine War, matching each other in their full-throated militarism and disregard for de-escalation or negotiation. The Labour Party's apparent concern for international law, which it invoked to denounce Russian president Vladimir Putin, would evaporate in the face of Israel's offensive in Gaza.

In one way, however, Starmer has proven himself to be even more doctrinaire than the Tories: he has refused to permit literally any discussion within the Labour Party that criticises NATO or government policy in Ukraine. In February 2022, Starmer penned a venomous opinion piece about the Stop the War Coalition, which had been launched in response to US president George W. Bush's 'global war on terror' in 2001 and played a key role in popular mobilising against the 2003 Iraq War. Starmer accused the organisation of giving 'succour to authoritarian leaders who directly threaten democracies'.[47]

This came as eleven Labour MPs indicated their desire to sign a Stop the War Coalition letter that criticised Russia's invasion of Ukraine but also called for an end to NATO's 'eastward expansion' along with rapid de-escalation and diplomacy. Starmer told the MPs that they would lose the whip if they signed this mildly worded letter; all did as they were instructed. Starmer had, of course, happily used images of the Stop the War Coalition march against the 2003 Iraq War in his 2020 leadership campaign promotional videos.

Starmer's *Guardian* letter was an eye-opening intervention that made him appear an even more worrying prospect on foreign policy than Blair, who, despite his many crimes and catastrophes abroad, still tolerated dissent from party colleagues and members at home.

LOBBYING, FREEBIES, AND CO-OPTION

Perhaps the clearest demonstration of the extent to which the Labour Party had accommodated the right was the enthusiasm with which business interests started knocking on the party's door—and Labour's eagerness to embrace them.

Past grandees of the Labour Together and Starmer projects were among the first to benefit. Ben Nunn, Starmer's political advisor who had been defended by Starmer against criticisms over his lobbying for the pharmaceutical industry, joined Lexington Communications in October 2021, before returning to the Labour fold in July 2023. Lexington helps corporate clients lobby 'decision-makers and stakeholders'.[48] Other Lexington newcomers included Mary Creagh, the former MP whose constituency received funds from the Ergon House scheme. Creagh was re-elected as a Labour MP in 2024.

The party's 2023 conference was notable for the influx of business delegates and Labour's courting of them, written up by much of the press as an uncomplicatedly good thing. The party's conference brochure boasted that of the twenty thousand attendees, 28 percent were from business—as compared with party members, who made up 22 percent. Representatives from trade unions made up a paltry 3 percent.[49]

A notable entry point for corporations into the party conference was the New Statesman Media Group, which had not long before publicly hitched its wagon to Labour Together. The outlet runs an events arm that put on sponsored talks at conference. One session backed by the defence conglomerate Babcock asked 'how we can make, buy and sell British'. It was hosted by Rachel Wearmouth, who had written about Labour Together and McSweeney in the past. Northrop Grumman, the US defence giant, sponsored an event on how to 'safeguard [the] UK's future national security'. Baroness Ruth Smeeth was a notable discussant. Palantir, the multinational firm with a history of involvement in mass surveillance by the US government, also sponsored an event on defence policy.

Labour Together got in on the action. It hosted several fringe events, including one about industrial strategy 'in association' with the industry body for human resources that featured McSweeney's old pal, Peter Mandelson. Wes Streeting, one of the 'brave' eight, fronted a Labour Together event on 'innovation in the NHS', held 'in association' with the Association of the British Pharmaceutical Industry. Another event, on tourism, was held with Airbnb, and an event simply about 'defence' with the shadow secretary for defence, John Healey, was hosted 'in association' with Capita, a private contractor to the UK military.[50]

These were only the most public displays of corporate sponsorship. Adam Ramsay and Ethan Shone of *openDemocracy*, alongside Solomon Hughes, have done excellent work tracking the extent of lobbyist and corporate co-option of the Labour Party. In one story, Ramsay reported that shadow business secretary Jonathan Reynolds, his wife (and senior parliamentary assistant), and Starmer's political director had accepted gifts of Glastonbury tickets from YouTube (owned by Google). Reynold's package for two was estimated at £3,377. Not long after, the Labour Party announced that it had dropped earlier plans to put a 10-percent tax on digital service providers like Google.[51]

In February 2024, just as the party was announcing that it would not reinstate the cap on bankers' bonuses or increase taxes on corporations and top earners, *openDemocracy* reported that the party had taken £2 million in donations from finance firms over the previous two years. The website described the party's plans as Labour's 'love letter to the City'.[52]

In the eighteen months prior to Labour coming into power, the party played host to a huge influx of staff seconded from private companies to the offices of shadow ministers and Starmer himself. Shone, in July 2024, calculated that the Labour Party had received seconded staff to the value of £1.8 million from 2022 onward. Remarkably this included secondees *directly* from lobbying firms, four of which sent staff to work in the offices of Anneliese Dodds (then the head of Labour's National Policy Forum), Tulip Siddiq, Rachel Reeves, and Jonathan Reynolds.[53] One of the lobbying firms providing these generous services was Global Counsel—Peter Mandelson's outfit. Shone reportedly asked every firm that had provided seconded staff to the Labour Party what they intended to get from the arrangement. 'We're yet to receive an answer—funny that'.[54]

The party attracted the attention of lobbying firms around the time of the Truss implosion, with many setting up dedicated 'Labour units' to advise their clients—and to start arranging meetings between their clients and the incoming government. Shone's investigation into a lobbying 'lovebomb', published in July 2024, revealed that lobbying firms had secured hundreds of meetings with Labour figures. The UK's lax transparency regulations require only government figures, not opposition MPs, to declare meetings with lobbyists. Shone only came to know of these meetings because people had bragged about them online. City lobbyists representing multinational asset management mega-firms like BlackRock and Macquarie alongside banks like HSBC secured more than twenty meetings with the most senior members of Labour's incoming front bench, such as Reynolds and Reeves.

The political website *openDemocracy* has also reported extensively on the presence of lobbyists within the newly selected cohort of Labour MPs. Of the roughly 215 prospective Labour Party candidates who had been announced by 2024, at least twenty (10 percent) were corporate lobbyists and communications advisers.[55] During the general election, one of the lobbying firms that had been most assiduous in employing future Labour MPs, Hanbury Strategy, bragged on LinkedIn that they had 'the most parliamentary candidates of any UK public affairs agency running in the general election'.[56] The post shared pictures of five Labour parliamentary candidates, including Chris Ward; the revealing story of how he was parachuted into a Labour safe seat in Brighton in the first week of the general election campaign is discussed in this book's final chapter.

By early February 2024, the party's embrace of business took a particularly gauche turn. On February 1, the party hosted a dinner at the Oval cricket ground in South London. Representatives of businesses ranging from Goldman Sachs to Google and big pharmaceutical firms paid £1,000 each to attend. The price of admission gave them direct access to Reeves, Starmer, and other shadow cabinet ministers—the sort of attention that ordinary citizens and constituents could never even contemplate. One Tory advisor and City lobbyist gushed, without any sense of irony, about how 'Labour have monetised business engagement in a way I've not seen before'.

It was clearly a good deal for the businesses for which £1,000 is the equivalent of loose change behind the sofa. Reeves told the assembled captains of industry that corporation tax would not increase under Labour and promised that 'your fingerprints are on every one of our national missions'.[57] Echoing New Labour's happy embrace of people getting filthy rich, Reeves reassured the audience that 'this Labour Party sees profit not as something to be disdained, but as a mark of business'.

STARMER'S LUXURY FREEBIES

As the Labour Party under Starmer has cosied up to big business, lobbyists, and the rich donor class, Starmer has personally benefitted in the form of luxury freebies.

Between early July 2021 and July 2024, Starmer was calculated to have taken £76,000 in freebies from businesses and rich gift-givers. This included donations worth £16,200 from Baron Waheed Alli (one of Starmer's earliest backers, and a former member of 'Tony's Cronies') for 'work clothing',[58] which would cause a scandal after the general election. As Adam Ramsay at *openDemocracy* noted, this meant Starmer had accepted more gifts than Tony Blair, Gordon Brown, Ed Miliband, and Jeremy Corbyn combined.[59] The speed with which Starmer broke this record is striking because, for the first year of his leadership, during the period of Covid lockdowns, he took no freebies. By comparison, Corbyn had taken just a single gratuity during his entire term as party leader: tickets to Glastonbury, so that he could famously address a supportive crowd from the Pyramid Stage. Corbyn had indicated he was not interested in taking giveaways as they can raise questions of conflicts of interest.

Starmer's freebies included many expensive football tickets, VIP comps to horse racing meets, luxury hotel stays, concert tickets to see Coldplay and Adele, and family holidays. Some of the donors were noteworthy. For example, Starmer accepted tickets worth £3,000 for six people to watch the Doncaster Races from Arena Racing Company, which runs horse racing tracks across the UK. Arena has lobbied against new measures that would force gambling companies to do affordability checks on customers to prevent repeat betters from gambling beyond their means.[60] Another notable donor was Matthew Moulding, who covered hotel accommodation worth £937 for four people (including breakfast, naturally). Moulding entered the billionaires list in 2021. He had previously donated £300,000 to the Tories since 2014 and reportedly lobbied Prime Minister Sunak to change listing rules for publicly traded companies.[61]

In 2022, Jonathan Goldstein gifted football tickets and hospitality worth a combined £1,650 to allow Starmer to watch his beloved Arsenal play Chelsea. Goldstein's property investment company, Cain International, gifted Starmer two tickets and hospitality worth £2,400 for the same fixture the following year. Goldstein had been the head of the Jewish Leadership Council for four and a half years from 2017 to 2021, during which period the JLC, and Goldstein himself, had branded Jeremy Corbyn and his followers an 'existential threat' to the Jewish community in Britain.[62]

On October 9, 2023, in the wake of Hamas' brutal attack on southern Israel (discussed later), Goldstein wrote that 'we must give our unstinting and total support to whatever action Israel determines in its absolute discretion as an appropriate response to this atrocity'.[63] Starmer enjoyed a luxurious £1,200-per-person trip to watch Chelsea versus Arsenal on October 21, 2023, only twelve days after Goldstein's article.

But perhaps the most disturbing, even grotesque, gratuity accepted by Starmer has been noted previously in relation to the resignation of Emma Dent Coad: the decision to accept football tickets worth £1,070 from the building firm Mulalley & Co in April 2023. The firm had been found guilty in September 2022 of designing and installing a defective cladding system in four tower blocks in Gosport and had been ordered to pay £10.2 million in compensation and damages.[64] The cladding, upon inspection following the Grenfell disaster, was immediately removed due to the unacceptably high fire risk it posed, while the blocks were put under twenty-four-hour fire watch.

Starmer would be pressed to explain his acceptance of freebies only in the final days of the general election: a mark of how little the media had scrutinised Starmer's record to that point. Starmer's defence was that all the freebies had been publicly declared. He further argued that he had to accept them because security concerns prevented him from watching football games like an ordinary person.[65] He did not explain, however, why he had taken free holidays and hotel stays, why it was necessary for the performance of his duties that he watch football at his leisure, or why his attendance at Arsenal matches outweighed the integrity of Britain's democratic governance.

CAPTURE, CO-OPTION, AND CORRUPTION

The Labour Party's rightward lurch on policy, its embrace of business and lobbyists, and Starmer's own predilection for luxuries donated by companies and the politically minded rich, together point to three disturbing features of the Starmer Project.

To begin with, they point to a troubling lack of political judgment. Starmer's pitch as leader has often centred on his image as a man of the law and of integrity. While Starmer's acceptance of freebies was legal, it is obvious that questions would arise about why he accepted the freebies and whether anything was expected in return. That something is legal does not make it ethical, wise or free from credible accusations of conflicts of interest.

Second, they point to the fact that the Starmer Project's war on the left did not just yield political control—it also allowed many of the project's allies and fellow travellers to earn salaries as lobbyists with access to the incoming government. Corbynism threatened a long-running and cosy relationship between the Labour Party, lobbying firms, and big business, all of whom were frozen out by a leadership that was instinctively hostile to the sort of corporate glad-handing the Labour right finds so comfortable. In defeating Corbynism, the Starmer Project returned the party to this Blairite political mode—a transformation that worked to the personal financial benefit of many of its most ardent supporters.

Finally, and most obviously, they suggest that the Labour Party under Starmer has arguably been co-opted by big business and the mega-rich—maybe even captured. This is likely to have serious and material implications for the party's policymaking in government. Indeed, the extensive corporate and lobbying relationships cultivated by the Starmer Project raise serious red flags pointing to the risk of corruption. Freebies may be legal, but they are also one way that companies and billionaires secure enhanced access to political figures, whom they can then lobby behind closed doors. Indeed, this is often how corruption starts: a few lavish meals here and there, lubricated with fancy wines and cocktails, where unscrupulous actors can suss out who in government might be open to collaboration. Similarly, a revolving door between lobbying firms, MPs, and Labour Party officials significantly blurs the lines between business and the state. This lowers public trust in the decisions made by governments, as it becomes questionable in whose interests these decisions are made.

CHAPTER 23

GAZA

Early on October 7, 2023, the Palestinian militant group Hamas broke through the walls of Gaza to launch an unprecedented attack on Israel. Hamas fighters engaged in a brutal massacre of civilians while taking some 250 people hostage. It was a major atrocity, no matter the context, marked by multiple war crimes. By the time the Israel Defence Forces (IDF) had quelled the attack, some 1,200 people—Israeli and other civilians as well as Israeli military personnel—had been killed. It was the largest single loss of Israeli life since the country was founded.

In response, Israel turned Gaza into 'hell on earth'.[1] The Israeli Air Force pummelled Gaza's civilian population with close to thirty thousand bombs in just the first hundred days, equivalent in force to three nuclear bombs. An IDF spokesperson explained on October 10 that, 'while balancing accuracy with the scope of damage, right now we're focused on what causes maximum damage'.[2]

The scale of devastation and human misery inflicted on Gaza's inhabitants was almost beyond description. By February 22, 2024—a date of considerable significance, as set out below—the United Nations Relief and Works Agency (UNRWA) reported that 1.7 million out of 2.3 million Gazans had been internally displaced, some of them multiple times.[3] Figures released a day later by the Gaza Health Ministry indicated that 29,514 Palestinians had been killed, 70 percent of whom were women and children. Nearly seventy thousand people had been injured.[4] The conflict was uniquely devastating for children, with fatalities and casualties at rates not seen in any other modern conflict.[5]

The physical destruction of Gaza was profound. By January 2025, almost 60 percent of all buildings in Gaza, and more than 90 percent of homes, had been damaged or destroyed.[6] 'Gaza is now a different colour from space', one expert explained, referring to satellite images of before and after Israel's assault. 'It's a different texture'.[7]

Israel repeatedly imposed a total blockade on Gaza that prevented any food, water, electricity, or fuel from reaching the civilian population. Acute food insecurity verging on famine became widespread as UN bodies along with human rights authorities accused Israel of systematically blocking humanitarian aid. In late February 2024, the UN special rapporteur on the right to food alleged that Israel was purposefully starving Gaza. 'In my view as a UN human rights expert, this is now a situation of genocide', he said.[8]

As of August 2025, it was unknown exactly how many people had been killed in Gaza. The destruction and collapse of health infrastructure—of nearly all infrastructure—precluded any comprehensive tallying of the dead. A group of forty-five international doctors who served in Gazan hospitals on humanitarian missions were all convinced the scale of death and injury had been underestimated and the targeting of children underreported. '[E]very one of us *on a daily basis* treated pre-teen children who were shot in the head and chest', the doctors informed President Joe Biden and his wife, Jill, in a publicly released letter in July 2024.[9] Some estimates have put the death toll at 186,000,[10] a figure still much debated but which comes close to 10 percent of Gaza's pre-October 7 population.

In 2025, *The Lancet* published a study calculating that the average life expectancy in Gaza had nearly halved between October 2023 and August 2024, dropping from 75.5 years to just 40.6 years.[11] This was the lowest life expectancy anywhere on the planet: a full 14 years less than in Nigeria, the previous holder of this ignominious record.

Dry statistics do not convey the visceral horrors, many of which played out each day on smart-phone and laptop screens around the world. Fathers carrying the remains of their children in plastic bags, toddlers missing limbs, ragdoll children staring out of lifeless eyes with the tops of their skulls blasted off and their brain cavities emptied—such images circulated relentlessly for months, forming a surreal if not crazy-making juxtaposition with speeches by Western officials defending Israel's 'right to self-defence' while expressing empty 'concern' for civilians.

In December 2023, the Republic of South Africa instituted proceedings against Israel at the International Court of Justice. South Africa accused Israel of committing genocidal acts and other breaches of the Genocide Convention in Gaza and petitioned the ICJ to order a halt to Israel's military operations pending the Court's final determination of the dispute. On January 26, 2024, the ICJ issued a remarkable, indeed historic, decision. Fifteen of the court's seventeen judges determined that the right of Palestinians not to be subject to genocidal acts was plausibly at risk.[12]

The court instructed Israel to put in place provisional measures to prevent genocide. 'Hague shmague', was the dismissive tweeted response of the far-right Israeli government minister Itamar Ben-Gvir to the ICJ's order.[13]

The ICJ quoted statements by high-ranking Israeli officials condoning or inciting genocidal conduct in Gaza. On October 9, 2023, for example, Israeli defence minister Yoav Gallant said he had 'released all restraints . . . We are fighting human animals . . . Gaza won't return to what it was before. There will be no Hamas. We will eliminate everything'.[14] Gallant said this after announcing a total siege that would shut off all electricity, food, water, and fuel to Gaza's civilian population.[15]

Three days later, Israel's president Isaac Herzog declared:

> It is an entire nation out there that is responsible. It is not true this rhetoric about civilians not aware, not involved. It is absolutely not true. They could have risen up . . . But we are at war. We are at war. We are at war. We are defending our homes. We are protecting our homes. That's the truth. And when a nation protects its home, it fights. And we will fight until we break their backbone.[16]

In December 2023, Herzog was pictured signing munitions due to be dropped on Gaza. 'I rely on you', he wrote, seemingly unmoved by the very real prospect that the shell would soon eviscerate innocent people.

These statements, like others quoted by the ICJ, were made right at the outset of Israel's onslaught. Any suggestion by Starmer or his associates that the devastation in Gaza was unforeseen or went further than expected have to be viewed in this light.

'THEY HAVE THAT RIGHT'

The Starmer Project unequivocally backed Israel's violent response to October 7 and eschewed sympathy for Palestinians, even as the early evidence indicated that Israel's retaliation would inflict mass death and destruction on Gaza's civilian population.

In a Sky News interview on October 11, Starmer was asked whether he had any sympathy for citizens in Gaza 'living under siege . . . no water, no electricity, no power? A word for them?' He answered, 'Responsibility is with Hamas . . . and I think it's very important that the world stands up and is clear about that and stands with Israel'.[17] Starmer declined to offer any sympathy for Palestinian citizens despite the prompting. By October 11,

Israeli strikes had already killed over nine hundred Palestinians and wounded five thousand more.

Starmer was interviewed by Nick Ferrari the same day, where he delivered what became one of the defining lines of his career as Labour leader until that point. After being asked whether Israel's response was proportionate, Starmer said, 'I'm very clear that Israel must have, does have that right to defend herself, and Hamas bears responsibility'. Ferrari followed up: 'A siege is appropriate? Cutting off power, cutting off water, Sir Keir?' Starmer doubled down:

> Well, *I do think Israel has that right*, it is an ongoing situation. Obviously, everything should be done within international law, but I don't want to step away from that sort of core principles that Israel has a right to defend herself and Hamas bears responsibility for these terrorist acts.

The context of this exchange was all-important: Starmer was explicitly being asked for his view on a comment by Israeli defence minister Gallant that the ICJ would subsequently adduce as evidence that a genocide was plausibly underway in Gaza.

Starmer's interview, which provoked widespread outrage, was publicly defended by Labour's shadow attorney general Emily Thornberry and shadow foreign minister David Lammy. Asked whether 'cutting off food, water, and electricity is within international law . . . ?' Thornberry responded: 'I think Israel has an absolute right to defend itself against terrorism'.[18] When Thornberry was told that this wasn't the question that had been asked, she said it was 'an answer to that question that you've asked, and it's an appropriate one at this time'. The subtext was plain—Israel's wrongdoing would not be acknowledged, let alone opposed.

Starmer did not appear in public for nine days after his statement. This gave the impression that he either meant what he said but was too afraid of public backlash to defend it, or that he was too cowardly to apologise for his mistake. In the end, he did neither. Starmer 'clarified' that he hadn't actually said what everyone had heard him say. Instead, he claimed to have been responding to the previous question, which he had already answered in full. It was a silly and mendacious response, yet typical of his method: say something clear and explicit one day, then deny saying it the next.

The new line was dutifully defended by the shadow cabinet. In an October 22 interview, it was put to Lisa Nandy, the shadow secretary of state for international development, that the Muslim community deserved an apology given its anger at Starmer's statement. By then, Muslim Labour councillors had begun resigning in serious numbers. 'We can't apologise for holding a position we've never held', Nandy retorted, effectively recasting authentic anger at Starmer's position as mere ignorance or confusion.[19] This came perilously close to gaslighting.

Even as the brutality of Israel's onslaught became increasingly obvious, Starmer and his team refused to entertain any meaningful talk about ending the violence. On November 15, 2023, the Scottish National Party moved a motion for an immediate ceasefire; it was opposed by Labour, which argued instead for a mere 'humanitarian pause'. This led to the largest rebellion against Starmer in his time as leader: fifty-six Labour MPs voted for the SNP's motion and multiple frontbenchers resigned their positions.

Future historians will no doubt have much to grapple with in explaining why Starmer and the party's instinctive response was to so aggressively back Israel. Two pieces of context are important.

The first, perhaps most obviously, was the 'antisemitism crisis' that had loomed large in Labour politics for so long. In January 2024, ITV aired a two-part documentary special getting 'up close' with Starmer. It explained Starmer's seemingly impossible bind: 'He is desperate to prove to the Jewish community that Labour has changed. But he also comes under massive pressure to follow Labour's leaders in London, Manchester, and Scotland in calling for a ceasefire'.[20]

It was a remarkable, maybe even obscene comment: Starmer, it was claimed, had to prove that the party was not antisemitic, and so could not back calls for a ceasefire in the context of a plausible genocide.

When this argument is viewed in the light of the revelations discussed in Part One above, it amounts to this: Starmer was compelled to support Israel as it inflicted a 'plausible' genocide in order to disprove alarmist claims of 'antisemitism' that had been fuelled, at least in part, by his own senior advisor, Morgan McSweeney, as part of efforts to discredit the Corbyn movement.

In fact, there were many in Britain's Jewish community who abhorred Israel's conduct in Gaza and demanded an immediate ceasefire. Still, the ITV analysis was correct that the party's 'antisemitism crisis' inflected, constrained, and disciplined the Labour Party's response to the Gaza catastrophe. Anyone with a detailed and granular understanding of the 'antisemitism crisis' knows that it remained in the gift of the Board of Deputies of British Jews to reignite a controversy that would have consumed even Starmer, and it didn't take a genius to predict they would be fiercely defensive of Israel's conduct in the wake of October 7.

Indeed, on October 27, 2023, the Board of Deputies and the Jewish Leadership Council released a joint statement decrying calls for a ceasefire and sending a clear warning to people outside of government (read: the Labour Party) to keep their noses out of grown-up business. 'Politicians who do not have a direct role in these diplomatic efforts [by the government] should focus on threats to community cohesion in the UK', the groups instructed.[21] In February 2024, the Board effectively told British MPs to get back in their box: 'the Board of Deputies reminds political parties that a long-term resolution to the conflict will not be brokered in Parliament but by Israelis and Palestinians themselves', it explained, referring to ongoing parliamentary ceasefire debates.[22]

The response of the Board of Deputies and JLC to the ICJ ruling was dismissive at best and obtuse at worst. The Board 'welcome[d]' the UK's official statement on the ICJ ruling. This statement expressed 'respect' for 'the role and independence of the ICJ' but then effectively dismissed its findings: 'Our view is that Israel's actions in Gaza cannot be described as a genocide, which was why South Africa's decision to bring the case was wrong and provocative', the government said.[23] The JLC, meanwhile, released a statement underlining that the ICJ had not questioned Israel's right to self-defence and had not ordered Israel to cease its military campaign.[24]

Arguably, the 'antisemitism crisis' had already pre-disciplined the party to tread carefully on the issue of Israel's response; in case any memories had lapsed, these statements would have made it abundantly clear that deviation from an accepted line would carry political costs.

The second important context was the Biden administration's full-throated support for, and co-participation in, Israel's onslaught. Multiple contemporary accounts agree that Starmer was keen to use the crisis in Gaza to demonstrate his reliability to the US security state.

Starmer's decision to follow US policy was confirmed in typical Westminster style: an anonymous and unsourced briefing to *PoliticsHome*.[25] In January 2024, the website reported that Starmer had told Labour MPs that he was in regular contact with Jake Sullivan, the US national security advisor. *PoliticsHome* reported that 'the party's current stance . . . has been specifically devised to mirror the US position following discussions with US figures . . . as a way of conveying the impression it is a government-in-waiting by factoring in the positions of key international players'.[26]

Tom Baldwin, Starmer's sympathetic biographer, reports that Starmer's response to Gaza was to 'seek to build relations with international partners who have real traction in the region. That meant proving to Joe Biden he would be a stable partner rather than one outflanking him for votes'.[27] A less charitable understanding of this impulse was that Starmer ignored members of his own party, who overwhelmingly supported an immediate ceasefire, in order to display fealty to the US.

This approach took its most absurd form after forces from Yemen began attacking and seizing ships in the Red Sea that were travelling to Israel, in response to Israel's destruction of Gaza. Britain joined the US in strikes on Yemen that amounted to a de facto declaration of war against the country. This followed a decade of conflict in Yemen that had been fuelled by British and US weapons; at least 377,000 people were killed in the violence.[28]

Starmer supported the bombing despite this violating his leadership campaign pledge (noted previously) to introduce a 'Prevention of Military Intervention Act'. He had explained in a 2020 interview that he would 'pass legislation that said that military action could be taken if first a lawful case for it was made, secondly there was a viable objective, and thirdly you got consent of the Commons'.[29] Prime Minister Sunak did not seek parliamentary approval for the strikes on Yemen, but Starmer did not object.

Starmer explained that there was no contradiction between his proposed legislation and his support for a military action that had been initiated without a go-ahead from parliament. His reasoning was that the strikes on Yemen did not involve a 'sustained campaign' or 'troops on the ground' and so could not be considered 'military action'.[30] It was obvious guff.

'SHAKING OFF THE FLEAS'

The Starmer Project's response to October 7 could not have been more carefully calibrated to appal much of Labour's own voting base and, in particular, the Muslim communities that had long formed the bedrock of many of Labour's safest seats. Four factors were arguably central to grassroots anger at the party leadership, the first of which was the party's intolerant and authoritarian response to dissent. On October 14, 2023, for example, General Secretary David Evans issued guidance and instructions to all CLP and branch secretaries. Evans brusquely informed the secretaries that the party had already advised (read: instructed) its elected representatives not to attend protest marches against the unfolding destruction of Gaza. He told CLP secretaries that they were bound by this guidance.

Evans explained that there was a threat that protestors might inadvertently 'share a platform with, or [get] close to, individuals that [*sic*] threaten to undermine the values and principles of the Labour Party'.[31] This stretched to breaking point the party's already problematic approach to guilt-by-association: people acting in good conscience were now instructed that they could not march in public lest they find themselves in accidental proximity to somebody insalubrious who they did not know, did not speak to, and did not endorse.

That same month, the whip was removed from Andy McDonald MP. At a protest march, McDonald had stated that 'we won't rest until we have justice. Until all people, Israelis and Palestinians, between the river and the sea can live in peaceful liberty'.[32] He was only readmitted after a lengthy suspension.

In February 2024, the party indefinitely suspended or expelled a host of councillors in Hackney and South London for breaking the party whip on the issue of a Gaza ceasefire. Multiple Hackney councillors lost the whip when they voted to allow a Green Party motion for a ceasefire to be debated in the council chamber.[33]

In Lambeth, one prominent and well-liked Black Labour councillor, Sonia Winifred, resigned after being suspended for breaking the whip and voting for a Green Party ceasefire motion.[34] Winifred had been a prominent campaigner celebrating the Windrush generation.[35] She resigned, believing that factional politics stood in the way of her being able to defend herself from the charges against her.

Another victim of the party's authoritarian bent was Martin Abrams, a self-identified 'Jewish socialist' councillor in Streatham. Abrams was indefinitely suspended because he broke the party whip by voting for an immediate ceasefire in support of a Green Party motion. Abrams explained that his vote was both an act of conscience, informed by his family's history of persecution in the Kyiv pogroms, and an attempt to reflect local and national public opinion, which supported a ceasefire.[36] In 2025, the party told Abrams that, as a result of this principled vote, he would never again be allowed to run for office on a Labour ticket.

Many, especially at the councillor level, resigned ahead of disciplinary action being taken. By early 2024, nearly a hundred Labour councillors had quit. The party lost control of multiple councils as a result, including in Oxford and Norwich.[37]

The second grievance stoking grassroots anger was the party's tendency to recast popular dissent and peaceful protest as forms of bullying and harassment.

On October 11, 2023, for example, Labour Friends of Israel (LFI) held a vigil at party conference, addressed by Rachel Reeves. Referring to nascent outbreaks of popular protest against Israel's onslaught, Reeves explained that the party would 'ensure that the police do everything within their powers to hold responsible' those engaged in 'antisemitism, the anti-Zionist and anti-Israel feeling that is allowed to flourish in some communities in Britain'.[38] In light of Israel's conduct in Gaza, it was extraordinary that Reeves wanted the police to intervene when 'some communities' expressed anti-Israel sentiments—but that wasn't even the most outrageous thing Reeves had said that week. Two days prior, on October 9, she asserted that 'Gaza is not occupied by Israel',[39] just as Israel was demonstrating its effective control by cutting off Gaza's electricity, food, water, and fuel.

The third factor was that the party's response to Gaza was arguably framed by, and then expressed, a hierarchy of racism that many in the party had long lamented. In the weeks following the mass resignations of Muslim councillors, for example, one unidentified but senior Labour source explained to the journalist Lee Harpin that the party was simply 'shaking off the fleas'. The party would later deny that the briefing had come from the Starmer leadership camp. But, as Andrew Fisher would point out, this would imply that they knew where the quote *did* originate—raising questions as to why no one was disciplined.[40]

According to Pogrund and Maguire's fly-on-the-wall retelling, Morgan McSweeney was unruffled when 'Muslim groups' began raising concerns. One of those groups was the Labour Muslim Network, which, as described previously, had long been sounding the alarm about Islamophobia in the party. When the LMN demanded Starmer apologise for his LBC comments, McSweeney responded dismissively on WhatsApp: 'LMN are not an affiliated organisation and are not good faith actors'.[41] It was an extraordinary thing to say about the largest Muslim group linked to the party, which had frequently been told by the party leadership over the years that its concerns were being taken seriously. Perhaps they never were.

Where the party attempted to smooth ruffled feathers, it did so in ham-fisted ways that quickly backfired. In late October, for example, Starmer made an impromptu appearance at the South Wales Islamic Centre. Starmer's Twitter account posted photos of him meeting members of the Centre, at which he apparently informed the (likely perplexed) attendees that Hamas needed to release Israeli hostages. Not long after, the Centre released a pained statement distancing itself entirely from Starmer's post, which had provoked criticism of the Centre for having potentially given Starmer a free pass on his statements about Israel's conduct in Gaza. 'We express our dismay at Keir Starmer's social media post . . . We wish to stress Keir Starmer's social media post and images gravely misrepresented our congregants and the nature of the visit', the Centre said.[42]

But it wasn't just the Muslim community that the party alienated. In January 2024, Starmer's Labour removed the whip from Kate Osamor MP, a Black member of the party's Socialist Campaign Group. Osamor's offence was to have released a statement on Holocaust Memorial Day that listed Gaza among the genocides that needed to be remembered.

She issued this statement one day after the ICJ had found that Israel was plausibly committing genocide in Gaza. Osamor quickly apologised 'for any offence caused by my reference to the ongoing humanitarian disaster in Gaza as part of that period of remembrance'.[43]

In a striking re-run of the Diane Abbott affair, Osamor's apology was rejected. The Board of Deputies praised the decision to remove the whip, regardless of Osamor's apology, and the Jewish Labour Movement said Osamor deserved to be removed as her 'subsequent non-apology rang hollow'.[44] These reactions were odd, perhaps, given how quick the Board and Starmer's Labour had been to absolve two white men—Steve Reed and Barry Sheerman—after they had made statements that were surely much more problematic.

Over the next weeks, *The Voice*—Britain's largest paper focused on the Afro-Caribbean community—carried stinging commentary alleging that 'Keir Starmer doesn't care about Black people'[45] and demanding Osamor's (and Abbott's) readmission. 'We see the double standard at play when it comes to how white MPs loyal to Starmer are handled compared to Black MPs, and we are watching closely',[46] Richard Sudan, a freelance journalist and activist, wrote in the paper.

The fourth and final factor was the tone-deaf and arguably outrageous response of the Labour Party's most faithful Israel devotees. Take the influential advocacy group Labour Friends of Israel, which was vice-chaired by Rachel Reeves and which listed Starmer as well as half of Labour Together's eight 'brave' MPs among its supporters.

In early January 2024, LFI sent a delegation of MPs, former MP, and supporters to Israel on a 'solidarity' visit. This took place while the ICJ was deliberating over its response to South Africa's application in the genocide case. The LFI delegation included some of the most prominent MPs who had driven the 'antisemitism crisis' in the Labour Party and who had vocally supported Starmer's approach on the issue: Louise Ellman, Ruth Smeeth (now Baroness Anderson), and Margaret Hodge.

The delegation was pictured smiling in a staged photo shoot with Israeli president Isaac Herzog.[47] By then, Herzog had already been cited in South Africa's ICJ application for his genocidal comments; the Court's judges would soon single out Herzog in their provisional ruling that Palestinians in Gaza faced a plausible risk of genocide. Herzog had also already been pictured in the press signing munitions bound for Gaza.

Ruth Smeeth's participation was particularly notable as she was, at the time, CEO of the Index on Censorship, which advocates for freedom of the press and the protection of journalists. At the time Smeeth stood smiling with Herzog, Israel had killed an estimated seventy-six journalists in Gaza over the previous four months.[48]

The impact of this photograph was profound, sending a clear message that some of the party's most senior and respected figures, closely allied with the Starmer Project, would defend Israel even as it faced well-evidenced charges of genocidal conduct.

At the same time that LFI was sending delegations to meet Herzog, it was also aggressively policing speech critical of Israel, in highly controversial and problematic ways.

In February 2024, for example, LFI posted a lengthy thread on X alleging that 'antisemitism on the left' manifested as anti-Zionism. The thread appears to have been inspired by the writings of David Hirsh and other authors who had contributed to a pamphlet the organisation published in mid-2023 about 'antisemitic anti-Zionism'.

Hirsh, a Jewish sociology professor and one-time member of Labour Against Antisemitism,[49] had a history of dismissing left-wing Jewish people as 'AsAJews'. In a *Jewish Chronicle* article published December 2020, for example, Hirsh argued that Jewish Voice for Labour should be expelled from the party in order to tackle antisemitism, precisely because they were anti-Zionist Jews:

> AsAJews parade their Jewish identities in an effort to give their views extra legitimacy in the eyes of a non-Jewish audience. It is an inversion of identity

> politics. They mobilise their identities in the service of silencing the Jewish consensus of reasonable concern about antisemitism. Anti-zionist Jews are not the useful idiots of left antisemitism, they are among its pioneers.[50]

LFI's February 2024 thread conflated antisemitism and anti-Zionism. LFI demanded that the Labour Party 'recognise that antizionism has no place in the Labour tradition'.[51]

The argument was pitiful in light of findings released by the Institute for Jewish Policy Research (JPR) a week prior to the thread. The JPR's survey of the British Jewish community, conducted in late 2022, had found that 62 percent of all British Jews identified as Zionist.[52] Of the remaining 38 percent, 8 percent identified as explicitly anti-Zionist and 15 percent as non-Zionist. The figures were starker for younger generations; only 59 percent of British Jews aged between twenty and twenty-nine described themselves as Zionist. It also found that 59 percent of Jewish Labour Party supporters were Zionist, although it did not break down how the remaining 41 percent was distributed.

Did this mean, according to the LFI, that a full 8 percent of British Jews—and maybe even 23 percent when non-Zionists were added—had 'no place in the Labour tradition'?

'BRITISH POLITICS AT ITS LOWEST'

The party's handling of the Gaza crisis reached its nadir in late February 2024 when Starmer and his allies broke with decades of parliamentary convention to kill a Scottish National Party motion that threatened to catalyse a rebellion against Starmer's leadership.

By then, popular opinion was firmly opposed to Israel's assault on Gaza. In mid-February 2024, a YouGov poll on British attitudes towards the conflict found that, between November 2023 and February 2024, the percentage of the British public that wanted Israel to 'stop and call a ceasefire' had increased from 59 percent to 66 percent.[53] Only 13 percent of the public, by February 2024, believed Israel should continue military action. In the same period, the proportion of people believing that 'Israel's attack on Gaza from October onwards is justified' fell from 29 percent to 24 percent of the population. By comparison, a full 45 percent of the British public believed that Israel's attacks on Gaza were not justified.[54]

The figures for Labour supporters were starker still. In February 2024, a mere 6 percent of people who voted for Labour in 2019 sympathised with 'the Israeli side' in the conflict, compared to 49 percent who were sympathetic to Palestine. Only 12 percent of the same cohort believed that Israel's actions in Gaza were justified, against 65 percent who said they were not, and only 3 percent believed that Israel should continue to take military action, compared to 84 percent who believed Israel should 'stop and call a ceasefire'.

It was in this context that the SNP used one of its rare 'opposition days' in parliament to put forward a motion for an immediate humanitarian ceasefire. The wording and intent of the SNP motion was notable for three key reasons.

First, the motion did not caveat or qualify its calls for an 'immediate ceasefire'. While the motion 'called for the immediate release of all hostages taken by Hamas', it did not make a ceasefire contingent on fulfilment of that demand. It simply required an immediate ceasefire in Gaza and Israel.

Second, the motion used damning language to describe Israel's assault and conveyed the realities of Palestinian victimhood. It described, for example, the 'slaughter' of innocent civilians and registered the extent of civilian harm with 'shock and distress'. It also referred to Rafah as the 'largest refugee camp in the world'.

Finally, and most importantly, the motion called for an 'end to the collective punishment of the Palestinian people'. This phrasing could have had serious consequences, particularly in terms of the UK's ongoing supply of arms to Israel, which are subject to arms export control regulations. These regulations forbid the export of weapons where there is a risk they may be used to violate international humanitarian law. Collective punishment is illegal. It would be very difficult for the government's lawyers to claim that there was no meaningful risk of weapons being used to collectively punish Palestinians in Gaza when a sizeable proportion of the country's own representatives were saying the opposite. Passing the motion, as a result, could have had tangible and immediate consequences for British policy.

The Labour Party refused to back the SNP's motion and tabled its own amended motion instead. By then, the party had begun to moderate its support for Israel in response to popular discontent, the ICJ provisional order, and a marginal shift in the language emanating from the Biden White House. Labour now acknowledged that an Israeli ground offensive in Rafah risked 'catastrophic humanitarian consequences', demanded that Israel implement the ICJ's provisional measures, and supported calls for an 'immediate humanitarian ceasefire'.

Starmer would later claim that he had personally drafted Labour's amended motion, and it is unsurprising that, as a result, it contained all sorts of slippery legal caveats and language. For example, the motion foregrounded the need for Israelis to feel 'assurance' that October 7 would not happen again, which was tacked onto the caveats and qualifications for a ceasefire. As a condition for a ceasefire, 'assurance' was a term of striking intellectual and legal woolliness: it implied that UK foreign policy would be made on the basis of how Israelis felt, rather than anything concrete, measurable, and actionable. It also begged the questions: When and how would Israelis feel safe? Were there any limits to what could be done to achieve this? And was it morally and legally justifiable for Israel to continue killing innocents in pursuit of an 'assurance' of safety? Certainly, there are many on the Israeli ultra-right who believe that Israel will only truly be safe once Gaza and the West Bank are emptied of their Palestinian populations.

Most importantly, the motion removed any reference to 'collective punishment' and did not, at any stage, either directly or indirectly, describe the violence inflicted by Israel in Gaza. The only Israeli violence it acknowledged was that related to Israel's illegal settlements in the West Bank. According to ITV's Robert Peston, the mention of 'collective punishment' was the issue that most exercised Starmer and which he most insistently rejected.[55] Of course, this was the only language that had immediate and material legal implications, whereas Starmer's motion was a lawyerly exercise in sounding plausibly upset at Israel while ensuring that nothing had to change.

The cynicism of Labour's amendment was inadvertently revealed by Starmer days after it was passed. He told Sky News that he had personally drafted the amended motion after having attended the Munich Security Conference to meet with allies in February 2024. Starmer claimed that while in Munich he had met with Antony Blinken, the US secretary of state and a staunch supporter of Israel, as well as unnamed representatives from Qatar and Israeli president Herzog.

Starmer seemed remarkably unruffled admitting that he had met and discussed matters with a man whose statements had been adduced as evidence by the ICJ that Israel was plausibly committing acts of genocide. After the ICJ issued its January 2024 order indicating provisional measures, Herzog made further comments that dismissed the Court and rejected its ruling.[56] On January 28, for instance, Herzog had dismissed the ICJ order and its criticism of his own statements as a 'blood libel that undermines the very values on which this court was established'.[57] This was weeks before Starmer's decision to meet with the Israeli president.

Starmer's Sky News interview strongly implied that his amended motion was drafted in light of these discussions and thus bore the stamp of their influence. It was certainly hard to listen to Starmer and avoid the impression that his personally crafted motion had adhered to parameters pre-agreed with Israel (then conducting its plausible genocide) and the US (which was enabling it).

The passing of Labour's amendment was a scandalous affair—and the first time the bureaucratic bad faith and cry-bully politics that had become the primary political mode of the Labour right was applied to the country as a whole.

Parliamentary convention held that the SNP was entitled, as part of its 'opposition day', to submit a motion. The precise rules are arcane, but the essential point is that only the (at this point Conservative) government would normally be able to challenge such a motion by amendment. Under normal circumstances, parliament would thus have debated only two motions: the SNP's Gaza motion and a Tory alternative. This created a major problem for Starmer, as over one hundred Labour MPs had already indicated that they were planning to vote for the SNP motion, which Starmer did not support. The clash could have led to the biggest parliamentary rebellion of Starmer's career and plunged the party into crisis over its handling of the vexed question of a Gaza ceasefire.

Starmer's faction set to work. On the day of the motion, supportive Labour Party MPs raised obtuse points of order and even forced a procedural vote: an effective filibuster to give Starmer's team time to fix the situation. It was reported that Labour's chief whip Alan Campbell used the delays to meet with the House of Commons speaker, Lindsay Hoyle, a former Labour Party MP for Chorley.[58] Hoyle was pressed to allow the Labour Party motion to be debated. The speaker is expected to run the House of Commons in a neutral and fair manner, applying parliamentary rules, conventions, and standing orders without fear or favour.

Hoyle was allegedly unmoved by Campbell's representations, and so Starmer was called on to personally intervene. A huddle of Labour MPs was reported to have heard Starmer loudly say he was 'going to fix the Speaker'.[59] Starmer allegedly entered Hoyle's office with Campbell, while Hoyle's clerks were told to leave. A few minutes later, Starmer and Campbell left the office smiling. Hoyle returned to the Chamber and announced, to the outrage of the SNP and others, that he had decided to break decades of parliamentary convention to allow the Labour motion to be heard alongside the others. In a highly unusual move, the clerk of the House publicly issued a letter explaining how 'long-established conventions are not being followed in this case'.[60]

Because of the vagaries of the motion system, Hoyle's decision resulted in the SNP's motion not being heard at all, while the Tory motion wasn't put forward as Tory MPs walked out in protest. The Labour motion, which should not have been heard in the first place, passed by default.

Hoyle later apologised for the fiasco. He professed that the eventual outcome had been unintended and that his primary aim had been to ensure the House could freely debate a matter of great importance. Hoyle hinted that he would make good by allowing the SNP's motion to be debated again. Yet, by the following week, Hoyle had decided to deny the SNP's appeal to use an unusual parliamentary protocol to move their motion afresh. The speaker was apparently no longer moved by the importance of ensuring that a plurality of views are heard. Dozens of MPs signed motions expressing no confidence in Hoyle.

Two reasons were offered for why Hoyle decided to break with parliamentary convention and save Starmer's blushes. Nick Watt, the political editor of BBC *Newsnight*, tweeted that he had been briefed by senior Labour sources.[61] They claimed Hoyle had been told that a future Labour government would have enough MPs to displace him, and that his position would be under threat if he didn't play ball. The party swiftly denied the allegation, but Watts was adamant that he had been briefed in this way. Pogrund and Maguire subsequently confirmed that this threat was, indeed, delivered by Starmer.

The other explanation was put forward by Hoyle and then amplified by Starmer and the Labour Party. According to Hoyle, Starmer had warned that if Labour MPs were denied the opportunity to vote for Starmer's caveated ceasefire motion, they would be exposed to serious and credible threats to their physical safety. Neither Hoyle nor Starmer presented any evidence to justify this assertion. It is striking that no police operation was mounted to investigate these purported threats, and that no proposal was made to subject Starmer and Hoyle's claim to proper scrutiny. Of course, the reporting by Watt as well as Pogrund and Maguire must cast serious doubt on the reality of the claimed threat to MPs' safety. For if Hoyle had been presented with credible evidence that MPs' physical security was at risk, would this not have sufficed to convince him without the need for Starmer to threaten the speaker's job prospects?

Unsurprisingly, Hoyle's explanation and Starmer's amplification inspired a flurry of Tory and far-right talking points. Suddenly the story of Starmer's shameful politicking was turned into a narrative about how the country's democracy was being undermined by violent protestors, many of them Muslim. The affair further dignified false claims by Tory ministers that months of peaceful protests for a Gaza ceasefire were actually dangerous hate marches, and that the country was being held to ransom by Islamists.

In the context of the Tories' wider legislative agenda, which sought to demonise and limit dissent, Starmer's rhetoric was not just dishonest but deeply reckless.

A week before the parliamentary drama, Israeli strikes had killed eight family members of Husam Zomlot, the Palestinian ambassador to the UK, as they sought shelter in Rafah.[62] The dead included two seven-year-old twins and a fifteen-month-old child. A photo of one of the dead twins, Sidra, had just gone viral. A picture showed her lifeless corpse dangling from a twisted metal bar near the top of the building she occupied, her legs torn into shredded, fleshy tassels.

Husam Zomlot announced her death on Instagram,[63] counterpointing her haunting image with a montage of photos of his now-deceased relatives. They had been a smiling, beautiful family.

'It is not a good day for the UK, not a good day for humanity', Zomlot told Channel 4 in the wake of Starmer's debasement of parliament. 'To see this chaos in the House of Commons . . . It is really, really, British politics at its lowest'.[64]

RISE OF THE INDEPENDENTS

The Starmer Project's takeover and remaking of the Labour Party, while often cheer-led by the media, had upset large parts of the party's own membership and alienated elements of its electoral coalition. Yet without the crisis in Gaza, it is not certain that this alienation would have catalysed any significant realignment in British electoral politics. Certainly, by mid-2023, there had been no realistic prospect of an independent challenge to Labour on the horizon, nor any seeming movement of voters from the Labour Party to left-wing challengers like the Greens; hence *Red Shift*'s confident prediction that the party could ignore the 'Activist Left' without consequence.

But Labour's response to Gaza accelerated the alienation of more progressive sections of its base from the party. This was particularly pronounced in ethnic minority communities, for whom Starmer's leadership had already been unsatisfying. Polling by Ipsos, reported on by Sky News, showed how Starmer's personal favourability ratings in such communities plummeted from a net of -3 in August 2023 to a net of -32 by December 2023.[65] Sky News dubbed this collapse the 'Gaza effect'.[66]

In early 2023, the party had enjoyed a position of seemingly unassailable strength. Now, it would be forced to campaign in the July 2024 election under more difficult circumstances than many had anticipated. It faced serious challenges in key seats from an insurgent movement ready to capitalise on localised but acute discontent with a leadership many considered to be both contemptuous of democracy and complicit in genocide.

PART SEVEN

INTO POWER AND OUT OF FAVOUR

CHAPTER 24

THE LOVELESS LANDSLIDE

At about 4:00 a.m. on the morning of July 5, 2024, Keir Starmer takes the stage in the swanky, glass-fronted headquarters of Camden council. It is four years, three months, and a day since he was elected as leader of the Labour Party on a pro-immigrant, pro-nationalisation, and Green New Deal-style platform that promised to retain the 'radicalism' of the Corbyn years. A throng of jubilant local Labour supporters mixes with a hubbub of media as Starmer addresses the country. He has just won his seat in Holborn and St Pancras, a seeming formality on his inexorable ascent to becoming prime minister. This time, Starmer has won on a platform of pro-business fiscal discipline leavened with commitments to tackle 'out of control' immigration. Television screens around the venue are confirming a Tory implosion and a historic Labour majority.

Starmer's acceptance speech does not diverge from the tone or talking points of the campaign. It is boring and wooden. The only memorable moment comes when Starmer promises, as he has done during the election, to return government to 'service' and end a culture of self-entitlement. 'Lies!' someone shouts from the crowd to widespread laughter. It briefly punctures the formal pageantry, reminding those in attendance that things are not as simple as they look. Indeed, it would take only months for Starmer's vaunted narrative of 'service' to crumble after his election, as the media finally started to pay attention to the glut of corporate and donor freebies that Starmer had accepted since 2021.

At the far end of the stage, Andrew Feinstein watches the crowd as Starmer makes his speech. Only minutes before, he had been called behind the stage, along with all the other candidates and their election agents, to be shown the outcome of the constituency vote. Feinstein had read the results while standing next to Starmer, and let out a bark of laughter—out of shock as well as amusement—when he saw what had happened.

Feinstein had run as an independent on a pro-peace and anti-austerity platform that celebrated immigration and centred pro-Gaza messaging. He had received 7,300 votes in the constituency, exceeding all expectations to come second with 19 percent of the vote. But what had tickled him was Starmer's tally: 19,000 votes.

'I could see him scanning the page', Feinstein says. 'I think we reached his result on the page at the same time, which is when I laughed. Starmer had a face like thunder. His security man put himself between me and Starmer and helped him to the stage'. Having been pushed to the back of the crowd of candidates, Feinstein could watch Starmer at a slight remove. 'I saw his fury turn into a fixed grin for the cameras. The strain seemed immense. I genuinely worried he would break his jaw, he was that uptight'.

While Starmer still won, his 19,000 votes were just *half* of what he had received in 2019 and a staggering 22,459 votes less than what he had received in 2017.[1] Turnout in the constituency had fallen to just 54 percent, down from 66 percent in 2019 and 67 percent in 2017. Starmer's result was, in fact, the lowest vote for a Labour candidate in Holborn and St Pancras, in absolute terms, since 2005, when the party was being punished for the Iraq War by a local Lib Dem surge—the last time, as well, that voter turnout there dropped below 60 percent. It was a shocking result for an incoming prime minister to have his local vote and turnout so dramatically reduced.

The results hardly inspired confidence in the level of real voter enthusiasm that underpinned Labour's overwhelming victory. They were also a powerful warning that the path to victory chosen by Starmer had seriously alienated broad swathes of the party's core support.

Feinstein had launched his independent bid to unseat Starmer only a day prior to Prime Minister Rishi Sunak's surprise dash through the rain in late May to fire the electoral starting gun. Like many others, Feinstein had anticipated that an election would only take place in October and thus expected to have six months to run his campaign, supported by an impressive online crowdfunding appeal. In the end, he had just six weeks (in reality, five, as the first week was bedevilled by logistical and IT issues) and, as a result of electoral regulations, could spend only £17,000 on his campaign.

But despite these hurdles, the significant online presence Feinstein had built through his activism on Gaza allowed him to attract hundreds of volunteers, from both the constituency and further afield. Many volunteers believe that if Feinstein had had six months, rather than six weeks, he would have had a real shot at pushing Starmer to the brink. Certainly, if Feinstein had captured the left-leaning Green Party vote in his constituency, this would have put him within touching distance of Starmer's much-reduced majority. Although this did not transpire, it was still a considerable feat for an independent candidate to go from a standing start to second place in the constituency in such a short period of time.

Feinstein's campaign was even more remarkable because of a de facto media blackout that meant independent challengers to the established political parties were all-but-ignored. In July 2024, Rivkah Brown of the independent *Novara Media* reported that *The Guardian*'s political correspondent, Aletha Adu, had initially planned to write a profile of Feinstein, until the piece was 'pulled by higher-ups'.[2]

Feinstein, originally from South Africa, had impeccable progressive credentials. The son of a Holocaust survivor, he had joined Nelson Mandela's African National Congress (ANC) in his teens before fleeing into exile. After apartheid ended, he was summoned by Mandela and 'deployed' to South Africa's first democratic parliament as an MP. He resigned after he was blocked by post-Mandela party elders from investigating a notoriously corrupt arms deal. For the last two decades, he has worked as an investigator and campaigner (alongside this author), exposing grand corruption and the consequences of excessive militarism.

Feinstein, who is Jewish, had long attracted the ire of those who had supported and amplified Labour Together's appalling Stop Funding Fake News campaign. He was a target of Labour Against Antisemitism, which accused him of promoting 'anti-Israel conspiracy theories' and of exploiting his family's history 'to substantiate his belief that Jeremy Corbyn is not an antisemite'.[3]

In 2021, Feinstein was sent a notice of investigation by the Labour Party in respect of a complaint that accused him of antisemitism. Party records show that this complaint was submitted by a non-Jewish member of LAAS in November 2020. 'He seems to constantly reference his dead family in order to undermine claims of anti-Semitism which is in common with others claiming Jewish heritage who have been expelled from the party', the non-Jewish member of LAAS alleged. Starmer's leadership, of course, directed the party to pay off LAAS activists named in the Leaked Report in 2023, and thanked LAAS for its contribution to the fight against antisemitism.

Feinstein submitted a lengthy and impassioned response to the allegation. The party did not bother to reply. Feinstein was informed only in 2023 that the investigation had been dropped, and then only because the law firm Bindmans had notified the party that it intended to bring a challenge against the party's complaints mechanism. It was, by any measure, a disgraceful way to treat a party member.

Feinstein had resisted local calls to stand against Starmer for years, not least because he had little desire to return to frontline politics after his history in the ANC. But Gaza had changed everything. Feinstein was persuaded to put his hat in the ring, leading to a period of exhaustive (and sometimes exhausting) local consultation to ensure that he had genuine community support. The Starmer Project had helped turn Feinstein, a former Labour member and Labour voter with no ambitions to hold public office, into Starmer's local rival.

It was a story repeated throughout the country as long-standing former Labour members and supporters stood as independents or volunteered for them, and many lifelong Labour voters either voted for left-wing alternatives to the Starmer Project or did not vote at all.

Just over the border of Holborn and St Pancras, in Islington North, Jeremy Corbyn announced his candidacy as an independent after the election was called, having been banished by Starmer from the Parliamentary Labour Party in 2020. Corbyn would eventually trounce his Labour opponent, Praful Nargund, a provider of private fertility services who had been selected as the Labour candidate in the teeth of the wishes of the local party. That campaign became a ghostly rerun of the 2015–20 era, as Corbyn's old nemeses flocked to canvass against him, unable to resist one more opportunity to twist the knife. In one photo posted to Twitter just days before the polls opened, Tom Watson was pictured canvassing for Nargund alongside Patrick Heneghan: a portrait of one of the slated beneficiaries of the pre-Ergon House secret funding scheme (Watson) beside one of its facilitators (Heneghan).

In the end, five independents would be elected to parliament—a historic record—all of them standing on a pro-Gaza and anti-austerity platform. If just a few hundred votes had been cast differently, the upset could have been even greater. The hugely impressive twenty-something Leanne Mohamad came within a whisker of beating Wes Streeting, one of Labour Together's eight 'brave' MPs and Starmer's future health secretary. Shabana Mahmood, another member of the 'brave' eight and soon-to-be lord high chancellor, scraped through after losing a staggering 40 percent of her 2019 vote, with her majority slashed from 68 percent to 9 percent. Mahmood had come within touching distance of losing what was once one of the top five safest Labour seats in the country.

The magnitude of Labour's overall victory meant that these warning signs were largely ignored in the election aftermath as many applauded the first Labour parliamentary majority since 2005. These developments suggested, though, that even as Labour now commanded an overwhelming parliamentary majority, the Starmer Project had chosen a route to victory that weakened the party's core base of support. This left the Starmer government vulnerable to scandal and political miscalculation.

Indeed, the triumphalist tone of the Starmer Project all but evaporated within three months of Starmer taking power as the country turned rapidly against his government. The policy decision to cut the Winter Fuel Allowance, the press' belated exposure of Starmer's penchant for luxury freebies, and an oddly disjointed and unpopular budget together caused Starmer's approval ratings to plummet.

These trends may reverse, and it would be foolish to write off a political project that already recovered from the disaster of Hartlepool and near-annihilation in Batley and Spen in 2021 to win a barnstorming majority three years later. The immediate task nevertheless remains to understand how and why the Starmer Project derailed so quickly after having finally come to power.

To begin with, the general election campaign provided a venue for the project to intensify its war against the party's left, which it conducted in ways that reflected the project's embrace of a hierarchy of racism. The last-minute exclusion of Faiza Shaheen, discussed below, and the early campaign controversy over Diane Abbott provided additional proof to many that the party had become a hostile place for left-wing BAME candidates. That internal conflict alienated much of Labour's core vote, as did the campaign's economically ungenerous manifesto, embrace of anti-immigrant sentiment, and soft-pedalling of climate issues.

What's more, the election campaign was strikingly similar to the campaign that had gotten Starmer elected as the leader of the Labour Party in 2020. It was, bluntly, another fraud. This time, however, the fraud was perpetrated on the general voting public instead of the party's once-sizeable membership. Thus, voters were told that the party had a plan to grow the economy and improve public services that was 'fully funded and fully costed' and which would require neither big tax rises nor austerity-style cuts. This was patently untrue, as nearly every serious economist repeatedly explained at the time. The new government's sudden 'discovery' of a 'fiscal black hole' was disingenuous and ham-fisted, yet was deployed to provide rhetorical cover for decisions that bore little resemblance to what had been promised on the campaign trail.

As taxes increased and pensioners lost their Winter Fuel Allowance, the real question became: If Labour had been honest with voters before the election about what it intended to do in government, would the result have been different? This repeated on a larger scale the question that members of the Labour Party had already been forced to confront: Would Starmer have won the party leadership in 2020 if he had told the truth about his plans to erase the Labour left and drag the party to the right?

A third proximate cause of the public's rapid disillusionment with the Starmer government was that Starmer's victory had been preceded by a near total hiatus of media scrutiny—another echo of Starmer's 2020 Labour leadership campaign. This time, the media had failed to raise, let alone meaningfully reveal and challenge, Starmer's personal history of taking freebies. The result was that almost as soon as Starmer was elected and this history was belatedly exposed, Starmer's one apparent virtue—that he would, at minimum, be less grubbily grasping than the Tories—lay in tatters.

FINISHING THE WAR ON THE LEFT

Sunak's surprise election announcement on May 22 accelerated the Starmer Project's long-running plan to transform the 'DNA' of the Parliamentary Labour Party. In practice, this involved the right-dominated National Executive Committee deciding that it would no longer put the majority of candidate selections to any form of local vote; the NEC would simply use its near-unlimited discretion to pick its favourites. This approach was, as noted previously, the total opposite of Starmer's 2020 campaign pledge to end precisely this sort of selection process. The result was a further degrading of party democracy, carried out in ways that also expressed the party's hierarchy of racism.

Two of the most high-profile victims of this process were Diane Abbott and Faiza Shaheen. Abbott, as noted previously, had the Labour whip withdrawn in 2023 following an ill-conceived but quickly retracted letter she had written to *The Observer*. The calling of the election led to renewed pleas for the whip to be restored to her, and to a grilling of Starmer by the media about the process that would decide this issue.

Starmer's responses to these interrogations were bunk. In an interview on May 24, Starmer explained that Abbott's case was being determined by an independent process, in which he could not get involved. 'It's not a question about what I want . . . the days when the leader rolls up his or her sleeves and gets involved in disciplinary cases are well and truly over. That's what Jeremy Corbyn did and it ended very badly', Starmer said.[4] Starmer, of course, had been closely involved in complaints on a systematic basis, as revealed for the first time in this book. Only once Abbott's case had been resolved, Starmer implied, would the NEC consider her candidacy.

Four days later, the BBC's Victoria Derbyshire broke the story that Abbott's disciplinary investigation had already concluded five months previously. Abbott had already been issued a formal warning and required to do an online antisemitism training course, which she had completed. Abbott was quoted as being 'angry, depressed and worn out' by the way the Labour Party had treated her.[5] By that evening, the party had formally lifted Abbott's suspension and restored the whip to her.[6] Once again, the party's 'independent' disciplinary process had delivered a result that just happened to coincide with what was politically convenient.

But twenty minutes before Derbyshire confirmed that Abbott had been readmitted, *The Guardian* reported, based on international party sources, that Labour still might decline to select Abbott as its election candidate. *The Guardian* reported that Abbott had liked a tweet posted by Jeremy Corbyn's wife, Laura Alvarez, about his decision to stand as an independent, and that this action could lead to Abbott's deselection.[7] The next day, Abbott told an impromptu rally outside Hackney Town Hall that she still wanted to stand, and vowed not to be 'intimidated or frightened' by Starmer's leadership.[8]

Abbott would eventually be confirmed as a parliamentary candidate on June 4, but only after weeks of humiliating treatment that dominated news headlines. Nevertheless, with her sizeable media profile and totemic status as the country's first Black female MP, and on the back of a huge mobilisation in the broader Black community, she was one of the few people to ever stand up against the Starmer Project and survive.

No such luck for Faiza Shaheen, one of the vanishingly few left-wing candidates to have been selected by the party since Starmer took control. Shaheen is a charismatic figure with a compelling rags-to-academic robes story. But many on the left believed that Shaheen's charm and qualifications had actually marked her card with the Labour right, which feared she could develop a troublesome political profile in the Labour Party as a popular and unifying progressive.

On May 31, as the Abbott affair rumbled on, Shaheen was informed in a Zoom meeting that she would no longer be the Labour Party's candidate for Chingford and Woodford Green.

Her interlocutors raised concerns about Shaheen's social media postings, including posts she had put out years before she was even a Labour Party member. As was typical of these sorts of processes, the 'problematic' posts that had been identified were anything but. One of her cited infractions was to have posted about her experience of Islamophobia in the Labour Party, in response to a Labour Muslim Network statement criticising the party's readmission of Trevor Phillips (discussed above).[9] Another of Shaheen's offences was to have 'liked' a post that shared an old skit by the American Jewish comedian Jon Stewart; Stewart's bit had poked fun at the tenor of the debate around Israel and Gaza.[10]

The online meeting was chaired by Wendy Nichols, who had helped to spike Anna Rothery's candidacy and chaired the NEC meeting that shuttered the East Ham and West Ham CLPs, as discussed previously. Another attendee of the meeting was NEC member Michael Wheeler, considered on the right of the party. Two days prior, Wheeler had been selected by his NEC colleagues as the MP candidate for the safe Labour seat of Worsley and Eccles without the courtesy of offering the local party members a say.

Shaheen, according to her recollection, had tried to navigate the unexpected criticism of her online conduct while trying to placate her crying newborn. Shaheen appeared in tears on the BBC's *Newsnight* that evening. 'Honestly I'm just so shocked right now to be treated this badly after being such an active member of the party', she said. [11] The party swiftly brought in a new candidate, Shama Tatler, a councillor from Brent who was also a member of the Jewish Labour Movement and co-chair of Labour to Win.[12]

Revealingly, it appears that the real decision-maker behind these scenes was Morgan McSweeney. In an interview with *The Guardian* in early June, Shaheen recalled that higher-ups in the Labour Party had tried to convince her not to do the *Newsnight* interview that broke the story. 'The decision might be reversed. Morgan might change his mind',

Shaheen claims she was told.[13] McSweeney, however, was not for turning.

Shaheen had spent years building up local support, raising the real possibility that she could have unseated the Tory heavyweight and former leader Iain Duncan Smith. He would end up retaining his seat after Shaheen, dropped by the Labour Party, decided to stand as an independent, effectively splitting the anti-Tory vote.

It did not take a genius to predict that many would detect an element of racism in the treatment of Abbott and Shaheen. This impression would no doubt have been reinforced by the party's line that these manifestly well-qualified candidates had been excluded because the party had adopted the 'highest standards'.[14] Martin Forde KC told *The Guardian* that the party was 'underestimating' the impact of its treatment of Abbott and Shaheen. 'There is still very much a feeling that if you step out of line as a black MP or councillor you get the book thrown at you', Forde explained with typical restraint. 'If you do so as a right-leaning supporter of the current leader, you'll be treated more leniently'.[15]

Less than a month later, *The Independent* broke the story of how the party had tried to 'gag' Forde from speaking about his own report, as discussed above. The story was based on documents given by this author to *The Independent*, confirming the appalling treatment meted out by the party to the very same Black KC it had asked to investigate allegations of racism. The silence that greeted the story in the wider news media was deafening.

Another notable victim of last-minute machinations was Lloyd Russell-Moyle, the left-wing MP for Brighton, Kemptown. Russell-Moyle, a popular community MP, had a particularly strong track record of scrutinising British arms sales. He had been elected as part of the Corbyn surge in 2017, when he won the seat for Labour from the Tories, who had held it since 2005. Russell-Moyle was also the first openly HIV-positive MP. He had announced his HIV status in 2018 to coincide with World

AIDS Day, in order to 'tell those out there living with HIV that their status does not define them'.

Russell-Moyle was suspended 'out of the blue' after a complaint was submitted about his alleged behaviour eight years prior, which Russell-Moyle believed was 'vexatious and politically motivated'.[16] He was convinced he would be 'exonerated', but the lateness of the complaint meant that his candidacy was terminated while the party investigated. Lo and behold, Russell-Moyle was later cleared by the party of the allegation months after the election had concluded.

The beneficiary of the decision to effectively deselect Russell-Moyle was Chris Ward, who was slotted into the vacant position by the NEC. As noted previously, Ward had worked with Starmer since 2015, including as the deputy campaign manager on Starmer's leadership bid. He stepped down as the deputy chief of staff in Starmer's LOTO in September 2021; three months later, in January 2022, he was appointed a director of Hanbury Strategy, a lobbying firm. Ward had headed Hanbury's newly created 'Labour Unit'. According to reporter Solomon Hughes, Hanbury's clients while Ward worked there included finance giants UBS and Blackstone, the gambling outfit Flutter Entertainment, and oil producer Navitas Petroleum.[17]

On Twitter, journalist Owen Jones alleged that Ward, his one-time friend, had long lusted after the Brighton seat. In late June, a reporter from *Bloomberg* claimed that Labour insiders had told him that Starmer had 'personally asked for Ward to be given a seat'.[18]

Other Starmer Project and Labour Together alumni also benefitted from the last-minute flurry of selections. Josh Simons, a Labour Together director since 2022 and its uncompromising public face since 2023, was selected by the NEC to represent Makerfield, one of the safest seats in the country: both Makerfield and its predecessor constituencies had been held by Labour since 1906.[19] Simons, as noted previously, was the Labour Together employee copied into correspondence with the reputation management firm that investigated my family and I after it emerged that I was writing this book. Luke Akehurst was selected by his fellow NEC members to become the candidate for North Durham. Akehurst, as noted previously, was the founding director of lobby group We Believe in Israel and a key figure in the candidate selection process up to that date. The Labour Party has held North Durham since the current version of the constituency was formed in 1983.

James Asser was chosen by his colleagues on the NEC to run for the seat of West Ham and Beckton. Local Labour Party members were unable to select their own candidate because the constituency remained under 'special measures' following the submission of the Gilles dossier, discussed above. Asser's local challenger, the independent Sophia Naqvi, was another former Labour Party councillor who had left the party. She was also one of the individuals whose private information was discovered and shared in Gilles' dossier.

Other NEC members selected by their NEC colleagues to run as Labour candidates included Michael Wheeler (who had participated in the Shaheen call with Wendy Nichols, as noted above) and Gurinder Singh Josan (one of Akehurst's Labour to Win allies).[20]

Closer to Starmer's home, one of his key local allies, Georgia Gould, was selected at the last minute to represent Queen's Park and Maida Vale. She would be appointed parliamentary secretary for the Cabinet Office upon her election. Gould, who boasted solid New Labour heritage,[21] had been the head of Camden council; reports suggested that Starmer personally wanted her to become a new MP.[22]

But perhaps the most striking new MP selection, and arguably the most concerning, based on what has already been discussed in this book, was Alex Barros-Curtis. According to a party statement, he was chosen through an expedited process by Labour's Welsh Executive Committee and 'representatives from the local Labour Party' in Cardiff West, an ultra-safe Labour seat. The process was sped up after the incumbent MP,

Kevin Brennan, announced he was standing down after the election was called.

Darren Williams had by this point been a Labour Party member for thirty-five years, a former member of the NEC, and a member of Cardiff West CLP. He claimed that the CLP was afforded 'no meaningful input' into the decision to select Barros-Curtis.[23] Williams resigned from the party almost immediately after Barros-Curtis was chosen. In a stinging letter to Starmer, Williams wrote that he could 'no longer bear to remain in a party that treats its members, representatives and voters with such contempt. I have witnessed some pretty unedifying behaviour by various party leaders over the years but you have outdone them all'.[24]

After winning the seat in the election, Barros-Curtis opened his maiden speech in parliament by acknowledging his own 'previous role', in which he had been 'proud to play my part in changing the Labour party'.[25] He said he had met 'countless constituents' who had told him that they wanted 'change with a purpose', for instance by 'making an offer for our country that is more positive, more hopeful and more honest'.[26] Companies House records show that, as of late May 2025, Barros-Curtis was still listed as the sole director of Movement for Another Future Limited, the company set up for Starmer's Labour leadership campaign in late 2019.

In October 2024, Barros-Curtis was elected by his Labour colleagues as a member of the House of Commons Justice Committee, which is responsible for scrutinising the government's approach to the rule of law. This appointment came just two months after the tribunal in the employment case brought by Halima Khan had commented on Barros-Curtis' 'astonishing behaviour' on the stand.

The veteran broadcast journalist Michael Crick, who had been highly critical of how the party had conducted itself over the preceding two years when selecting candidates, responded with palpable anger and disbelief to the spate of last-minute resignations and rushed-through selections. Railing against a process effectively run by a 'ruling group around Morgan McSweeney',

Crick commented that 'it will go down, I think, as one of the most disgraceful episodes in modern Labour Party history . . . Traditionally, I'm a Labour right-winger. I regard myself as a bit of a Blairite. I won't be voting Labour in this election'.[27]

THE MEAN MANIFESTO

The centrepiece of Labour's electoral offer was its manifesto, which was launched on June 13.

The manifesto, simply titled 'Change' and padded out with thirty-odd full-page photos of Starmer, pitched a programme of limited ambition that would have gotten few hearts racing.

A language model analysis found that the 'Change' manifesto had more in common, at least discursively, with Ted Heath's Conservative Party manifesto from 1974 than anything put out by Labour's previous administrations.[28] Thus, the word 'business' appeared sixty times and 'growth' forty-seven times, while 'inequality' appeared precisely once—the same number of times as 'Gaza', where Israel's plausible genocide continued to unfold. Labour's 2019 manifesto had mentioned inequality thirty-one times.

'Economic stability' was the overarching promise that coloured and framed all of the manifesto's specific policy offers. Stability would in turn be achieved by adhering to strict 'fiscal rules', which were declared 'non-negotiable'.[29] These fiscal rules essentially constrained how much debt the government could take out. In practice, this meant that virtually any new spending (besides a small amount borrowed for the party's Green Prosperity Plan, discussed below) would have to be financed by higher taxes.

But the need for economic stability was also deployed to explain that the party did not intend to significantly hike taxes, and certainly not on big business or the rich. In total, the manifesto promised to raise £9.65 billion in new tax revenues a year: a mere 6.3 percent of the *increase* in wealth of the UK's billionaires between 2020 and 2022. In the context of the UK's GDP of £2.27 trillion, and UK billionaire wealth of more than £650 billion, the newly raised tax revenues would amount to barely a drop in the ocean.

Without raising taxes or taking out debt, the party's election offer was inevitably meagre. In total, the party proposed to spend just £4.8 billion of new tax revenues on public services. In addition, certain new policies would be funded by reallocating existing allocations. It was for this reason that the Institute for Fiscal Studies (IFS) declared that Labour's planned 'public service spending increases . . . are tiny, going on trivial'.[30]

The party's offer on economic investment was also limited. In total, the party promised to spend just £4.7 billion per year on its Green Recovery Plan, considerably less than the £28 billion per year that Reeves and Starmer had pledged early in Starmer's leadership. It was a meagre sum considering the scale of the crises it sought to tackle: anaemic national economic growth and the existential threat of runaway climate change. Proposed funding for the plan amounted to less than one-tenth of the UK's defence spending in 2022/2023.[31]

But this is not to suggest that the party promised no meaningful change. In fact, the party and Starmer repeatedly pledged that their unique managerial skills and prudence would materially change people's lives for the better.

This mean and limited offer meant that Labour's manifesto ended up playing an odd role in the party's fortunes. Polling suggests that it had almost no effect in convincing people to vote for the party (this is discussed further below). Instead, the manifesto's main impact was likely that it confirmed to anyone on the left that the party had long dropped any pretence to economic radicalism, further alienating a core component of the party's traditional base.

Yet the manifesto would ultimately become a burden for the party. Much like the 'Ten Pledges' of Starmer's Labour leadership campaign, the manifesto would endure as incontrovertible proof that the party had made promises to voters that it subsequently and shamelessly broke.

'COMPLETE ALIGNMENT'—LABOUR AND THE EMBRACE OF THE BILLIONAIRES

The only demographic that showed any real enthusiasm for Labour's offer were the mega-rich, who poured huge sums into Labour's election campaign. By comparison, the trade union Unite, long affiliated with the party and the party's most generous funder in the Corbyn period, refused to endorse the 2024 manifesto and did not contribute to Labour's election fund.

The Starmer Project's unique appeal to billionaire capitalists was memorably confirmed by John Caudwell, the 109th richest person in the UK[32] and one of the 1,500 richest people in the world.[33] Caudwell had previously donated £500,000 to the Tories' 2019 election campaign and famously threatened to move to Monaco if Corbyn won in 2019. 'Why would we stay and be raped?' Caudwell had asked in response to Corbyn's tax-and-spend plans, comparing mild progressive taxation to sexual violence.[34]

Six days after the manifesto was released, Caudwell appeared on *Newsnight* to announce that he was now backing the Labour Party, on grounds that neatly summarised and confirmed a central thesis of this book: 'What Keir has done, as far as I can see, is take all of the left out of the Labour Party, and he's come out with a brilliant set of values and principles and ways of growing Britain, in complete alignment with my views as a commercial capitalist'.[35]

As a result of the generosity of its mega-donors, the Labour Party raised £9.5 million during the election period—more than all other parties combined. The Tories raised just £1.9 million.[36] The amount donated by the two unions UNISON and USDAW (just over £2 million) was massively overshadowed by donations from wealthy individuals. The biggest individual donors were Lord Sainsbury (£2.5 million), Gary Lubner (£900,000), Martin Taylor (£700,000), and Stuart Roden (£570,000).[37]

Roden was a relatively new Labour donor. Worth an estimated £280 million, Roden is the co-founder and chair of an

Israeli venture capital firm, Hetz Ventures.[38] Hetz describes itself as 'the first choice investor for ambitious early-stage Israeli startups'. Roden had formed Hetz in 2018 alongside Lord Feldman (once described as David Cameron's 'oldest political friend') and a former Israeli special forces officer, Judah Taub.[39]

This support was buttressed by a huge influx of cash as well as non-cash donations from Labour Together, which, beginning in early 2024, had started making transfers to prospective Labour MPs or their CLPs. In total, Labour Together donated £1,556,796 to the Labour Party, individual MPs, and CLPs between January and the end of June 2024, about half of which was spent on party staff and consultancy costs. A handful of big dogs in the Parliamentary Labour Party also continued to receive substantial support from Labour Together in the form of consultancy services, including Yvette Cooper (£33,750 in January 2024), David Lammy (£40,440 in April 2024), and Rachel Reeves (£18,398 across two donations in March and April 2024).

Dozens of MPs or their CLPs received smaller donations, with many £5,000 and £10,000 contributions being distributed to the prospective new intake starting in March 2024. Amongst the recipients of Labour Together's largesse was Imogen Walker, Morgan McSweeney's wife, who had been selected in July 2023 as Labour's parliamentary candidate for Lanark and Hamilton in Scotland. She received £10,000 from Labour Together to pay for 'direct mails and digital campaigning', in addition to £15,000 directly from Labour Together's generous backer, Gary Lubner.[40]

Another beneficiary of Labour Together's support was Kirsty McNeill. McNeill was selected as Labour's candidate for Midlothian in Scotland, after which her CLP received donations from Labour Together. McNeill was voted in as an MP in July 2024 and was rapidly transitioned into the cabinet as parliamentary under-secretary for Scotland—a considerable honour for a newly elected MP. McNeill was appointed a director of the Labour-Together-associated Center for Countering Digital Hate in September 2019. She served in this role until her resignation in July 2024.

The party could also draw on substantial resources provided—for free—by a large cohort of lobbyists. In another excellent piece of reporting, *openDemocracy*'s Ethan Shone revealed that more than a dozen lobbyists went to work for the Labour Party for free during the election campaign. This did not have to be declared, because the services were offered pro bono; Shone was able to reconstruct the gigs based on social media postings and other evidence. He noted that the lobbyists worked at firms 'representing private healthcare companies, the financial services industry, private rail operators and major polluters'.[41]

Shone would also break the story, following the election, that the Labour Party's campaign had been funded by a mammoth £4 million donation from Quadrature Capital, a sophisticated algorithm-driven hedge fund owned by two billionaires, Greg Skinner and Suneil Setiya.[42] The *Sunday Times Rich List 2024* named Skinner and Setiya as the joint-161st-richest people in the UK.[43]

Quadrature's donation was the single largest donation the party had ever received and one of the largest donations in UK political history. But because of the way it was reported, voters were completely unaware that the fund was the largest contributor to the Labour Party's election campaign. Quadrature's payment had been made during a week-long window between Sunak's announcement of the election and the beginning of the 'pre-poll reporting period', during which all large donations would have to be published weekly. This meant that it was not declared publicly during the general election itself. It was eerily reminiscent of the Labour leadership contest in 2020, when Starmer had waited until after the election to report his full set of mega-rich donors.

If Quadrature's donation had been contemporaneously disclosed, voters might have learned about its investment history and considered the potential implications of this for the priorities of a future Labour government. In 2023, for example, *The Guardian* reported that Quadrature held shares in forty-five separate fossil fuel companies.[44] This included a $24 million stake in ConocoPhillips, which had been named by *The Guardian* in 2019 as 'one of the world's most polluting companies'.[45]

My own investigations into Quadrature, published by *openDemocracy* in October 2024, revealed other controversial shareholdings. An analysis of filings submitted by Quadrature with the Securities and Exchange Commission in the US showed that it held shares in multiple arms companies that were linked to the ongoing 'plausible' genocide in Gaza, such as Lockheed Martin and Boeing, and that it held on to these shares after the October 7, 2023, attacks.[46] Pleas for the party to return the £4 million pound donation—denounced as 'blood money' by the Stop the War Coalition[47]—went unanswered.

Quadrature responded by explaining that the SEC filings did not reflect its full 'long' and 'short' market positions and also noted that its investments had been made on a 'fully automated' basis.[48]

MAKING THE NEGATIVE CASE FOR IMMIGRATION

Alongside a war on the left and a miserable manifesto hemmed in by fiscal orthodoxy, the party also communicated a tough and uncompromising message on immigration—a world away from Starmer's 2020 promises to make a 'positive case' on the issue.

Labour's tone had already been set prior to the election. On May 8, 2024, just under two weeks before Sunak's election announcement, the Labour Party welcomed Natalie Elphicke to its benches. Elphicke crossed the floor from the Tories; she had intended to stand down at the next election, in any case, so the defection was primarily a PR coup for the Labour Party and an opportunity for Elphicke to distance herself from a tanking Tory leadership.

Elphicke was on the right wing of the Tory party. She had joined the pro-Brexit European Research Group upon her election and had backed Liz Truss for leader. She had previously been strident in her attacks on Labour's immigration plans[49] and had regularly highlighted the urgent need to 'stop the boats' of asylum seekers crossing the Channel. By 2024, however, she was convinced that Starmer was better placed than Sunak to ensure 'the security of our borders'.[50] At the time of Elphicke's defection, lifelong Labour representative Diane Abbott still had not had the whip returned.

Elphicke's arrival was taken as an opportunity to rehash the party's immigration and border policy, which promised to 'create a fair system and stop the small boats crossings', the latter to be achieved by 'smashing' the criminal gangs Labour entirely blamed for the crisis.[51] Pointedly, Starmer explained that 'safe routes' were not the 'answer',[52] a response to the (reasonable) idea that asylum seekers would stop using deeply dangerous small boats to enter the UK if the country provided safer and more humane routes of travel.

Labour took aim not only at small boats but at immigration of all kinds. 'Every time the Tories have faced a choice between raising skills and working conditions here in the UK or issuing more visas, they choose [*sic*] the higher migration option', the party complained. 'The Conservatives have promised to bring down net migration countless times but it has more than tripled since the last election under their watch'.[53] This rhetoric was, of course, the diametric opposite of the kumbaya pro-immigration mood music of Starmer's 2020 leadership campaign.

Starmer and the party stepped up the anti-immigrant rhetoric during the election. On June 1, while the party was humiliating Diane Abbott and one day after the Faiza Shaheen story broke, Starmer was interviewed in *The Sun*—the same right-wing tabloid he promised not to give interviews to during his 2020 Labour leadership bid. 'Read my lips—I will bring immigration numbers down', Starmer promised. 'I will control our borders and make sure British businesses are helped to hire Brits first'.[54]

Soon after, Starmer would trot out a clearly rehearsed line during a televised leadership debate with Sunak. Sunak, who had endorsed and tried to implement the Tories' Rwanda scheme, was attacked by Starmer as being 'the most liberal prime minister we've ever had on immigration'.[55] Nesrine Malik, writing in *The Guardian*, despaired at how Starmer had rendered immigration a 'dirty word that can be hurled like a slur'.[56]

In their language, if not their specific policies, the Labour and Tory campaigns were barely distinguishable on the issue of immigration—a striking fact, given that the Tories had, for years, been moving ever rightward on the issue for fear of being outflanked by Nigel Farage's Reform. Labour and the Conservatives agreed that legal and illegal immigration was problematic, and that immigration numbers were too high. Each offered a tough, law-and-order-style response to the humanitarian issue of asylum: deportation to Rwanda from the Tories, plans to 'smash the gangs' from Labour. Both accepted that the hot-button tropes of the far right articulated legitimate concerns, whether it was the need to 'stop the boats' or complaints about how asylum seekers were living high on the hog in hotels. When far-right riots broke out in the weeks after Starmer's election, it was striking how many rioters voiced these concerns.

The generalised attack on immigrants took a more specific and ugly turn on June 26, as the campaign entered its final run. Starmer appeared on a televised panel hosted by *The Sun* and was interviewed by the newspaper's editor, Harry Cole. Pressed on how he would reduce immigration, Starmer responded, 'I'll make sure we got [*sic*] planes going off . . . back to the countries where people came from'.[57] When asked where he would send them back to, Starmer reached for Bangladesh: 'At the moment, people coming from countries like Bangladesh are not being removed, because they are not being processed'.[58]

One of Starmer's shadow ministers, Jonathan Ashworth gave an unpleasant interview that same day, in which he promised that Labour would send immigrants 'from Bangladesh or wherever back to their country of origin . . . People coming here from the Indian subcontinent do not get returned. They get put up in hotels, and they can stay in these hotels for the rest of their lives. That's the Tory policy'.[59] Not much more than a month later, far-right rioters would try to set hotels hosting asylum seekers on fire.[60]

Bangladesh's high commissioner to the UK sent a letter to Starmer regarding his 'concerning' remarks. The letter pointedly informed Starmer that Bangladesh did not feature in the top twenty countries of origin for small boat arrivals. In fact, the letter pointed out, 'during a recently concluded first meeting of the Bangladesh-UK Home Office Joint Working Group [it was testified] that not a single case of returns is pending to date'.[61]

The high commissioner's letter, coded in diplomatic niceties as it was, underplayed the widespread hurt, alarm, and 'absolute outrage' that the comments raised in the UK's largely Muslim Bangladeshi community.[62] Multiple independent campaigners, including in Starmer's Holborn and St Pancras constituency, reported anecdotally that the comments had galvanised a flurry of activity.[63] The Bengali community constituted the single largest ethnic minority group in Camden, the heart of Starmer's constituency, and a sizeable portion of the population of Ashworth's constituency in Leicester.

THE LOVELESS LANDSLIDE

On the evening of July 5, 2024, Starmer triumphantly strode into Number 10 Downing Street. Television footage showed him walking past crowds of Labour loyalists, members, and insiders, all looking to shake his hand as he became prime minister in control of a mammoth parliamentary majority—a majority that one journalist, however, quickly dubbed a 'loveless landslide'.[64]

There is no doubt that in pure parliamentary terms it was a barnstorming victory. The Labour Party won 411 out of 650 seats in parliament, more than double the 202 seats won by the party in 2019. The Conservative Party collapsed to a low of 121 seats, losing 244 of the 365 seats it had won in the 2019 election. It was the Tories' worst result since the nineteenth century.

Retirements and last-minute stitch-ups meant that well over half of Labour's incoming MPs had been freshly selected by advisors under the direction of Morgan McSweeney. These officials had 'maintained a vice-like grip on the selection of Labour candidates' over the preceding two years.[65] This was, in all the ways that mattered, as much McSweeney's Parliamentary Labour Party as it was Starmer's.

Labour Together alumni and associates would dominate Starmer's newly appointed cabinet. Fully seven of the eight 'brave' MPs associated with Labour Together were given cabinet and front bench roles; the most senior positions went to Rachel Reeves, now chancellor, and Shabana Mahmood, the new lord chancellor. Five candidates linked to Labour Together as research fellows or employees (Josh Simons, Chris Curtis, Miatta Fahnbulleh, Hamish Falconer, and Gordon McKee) were also elected as new MPs. Fahnbulleh and Falconer were appointed as junior ministers in Starmer's government, while Simons is rumoured to hold considerable sway on the backbenches.

But the impressive seat return disguised a more complex and less flattering picture for the Starmer Project. For one, turnout at the election was only 59.9 percent of all registered voters, the lowest since 2001 and the second lowest since 1918.[66] Only 52 percent of all eligible adults in the UK voted in the election—the lowest population share since the introduction of universal suffrage.[67] The reality behind Labour's vaunted electoral 'efficiency' was widespread popular disengagement from the political process.

The Labour Party's absolute and relative vote returns were also less-than-stellar. Starmer's party received fewer absolute votes than in both 2017 and 2019 and a much lower proportion than in 2017. In fact, the result of the Labour Together and Starmer projects' seven-year programme was that Labour's national vote share in 2024 was 6.3 percent *lower* than what it had achieved in 2017, and only 1.7 percent higher than what it had managed in 2019.

As this suggests, there was a significant disconnect between the size of Labour's vote and the number of seats it secured. Indeed, Labour's victory was, according to the BBC's Verify unit, the most disproportionate on record, as the party won 63 percent of parliamentary seats on just 33.7 percent of the vote.[68] When considered against turnout, the Labour Party's vote share was even more striking: the party's 33.7 percent share of the vote meant that only 20 percent of the registered adult population voted for Labour.[69]

In the context of Labour's twenty-first-century performance, the absolute and relative vote achieved by Starmer's party was (literally) middling. As shown in Table 5, the only Labour leaders to secure more than ten million votes and a vote share of 40 percent or above in the twenty-first century were Tony Blair and Jeremy Corbyn. By comparison, Starmer's percentage vote share was distinctly average.

TABLE 5. Labour Party Election Results in the Twenty-First Century

Election Year (Labour Party leader)	Votes Won (change on previous election)	Vote Share (change on previous election)	Seats Won (change on previous election)	Voter Turnout (change on previous election)
2001 (Blair)	10,724,953 (-2,793,214)	40.7% (-2.5)	412 (-6)	59.4% (-11.9)
2005 (Blair)	9,552,376 (-1,172,577)	35.2% (-5.5)	355 (-48)	61.4% (+2)
2010 (Brown)	8,609,517 (-942,859)	29% (-6.2)	258 (-91)	65.1% (+3.7)

(continued)

Election Year (Labour Party leader)	Votes Won (change on previous election)	Vote Share (change on previous election)	Seats Won (change on previous election)	Voter Turnout (change on previous election)
2015 (Miliband)	9,347,234 (+737,717)	30.4% (+1.5)	232 (-26)	66.4% (+1.3)
2017 (Corbyn)	12,877,918 (+3,530,684)	40% (+9.6)	262 (+30)	68.8% (+2.4)
2019 (Corbyn)	10,269,051 (-2,608,867)	32.1% (-7.9)	202 (-60)	67.3% (-1.5)
2024 (Starmer)	9,708,716 (-560,335)	33.7% (+1.7)	411 (+211)	59.9% (-7.4)

Also notable was the disjuncture between the party's vote share and pre-election polling. Prior to Sunak's announcement, the aggregate polling suggested that just over 40 percent of the country intended to vote for the Labour Party. While variables such as tactical voting and the large number of unregistered voters necessitate a somewhat nuanced interpretation, one takeaway from the election campaign was that the more people saw of Starmer and the Labour Party, the less they liked. It was a trend that would continue and intensify after Starmer's government took power.

Polling certainly indicated that there was very little love for Labour or Starmer. On the eve of the election, YouGov asked individuals who said they were going to vote Labour why they would be doing so. Nearly half (48 percent) answered that they wanted to 'get the Tories out', while 13 percent said that 'the country needs a change'. A mere 5 percent said they would be voting Labour because they agreed with its policies. Just 1 percent cited 'Keir Starmer's leadership'.[70] In 2017, two of the top three reasons given by people to explain their intended vote for

Labour were its manifesto policies (28 percent) and the leadership of Jeremy Corbyn (13 percent).[71]

The public never warmed to Starmer. On July 8, 2024, YouGov polling found that Starmer's personal net approval rating, which had bounced upwards upon his election, was still at -3 percent.[72] While Starmer's parliamentary landslide had had echoes of Blair in 1997 in terms of seats won, the difference in the public perception of the two could not have been starker; Blair, on his election in 1997, had an astonishing +65 percent approval rating.[73]

More broadly, the distribution of votes in 2024 indicated a serious fracturing of the Labour-Tory duopoly. The Tories and Labour had received a combined 57.4 percent of the vote, the lowest such figure for nearly a century. The right-wing Reform UK and the left-wing Green Party had received 14.29 percent and 6.39 percent respectively, while the Lib Dems had gotten 12.2 percent.

Despite all of the blandishments about voter efficiency and voter spread, treated as evidence of McSweeney's unrivalled genius, the picture that emerged from the election was more banal: 'this looks like an election the Conservatives lost more than Labour won', the respected psephologist Sir John Curtice put it.[74] Apart from a genuinely impressive increased Labour vote in Scotland, the Labour Party's total and percentage vote share remained static through much of England and Wales. In fact, when compared to the 2019 election results, the party's 2024 vote share was just a half-point up in England and down 4 points in Wales.

The Labour Party thus won primarily by staying in place (except in Scotland) while the Tory vote collapsed to its lowest level in close to two hundred years. This Tory collapse was driven mainly by the rise of Reform UK, which caused the right-wing vote to split.

INTO THE FUTURE

When the 2024 election results were announced, Keir Starmer was not the only senior Labour figure to find themselves in for a shock.

Across a wide range of mostly urban constituencies, seats that had been unchallengeable Labour strongholds became marginals as Labour's vote share collapsed. Shabana Mahmood and Wes Streeting, for example, barely held on as their percentage vote shares plunged by 40 points and 20 points respectively. In Bethnal Green and Stepney, Labour's share of the vote fell from 73.5 percent in 2019 to just 34.1 percent in 2024, and the party would likely have lost the seat if the constituency's pro-Gaza, anti-austerity independents and the Green Party had come to an electoral agreement. Jess Phillips, too, came within seven hundred votes of losing her seat of Birmingham Yardley. Her constituency vote share fell by 26.9 points. Naz Shah, sitting in Bradford West, saw her vote share slashed by an astonishing 44.6 percent, barely scraping through as the independent vote split.

Other Labour bigwigs were less fortunate. In Bristol Central, Thangam Debbonaire was defeated by a remarkable swing to the Green Party. Debbonaire had long been tipped for a future cabinet position after serving as shadow minister for culture, media, and sport under Starmer. Debbonaire's 2019 percentage vote share was cut by more than 25 points, while Green Party co-leader Carla Denyer increased her percentage vote share by over 30 points—an amazing fifty-point swing against Labour even as the latter romped to power nationally. Debbonaire was nevertheless appointed the following year to the House of Lords, a body Starmer had promised to abolish five years prior during his leadership election campaign.

But perhaps the most unexpected loss was Jonathan Ashworth, who had become a major player in Starmer's campaigning team and was tipped for a senior cabinet position. Ashworth lost his seat of Leicester South to the relatively unknown, soft-spoken optometrist Shockat Adam. Ashworth's share of the constituency vote had fallen by 34.1 points.

Ashworth would enjoy the ultimate soft landing as he was appointed the new head of Labour Together only days after his electoral defeat, replacing its former head, Josh Simons, who had just been elected to a safe seat he had been parachuted into at the last minute. Ashworth would go on to a cut a garrulous figure, appearing regularly on breakfast politics shows and the like, where he simultaneously defended the Starmer Project and complained about his defeat.

The growth of the Green Party's vote in London and other urban centres, together with the success of independent campaigns, points to three notable trends. The first was that the Labour Party, in pursuing its (successful) electoral strategy of shadowing the Tories, had alienated many progressive supporters. In London alone, the Green Party came second in eighteen constituencies, seeing substantial vote share increases as Labour's majorities fell. While Labour still held many of these seats comfortably, and had started from a position of considerable dominance, the trend away from the party and towards left-wing alternatives was clear.

All told, the Green Party had come second in an astonishing forty seats across the country; in every one of those seats, they had come second to the Labour Party. By comparison, in 2019, the Green Party had come second in just three seats. The Green vote had surged, largely on the back of growing popular disaffection with the Labour Party.

An equally striking statistic, first highlighted by the journalist Richard Sanders, was that independent or Workers Party candidates came second in seventeen seats; again, in each one, they were second to the Labour Party.[75] This was in addition to five left-wing independent candidates winning their seats, incredible achievements given the difficulties inherent in running campaigns outside of party-political structures. 'That's 57 constituencies where voters now know that a vote for the Greens or an independent is no longer an empty gesture but can have a real impact', Sanders notes.[76]

The second trend, likely related to the first, was that the Labour Party had lost the votes of many young people. Although still handily beating the Tories, who received negligible votes from younger voters, the party lost 22 percent of its support from those aged between eighteen and thirty-four.[77]

The third trend was perhaps the most profound: a collapse in the Labour Party vote amongst ethnic minority communities throughout the country. Ipsos polling conducted for *The Independent* showed that the party's support amongst ethnic minority voters had fallen from 64 percent under Corbyn in 2019 to 46 percent in 2024, meaning that the party 'shed nearly a third of its 2019 voters among the cohort'.[78] Strikingly, Labour's vote share amongst self-identified 'Asian' heritage voters had fallen to less than 40 percent. Writing in *The Guardian* about the fragility of Labour's coalition in the wake of the election, Aditya Chakrabortty would note that 'Starmer's team is speedily converting safe Labour territory—Muslims and other ethnic minorities—into marginal voters'.[79]

At the same time, the party now faces a hard-right surge in the UK, in line with a similar shift throughout the world. Reform UK's 2024 vote share of just under 15 percent was not far from half of the Labour Party's vote. Nigel Farage, arguably the most successful and influential politician of the past decade, now sits in parliament, which gives him an even louder platform for his unique brand of right-wing populist agitation. 'We're coming for Labour—be in no doubt about that', Farage promised on his election. Reform UK had come second in ninety-eight seats, of which eighty-nine were won by the Labour Party.[80]

A HUNDRED AND EIGHTEEN DAYS OF DISAPPOINTMENT

Labour's thumping parliamentary victory generated an air of triumph and confidence around the party. Starmer's 'King's Speech', delivered less than two weeks after Labour's victory, was presented as a muscular mission statement of a party ready to roll up its sleeves and get things done. Ian Dunt, a long-time media cheerleader for the Starmer Project, enthused that the speech had buried the Tories 'for a decade'.[81]

It certainly buried what remained of Labour's Corbynite left. Seven MPs associated with the party's socialist bloc decided not to vote in support of the King's Speech. Instead, they backed an amendment calling on the government to scrap the two-child benefit cap. All seven MPs had the whip withdrawn in another of the Starmer Project's ritualistic public humiliations. Among those who lost the whip was John McDonnell, Corbyn's one-time shadow chancellor, who voted for the amendment along with Corbyn and the new crop of independent MPs. Thus, within less than five years of Starmer's election as a Labour leader promising unity and an end to factionalism, the Starmer Project had exiled Starmer's immediate predecessors as leader and shadow chancellor—an unprecedented situation in Labour Party history.

But already by autumn, the brash confidence that had allowed the Starmer Project to respond so uncompromisingly to even minor and polite disagreement had dissipated as public support had tanked. By mid-October, Starmer's personal popularity had cratered. Opinion polls show that the public had initially taken a wait-and-see approach to Starmer, giving him some benefit of the doubt upon his election; this had allowed his net approval rating to climb to just about even. By October 5, however, YouGov polling put Starmer's net approval at -36, with 63 percent of the country holding an unfavourable opinion of him against just 27 percent who held a favourable opinion.[82] Strikingly, Starmer's approval rating a hundred days into the job was one of the lowest recorded since modern polling began in the Thatcher era; his only meaningful competitors for this questionable accolade were Liz Truss (-59 after 26 days), Rishi Sunak (-25 after 118 days), and Boris Johnson (-9 after 117 days). There are serious questions to be asked about the health of British democracy when the country's last four leaders in a row have proven to be so disappointing to the general public.

Public disaffection extended beyond Starmer to the Labour Party as a whole, which sank to a net approval of -41 percent by early October—down from -4 immediately after the election.[83] These figures were not far off those achieved by the preceding Tory government, which had just suffered the worst performance in Conservative Party history. By the time they were finally dispatched, the Tories' public approval ratings had reached -56 percent. Starmer's performance was thus a continuation of a disturbing political trend in which the public comes to thoroughly dislike and distrust those that govern them.

Behind this collapse in support for Starmer and the party was a widespread sense of disappointment and betrayal, as people came to realise there was little connection between the party's election sales pitch, its historical character, and what it planned to deliver. While it is true that the voting public did not express great enthusiasm for what Labour offered in its manifesto and during the campaign, there was still arguably an underlying belief that the party would largely stick to its promises and messaging: that it would neither countenance serious tax rises nor contemplate a return to austerity, and that a rise in living standards would be achieved through diligent and sober management by a professional political class free from the sleaze and corruption that had come to taint the Tory brand.

The latter promise was discredited almost immediately after Starmer's election, as the press began to report luridly on the tens of thousands of pounds in freebies Starmer had received since becoming Labour Party leader. Much of this coverage lingered on free clothes and accessories gifted to Starmer by Lord Waheed Ali, and the free box-seat tickets Starmer had accepted to watch his beloved Arsenal. It spawned a new nickname—'Free Gear Keir'—and completely undermined the image of Starmer as a dour yet upright technocrat. When it emerged that others in Starmer's cabinet had taken freebies in ways that raised questions about conflicts of interest—like Steve Reed, who denied there were any such conflicts—the taint of self-serving grubbiness spread to the whole Starmer cabinet.[84]

Despite vociferous public denials, the freebies row bore the stamp of a factional manoeuvre aimed at removing Starmer's chief of staff, Sue Gray. Certainly, the whole affair appeared to be driven by relentless hostile briefing against Gray, who somehow became responsible in the public eye for Starmer's relationship with Waheed Ali. Those in Labour circles, meanwhile, blamed Gray's media management for the failure to squash the story. Both criticisms were unfair on Gray: Ali's support for Starmer stretched back to the 2020 leadership election, long before Gray was on the scene, while it was hard to see how media planning could have mitigated the genuine popular outrage at the decision to cut the Winter Fuel Allowance, described below.

It was striking that the freebies affair ended up focusing entirely on Starmer's relationship with Ali and barely registered Starmer's arguably more problematic receipt of gratuities from gambling companies and construction firms. It was equally striking that when Gray finally departed, the media scandal abruptly ended, even if its effects in the public consciousness lingered on.

The whole debacle reflected extremely poorly on the media. Starmer's history of accepting freebies had hardly been obscure—it could have been identified long before the election by simply searching his parliamentary register of interests. Outlets like *openDemocracy* had been raising it as an issue from at least 2023. I was so frustrated by the mainstream reporting failure at the time that, despite my discomfort in front of the camera, I appeared in a video for *Double Down News* during the election campaign, in an attempt to raise concerns about the influence of wealthy interests on the Starmer Project.[85]

Yet the mainstream media, for reasons yet unknown, simply did not report on the issue in any substantive way prior to Starmer's election. In fact, the story was broached only once during the entire election campaign—by the *Financial Times* on July 1,[86] three days before the polls opened. Starmer was asked about the issue by the media pack for the first time a day after the *Financial Times* piece—just two days before the polls opened. The media's failure to conduct the most basic due diligence on the future prime minister recalled the hiatus on scrutiny that had preceded Starmer's election as leader of the Labour Party.

The result was an electorate seriously under-informed, and maybe even misinformed, about the man they were about to vote into power. Is it any surprise if the public was then incensed to learn, only weeks after the vote, that the man they had just elected was a very different sort of person than they had been led to believe?

Gray's departure meant that McSweeney came to hold a 'position of power unparalleled in Labour history', as veteran political commentator Andrew Marr noted.[87] Not only was McSweeney made the uncontested top dog as Starmer's chief of staff, but his wife, Imogen Walker, was appointed parliamentary private secretary to Chancellor Rachel Reeves. After David Evans quietly stepped down as general secretary (soon to be appointed to the House of Lords), he was replaced by the long-time Labour staffer Hollie Ridley, who McSweeney had championed.[88] In light of what is now known about the appalling projects he led for so long, McSweeney's reach and power is chilling.

One of those appalling projects, the electorate would soon discover, was Labour's 2024 general election campaign, which replicated the methodology of Starmer's 2020 leadership bid: say and promise whatever it takes to win power, and then do something totally different.

The heart of the Starmer campaign's mendacity was the party's manifesto and its promises on the economy, some of which have already been explored above. Here, cutting through the jargon, the party made five promises: fix public services through reform, avoid substantial spending increases, no return to austerity, no substantial tax rises on 'working people', and that this plan was 'fully funded' and costed. In short, the party promised to improve public services and people's living standards through prudent financial management.

But it was all nonsense, as many economists made clear at the time. James Meadway, the left-wing economist and host of the Macrodose podcast, explained to me that the manifesto's figures were simply 'not credible'. This was because they were totally silent on the very well-known fact that the Tory chancellor's 2023 Autumn Statement had identified a massive £20 billion hole in the country's finances that would *have* to be resolved through some combination of tax rises and spending cuts.[89]

Paul Johnson of the Institute for Fiscal Studies was damning of both the Tory and Labour manifestos. He called their failure to acknowledge economic reality a 'conspiracy of silence'. He also made the very reasonable point that it was simply not believable for Labour or the Tories to claim that they would cut NHS waiting lists and fix public services without spending any real money. 'Promises to deliver much-needed improvements to the NHS are essentially unfunded commitments . . . These "fully costed" manifestos appear to imply this can be delivered for free. It can't. You can't pledge to end all waits of more than 18 weeks, allocate no money to that pledge, and then claim to have a fully costed manifesto', Johnson argued.[90]

Johnson presciently noted that, '[r]egardless of who takes office following the general election, they will—unless they get lucky—soon face a stark choice. Raise taxes by more than they have told us in their manifesto. Or implement cuts to some areas of spending. Or borrow more and be content for debt to rise for longer'.[91]

Some commentators even had the audacity to *hope* that the Labour Party was lying. As Andrew Marr told a *New Statesman* podcast in 2023:

> We are all hoping that they are saying one thing before the election, and will be doing something slightly different afterwards because we all know . . . we know that they will have to do radical things if they're going to be a successful government, that they are not talking about now for electoral reasons. So, in

> a sense, we are all complicit in a certain dishonesty in British politics.[92]

By March 2024, after the IFS pointed out that tax rises and/or spending cuts would simply have to be made in light of the looming hole in public finances confirmed by the Treasury, Marr would express 'despair' at the 'fantasy politics' on offer from both the Tories and Labour. He said that both parties were 'selling an illusion' that a modern functional government did not require 'hard choices' between either cuts or tax rises. 'They spoon-feed us honey and aspirin', he lamented.[93]

Sure enough, upon entering office, Starmer's government suddenly wailed that there was a £22 billion 'black hole' in the public finances that needed to be filled, upsetting all their pre-election plans. They had supposedly discovered this only when they got to see the 'real books' the Tories were nefariously hiding at the back of the drawer. It was an unconvincing pantomime made more galling by Labour claiming that they now owed it to the electorate to 'tell it straight'—*after* having done the precise opposite to get elected.

In what may become a defining example of political self-sabotage, Reeves announced at the end of July that the party was scrapping the Winter Fuel Allowance (WFA) for all but the poorest pensioners as a first step to plugging this newly discovered fiscal black hole. The WFA, a universal benefit for the over-65s, paid money directly into people's accounts. For many hard-up pensioners it was a lifeline, especially in the context of the spiralling costs of living that had dominated the last years of the Tory government. The charity Age UK estimated that as many as two million of the country's pensioners would lose out on a benefit that was literally keeping them warm and fed;[94] figures belatedly released by the government in November 2024 showed that the government's estimates at the time of the announcement were that at least an additional fifty thousand pensioners per year would be pushed into absolute poverty by the cuts starting in 2025/2026.[95]

The cut in the WFA was austerity of the most blunt and brutal kind, brought in by a party that had been elected after repeatedly promising that austerity was not on the cards. Even for those cynical about the party's rightward lurch towards orthodox economics, this was hard to process: a *Labour* government was impoverishing some of the most vulnerable and poor people in society. Not only that, but it was doing so in the midst of a freebies scandal that exposed the Starmer Project's predilection for luxuries gifted by millionaires and billionaires. Many would rightly wonder what role this generous flow of gratuities played in the party's decision to push pensioners into poverty rather than countenance tax increases on the mega-rich.

When Reeves finally delivered her maiden budget, it bore little to no resemblance to the economic promises the party had made during the election. Spending was significantly increased, in particular on the NHS, while taxes were raised substantially, with the bulk levied through an increase of employers' national insurance contributions. The latter decision was bitterly received as many interpreted it as precisely the sort of tax on 'working people' the Labour campaign had specifically disavowed. It did not help that what followed was another unedifying episode of small-print politics as Starmer and others sought to redefine what and who 'working people' were.[96]

There are, of course, good reasons why the government had to increase spending on public services and public wages. It was unthinkable that the damage done by fourteen years of austerity could be remedied without turning on the fiscal taps, and it would have been a different sort of disaster if this had not been done. Ironically, those who could have provided the Starmer Project with cover on these points and compellingly made the argument for a renewed and revitalised public realm were exactly the sort of left-leaning voters and supporters the party had wilfully alienated—or simply thrown out.

But this was not the point. The point was that the Starmer Project had promised things in order to win people's votes.

Once it had gotten those votes, it broke those promises, just as Starmer had done to become Labour Party leader in 2020.

Then, the disappointing realisation that Starmer's leadership pitch had looked nothing like what followed had triggered an exodus of members from the party. Will the electorate now do the same and abandon a party and project that many voted for without love or enthusiasm?

WHAT DO YOU THINK?

This, then, is the result of the Labour Together and Starmer projects: a massive electoral majority built on sand, bought at the price of alienating the party's core constituencies; a party and government apparatus wide open for corporate and donor capture; and a Labour government that was already disliked, distrusted, and on the defensive after just six months in power.

This political project now faces acute challenges both at home and abroad.

About one-fifth of the UK population lives in poverty—a 50 percent increase from the 1970s.[97] In March 2025, government figures showed that a third of all children (over four million) in the UK lived in relative poverty (after housing costs were factored in); 72 percent of these came from working families.[98] The widening of wealth and income inequalities continues unabated. As of early 2024, Britain's richest fifty families held as much wealth as the entire bottom half of the population.[99] Gas, electricity, and water prices are predicted to increase, even as the water industry dumps an estimated twenty million tons of raw sewage into our rivers every year.[100] Significant economic growth has proven illusory since at least the mid-2010s, while the benefits of what little growth there was have been unequally distributed. Due primarily to the combination of Long Covid,[101] a decade of austerity, and a cost-of-living crisis,[102] significantly more people in the UK suffer from long-term illness and disability,[103] a trend exacerbated by alarming health inequalities and the impacts of widespread relative deprivation.

Over the last decade, many people in Britain became poorer and sicker. For a significant number, the first six months of a Labour government cutting the WFA and removing important cost-of-living support (like bus subsidies) made this worse. All this in the world's sixth-largest economy by Gross Domestic Product.

Internationally, the UK will have to navigate the chaotic eddies generated by a Trump presidency that threatens to induce a global surge in support for the populist and authoritarian right. War and crises continue to ravage the Middle East. Israel's genocide in Gaza continues at the time of writing, with the Labour Party effecting only token gestures to restrain Israeli leaders increasingly confident that the world will do little to stop them. The scientific consensus is that insufficient global action will likely see the climate exceed 1.5 degrees of warming, potentially triggering amplifying feedback loops and catalysing a state of constant crisis and instability.

How will the Starmer Project address these interlocking challenges? How will it react if Rachel Reeves' 'securonomics' produces neither economic security nor transformative growth? How will it protect its sandcastle majority as the electorate splinters away from the two-party politics of old? How will it respond to disaffection on its left and intransigence on its right?

Will it look to rebuild its centre-left coalition, recreating a broad church that can assuage the disquiet of the voters who, in constituencies like Starmer's own, voted for independent challengers or didn't vote at all? Will it reach beyond the technocratic solutions that appeal to the lobbying class, and grasp the nettle of redistribution and radical intervention on climate change?

Will it seek to forge a new middle-ground consensus by forming alliances with soft Tories, if any of those still exist?

Or will it instead race to the right in an effort to hold on to the eighty-nine seats threatened by Reform UK? Will it tear up the UK's already insipid regulatory regime in a desperate attempt to secure investment? Will it shadow Farage's anti-immigrant incitement while continuing its long war against the left? Will it embrace nationalist jingoism and unrestrained militarism, draping itself in the flag and increasing defence spending even as it slashes public services? Will it launch a fresh round of austerity by cutting disability and out-of-work benefits to send the 'right signals' to capital in a desperate search for growth? Will it water down its already meagre commitments to tackling climate change as the right wing rails against the evils of 'net zero'?

Will it meet a left-wing challenge fairly on the battlefield of ideas? Or will it use the power of the state in a similar manner as it used the Labour Party machinery: to crack down on dissent and criminalise solidarity through proscription?

Are there any limits to the lengths the Starmer Project might go in order to keep its grip on the power it wrested through a near-decade-long campaign of misdirection, political subterfuge, outright lying, and anti-democratic stitch-ups?

Having read this book, what do you think?

REFERENCES

The supporting references for this book may be viewed online at: www.thefraud.info

ACKNOWLEDGMENTS

This book exists thanks to the collective work, support, bravery, and love of a huge range of people.

Much of what is revealed in this book has relied on whistleblowers and sources who have agreed to talk and to share documents. Some have taken real risks to reveal the truth of the political projects I describe in these pages. Many have suffered severe stress, worry, mental health issues, and genuine hardship as a result of their bravery. You know who you are; know, too, that you are heroes.

There are a number of insiders who I have quoted anonymously and who have been generous with their time. It's a sad reflection of the retributive nature of our politics that so many people felt uncomfortable putting their names to even mild criticism of these projects. My thanks to all of you.

My thanks, as well, to everyone who agreed to be interviewed and quoted on the record.

I am hugely indebted to the victims of the Starmer Project, so many of them Jewish, who have spoken to me even though it was hurtful for them to relive their mistreatment. I am especially grateful to Stefan Povolotsky, who gave so much of his time and emotional energy to tell me the story of his mother, Riva Joffe. I only hope that it leads to some sort of resolution in this case of obvious injustice.

I am incredibly grateful for the team at OR Books, who backed this project despite its at-times labyrinthine complexity. My particular thanks to Colin Robinson, who agreed to take on this book despite the risks and complications, and to Jamie

Stern-Weiner, my eagle-eyed editor, who has brought both diligence and insight to a once-unwieldy manuscript. My thanks as well to Ana Ratner, Gloria Dawson, and Georgie Carr, as well as Alex Nunns, who kindly introduced me to Colin.

My friends and colleagues at Shadow World Investigations have been nothing but supportive and patient as I've gone down this rabbit hole. Andrew, Rhona, Ruth, Jack, and Anna, as well as our long-suffering board members: you guys are the best team I could have ever hoped to work with.

My big thanks, too, to the team at Bertha, who provide such invaluable support for an impressive array of organisations; and a particular thanks to Sophia, who makes sure everything *just works*.

Richard Sanders and Andrew Murray have been extremely generous with their comments, help and insights.

My thanks to Matt Taibbi and Paul Thacker. Matt worked tirelessly to knock into shape my investigations into CCDH, SFFN, and Imran Ahmed, while Paul has been incredibly dogged in digging into an organisation that deserves much more scrutiny.

I am grateful to Rhiannon James at Keystone Law, who provided invaluable insight into the UK's libel regime.

I am also grateful to Professor Robert West, who took a pruning shear to my earliest manuscript drafts. Robert was kind enough not to lose his mind after he watched me replace the tens of thousands of words he had removed with a few ten thousand more.

My family, both immediate and extended, have been constant in their support. My daughters, Zoe and Farah, to whom this book is dedicated, fill my heart with joy and root me in the present.

My love to Susan (who keeps us *all* going), Andrew, William, Mark, Clare, Otto, Jack, Heidi, Vincent, Shannon, Rio, (Gr)Anna and Sally, Laura, Sam, Maeve, Jeremy, Deena, Quinn, and the rest of the Murray-Michie clan. My love to all my friends, both old and new, like Tymon, Hennie, Marion, and the rest of the Wits bench-by-the-trees team.

My biggest thanks are reserved for Jessica. Not only is Jessica my favourite person (well, third-joint-favourite), she is also the best investigator I have ever worked alongside, with an extraordinary nose for a story and a preternatural ability to spot a lie. She is extremely gracious about how frequently and outrageously I take her best insights and pass them off as my own. This book would not have been possible without her.

Jess: you are the most wonderful mother, partner, and collaborator a silly sod like me could wish for.

AUTHOR'S NOTE

In the interests of transparency, I think it is important that I declare my family and work relationships.

First, I have a family connection to Andrew Murray and Laura Murray. Laura was a Labour Party official, while Andrew advised Jeremy Corbyn while serving as Unite the Union's chief of staff.

Andrew does not appear in the text, but I do refer to Laura in relation to the Leaked Report, the Corbyn administration's handling of the issue of antisemitism, and the tasks Laura was asked to perform by the Labour Party once Keir Starmer was elected leader. Laura was sued for libel by another person whom I write about in this book, Rachel Riley. I discuss the matters travailed in that case and the inferences to be drawn about Riley's conduct. But I accept the findings of the courts in that matter.

Second, my closest work colleague over the last fifteen years has been Andrew Feinstein. My understanding of the 'antisemitism crisis' in the Labour Party has been shaped by discussions with Andrew and by his treatment by the party. The son of a Holocaust survivor, Andrew served in South Africa's parliament under Nelson Mandela and was the first person to dedicate an address to the Holocaust in South Africa's parliament. He has also spoken at Auschwitz about genocide prevention, and was investigated by the party for years for alleged antisemitism. He was only told the case had been dropped on threat of legal action, two years after he had been told he was under investigation.

In June 2024, Andrew stood against Starmer as an independent in Starmer's constituency of Holborn and St Pancras. I provided ad-hoc input to Andrew's campaign, although I was not formally part of it.

This book is entirely my work and none of the people I mention above are responsible for its content.

Paul Holden has over a decade of experience in investigating cases of grand corruption and corporate malfeasance, including as the senior researcher on the book and feature documentary *Shadow World: Inside the Global Arms Trade*. He has published six books, three of them bestsellers in his native South Africa, and has written for publications including *The Guardian* and *The Independent*. He is a Network Fellow at the Safra Centre for Ethics at Harvard University.

www.ingramcontent.com/pod-product-compliance
Lightning Source LLC
Jackson TN
JSHW080723050626
103385JS00001B/1

* 9 7 8 1 6 8 2 1 9 5 9 8 7 *